The Gap in God's Country

The Gap in God's Country

—— A Longer View on Our Culture Wars ——

Laurie M. Johnson

CASCADE *Books* · Eugene, Oregon

THE GAP IN GOD'S COUNTRY
A Longer View on Our Culture Wars

Copyright © 2024 Laurie M. Johnson. All rights reserved. Except for brief quotations in critical publications or reviews, no part of this book may be reproduced in any manner without prior written permission from the publisher. Write: Permissions, Wipf and Stock Publishers, 199 W. 8th Ave., Suite 3, Eugene, OR 97401.

Cascade Books
An Imprint of Wipf and Stock Publishers
199 W. 8th Ave., Suite 3
Eugene, OR 97401

www.wipfandstock.com

PAPERBACK ISBN: 978-1-6667-3740-0
HARDCOVER ISBN: 978-1-6667-9681-0
EBOOK ISBN: 978-1-6667-9682-7

Cataloguing-in-Publication data:

Names: Johnson, Laurie M., author.

Title: The gap in God's country : a longer view on our culture wars / by Laurie M. Johnson.

Description: Eugene, OR : Cascade Books, 2024 | Includes bibliographical references and index.

Identifiers: ISBN 978-1-6667-3740-0 (paperback) | ISBN 978-1-6667-9681-0 (hardcover) | ISBN 978-1-6667-9682-7 (ebook)

Subjects: LCSH: Church and the world. | Christianity—United States.

Classification: BR517 .J66 2024 (paperback) | BR517 .J66 (ebook)

VERSION NUMBER 10/16/24

Scripture quotations are taken from the New American Bible, revised edition, © 2010 Confraternity of Christian Doctrine, Inc., Washington, DC. All rights reserved.

To the John Paul II Catholic Worker Farm
and all who work, love, and support it

Contents

Abbreviations | viii
Introduction | 1

Chapter 1: Theory Streams | 22
Chapter 2: Unsettling 1: Leaving the Farm | 57
Chapter 3: Unsettling 2: Nonstop Change | 94
Chapter 4: Secular v. Sacred | 121
Chapter 5: Ideological Strong-Arming: Free to Choose | 157
Chapter 6: Religious Strong-Arming | 194
Chapter 7: The Role of the Church and Christian Economies | 231
Chapter 8: Conclusions | 270

Bibliography | 289
Index | 317

Abbreviations

AEI   American Enterprise Institute
BSac   *Bibliotheca Sacra*
EvQ   *Evangelical Quarterly*
JFSR *Journal of Feminist Studies in Religion*
JSSR *Journal for the Scientific Study of Religion*
NCS   National Congregations Study
TS   *Theological Studies*

Introduction

THESE DAYS IT IS quite common to hear of people who have suddenly switched political directions, or if they haven't exactly switched, they've intensified their political views in ways that seem drastic, even fanatical. It's also not uncommon for these dramatic turns or intensifications to come from "going down a rabbit hole" on the Internet. One day, your friend is a "moderate" and the next she's preparing to defend her freedom against the "Great Reset." While there are many in the US who have not gone down any rabbit holes, the number who have seems to be on the rise. This book is for them and the people who love them, or want to, which should mean all of us.

This book's subject is admittedly the hardest: finding common ground in a highly divisive social climate. It's about holding on to what is right about our current political upheavals and swings while moving away from what doesn't serve us. When it comes to why people can change ideological orientations quite dramatically, why they can grow to distrust mainstream authorities, and why that signals a problem beyond them, my own history may be instructive. I offer it here partly as a mea culpa and partly as an entry point. In a nutshell: I was a "liberal," then I was a "conservative." Lastly, I became something not in between those two—not a "moderate," but someone who melds ideas from serious forms of leftism and a different and older form of conservatism. That unusual turn put me into the territory of thinkers like Christopher Lasch and Jacques Ellul. That's where I'm at now to the extent that I can locate myself on an intellectually recognizable political spectrum.

I grew up in Rock Island, Illinois, a working-class town on the Mississippi River and part of a metro area of about five hundred thousand people. The farm implement industries of John Deere, J. I. Case, and International Harvester dominated the local economy when I was young. My dad was a high school teacher, and my mom was a substitute teacher and secretary. Dad was also a veteran of WWII and the Korean conflict. In his youth, he'd left rural Kentucky to join the army. He was, as far as I know, the first person in his family to earn a college degree, thanks to the GI Bill.

A bit more on my dad is warranted because I think his own story shaped the political trajectory of our family. My dad grew up poor, and he learned great mechanical skills from his dad. His dad, whom I never met, was a skilled roofer and carpenter. But he was also an alcoholic. His family moved whenever they couldn't pay the rent, which meant they moved a lot. Dad learned how to forage for food in the abundant countryside and grow food when he could, out of necessity. He cooperated, when possible, with relatives and neighbors to grow food, so growing up I learned strategies of that kind of cooperation from him. As a kid, along with my brother and sister, I helped him grow a rather extensive garden in our backyard. I also learned from his mechanical know-how, and I'm still doing so, because he's ninety-seven and living right next door. My mother passed in 2022, at the age of ninety-four. She came from a middle-class background. Her father, whom I also never met, was an International Harvester dealer in Iowa. A veteran of WWI, my grandfather on Mom's side had alcohol problems, but managed to keep it together so that the family was at least financially better off than my dad's. Both my parents were children during the Great Depression, and they remember what it was like to be insecure and relatively deprived. Because of my parents' backgrounds, I grew up frugal, self-reliant, somewhat handy, and inclined to grow food. I was taught that this kind of capability was an insurance policy against unpredictable times, and I've retained that perspective throughout my life.

My mom came from a Republican family, but my dad, because he was from the South and had a working-class background, was a Democrat. When he was a boy, Democrats ruled the South, and that only changed when the civil rights movement caused people to take sides on desegregation. When the Democratic Party decided to get behind the civil rights movement and women's rights, it precipitated a major party realignment.[1] The party that had fought to free the slaves, the Republicans, moved into the South to collect the constituents who weren't ready to be that era's version of "woke."[2] This is why the South shifted red. After a while, Southerners absorbed the rest of the Republican ideology, including free-market economics—but that more thorough embrace of what Americans would now identify as "conservatism" came long after my dad had moved north.

Dad remained a Democrat for another reason. Because of his family background, he aligned easily with blue-collar people. As a high school business teacher, he taught his students skills so that they could get "white-collar" office jobs, but he saw people with those types of jobs as essentially working class too. They were, by economic measures. Many of his students were young, poor, Black, and female. He was convinced that because of our country's history of racism and sexism, we needed to make sure that they got the education they needed to get ahead. More than that, he thought that the working class, people of every color and creed, needed to be supported in their quest for equal respect and opportunity within our economic system. During the '80s, he loudly criticized Republicans for trying to peel away the social safety net to benefit the rich. I absorbed all of that.

I went to college in the mid-'80s and I didn't like Ronald Reagan. I became interested in political science as an undergraduate at Northern Illinois University, and after graduating, I decided to go for a master's degree. At that point, the United States was still in a recession. There were few jobs and I figured I didn't have much to lose by going to graduate school, especially since I was able to get a position through the NIU Political Science Department, which paid for tuition and gave me a small stipend. As I learned more about political philosophy at NIU, I was introduced to intellectual conservatism. I was skeptical of conservatives, though, and remained progressive for the rest of graduate school, conducting lively debates with well-read and intelligent conservative students and faculty. But as I neared the end of my degree program, several things happened that changed my mind about being a progressive.

---

1. For a unique take on the multidimensional character of the great realignment, see Self, *All in the Family*.

2. This term originated in the Black community as an appeal to other Black people to stay awake and to see and fight prejudice against them. For the history of the term, see Montanaro, "What Does Word 'Woke.'"

First, when applying for jobs, I was treated by many left-leaning faculty hiring committees as a "token woman." When meeting them for an interview, I was an obvious disappointment. I had an education in classical political philosophy. My dissertation was a comparison of the ancient Greek historian Thucydides and the seventeenth-century British social contract theorist Thomas Hobbes. I had not had a single class in feminist theory. It wasn't that I actively disagreed with feminist theory, or that I wasn't myself a feminist in the sense that I wanted women to have equal rights. I was just more interested in other things. But I found out that it was unacceptable in progressive university settings on the East Coast to be interested in other things if you were a female faculty member. I was treated rudely, dismissively, and with incomprehension by many interviewers who clearly hadn't even bothered to look at my résumé before asking me to fly out. The assumption of what I would be—left wing and feminist—was so strong that they couldn't imagine another possibility. It was a scary experience for a young job candidate. I ended up working for a year at a college in Virginia thanks to the connections and recommendation of one of my professors. There, I was the only female faculty member, but the rest of the faculty didn't care that I couldn't teach feminist theory, and we got along quite well. I was trusted to teach as I wished.

While I found a tenure-track position at Kansas State University the next year and was able to teach in my area of expertise, I never forgot that harrowing first job search. The mean-spiritedness and tokenizing attitude of those interviewers took the sheen off the academic left for me. In academia, for about the first half of my career, progressive faculty were often intolerant, rude, and frankly not too well informed when they encountered a contrary opinion. What these superficially lefty professors—and I—didn't realize at the time is that progressive academics had already been politically sidelined outside the university boundaries (and even within them). They had comfortable positions, but they would have less influence than they believed they had in the coming decades. Certainly, they became foils for anti-elitist "conservatives" who were building an ideological empire in think tanks, campus organizations, and gift- and grant-making foundations. Academic progressives in turn became ever more anti-conservative. But these same left-leaning academics adopted more and more professional standards that kept them mainly talking among themselves in obscure journal articles and books, most of which

INTRODUCTION

were never read by nonacademics.³ Whether progressive professors knew it or not, they would largely be confined to creating a cultural sideshow that aided the system they obliquely and fruitlessly criticized.

After being hazed by narrow-minded prospective employers, I had a moment—an "I don't want to be a part of that club" moment. Once that happened, I reevaluated (and revalued) everything I believed. I started to read more widely in contemporary conservative literature, including some of the ideas of prominent Black conservative Thomas Sowell and conservative libertarian Walter Williams. I began to question why in all the decades since the New Deal, the Great Society, and the civil rights movement, our country still had a huge problem with poverty, and particularly with Black poverty and social inequality.⁴

Conservatives had a ready answer to those questions: the culprits who kept people down were liberal "elites," who had made homes for themselves not only in academia but more generally in government service. This was the message of Rush Limbaugh, the radio personality who was just coming into mainstream awareness in the late 1980s, and whom I listened to until I got bored, which actually didn't take long (Limbaugh had a predictable playbook).⁵ According to Limbaugh, as well as Sowell and Williams, progressive elites had no real interest in finding solutions to poverty, maybe especially Black poverty. Instead, they *wanted* to keep minorities dependent so that they could keep their elite "fix-them" jobs. They took their female and minority constituents for granted. They sold them hope with each election, but never really delivered.

After realizing what middle-class people actually paid in taxes by paying them myself, I was indignant that Democrats had failed to deliver on their promises to raise people out of poverty, improve public

---

3. The long debate about open access to scholarly journal articles and books is a sign of the wall that exists between the academic world and the public. Even within the academic world, disciplines are "siloed" so that engaging outside of one's discipline is not rewarded. There is an ongoing debate about whether both phenomena are changing and whether they are good or bad for society. See Fecher et al., "Reputation Economy."

4. Sowell and Williams are both still going concerns in our culture. In fact, I have been told that Sowell is having another "moment." For more information on Sowell, see https://www.tsowell.com/; for more information on Williams, see http://walterewilliams.com/. Sowell wrote many books, among them, *Black Rednecks and White Liberals*; Williams wrote, among many other works, *The State against Blacks*. Williams passed in 2020, and Sowell is still alive.

5. You can still listen to Rush Limbaugh on his podcast, *Timeless Wisdom*. Limbaugh's first of seven books, and arguably the most influential because of that, was *The Way Things Ought to Be*.

education, and provide an even playing field for people who wanted to get ahead in America through hard work. It made me an early fan of this new breed of conservatives, especially of Sowell. I must note: these men's conservative accusations against US Democrats and progressives were not entirely wrong. Democrats did fail to really fix the problems of the urban poor, racial discrimination, race-related poverty, and general discrimination against Blacks, other minorities, and women. I do not need to cite statistics to prove this. Just drive through the parts of any major city that are not on the preferred byways of those with cash to spend. There probably is a great deal of truth in the Reagan conservative's argument that people in power do not have a strong incentive to change things drastically, because positive change would dislodge them from their comfortable positions (the problem of the "managerial elite").[6] There's also a lot of truth to the idea that, over the decades, Democrats moved away from championing the working class and rural citizens who had previously benefited from the New Deal programs that my dad remembered.

Over the decades after the great party realignment, Democrats in effect moved to the right, though neither Republicans nor Democrats had an interest in pointing that out. They are rarely openly critical of capitalism or the rich. They no longer strongly identify with labor unions. They seemed relatively unconcerned as those unions were decimated by Republican policies in the '80s.[7] They began talking about race, gender, and sexual orientation more than economic class, with the effect that they could move ever rightward in their economic policies while sounding left wing.[8] This became their low-cost, low-action strategy of cultural signaling. It was the origin of the "identity politics" of race, gender, and sexual orientation consciousness that still embroils Democrats and Republicans today in our seemingly endless "culture wars."

Actually, *identity politics* was a term originating in Black feminism, which aimed at building coalitions among people of different identities for real material change.[9] But the political strategy loosely associated with that origin was adopted at a superficial level by progressives

---

6. Frank, *What's the Matter*.

7. Thomas Frank argued that Democrats started to let go of unions as a "premiere interest group" as early as the 1960s and '70s (*Listen, Liberal*, 46).

8. Frank calls this "cultural liberalism," which he says predominated in the post-McGovern Democratic Party (*Listen, Liberal*, 57).

9. Táíwò, "Identity Politics."

INTRODUCTION

for aims that were often psychological and emotional in nature. Much of the discourses, concessions, and victories of the movement in the United States were and are experiences and concerns of middle- and upper-class professionals. This adoption of the strategy by people perceived as cultural and economic elites has led to the co-optation of the term by the people on the right, who see these discourses, concessions, and victories as threatening to their own identity.[10]

Much of the cultural change elicited by identity politics in the US has been rhetorical and stylistic. Guy Standing points out that in Europe, things were and are a little different. The European working poor, including many migrant workers, gathered strength prior to, and stood up in, the Euro Mayday protests of 2008. Their leaders tried to forge a sense of common ground with which to fight for meaningful material change in their conditions—better pay, more security, and social welfare provisions. But even in this example, which involved the working poor and not mainly the professional classes, nothing of a material nature changed very much. Standing writes of the protests of 2008: "But as a leftish libertarian movement, it has yet to excite fear, or even interest, from those outside. Even its most enthusiastic protagonists would admit that the demonstrations so far have been more theatre than threat, more about asserting individuality and identity within a collective experience of precariousness. In the language of sociologists, the public displays have been about pride in precarious subjectivities."[11]

Like what Standing points out regarding the European scene, in the United States, more people in lower economic classes of all colors and identities have been employed in areas not easily unionized. Many of these jobs are in the service economy (food, retail, low-paid office work and technical support).[12] These are the dynamics that created the new "precariat" class, in his view. This class of people often live on the

10. See Lilla, *Once and Future Liberal*.

11. Standing, *Precariat*, 4.

12. According to the Bureau of Labor Statistics, as of 2020, Blacks and Hispanics are disproportionately represented in the service sector, and in production, transportation, and material moving. They were also more likely to be unemployed. See Bureau of Labor Statistics, "Labor Force Characteristics." The Congressional Research Service reports a general historic decline in union membership across sectors, but these occupations have either never been heavily unionized (services) or are rapidly declining in unionization. "For workers in the Transportation and Material Moving occupational class, union density was highest for RLA covered workers and had a statistically significant 18.2 percentage point decrease (from 75.0% during 1984–1986 to 55.2% during 2020–2022)" (Romero and Whittaker, *Union Membership Data*, 8).

financial edge—one paycheck away from not making rent, car payments, etc., and having no retirement plan other than Social Security.[13] In the US, Democrats don't seem to know how to communicate with these new types of workers, but Republicans do.[14]

To get back to my own story, by the early '90s, I was becoming quite troubled by the Democrats' disregard (and sometimes outright disdain) for people in lower income groups. I still had the same concerns I had inherited from my father. The poor in our community were trapped in a vicious cycle in America. The Democrats' lack of focus on real economic change was beginning to be felt not just by the unemployed and underemployed in the Black community, but by many whites, Hispanics, and others too. Working-class whites picked up on Democrats' rhetoric of identity politics and grew resentful that *their* identity, as well as their working-class economic situations, no longer received the party's attention.[15] So, they turned ever more to the Republicans, who, after Ronald Reagan's success at peeling them away from Democrats, continued to make very concerted efforts to recruit and retain them.

Republicans told their new constituents that it was big government that blocked economic growth, a point that is at least half true.[16] And, they argued that if we could shrink its power, opportunities could be unleashed that would lift everyone, white males as well as women and minorities. They also preached, until the Trump era, that race consciousness was an obstacle to the country's success, but they tended to turn this message toward minorities who needed to be liberated from what Republicans considered their overly race-based approach to politics.

---

13. Standing, *Precariat*.

14. See Borquez, "Reagan Democrat Phenomenon."

15. For this dynamic, the feeling that others were "cutting in line," see Hochschild, *Strangers in Their Own Land*.

16. The problem is, Republicans tended to define "economic progress" in terms of some universal metric like gross domestic product (GDP) that doesn't reveal who benefited the most. While Republican tax and monetary policies might have stimulated the economy in the '80s and into the '90s, it was at the expense of growth in small and medium-sized businesses and in favor of corporate business organizations, often with a global reach. "Between 1997 and 2012, the number of small construction firms declined by about 15,000, while the number of small manufacturers fell by more 70,000. Local retailers also saw their ranks diminish by about 108,000—a drop of 40% when measured relative to population. As recently as the 1980s, independent retailers supplied about half of the goods Americans bought in stores; today their share is down to about one-quarter" (Mitchell, "View from the Shop," 502). For a perspective on how and why big government discourages a thriving small business sector, see Salatin, *Folks, This Ain't Normal*.

Minorities simply needed to think more about their bottom lines and take advantage of available opportunities.[17]

Notice that, strangely enough, the pre-Trump Republicans gained more and more power by making an argument that was previously Democratic territory. They were making a type of economic class-based appeal. The Democrats moved further into largely rhetorical territory where equal rights for various groups took center stage at a cultural level, but concerns about economic inequality receded. Perhaps without intending to, at least at first, Democrats ceded the ground for endless corporate growth, consolidation, and globalization at the expense of the middle class, the working class, and the poor.[18]

I remained quite conservative through my early years working in academia. I often complained about the academic left, partly because they had caused me so much personal aggravation, and partly because at that point, I overestimated their influence. Academics, like a lot of people, tend to live in a bubble and see their impact on the wider society as bigger than it really is. For many academic conservatives, it was a huge deal that university students were being exposed to left-wing ideas in their literature classes. I joined groups that promised to push back the leftward tide in academia, but it became clear over time that many of these groups were just shills for the right-wing juggernaut attempting to make academia *safe for business, not ideologically evenhanded*. Over the years, I have noticed that rather than breeding a leftist culture on campus, so-called progressive faculty and administrators give way at every turn to corporate and political influences from the right. Their leftism, such as it is, must be rendered harmlessly compatible with the corporate funding and priorities that keep many state schools open. This need for funding has had a particularly large impact on the natural, medical, and agricultural sciences at universities that take ever more corporate financing for their research.[19] Red-state universities increasingly need corporate money because their legislatures keep cutting taxes and reducing funding.[20]

---

17. Kanye West is a recent example of an African American attracted to Republican ideology partly due to the desire not to be stereotyped and taken for granted.

18. Lasch, *Revolt of the Elites*, 27.

19. Enders and Jongbloed, *Public-Private Dynamics*, 301–28.

20. This is a general rule. Red states vary. For instance, Texas spends quite a bit more per full-time student than Kansas. As of 2021, Kansas spent $4,999 per full-time college student, and Texas spent $6,020. But both states were in the bottom two quartiles when it came to state funding; Wyoming spent $16,284 and Connecticut $13,604, putting both in the top quartile. The Wyoming example shows that

These moves are highly compatible with their constituents' general distrust of higher education and lack of desire to "even the playing field" for those who cannot afford higher education without aid.[21]

Back in the '90s, when I first got started, most university professors were probably still progressive in their politics, but academic programs were increasingly about just "getting a job," emphasizing STEM (science, technology, engineering, math), teaching only corporate-approved business and farming methods, and making money from inventions and patents that could be sold to the highest bidder. Over the years, I was forced to notice that supposedly left-leaning professors were having no effect on my university's overall intellectual culture, or the trajectory of most of its students. They got trotted out as window dressing for meaningless "town halls" or other bull sessions, special events, the dedication of a new building, or the initiation of some new program. These performative exercises were conducted so universities could say they were doing something about issues like systemic racism while not making any material difference. The financial power of the right in the form of both state and corporate funding vastly outweighed the "achievement" of some professors' obscure scholarship. Chasing after the highest "impact factors" for our pay-walled journal articles kept us all busy, and invisible.

Meanwhile, over the course of my career, well-funded right-wing organizations blossomed on college campuses all over the country to fight for US conservatives' right to speak freely and to not be confronted by left-wing nonsense.[22] We entered a world in which everyone's skin became so thin that even the mention of a disagreeable idea caused protests, grievances, and lawsuits from both sides. The right-leaning students and faculty became "snowflakes" just as much as those on the left. And in fact, because they often have more money and external organizational power than their left-wing counterparts, right-leaning students and faculty have become particularly dangerous whiners.[23]

---

a red state with a rather low cost of living can still provide a much higher level of support than other red states. See https://ncses.nsf.gov/indicators/states/indicator/state-support-for-higher-education-per-fte-student.

21. For more on attitudes towards higher education in red and blue states, see Parker, "Growing Partisan Divide."

22. Turning Point USA, Young America's Foundation, Young Republicans, the Leadership Institute, Young Americans for Liberty, Young Americans for Freedom, Young Republican National Federation, etc.

23. The current star of the academic right is Jordan B. Peterson, whose whining is now an industry.

INTRODUCTION

Turning Point USA cadres now "out" perceived left-leaning professors on their website, a move that is a technological echo of the tactics used by the Maoist youth during the Cultural Revolution (their low-tech equivalent was to parade professors down the street in dunce caps as class traitors).[24] It took a while, but eventually my vision completely cleared. What I see now is right-wing strong-arming, threatening, and bullying of largely impotent academics who only marginally influence our culture. These "conservatives" and their corporate allies are no better than the politically correct bullies I had encountered in my early days as a university professor. At the point I received this insight, I stopped identifying as primarily conservative or liberal.

My subsequent feelings of dismay were greatly amplified by the candidacy and election of Donald Trump. I'm not going to lie—I was an early "never Trumper." I was a registered Republican until about two years into Trump's term, but I had voted with no enthusiasm for Hillary Clinton because she seemed to me the least harmful choice available. However, I understood that the 2016 election was between a virtual Republican (Hillary Clinton) and an ill-equipped, seemingly unbalanced nationalist populist of some kind (Donald Trump). Trump was a different kind of candidate, and part of a growing international trend towards right-wing capitalist-friendly ethnically based populism.[25] Again, as I realized that the people I had identified with were embracing a narcissistic and unstable reality TV show host for president,[26] I decided not only to leave the Republican Party, but to further rethink my politics. In the process, I tried hard to figure out why so many people had decided to vote not for the de facto Republican, Hillary Clinton, but for a nationalist/populist.

I finally realized that my personal reactivity had contributed to our country's political problems for at least half my adult life. I should not have allowed my politics to be so tied up with whether I was personally liked or respected by representatives of a particular political view. Just because some or even many of its adherents are rude doesn't mean that a political position has no merit. And so, I began a conscious effort to read and discuss across a spectrum of political and economic thought that I'd previously avoided, including what could be called "far left" and "far right." I also rediscovered some literature that had meant something

24. See https://www.professorwatchlist.org/.
25. Brajer and Schütz, "3 Old Concepts."
26. Swogger and Miller aptly referred to candidate Trump, before he was elected, as a potential "Narcissist-in-Chief." See Swogger and Miller, "Donald Trump."

to me in my college years, in particular the ideas of Christian anarchist Jacques Ellul, psychologist Carl Jung, and political theorist Christopher Lasch. I picked up Charles Taylor's *A Secular Age*, which helped me think about a longer historical trajectory in which the Renaissance, Reformation, Enlightenment, and Industrial Revolution changed our experience of religion in ways that set us up for societal alienation. Thanks to an environmentally minded friend, I became interested in agrarian activist Wendell Berry and learned a lot about the environmental and food system threats we face. I realized that we had huge problems that could not be answered by our pathological right-left polarity. Why I hadn't realized this sooner is *the* question for me. I realize that I am far from alone in only lately being deeply troubled by the irreducible complexity of our situation. The fact that most of us never even think hard about the problems we face or spend most of our lives supporting "one-way" or "simple-solution" thinking about the world is the problem of our time. There's a good chance it's going to ruin our children's chances for a better future if we can't finally get past it.

We can no longer afford to reject an idea just because the "other side" happens to talk about it. We also cannot afford to be fighting the Cold War in the twenty-first century. We can probably not afford to think that standing in a crowd shouting and holding posters will stop any threat to our future. These days, the old categories are showing just how old they are. Not only the political parties but the country itself are in a crisis of decrepitude, an inability to come to grips with challenges, a lack of hope, a lack of concerted thought and effort. Under our current circumstances, we have an obligation to rethink everything. Towards the goal of rethinking, I am going to practice *détournement*. *Détournement* is taking ideas and working creatively with them to come up with something new and appropriate for the situation. Great ideas are not monuments to be worshipfully preserved in all their purity. They are streams that can—and should—be diverted and recombined. My way of thinking is syncretic. If you hold the opinion that I don't have classical or contemporary conservatism, Marxism, anarchism, Christianity, or any other way of thinking just right, my answer is "fine." That's not my aim in this book. I've done my share of narrow but safe and sure scholarship, and I consider it a useful occupation only to get ready for this.

INTRODUCTION

The Plan

I will begin with an explanation and defense of drawing from different theory streams that people usually assume cannot be combined: conservatism, leftism, psychology, and Christianity. This chapter will appeal immediately to bridging divisions by showing how seemingly very different ideas can work together and be brought to bear productively on major social problems. As we all know at some level, refusal to ever fraternize with "the enemy" leads to imprisonment in looping arguments and dramas that go nowhere, and therefore support the status quo. If you want to make sure that you will not be a part of any solution, simply enjoy the social benefits of being a team player and the psychological benefits of feeling a certainty that does not exist. Just don't expect to win even the histrionic spats that now characterize the American "culture wars." I hope to get across that this type of Facebook and Twitter (X) "winning" is losing, which hopefully will pique the reader's interest in learning more about how these major theoretical streams can be combined.

In the second chapter, whose title "Unsettling 1: Leaving the Farm" is inspired by Wendell Berry, I'll turn to a story of displacement in the United States, one that has had huge ramifications for our political scene. A mere sixty years ago, rural life in Kansas, my home state, was close to what people today (wrongly) might consider communalism/communism. I will base this surprising claim on social science research, but also the stories of people who grew up in rural areas and lived through the transformation of the food production system from diversified family farms to large-scale agricultural industries. Now, rural areas have been decimated and deracinated by the "get big or get out" trend in agriculture and business. Back then, when there were more people and intact families, apparently, it was possible to ask a neighbor not only for equipment but also for free labor at certain crucial points of the year, such as harvest, or when there was some sort of crisis. In fact, sometimes people didn't even ask—help was just expected and miraculously appeared. Labor and goods were often provided freely, without money exchanging hands, and with no expectation of repayment other than the knowledge that those who gave would receive if they needed help.

Rural small-town life was inconvenient by today's standards, but it did tend to bring out a naturally communal mentality in people who knew that they needed each other, not the "Wild West" way of thinking the US is best known for idolizing now. The role of the church was a bit different, but not as much as people think. What was different was the level of simple neighborliness. While we can't and probably don't want to go back to the "good old days," examining earlier lifeways suggests that people can think far differently about privacy, private property, and "success" than they do now. Exactly how and why did rural America change so rapidly and fundamentally, displacing so many people and causing the major cultural shift that we're struggling with today?

In addition to providing statistics and facts to try to answer that question, I'll look at how this shift was justified and even glamorized in our entertainment industry, via a look at America's beloved nuclear family, the Cleavers of *Leave It to Beaver*. This was the birth of the "white picket fence" ideology of a wholesome family with a professional man at the head, who could provide for his family all on his own income, without getting dirty and without asking his neighbors for help. What allowed this development? To answer that question, I will turn to the so-called "green revolution," in which the achievement of plant breeding allowed for much higher yields with less disease and insect predation, making it easier for fewer and fewer people to work the land. Tragically, green revolution founder Borlaug's achievements got caught up in US foreign policy, in the desire to use "food as a weapon" via international trade and aid. With this in mind, we can see that the aspiration for Cleaver-style white picket fences occupied the social imaginary while an emerging international agricultural industry worked to create more profits for everybody but farmers, who now need to be heavily subsidized by the government just to stay afloat. The result was more agricultural power and more food but less food security for everyone. A brief excursion to the case of India, whose farmers recently successfully fought the international agricultural industry, will hopefully help make that point.

Also inspired by Wendell Berry's scholarship, and insights from classical conservatism, the third chapter is "Unsettling 2: Nonstop Change." It will further track the story of displacement via rapid and drastic change in our economy through a discussion of the impact of ever-increasing automation. Automation, of which industrial agricultural practices are a subset, has instigated a social dislocation and disembedding (Charles Taylor's usage) that has had real and long-lasting economic and cultural consequences, which in turn have led to psychological and spiritual disruptions in rural and suburban areas where the political maps trend red. In an environment of stress, people look for answers and stability, and often find them in strong ideologies that engage in scapegoating. I use some of the data and information Jakob Hanschu and I collected in 2019, along with other studies, to show that there's been a cataclysmic shift in a short period of time, depopulating and impoverishing rural America and sending many people into suburbs and cities to do low-paid/low-security work. All this dislocation has been, and continues to be, promoted by Republican and Democratic policies alike, for decades. I will use the latest electoral results as a backdrop to clarify why these demographic shifts are extremely relevant for understanding the deep divisions that we face moving forward.

To deal with the real reason automation is a problem for us, when it should be a blessing, I take a step back in this chapter to explain the agrarian origins of capitalism as it developed out of enclosure of the land and tenant farming in England. The emergence of "market imperatives" in rent and farming, in a dynamic, competitive environment, began to force people even back then to "get big or get out." Though people had owned private property and engaged in markets for millennia, it was only at this point that we entered a system that systematically forced us to behave in a certain way to survive economically. It is at this point that we find more and more people coerced to leave the relative material security of land, from which they could at least feed and house themselves, and to move to urban areas in hopes of replacing all that by making money, and perhaps enough money to live a more comfortable life than a peasant farmer. This chapter will also deal with the human cost of all this—dislocation, constant retooling, social isolation, more and more personal debt, and the depletion of inheritances.

While these events are often depicted as inevitable, I want to again drive the point home that government intervention is necessary to create conditions in which corporate business is favored over small and medium-sized business. So, I'll take a look at how American politics is driven by big money, so much so that we no longer use antitrust measures to ensure a competitive business environment, and so much so that Democrats no longer champion labor unions. Corporate power has become indispensable not only to the US projection of power around the world, but to our politicians. I will spend some time toward the end of this chapter discussing how and why the Democrats, supposedly the allies of the "little guy," have abandoned class-based politics for superficial, unproductive identity politics. Both parties now disregard the needs and aspirations of the growing "precariat" (more on this new class later) while continued cooperation with the system is ensured by a welfare system designed to keep them in their place. The final part of this chapter will focus on the political ramifications of all these developments in the emergence of a strong red/blue, or rural/urban division.

In chapter 4, "Secular v. Sacred," I will turn back more explicitly to political theory by exploring the nature and impact of the drive towards secularity in the modern world through four thinkers: Carl Jung, Leo Strauss, Charles Taylor, and D. C. Schindler. Jung was at the center of my last book, *Ideological Possession and the Rise of the New Right*, in which I traced his theory that the archetypes of the collective unconscious were functionally well expressed by genuine religion, especially Catholicism, but had become expressed in a dysfunctional way in modern times, in destructive ideological mass movements. Many would not tie him to insights from Strauss, Taylor, and Schindler, and indeed none of these authors would necessarily enjoy each other's company, and yet all of them are trying to explain the reasons for, and the impact of, the Western world's modern turn, a secularizing turn that changed the human trajectory in remarkably positive but also shockingly negative ways. Each in their own way is dismayed by the collectivizing tendencies of the modern state, and the ways in which we have come to treat human beings, not as spiritual and social animals, but as malleable cogs in organizational and economic structures that they fuel but over which they have little control. The ideas of Jacques Ellul will also enter the discussion of the dehumanizing effect of human management "technique."

Continuing the line of argument that began in a previous chapter, the fifth chapter, "Ideological Strong-Arming: Free to Choose," will detail how major economic interests were and are benefited by the promotion of a certain type of "free market capitalism" ideology, an ideology that resembles a religion. Perhaps unwittingly, proponents of this ideology promote a narrative about the US economy that isn't true anymore, if it ever was, but that expresses the aspirations and hopes of people who are increasingly on the economic outs (part of the "precariat" rather than the professional elites). This imaginary, compellingly formulated by the father of neoliberalism Milton Friedman for a PBS audience in the 1980s, was so strong, and so attached to the pride and desire for self-reliance of people in danger of being left behind, that it obscured the reality of their relative and growing poverty, aggravated by the same sort of social ills that plague the urban poor. Friedman consciously promoted this ideology as a "faith." This imaginary has served over the years to aim "red" people's ire at imaginary "socialists" who want to change the economy in a totalitarian direction. The US economy, however, is highly socialized and arguably trending totalitarian already, so part of the aim of this chapter will be to show how the type of socialism we have adopted amounts to corporate socialism—i.e., the state's propping up big agriculture and big business at the expense of the poor and middle-class citizens. The question should not be whether we want government involvement in our economy, but what kind of involvement, because there is no turning back the clock to a time when the government was not heavily involved.

Next, I will explore how American Christianity has picked up on the religious nature of Friedmanian neoliberal ideology and made it their own, melding it in certain ways with their previous faith. This is not a surprising move—human beings are religious creatures, and the neoliberal narrative resembles the mythologies and belief systems people have and continue to believe—good v. evil; the need to expiate evil and sin by "responsiblization" (more about this later, too); the motive to remove the unclean by scapegoating; the tendency to color every part of life with religious meaning; purification of public spaces; the promise of perfect peace, security, justice, and abundance for those who stay faithful; etc. These dynamics help explain the meteoric rise of a new kind of ideological leader—the information technology–abetted warrior—from Rush Limbaugh to Nick Fuentes, the ideological TV preachers of our divisive era. How we got from the Reaganite Limbaugh to the openly ethnonationalist Fuentes will be explained, at least partly, through a deeper look at why and how US progressives abandoned economic class issues in favor of superficial identity politics, and how that abandonment is partly responsible for the rise of Donald Trump. A look at a few of Trump's official speeches will remind us of the themes that caught the imagination of his supporters back in 2015–16. The irony is, Trump tapped into class-based issues and spoke to the trends I've discussed in previous chapters, which have impacted rural areas of the country hard.

The sixth chapter, "Religious Strong-Arming," will deal with the problem of Christian nationalism, which largely reflects the ideological strong-arming described in the previous chapter. I will argue that this development is a result of the need for an ideological explanation/handling of the economic changes that are impacting so many Americans, leading to precarious employment and a deep feeling of insecurity and lack of community. In this environment, we have Christians who are confusing the imaginary of "free market capitalism" and American patriotism with the tenets of Christianity, leading to events like the one in Lebanon,

Kansas, in which Americana iconography replaced Christian imagery as the visual focus of a Christian rally.

I will illustrate how churches send the message that members should be good corporate citizens and consumers and should fulfill their Christian duty by voting the right way and writing checks. Not only have churches emphasized easy ways of feeling right with God, but they have largely adopted the corporate model of leadership and provision, treating their members as consumers and followers whose habits, money, and time should all be heavily influenced by the church. I will trace how Christian nationalism emerged through the intersection of religion and politics in America through the country's strong civil religion, which has been there since its founding. America's civil religion has been substituted for orthodox faith, leading to spiritual abominations like the "Patriot's Bible," and the spiritual direction of Pastor Paula White, who assured Donald Trump that America's evangelical Christians were on his side, though he did not appear to know much about evangelical Christianity.

The metastasizing of this general trend is to be found in the large, politicized megachurch phenomenon. John MacArthur's Grace Community Church in Sun Valley, California, becomes a case in point for this chapter. MacArthur's megachurch embraces the corporate model and fully embraces the MAGA politics of the moment, including a full-throated endorsement of Trump himself and the promotion of vaccine resistance during the pandemic. Before all that, the church had promoted a right-wing political and social worldview that pushed women into second-class status and sometimes publicly called them out for trying to leave their abusive husbands. For the true believer, the church offers everything—answers to all of life's questions, including financial ones. It offers education for your children, an organized social life, and counseling for your failing marriage or any errant thoughts. It creates a kind of community, but one that seeks to control thought and behavior, and threatens nonconformity with social ostracism.

I will argue that this model is an impoverishment of the Christian way of life that is nonetheless an understandable development in a world in which dislocated, deracinated subjects are looking for answers, belonging, and some sense of higher purpose and meaning. To that end, I will explore how and why people get drawn into abusive relationships and cultlike religion and institutions. Far from being an anomaly, joining something cultlike is second nature to people, especially people who are hurting, lonely, and in need of support. I will

INTRODUCTION

explore this well-known phenomenon through a story of an abused wife, the calling out of abused women at Grace Community Church, the recollections and analysis of a former member of that church, experiments like the Milgram study and the Stanford prison experiment, and beyond. Which mechanisms of the human mind are triggered, and how, to create strong motives to obey and conform? And, drawing partly on my previous book, *Ideological Possession*, how can cultlike dynamics go further, and become political mass movements?

This chapter will make a forthright argument that remaining in a cultlike church, or a cultlike mass movement, is a fundamental (though understandable) mistake about whom to worship. Theological insights from thinkers like Walter Brueggemann, Jürgen Moltmann, and Brian Zahnd will provide a background for a different understanding of Christianity that could support the rebuilding of community and a bridging of the ideological and cultural divide between red and blue Christians. How can individuals get out of social entanglements that envelop all aspects of their lives and threaten to leave them bereft of any social and even financial support? How can Christians who are susceptible to those dynamics break free of the politics, which are really a form of idolatry and heresy, that hold them in sway and keep them from being able to be guided by Jesus rather than "John Wayne"?[27] I will turn to an examination of the theological insights of thinkers such as Walter Brueggemann, Brian Zahnd, Jürgen Moltmann, Eugene McCarraher, and of course, the Bible itself, in an attempt to answer that question.

The seventh chapter, "The Role of the Church and Christian Economies," will critically examine the institution of the church. Having discussed the mistake of Christian nationalism, I will argue here that a reorienting of the Christian church could yield some very promising results. While church attendance and denominational identification are waning among the young perhaps largely because of the negative trends addressed above, Christian churches remain among the most prevalent and strongest of nongovernmental organizations in this country. I will examine here why a growing number of people who used to be churchgoers are becoming "nones," or "nonverts," and how the politicization of churches across the political spectrum is partly to blame. Following on that point, I'll examine the "exvangelical" movement, focusing on evangelical Christians who are rejecting Christian nationalism. That example

---

27. See Du Mez, *Jesus and John Wayne*.

will reinforce just how hard it is for American Christians to depart from the liberal political framework. Churches, like businesses, are consolidating. They're getting bigger and more corporate in nature, while smaller churches struggle and die. Just like the rest of the world, they operate on a largely liberal model that is unnoticed and in the background, even in the application of Christian charity itself. This liberal charity model is better than nothing, but it is arguably not the best Christians could do. If politics weren't seen as the main means of getting things done at the societal level, and money were not the main vehicle of aiding people at any level, what would have to change?

To begin to answer that question, I will turn to my own experience with trying to engage church leaders and members at the level of direct mutual aid. I will bring in thinkers like Walter Brueggemann and Stanley Hauerwas, and examples of movements whose origins are in Anabaptism such as the Amish and Bruderhof. Among the influences in this chapter will be the thoughts and lives of Dorothy Day and Peter Maurin, the founders of the Catholic Worker movement. The movement as it exists in the US today does not fulfill all its founders' fullest aspirations, having become largely (admirable) houses of hospitality serving the poor daily but falling short of developing stable self-governing communities. Catholic Workers interact with the poor primarily within the framework of liberal charity rather than mutual aid for a variety of reasons, and they spend much time petitioning the government for redress of grievances. Arguably, a protest that bypasses both of those things in direct mutual aid may be more adaptive to our world today, a world in which it is increasingly clear that protests have not stopped the global war machine, violence, including racially motivated violence, homelessness, and generational poverty. These things, if anything, have only grown bigger and harder to stop. Arguably, also, charity with time and money directed to those in need helps ameliorate the situation in the moment but also perpetuates the economic system upon which it depends. For these reasons alone, the Catholic Worker movement is a perfect case study for what is right and what is missing in those who are quite serious about Christian action. The fact that the movement exists at all, and the founders' enduring vision, makes it a great potential source of Christian solidarity.

In the conclusion to this book, I will not summarize again what I've written (this introduction serves as a sort of summary). I will point the way to some concrete measures that can be taken by conservatives, progressives, and Christians of all kinds to make the situation better. For conservatives, this means (among other things) coming to grips with economic reality and redefining conservatism to fit our current needs. For progressives, this means also coming to grips with economic reality and reevaluating their core mission towards addressing economic disparity, lack of opportunity, and belonging much more aggressively. For Christians, this means a fundamental reorientation towards living Christianity rather than having faith mediated by politics, ideology, institutions, or money.

Many people have been helpful in the long process of writing this book. Special thanks to Alex Partin for her work in formatting and proofreading this manuscript; Natalie Jabben, Erica Beebe, and Alex Ralston for their help with interviews; Jakob Hanschu, Spencer Hess, and Emily Larner for reading and giving feedback on parts of this manuscript. Thanks also to followers of the Maurin Academy who gave me such good feedback on segments of this book during chapter workshops, and thanks to Word of Life Church, St. Joseph, Missouri, for providing a fuller and more informed Christian life, even for Catholics like me.

1

Theory Streams

I WILL BE MAKING use of four ways of thinking and being: classical conservatism, Marxian critiques of capitalism, Christian theology, and political psychology. There is something to hate here for everyone, but there is no necessary reason why any of these streams of thought must be rejected out of hand or be seen as entirely at odds with one another. Over the course of this book, I hope to show how, if not taken dogmatically, they can support and inform each other. Practicing heterodoxy can help us build a different political and cultural worldview that may forge a path beyond society's current malaise.[1]

Classical Conservatism

I was first exposed to classical conservatism when I took a class on Edmund Burke's *Reflections on the Revolution in France*. The fact that we devoted an entire semester to that single eighteenth-century work gave me time to contemplate the significant difference between Burke's conservatism and the "conservatism" popular in the US from the 1960s onward. Learning how Burke viewed the classical liberalism of the American and French Revolutions[2] was my first glimpse into a practical way of thinking that I have continued to find compelling.

---

1. I use the term in the sense of Taylor's *Malaise of Modernity*.

2. For those who have not studied political philosophy, terms like "classical liberal" and "liberalism" can be confusing. Strictly speaking, *liberalism* refers to the type of

The first thing Burke taught me is that the American and French Revolutions were radical events. While he thought the French Revolution was even more radical than the American Revolution, neither of them was a celebration of tradition. From Burke's perspective, the French Revolution stood out for its strong currents of extremism and fanaticism. Both revolutions, however, because they were liberal, represented breaks with past institutions and traditional sources of authority. They were bourgeois revolutions, seeking to overturn the aristocratic order that had governed for centuries. In Burke's view, they promoted experimental, materialistic, often anti-religious ways of thinking and living.

These bourgeois revolutions did contain some values that Burke found compelling, such as human equality and freedom (both, to a point), but many more values that he found highly objectionable. One idea to which he strongly objected was the liberal primacy of material self-interest as a one-size-fits-all motivation for action in the marketplace and politics.[3] The damage to religious faith caused by radical Enlightenment thinking gave Burke even more concern.[4] He thought that people benefited spiritually but also socially from the guiding thread of a living religion in their lives.[5] He taught that the benefits of religion included personal and social stability, concern for others, a sense of duty and responsibility, and the humility born of the fact that there is something in life greater than oneself.[6] Burke seemed to think that if we

---

thinking embraced by the American founders—based on individual rights and liberties, structured in a "social contract," and embracing free trade and market economics. Today, Americans use the term "liberal" to refer to Democrats and progressives. However, unless those on the left are Marxists, they are liberals. Using the original meaning of the term, most Republicans and Democrats in the US are liberals.

3. Burke famously critiqued the "money-jobbers" of his day who used money to create more money and enrich themselves, especially with public funds, accusing many in France of having these ulterior motives in supporting the revolution. He warned, "If this monster of a constitution can continue, France will be wholly governed by the agitators in corporations, by societies in the towns formed of directors of assignats, and trustees for the sale of church lands, attorneys, agents, money jobbers, speculators, and adventurers, composing an ignoble oligarchy founded on the destruction of the crown, the church, the nobility, and the people" (*Reflections on the Revolution*, 171–72).

4. He admonished his own people that they should not imitate the French in the politicization of faith, opining, "No sound ought to be heard in the church but the healing voice of Christian charity" (*Reflections on the Revolution*, 10–11).

5. See Deneen, *Why Liberalism Failed*, for a traditionalist and often classical conservative critique of America's love affair with Enlightenment liberalism.

6. Burke went so far as to recognize the function of the French Catholic Church in this regard, noting the sordid motivations for confiscating church lands during the

could only embrace that humility inherent in religious faith, we could avoid much self-inflicted grief.

Classical conservatism is a *way of thinking and acting* more than it is a set of rules, a formula, or an ideology. For instance, it has an attitude that is wary of social change. At the same time, it does not endorse standing still or going backwards toward some supposedly ideal past. During and after the bourgeois revolutions (American and French), reactionaries wanted a return to the golden age of absolute monarchy. Burke was not a reactionary. He wanted to adapt the English constitution to the popular, more democratic currents of his time, but without losing the cultural unity and stability the English monarchy provided. This is why he was particularly horrified when the French first deposed and then killed their king and destroyed many monasteries after confiscating their property.[7]

Oakeshott argued that "to be conservative . . . is to prefer the familiar to the unknown, to prefer the tried to the untried, fact to mystery, the actual to the possible, the limited to the unbounded, the near to the distant, the sufficient to the superabundant, the convenient to the perfect, present laughter to utopian bliss."[8] When we decide that we know without a doubt what is best in every instance, when we call all previous ways of life entirely wrong, when we propose to change everything suddenly to something much more "rational," the classical conservative senses that we are not thinking objectively but ideologically. If a society has managed to survive for centuries with a monarch, for instance, then an objective thinker whose goal was success would ask, with some humility, "What functions did that monarchy serve?" Burke (somewhat like Confucius) noted that many long-standing purposes of cultural and governmental institutions were reasonable, but people had forgotten the reasons. Instead of being thrown out, the reasons behind the institutions need to be recovered so that people can make wise decisions about what to keep and what to change.

To continue with this example, there are many reasons for wanting to abolish monarchy. Monarchies perpetuate inequality, and we have decided that we want less inequality because ordinary people have rejected slavery and serfdom. But monarchies also serve to unify people around a

---

revolution, an ingredient in the further destabilization of the country (*Reflections on the Revolution*, 108–9).

7. Burke, *Prospect of Regicide Peace*. See Beales, "Edmund Burke and Monasteries."
8. Oakeshott, "On Being Conservative," 408.

meaningful cultural symbol. Because they can unify people, monarchies may sometimes allow citizens to give more time to their families, communities, and livelihoods and spend less of their time on futile political battles. Maybe monarchies also create a situation in which leaders want to appear morally upright because they know that their behavior sets the cultural tone for an entire nation.[9] If we eliminate monarchy, like the French (and before them the English, temporarily) did, then both the harmful *and* the beneficial effects of having a monarchy are suddenly erased. As a matter of fact, in the subsequent man-made cultural vacuum, we might inadvertently cause a worse type of leader to step in—an Oliver Cromwell, for instance.[10] Now perhaps the fact that the British have retained their monarchy as a relatively benign cultural institution makes some sense, even as the royals feud over popular support.[11]

During the 1980s and '90s, US conservatives (from now on I will refer to them as "right liberals" because they are—or in some cases were[12]—right-leaning classical liberals and not actual conservatives) proposed some drastic changes to reverse the similarly drastic New Deal changes the US had gone through because of the Great Depression. Republicans initiated two culture-shattering shifts in one century. Not only did they try to reverse the welfare state, but they promoted a rationalistic, free-market way of doing business that optimistically claimed that market incentives could cure *all* human problems, including racism, poverty, and environmental pollution.[13]

Here is an example of how sudden change that purports to be "rational" can backfire. In the 1980s, right liberals argued that all the regulations on political donations adopted in the 1970s in the wake of the Watergate scandal were ineffective, and many ought to be removed.

---

9. Thomas Hobbes makes arguments like these to support monarchies as superior to oligarchies and democracies in *Leviathan* (ch. 19).

10. Hobbes certainly made this point in his *Behemoth*.

11. For a great example of that, see Harry, *Spare*.

12. I use the past tense here because in the era of Trumpian politics we are seeing a rise in nationalists, ethno-nationalists, open racist/identitarians, and economic protectionists who vote Republican and who may be initiating another party realignment in which the right liberals will flow towards the Democrats, turning the Democratic Party even more rightward and making the way for a new party that is more leftist in its orientation. Russell Kirk would be a good example of an American classical conservative. See Birzer, *Russell Kirk*.

13. For a great example of the naive optimism of the beginning of this era, see Friedman, *Free to Choose*, a PBS documentary from 1980 that championed the rationality of the free market.

They filibustered and otherwise resisted any attempt to strengthen and expand existing regulations and limits on campaign financing and spending. Their response to critics, who were afraid that their vision would make corporate political influence too strong in our politics, sounded promisingly rational. They argued that the transparent and free marketplace of political donations would increase the diversity of donations and reduce the influence of any one donor. Second, they argued that with full transparency about who gave what, each voter could freely decide whether the donations that candidates received mattered. In the free marketplace of information about donations, if a voter didn't like where the candidates' funds came from, she could just vote for the other candidate, or so the reasoning went. Stephen Harder, for instance, argued, "Left unregulated, the market for political finance is of such breadth and competitiveness as to afford almost no chance for illegitimate economic coercion of political authority."[14]

That idealistic argument for a free marketplace of information would work if all voters were highly and accurately informed rational actors who spent a good part of their days reading up on campaign contributions and studying which laws their representatives were proposing and which policies political candidates were advocating. Enlightenment liberal thinking tends to assume such rational actors—a way of thinking Oakeshott called "rationalism," as opposed to rationality.[15] But, as we know, most voters (just like most buyers of commercial goods) are not that highly informed. They have jobs and lives to live. Nor are they consistently rational—no one is. The result is that corporate and otherwise wealthy donors, especially since Citizens United v. FEC (2010), have gained much more clout in our electoral system.[16]

Citizens United v. FEC established that corporate donations to political campaigns cannot be limited under the First Amendment freedom of speech clause. This applies to political action committees (PACs), nonprofit organizations, labor unions, and other corporate entities. The result has been huge influxes of money into political campaigns, protracting those campaigns to an almost endless duration in American culture. Scholars disagree about just how much influence PAC and other spending has had since Citizens United, but the public understandably

---

14. Harder, "Political Finance," 63. See Winter, "Political Financing."
15. Oakeshott, "Rationalism in Politics."
16. Federal Election Commission, "Citizens United v. FEC."

perceives big money in politics to be a corrupting influence.[17] This has contributed to more and more public cynicism. The subsequent influence of big money on our political process has helped create the open corruption now fondly referred to as "the swamp." Edmund Burke would not be surprised. He did not think that human beings were the rational maximizers that classical liberal theory assumed they were.[18] He understood that people's estimation of the legitimacy of their leaders mattered. Because of this, Burkean classical conservatism would be skeptical of the Milton Friedman–style right liberalism that holds sway among many of today's Republican champions of the liberal ideology.

It is true that right liberals tend to argue in a less-than-liberal direction on social issues such as abortion, gay marriage, affirmative action, and drug legalization.[19] They do realize at one level that society is changing rapidly in its cultural dimensions: the older ideals of the heterosexual nuclear family; monogamous marriage for life; Anglo-Saxon dominance of the US culture and economy; and traditional relationships among men, women, youths, and elders are waning. They even sound a bit like classical conservatives in their complaints about the rapidity of these changes. There is *some* similarity in their way of thinking, but only so much. Republicans want to idealize the nuclear family, to campaign for a type of family that has never been fully realized, and to somehow go back to an allegedly more wholesome era. In this respect, today's Republicans are more like eighteenth- and nineteenth-century reactionaries, and they have a similar chance of reversing social change as their precursors.[20] And, like previous reactionaries, the fact that they complain about social and cultural disruptions does not mean that they necessarily understand why these disruptions are happening. On the contrary, I will argue that liberal "free market" capitalism has created the very conditions to which they are reacting, conditions in which all sorts of traditional institutions,

---

17. See DeBell and Iyengar, "Campaign Contributions." On the mixture of opinions regarding PAC contributions and political influence, see Peoples, "Contributor Influence in Congress."

18. Burke advocates for a "monarchy directed by law, controlled and balanced by the great hereditary wealth and hereditary dignity of a nation," as preferable to a "pure democracy," because it provides more social and cultural stability (*Reflections on the Revolution*, 108–9).

19. For a breakdown of right- and left-liberal positions on issues like this and why they are self-contradictory and partial, see Taylor, *Malaise of Modernity*, ch. 8.

20. For a great discussion of the motivation, content, and importance of reactionary ideas, see Berlin, *Crooked Timber of Humanity*.

values, and ways of life are upended. Right-liberal ideology and institutions are, for better or worse, wrecking balls for traditional values.

Philosopher Charles Taylor describes the irony of the situation this way: "In their economic policies they advocate an untamed form of capitalist enterprise, which more than anything else has helped to dissolve historical communities, has fostered atomism, which knows no frontiers or loyalties, and is ready to close down a mining town or savage a forest habitat at the drop of a balance sheet."[21]

Right liberalism is a form of classical liberalism. Classical liberalism is built around the individual as the main political and economic actor. In classical liberal ideology, the individual's rights are all important.[22] The economy thrives to the extent that individuals act upon their self-interest in the workplace, business, and in consuming products and services. The right liberal economic imaginary is based squarely on free individual choice, but the reality is that continual growth can be attained only with ever-increasing stimulation of individuals' acquisitional desires through marketing. Why *wouldn't* "consumers," who are told that their individual rights and self-defined interests are paramount, and that American freedom equals ever-increasing access to abundant goods at low prices, *also* want to break loose from society's hidebound moral rules, particularly any restrictive ideas of how they as individuals ought to behave?[23]

Economic and cultural liberation are not only coincidental but mutually reinforcing. Common sense tells us that aspiring to ever-increasing choice and change in products to consume will raise expectations in other areas of life for more variety and change, making solid, lasting relationships seem particularly boring and stultifying. The breakup of relationships and families and the loosening of social bonds certainly puts people into a position of needing more goods and services in their relative personal independence and social isolation. These observations—succinctly summed up by the dominance of dating apps on our social scene, apps through which people shop for their next mate—validate Burke's classical conservative warning of "unintended

---

21. Taylor, *Malaise of Modernity*, 95.

22. That is how a Republican school board candidate can honestly make the statement "Our students are being taught that they don't have individual responsibility for their actions, that they're part of a community instead" and not see the irony (Dome, "Manhattan City").

23. See Lasch, *Haven in Heartless World*; Lasch, *Culture of Narcissism*. See also Hofstadter, *American Political Tradition*.

consequences" coming from seemingly "rational" policies. In this case, the unintended consequences have destabilized families, communities, and cultures in the US and around the world.[24]

The intended consequences of capitalism were too materialistic, and the relentless pursuit of "mammon" in our society, which leaves us all frayed and empty, is the unintended result.[25] Burke disdained people who thought of making money more than they thought of their familial or social duties, contrasting life before and after the advent of finance capital and the end of traditional arrangements in landed property.[26] Now, we tend to disrespect people who choose to stay in place, whether on their family's farm or in their hometown. The motivation to stay for the sake of family is problematic if it gets in the way of an aspiring professional's career.[27] In our contemporary cultural framework, it is a lot to ask of the autonomous individual to forgo greater financial success and status to stay in place.

The unintended cultural consequences of free-market ideology, including increasing acceptance of previous taboos such as gay marriage, acceptance of the rights of people with different gender identities, and (before those rose in social consciousness) equality for minorities and women, may be better results than the material abundance we find amid poverty and alienation. Most of today's right liberals would disagree with that observation, but whether all these changes are good or not, it is still the case that they stem from economic developments that right liberals support. Here is an example that may help illustrate the connection between right-liberal economics and the breakdown of traditional social order:

During and after WWII, women moved into the workforce, something that is usually celebrated as a move toward equality. Women's

24. See Thomas et al., "99 + Matches."

25. For a treatment of the history of the worship of mammon in the US and its cooptation of the Christian religion, see McCarraher, *Enchantments of Mammon*.

26. Henry Heller writes that "the views of Burke, the leading counter-revolutionary theorist of the time, are impressive in their grasp of the new post-revolutionary power of finance capital and the concomitant transformation of landed property into capital. Likewise, Burke understands the link between the immediate crisis and the longer-term conflict between rival economic orders, the one based on traditional control of land, and the other based on finance capital" (Heller, "Bankers, Finance Capital," 188).

27. Hendershott, *Moving for Work*; Hektner, "When Moving Up Implies Moving Out." With the advent of more remote work, this may begin to change, but it is too early to tell.

entrance into the labor market grew the economy by bringing more money into circulation and expanding the consumer base. It also stimulated growth by increasing demand for convenience food and other items that eased the burden on them and their families.[28] While it is not the case that the entrance of women in the workforce is responsible for the ever-increasing cost of living, it is also true that to live a middle-class lifestyle, both spouses in a marriage often must work. Partners in these two-earner families are now faced with increasingly expensive childcare options, and the US does not enjoy the level of social support for this, maternity and paternity leave, and other family care needs. Amanda Weinstein writes, "The United States is the only industrialized country without a paid maternity leave policy (Human Rights Watch, 2011) and only five states provide income replacement for maternity leave."[29] Without these benefits, families (those no longer able to ask relatives nearby for help) must make hard choices, which may mean that children and the elderly inhabit substandard day care centers and assisted living facilities. The outcomes of both partners working have been mixed if we consider overall expenses and often difficult choices about care, but positively, women are now more accepted as equals in our society—equals as workers.[30]

Women closing in on complete economic equality is an example of how capitalism makes social roles that once felt unchangeable become obsolete and retrograde. The resulting changes feel liberating, and to that extent capitalism has been beneficial for women *and* men. However, the liberation afforded by this commercial inevitability goes only so far and, arguably, does not free women in their full humanity, but only as workers, consumers, and subjects of contracts. Rights movements are good but imperfect. They are good because they bring a certain type of emancipation for a lot of people. They are imperfect because so often they begin and end with the demand to engage in the same type of self-interested activities that the existing order finds acceptable, creating a lot of conflict and waste along the way. Realistically, acceptance of a person's right to choose work or a career path beyond the home is perhaps the first step towards full acceptance of all human beings as equal children

---

28. Rutherford, "Making Better Use of U.S. Women."

29. Weinstein, "Working Women," 607.

30. Some feminists reacted to this dilemma early on by demanding, instead, wages for domestic work. For a good summary and update on proposals to compensate domestic work, see Sedacca, "Domestic Workers."

of God. As such, acceptance of equal rights for women perhaps points us in the direction of a more fully human community. A classical conservative response to these types of cultural developments, when they have become mainstream, is acceptance, but also a realistic acknowledgment that legal equality is not a miracle fix for all that ails humanity. Instead, the classical conservative would see these types of changes as mixed but necessary adaptations to the current environment.[31]

Classical conservatism has a concept, "the social fabric," which argues that all human beings are woven together in a complex tapestry that includes the dead (their legacy), the living, and those yet to be born.[32] If some pull off in the direction of their self-interested and purely individual rights, so will others, fraying the fabric.[33] Once the cloth is damaged, it is impossible to perfectly repair it, and the disruption leads to confusion, conflict, and decline. If the social fabric is not to be torn, we must have enough societal cohesion based on mutual self-control, regard, and care so that people do not feel like pulling so far away from each other.

As Oakeshott puts it, "Changes are without effect only upon those who notice nothing, who are ignorant of what they possess and apathetic to their circumstances; and they can be welcomed indiscriminately only by those who esteem nothing, whose attachments are fleeting and who are strangers to love and affection."[34] In our current context, the uncompromising anti-mask protester and pro-choice activist who brooks no barriers to abortion at all are like "those who esteem nothing." They share a mutual desire to pull away, to not be encumbered by anyone else's concerns, cares, wishes, or demands, indeed a desire for complete bodily autonomy.[35] We must acknowledge that the impact of a pregnancy on a woman's body and life is by far greater than the impact of a face mask. The larger point, though, is that with the insistence of complete individual

---

31. For a good summation of the classical conservative perspective, including incrementalism and slow, reversible adaptation, see Oakeshott, "On Being Conservative."

32. Burke accuses revolutionaries of "destroying at their pleasure the whole original fabric of their society, hoarding to leave to those who come after them a ruin rather than a habitation" (*Reflections on the Revolution*, 83). He argues that it was a mistake to think that the entire social and political structure of France's "whole fabric should be at once pulled down and the area cleared for the erection of a theoretic, experimental edifice in its place" (111).

33. Contemporary classical conservative (of sorts) David Brooks uses the term in his Weave: The Social Fabric Project, whose mission is to get people in the United States to build healthy relationships as citizens. See https://weavers.org.

34. Oakeshott, "On Being Conservative," 409.

35. See Bluth, "My Body, My Choice."

autonomy, as Burke alluded, comes a brittle vulnerability stemming from the subsequent undermining of a true, supportive community.

Classical conservatives value flesh-and-blood people above abstract ideas. This is the chief reason they do not advocate pushing people to change beyond their current capability. As Russell Kirk, another classical conservative, wrote, "The intelligent conservative endeavors to reconcile the claims of Permanence and the claims of Progression. He thinks that the liberal and the radical, blind to the just claims of Permanence, would endanger the heritage bequeathed to us, in an endeavor to hurry us into some dubious Terrestrial Paradise. The conservative, in short, favors reasoned and temperate progress; he is opposed to the cult of Progress, whose votaries believe that everything new necessarily is superior to everything old."[36]

To be clear, classical conservatives are not arguing that people should not change at all. Burke was a member of the Whig Party in England, and as such, he was an apologist for the changes that happened during England's Glorious Revolution. That event moved England away from absolute monarchy and toward parliamentary supremacy, but still within a monarchical framework. Burke saw these changes, including increasing political and legal rights for men regardless of property, and a slowly expanding franchise, as evolutionary moves to fulfill the potential inherent in the English constitution. But he knew these changes were possible because the social and commercial development of the English people at his time had laid the groundwork for them. What Burke opposed, and what he saw happen during the French Revolution, was people forcibly imposing abstract and radically different ideas on a population that was not ready for them.[37] When a minority of people in a society have a grand scheme for change and are willing to use force if necessary to get that scheme accomplished, they are extremists. They embrace the idea that

---

36. Kirk, *Politics of Prudence*, 25.

37. For instance, Burke called Rev. Richard Price, who was advocating for the revolution to come to England, the "archpontiff of the rights of man" (*Reflections on the Revolution*, 12). He depicted him as someone who was willing to gamble with others' stability and relative happiness for an abstract social ideal.

you must hurt people to help them.[38] As Rousseau famously argued, radicals force people to be free (he was in favor of it).[39]

To avoid the harm that comes with sudden drastic change, conservatives argue for incrementalism.[40] Instead of imposing a one-size-fits-all blueprint, classical conservatives take a small-scale experimental model for change. If a small change doesn't work, it is to be examined and changed again. There should always be an exit strategy, a way of moving back to a position that works better. This way of dealing with necessary change comes from a place of humility, rather than the typical "we've got the one right answer" mentality. In addition, the classical conservative way of thinking rejects universalism when it comes to change. It's willing to admit that what works in one place or time may not work in another because the conditions are different and/or the people are different.[41] This need not indicate "moral relativism."[42] It is an acknowledgment of the reality "on the ground," and also the fact that there are multiple (but not infinite) ways to obtain beneficial results, all of which may prove their utility in the places they are tried.

In the US, we are now seeing the effects of a radical, universalistic, "one-answer" mode of thinking. Free-market liberalism insists that marketplace thinking works equally well for *all* people in *all* times and places, and even works best to organize people and solve problems in areas previously deemed beyond the market, such as schools, churches, family and community life.[43] In this way, it shares some of the totalitarian aspects of more openly apocalyptic revolutionary regimes.[44] We see liberalism in the insistence that farmers need to "get big or get out," and

---

38. The most jarring example of this in recent memory is the attack on the US Capitol, the "Capitol Insurrection" that occurred on January 6, 2021, when a motley but deadly horde of MAGA followers, QAnon conspiracy theorists, ethno-nationalists and other militia-types broke into the US Capitol in a failed attempt to overturn the 2020 electoral victory of Joseph R. Biden.

39. Rousseau, *On the Social Contract*.

40. As Oakeshott puts it, "he favours a slow rather than a rapid pace, and pauses to observe current consequences and make appropriate adjustments" ("On Being Conservative," 412).

41. A good example of this would be Edmund Burke's defense of Indian culture in his parliamentary impeachment speeches against the colonial aggression of the Hastings governorship. See B. Smith, "Edmund Burke."

42. This is a tricky question, though, as indicated by Holston, "Burke's Historical Morality."

43. See W. Brown, *Undoing the Demos*.

44. Wolin, *Democracy Incorporated*.

that if it is no longer economically feasible to run their family farms and pass them down to their children, they should simply "retool" and join another sector of the economy. We see it also in churches that use marketing strategies to raise funds for their "capital campaigns" and engage in Madison Avenue advertising to attract members. We see it in higher education when parents and professors alike generally agree that studying history, reading literature, and making art and music waste students' time because they aren't immediately lucrative. Right liberals in the US complain about the decline in active and informed citizenship and aesthetic tastes without understanding the connection between cultural decline and the imperative to study just for employment.

Do today's Republicans really want to support an ideology whose more dire consequences contribute to the dissolution of community, culture, family, and citizenship? Do they really want to identify individual rights just with consumer freedom? Does religious piety really go along well with an ardent faith in the power of capitalism and right-wing politics to solve all problems? Do their attempts to curb cultural change really go along with the capitalism they support, whose imperatives are endless change and unbridled growth? This book will take an unflinching stance on the contradictions inherent in the current right-liberal positions and try to argue for their correction.

Marxian Critiques

We are living through times of incredible challenges, challenges that are largely a product of previous ideological choices. During the Cold War, both communism and capitalism emphasized technological innovation and economic growth. Both tended to reduce the vision of human life to materialistic matters, and both held goals that, in practice, amounted to material progress. For both capitalists and communists, the promise was human emancipation—the idea that only when human beings lived free and prosperous could they actualize themselves. But actualization always remained distant, no matter how much licentiousness or material growth occurred. For the capitalists, material progress became an end in itself—the superabundance of production as a source of pleasure and pride. As exiled Soviet dissident Aleksandr Solzhenitsyn said of the United States in his famous Harvard commencement speech in 1978, "The constant desire to have still more things and a still better life and the struggle to this end imprint many Western faces with worry and even depression, though it is customary to carefully conceal such feelings. This active and tense competition comes to dominate all human thought and does not in the least open a way to free spiritual development."[45] For communists facing the West's frenetic push for growth, it soon became about producing consumer products on the scale of the capitalist West to show that communism was the better system.

Now that state-dictated communism has largely become a thing of the past and capitalism has won the world stage, the constant concern of American economic analysts is still growth, and not just growth but the *rate* of growth. We're not doing well unless the curve on the chart keeps getting steeper, which at a certain point, is *practically* impossible.[46] The truth is that endlessly increasing rates of growth, even if they were possible, are not only culturally, economically, and environmentally unsustainable, but also bad for the human spirit. Higher human goals like emancipation and human flourishing are largely spiritual, and they tend to get completely eclipsed in metastasized economic growth. When times are good, materialistic dreams keep people from deepening and stretching their character and helping others do the same. When times are bad (and in capitalism, these times come around cyclically as a part of the deal), the nightmare of insecurity blocks out all other aspirations. Good times or bad, there's not much room for *human* growth. As friends, lovers, fellow citizens, thinkers, creators, dreamers, and recreators, we are human beings; as "workers" and "consumers," we are mere animals.[47] If we can admit that capitalism has itself done much damage physically and spiritually, then why must we reject critiques from the left altogether, as though they are entirely wrong?

---

45. Solzhenitsyn, "World Split Apart," para. 12.

46. Beaudreau and Lightfoot, for instance, argue that continuing to increase the rate of economic growth would require a concomitant increase in the rate of energy output, leading to a physical limit ("Physical Limits").

47. Marx theorized that work was man's highest activity because we could achieve self-awareness in our work through active participation and hopefully creative participation. While that might have been true, and still is for the craftsman, for a worker in a highly mechanized and automated system, whether factory or office, that is simply not the case. Marx never made a convincing case that communists would more humanely use the collectivized system of labor created by capitalism. Labor organized by technical rationality, broken down into highly routine and mindless actions, devoid of opportunities to problem solve and innovate, cannot be something in which we can contemplate our full humanity.

Even though times have changed, many still tend to think that the history of the Soviet Union and the People's Republic of China makes it impossible to entertain any element of Marxian analysis. But Marx's analysis of capitalism can be separated not only from his predictions of future communism but also from what ideologues later made of those predictions in the Soviet and Chinese regimes.[48] Everyone agrees that the history of communism in the twentieth century was largely bad. But capitalism is, in its own way, not much better, and this is a much harder truth to accept. Marxian theory helps us understand why this is the case. Capitalism has done a better job of producing more material goods in the long run, but among its by-products are unemployment, low wages for many workers, increasingly deskilled jobs for millions of people, more weather-related disasters, floating plastic islands, cancer, obesity, ungovernable technology-obsessed children, broken families, chaotic boom-and-bust cycles, empty secularism, boredom, anxiety, global epidemics (because of the globalized economy), and an incredibly expensive and violent international empire that is often deeply resented.[49]

Simply put, we all hold a prejudice for the system we are embedded in now. We sense that to be on our team means we must love all things capitalist regardless of harm, and hate the "communists," though they largely don't exist anymore. But to be fair, our tendency to steer away from leftist thought is also based on fear of left-wing cruelty. We know of the cruelty and mass murders of Soviet- and Chinese-style communism, and no one wants to consider a move towards these failed systems in which people suffered so much and did not receive even the worldly rewards promised to them. While not nearly as bad, today's politically correct "social justice warrior" is reminiscent of witch hunt–style Puritanism, and people understandably do not relish the thought of a regime headed by censors, cultural bullies, and killjoys.[50]

Does all this mean that there is nothing we can take away from the large deposit of learning and information from Marxist sources? There is quite a lot that can be gained, once we realize that neither totalitarian

---

48. The theory of Moishe Postone, for instance, deals with economic analysis and moves past any tendency to predict some determinate historical outcome based on dialectical theory (*Time, Labor, Social Domination*).

49. A recent heartbreaking example of this dynamic is the US government's long and destructive involvement in, and abrupt pullout from, Afghanistan.

50. Which we already have to a certain extent under the moniker of the "managerial elite." See Lind, *New Class War*.

communism nor social justice warrior–style Puritanism are the only products of leftist thought. In fact, the "SJW" is a product of left liberalism, not the Marxian left. SJWs are what liberalism produces when people are inclined to the left but do not want to substantially change the economy to address social problems—they remain at the level of changing attitudes, laws, and regulations. Because many people largely benefit from the capitalist system as it is, they end up surrendering to it, but with considerable guilt that they need to expiate somehow.[51] True leftism is not about simply demanding equal recognition for individuals or members of a group, or being accepted within the existing system, and it is also not about claiming status as a victim of past injustices. True leftism provides an unblinkered analysis of the downsides of capitalism from which everyone suffers. At its best, it also provides visions of different, and better, ways we could live.[52]

Marxian thought helps us understand why capitalism has devastating cyclical downturns, recessions, and depressions. Capitalism is a way of producing and distributing goods and services that is particularly vulnerable to shocks. The more refined and "just in time" it becomes, the more vulnerable to shocks it is. Marx brings to our attention capitalism's "crises of overproduction." These happen when more things are produced than can be sold, and more capital has been invested in production than can be profitably absorbed. Prices sink, and producers can't make a profit. People lose jobs. Crises of overproduction occur because of the nature of capitalist competition itself, not because of mistakes companies make but could avoid if they were smarter.[53] Capitalists must compete with others to sell their goods, so they are always looking for ways to cut costs and reduce prices but still make a profit, and indeed a larger profit. To cut costs, business owners try to pay workers as little as possible, hire workers from other lower-cost regions, and replace workers with machinery. Capitalism naturally incentivizes the use of undocumented laborers and

---

51. Provocative Marxist philosopher Slavoj Žižek makes this point about "political correctness" and "SJWs" frequently in his books, articles, and talks. See, for instance, "Sex, Contracts and Manners." For an example of Žižek at his best, and at his most politically incorrect, arguing that Donald Trump's election might not be a sign of regress, see *Sex and Failed Absolute*. For a good example of a true left perspective on progressive identity politics, see Nagle and Tracey, "First as Tragedy."

52. For a good example of leftist thought rejecting "culture war" politics, see Guastella, director of operations for Teamsters Local 623 in Philadelphia ("We Need Class War").

53. Kotz, "Contradictions of Economic Growth."

the transfer of factory jobs to other countries where labor costs are lower. In many cases, even the liability of paying for factory machinery and its maintenance is now "outsourced" to foreign owners.[54]

Once we understand dynamics such as these, we can see that foreign labor taking US jobs is not the fault of anyone, not capitalists, and least of all the workers in other countries (or immigrant workers who come to work in domestic farms, meat-packing plants, and other employment). It is baked into the system due to the coercive nature of capitalist competition, that is, "market imperatives."[55] Marxian thinkers do not place blame or use moralistic arguments against individual capitalists or countries. They identify the capitalist economic *system* and its imperatives as the cause of economic crises and inequality, not the people inevitably involved in it. By examining how market imperatives necessitate choices that are bad for society, they point towards how the economy might be run in the future to serve the interests of everyone rather than simply some people's profits. Leftist economic analysis thus provides a possible way past the endless moral blame and division that currently paralyze our culture.

A globalized workforce creates cheaper consumable goods, which everyone likes, but is also a problem for workers in the West who cannot live on the type of wages that, say, workers in Vietnam can indeed live (poorly) on. Automation is a real problem for working-class people all over the world. It often leaves them without job security or benefits, laid off, stranded without a job and with the need to move and/or "retool," propositions both personally costly and risky. When they are not eliminated, the jobs that people do get in the manufacturing, retail, and service sectors pay less and less because they're automated enough to require fewer skills—workers become more and more interchangeable. Think of the checkout person at the big-box hardware store who now stands between lines of eight to ten customer-operated cash registers and looks on in case anyone has a problem. Not only are the customers now working for the store, not only has the checkout machinery replaced eight to ten cashiers, but the one employee left now has a job that is not as interesting as a cashier's job. Much of his work involves simply observing and only minimally interacting with either the people or the machines.[56]

---

54. Wark, *Capital Is Dead*; see also Standing, *Precariat*.
55. Wood, *Origin of Capitalism*.
56. Standing, *Precariat*; Ikeler, "Deskilling Emotional Labour."

Automation may seem like a blessing for employees who are still employed. They have less work to do and still get paid for practically just standing there, at least in some cases. But from another angle, this minimization of effort is a great misuse of a good person's time. Such jobs do not allow people to display their full range of abilities. Work can be enjoyable on many levels, including being able to show what you know; to have the chance to learn and develop new skills; and to take the opportunity to interact with coworkers, customers, and clients.[57] More and more, though, work is monotonous and isolating, and yet we spend eight or more hours a day, at least five days a week, doing it. This is a product of the competitive drive for efficiency at which capitalists excel. Capitalism provides fewer and fewer high-paying and secure jobs, and more boring jobs for lower-wage employees. At some point, the system starts to bite itself in the tail. Who will have enough money to purchase things at the necessary rate to keep the charts moving ever upward? Huge amounts of consumer as well as government debt have been accrued in the pursuit of endless growth for this very reason. Some are now talking about the inevitability of a fully rental economy (in which most people never really own anything) because of this dynamic.[58]

Leftist thought provides us with a better and less moralistic understanding of the pitfalls of cost-cutting competition and automation. It also helps us get away from the trap of blaming the effects and not the cause. We blame the effects when we think that racism is the primary problem and not an effect of stress that causes people to seek scapegoats. We blame the effects when we say that Mexican or Somali workers are taking American jobs and causing domestic unemployment. In addition to blaming racists, progressives in the US tend to condemn "the rich" for economic problems like unemployment and underemployment. Again, Marxian thought generally assumes that no one is morally guilty for the massive destabilizing effects of global capitalism, not even "the rich." The problems, from this point of view, are systemic in nature. Yes, we have corrupt politicians and greedy short-sighted business leaders, but even if we eliminated everyone with character flaws and somehow replaced them with either morally upright people or robots, we'd still get the same dynamics from the system.[59]

57. Sennett, *Craftsman*.

58. See Rinne, "Sharing Economy."

59. This point is what Trump sometimes tried to convey when he explained why he tried to dodge taxes. He was saying that everyone did what it took to survive in a corrupt system, including himself.

At the international level, capitalism splits up extended and nuclear families in developing countries and eliminates the traditional ways of life that allow people to feed and shelter themselves with less need for cash. Like what happened to nineteenth- and early twentieth-century Europeans described by G. K. Chesterton in *The Outline of Sanity*, people in developing countries lose the support of their families, tribes or communities, extended families, and means of local food production as they join the globalized production and consumption market. They become extremely vulnerable, even with their manufacturing income.[60] There is a lag between the beginning of the integration of local economies into the global economic system and where that integration naturally ends. The United States has already lived through this transformation away from strong local communities whose members could work together to supply each other's needs. People in the developing world are getting there even faster and without the same level of wealth built up in the form of inheritances, and a reliable welfare state to cushion the blow. We are living through times in which the developing world's tribes, extended families, and local communities are unraveling in the face of the same economic pressures that leveled rural life in America, and the Native American way of life before that,[61] giving rise to extremism, terrorism, civil war, and mass migration. All of this is also exacerbated by climate change producing disruptions in agriculture and destroying places people used to be able to live.[62]

An argument that points out all the cultural destruction caused by economic trends could be made *only* via an intersection of classically conservative and leftist analysis. The classical conservative cares the most about what happens to extended family, nuclear family, and local community; the leftist keeps his eye on the economic forces doing the damage.[63] The conservative tends to propose changes to restore traditional social institutions, even if on a new cultural footing. The leftist tends to look towards solutions that do not restore these older social institutions but repurpose and maximize the value of built-up capital and technological know-how, though what constitutes progress is always debatable.

60. Chesterton, *Outline of Sanity*.
61. Berry, *Unsettling of America*.
62. IOM and UN-OHRLLS, *Climate Change and Migration*; Lennox, "Climate Change and Globalization"; Dell'Angelo et al., "Tragedy of Grabbed Commons."
63. Christopher Lasch is an example of this kind of thinker. See for instance Lasch, *Revolt of the Elites*.

Though the best of leftist thought takes blame out of the equation, it does shine a light on the political level, where left- and right-liberal politicians do their best to stop any sort of popular push for real systemic economic change. Even here, though, we must realize that because of the way we've set up our political systems, politicians must compete to survive as well, and a large part of that competition comes in the form of obtaining enough funding to campaign against and beat their rivals. To do that, politicians naturally take money from corporate interests and then listen to them more than other constituents. This is a leftist political insight, although it's one that is so familiar that many people who agree with it may not realize they're thinking like Marx.[64] Political corruption makes it difficult to change the capitalist system that Mark Fisher called "capitalist realism." Fisher simply meant that no one can even imagine a different way of running things.[65] But some can envision a better way of life.

Marx theorized that all countries would eventually pass through advanced capitalism and then, in a great revolution, they would move into a stateless global communism.[66] That has not happened. But Marx's vision of what communism would be like was quite different and much more attractive than what happened in countries like Russia and China. In Marx's view, future communists would collectively control the economy, including the factories and other productive forces, the means of transportation and distribution. He credited capitalism with creating the capability for all to live in material abundance through mass production, with its technology to lighten the workload and speed up manufacturing. He also argued that capitalism had socialized labor by amassing an industrial army of workers, all directed and aimed at a common (corporate) cause. But he thought it more than ironic that this capitalist army of workers, already collectivized through their highly organized labor, could toil all day but obtain only a small fraction of the benefit. Even more ironic was the situation that periodically occurred in which most workers were paid so little that they could not afford to buy the very things they produced.[67]

---

64. See the classics of this way of thinking: Parenti, *Democracy for the Few*; Beard, *Economic Interpretation of Constitution*.

65. Fisher, *Capitalist Realism*.

66. Marx and Engels, *Communist Manifesto*.

67. See Marx, "Critique of Gotha Program."

For Marx, capitalism was the goose that laid the golden egg—increasingly automated mass production—but the egg was in danger of never being hatched because the capitalist system would not allow it to achieve its ultimate end. In his view, the amazing technological improvements and economic growth spawned by capitalists were being used, not to benefit everyone involved, but to benefit a few who had amassed most of the capital in their hands. We all know there is a tendency in capitalism for wealth to be increasingly concentrated and for monopolies to take away the very competition that the system relies on to spread the wealth more broadly.[68] Only governments can slow this process down by regulating businesses and breaking up monopolies. But we also know why this doesn't happen much anymore—politicians are beholden to the ultimate collectivized system (huge corporations, which are now, in many ways, more powerful than our governments). It is becoming harder to make the distinction between commercial and governmental power. This entanglement no doubt partly accounts for the rise of populist anger about elections, even if the people involved cannot put their finger on why they feel like they are not really being represented.[69]

Marx thought we should take capitalism's greatest accomplishments—increased automation and collectivized/socialized labor—and finally make them work for instead of against human goals. At a higher level of economic development, the necessity of hurting workers (who are also "consumers") by cutting costs would no longer drive us. His vision of the future is the ultimate Enlightenment vision of a completely rationalized economic system, which reduces the working day, makes the work people do more social, involves the collectivized workers in the decision-making process every step of the way, and finally brings material abundance and leisure to every human being, not just the few.[70]

This all sounds desirable in its simplicity, and it does reveal the inner demons of the capitalist system. But notice that the Marxist vision embraces the goal of ever-increasing rates of growth, and it also has relatively little to say about the pollution and existential threat of climate change that have emerged as the worst unintended consequences of capitalist and communist economic striving. Marxism also does not concern itself much with whether families and communities change drastically, and it doesn't adequately address the luxury question. What do people in the

---

68. Elliott, "Karl Marx."
69. Mouffe, *Return of the Political*.
70. Chris Cutrone captures this idea well ("American Revolution and Left").

automated and efficient communist future do with all that time?[71] On the one hand, Marx thought work should be satisfying, because if done well, it would develop people's humanity. On the other hand, he thought that work time and workload would be reduced by automation, leaving people with more free time. Would they use that free time well? With hindsight, we surely must admit that when people are faced with more leisure time, they don't automatically do enriching things with that time.[72]

From Marx's perspective, technology was problematic only because it was being used for profit, creating a perverse incentive to make junk, hire fewer workers, and pay them less. But other streams of leftism do think that technology is inherently problematic. This is where, again, leftist insights can begin to merge with certain streams of conservative thought. Most right liberals today think that technological innovation is our salvation and, while it does create some problems, it will in due time solve all the problems it causes. Leftists like Jacques Ellul disagreed.

Ellul was a twentieth-century Christian anarchist. He authored *The Technological Society* to warn the West that what he called *technique* pervaded both state communist countries like the Soviet Union and liberal capitalist countries like the United States.[73] *Technique* for Ellul meant not only machine technology that escapes human control and assumes a destructive life of its own, but also the mentality pervasive in the East and West that embraced efficiency as a primary value, and specialization and bureaucratization as a way of life. Other authors call this phenomenon "technical rationality."[74] Modern governments and corporations use *technique*, splitting work up into discrete tasks done by different people or units in ever larger factorylike organizations, which has the effect of making no one responsible for the finished product. Many of the people involved do not even know exactly what the finished product will be, or how it will be used.[75] At a certain point, even efficiency is sacrificed as the organizational bureaucracy grows larger, because it too has taken on a life of its own.

Ellul's lifetime of work formed a passionate plea for us to become aware of the dehumanizing power of *technique* and to realize how much we

71. See Bastani, *Fully Automated Luxury Communism*; and Sennett, *Craftsman*, for two different takes on the prospects of a fully automated future.
72. See Sharif et al., "Too Little or Too Much Time."
73. Ellul, *Technological Society*.
74. Balfour et al., *Unmasking Administrative Evil*.
75. Even if it is only an idea, policy, software code, song, or brand.

need, somehow, to get it back under human control. Often, Ellul despaired of our ability to do so. Both communist and capitalist countries have a lot of bureaucracy, and capitalist countries have it not only in government at all levels but also in their supposedly separate "free market" sectors.[76] With bureaucracy comes less, not more, popular control of government and corporate power. When a corporation moves manufacturing overseas because it is beholden by law to its stockholders to make the maximum profit, no one person or unit made that decision, no individual is to blame, and no one can decide to change the outcome.[77]

We need to recover insights from Ellul and others who are even harder to categorize and are often forgotten in our current polarized discourse. Some examples of heterodox thinkers include historian and social commentator Christopher Lasch, agrarian activist and poet Wendell Berry, and nineteenth-century Romantic authors like William Blake. It is somewhat chilling to remember what people during the inception and development of collectivized factory and factory farm production had to say about how it changed their world. What they wanted instead of increasing scientific and technological tinkering, mass production, efficiency, and economic growth was beauty and peace of mind. Blake, for instance, wondered where God was to be found in this new polluted and ugly terrain when he wrote this:

> And did the Countenance Divine,
> Shine forth upon our clouded hills?
> And was Jerusalem builded here,
> Among these dark Satanic Mills?[78]

Political Theology

It's hard not to agree with William Blake, even in the twenty-first century. Our technological creations blur our vision of the Divine now more than ever. Our "dark Satanic mills" were born in the Enlightenment from faith in human reason and the goodness and inevitability of technological "progress." But faith more rightly implies belief in the ultimate goodness and desirability of God and creation, not human reason. From a Christian perspective, faith in anything or anyone other than

---

76. I will be arguing that the market in "free market" markets is not free.
77. Mander, *Absence of the Sacred*.
78. Blake, "Jerusalem," stanza 2.

God is idolatry, even if it's an idea like progress. Our modern secular idols include science, technology, bureaucratic organization, and belief in progress itself.[79] As opposed to secular religions—political ideologies—Christian faith *does not* require people to have no doubts about human schemes (or even about God's providence). Those who embrace secular gods *do* tend to portray the goodness of their ideas and proposals as obvious and beyond rational doubt. Yet without deep doubt about the value of science, technology, and bureaucratic organization, we will continue to believe in things that may be useful in some ways but cannot deliver the fulfillment they promise.

We don't have to look very far to find evidence of the recklessness of our misplaced faith in modern idols. Think of the ways in which the fruits of science and technology have posed existential threats to humanity—from potential atomic/nuclear Armageddon to environmental change that brings more floods, wildfires, and species extinctions. Think about how science and technology have been used for decades to make our food ever more palatable and ever more unhealthy, fast, and cheap, leading to low-wage jobs, rampant obesity, heart disease, cancer, and other physical afflictions.[80] Think about how many reputable scientists and scientific institutions were involved in helping us accept cigarette smoking as safe and even healthy.[81] Contemplate again the increasingly mind-numbing, simplified, and automated work that many of us do each day thanks to technology and scientific management techniques that are routinely presented as major humanizing advancements.[82]

Given all of this, it is sheer hubris for scientists to argue that people should simply accept their authority and believe that they are obviously and exclusively working for humanity's well-being. Only unquestioning *faith* in science would blind people to the checkered history of our scientific and technological innovations.[83] The truth is that the history of science is partly why it is now so hard for people to accept any sort of authority as legitimate. Technically knowledgeable authority has repeatedly

---

79. Brueggemann, *Out of Babylon*.

80. Most scientists work for industries and not for the public at research institutions, and even the ones at research institutions are often working on corporate grants. They are not free to seek the truth wherever it leads or to question the goals of technological progress.

81. Oreskes and Conway, *Merchants of Doubt*.

82. McCarraher, *Enchantments of Mammon*.

83. See Kuhn, *Structure of Scientific Revolutions*, for an understanding of how the human and often very creative process of scientific advancement really takes place.

let us down. This sense of disappointment is, I believe, behind much of the skepticism over vaccines, masks, and other policies promoted by scientific and political authorities in recent memory. Moreover, the questioning of science and authority is not inherently bad. In fact, it is a sign that people still are human—deeply skeptical, attempting to think for themselves, unwilling to simply believe what they are told. But at this point, our culture's growing anti-authority stance has paralyzed us just when we need objective science the most to deal with problems such as climate change and deadly pandemics. Scientists' repeatedly asking why people do not trust their knowledge is not helpful in this situation.

Questioning the goodness or inevitability of our culture's idea of progress does not mean that there can never be improvement or that the "clock" must be "turned back." Quite the contrary—only if we let go of our idea of the *inherent* desirability of *all* technological and organizational advancement can we hope to truly improve our situation even in the areas of technology and organization. Brueggemann has said that "the dominant script of both selves and communities in our society, for both liberals and conservatives, is the script of therapeutic, technological, consumerist militarism that permeates every dimension of our common life," adding that he uses the term "technological" "following Jacques Ellul, to refer to the assumption that everything can be fixed and made right through human ingenuity; there is no issue so complex or so remote that it cannot be solved."[84] These "sayings are hard" (John 6:60), easily misunderstood, but they should be better understood than they are by those informed by Christianity. If Christians do not consistently refer to Christ as the ultimate measure of what is truly an improvement in all areas, if they unthinkingly equate Christ's moral stance with economic growth and technological advancement, Christianity will be of no help when economic "progress" is actually dangerous, harmful, alienating, or dehumanizing.

Why is the church often mute or at least very tepid when it comes to criticizing much of what harms individuals, families, and communities? Perhaps it is because a commercialized and thoroughly money-integrated Christianity that verges constantly on idolatry has no ability to oppose whatever promises "economic growth."[85] This type of

---

84. Brueggemann, "Counterscript."

85. Brian Zahnd's personal journey of struggle with the American Christian church will come through in this book from time to time, much of it surrounding this issue of idolatry. See, for example, Zahnd, *Postcards from Babylon*.

Christianity is critical of the fruits of science on a few hot-button issues like abortion or the theory of evolution, but it mostly ignores all the ways in which rudderless science and technology cause death, illness, dislocation, and poverty. Sadly, compromised Christianity has been around for a long time.[86] Today, it often serves to mobilize people to contribute their time and money to political interests that do not deliver a better world. Instead, donations often result in things Christians wouldn't normally support. These include the abuse of power corporations wield over employees and customers,[87] a globalized economy that outsources jobs, environmental harms that threaten the livelihoods of farmers and many other people who rely on the land (not to mention everyone's food sources), and the necessary price of world dominance—a costly and deadly US military involvement around the world that inevitably kills innocent people.[88] The enticements into this Faustian bargain are old but reliable hot-button single issues like being pro-capitalism, pro-life, or advocating for gun rights and "liberty."

Christians in the US don't often grapple with the reality that they have become political tools. To use explicitly theological language, they are too often manipulated by those with an interest in death and slavery—death because they literally cause death and pull people away from life in God, and slavery because the people who get entrapped in these ideological battles are really working for someone else without compensation. They've been enticed into a shell game—they focus on one shell, try to follow it, and forget about the rest of the shells full of mind-blowing, catastrophic, death-dealing chaos. To add insult to injury, people who get caught up in this game line corporate pockets in the process.[89] Most do not fully appreciate that the cultural problems the right wing focuses on, such as endangered marriages and abortions, are *never solved* no matter how many Republicans get elected, or even when the Supreme Court overrules Roe v. Wade. They have faithfully donated, purchased, posted, and emailed but, if anything, cultural decay just gets more pervasive and complex, and people get more divided.[90] This is proof of the insight that the most powerful way

---

86. See McCarraher, *Enchantments of Mammon*.

87. See indictments of Amazon, Walmart, etc., at United for Respect, "Fight for Good Jobs."

88. Zahnd, *Farewell to Mars*.

89. For an example of how leaders with ulterior motives can manipulate people into enthusiastically supporting their lifestyle, see Mak, "New York Attorney General."

90. See Douthat, *Decadent Society*, for an admirably complete description of our state of decadence.

to get people to obey is to make them think that it's their idea, and the best way to do that is to keep them in a constant state of moral crusade.[91] The crusading spirit is narcissistic, oppressive, and repulsive, as we try to do the impossible and bring heaven to earth.[92] It is a manifestation of what Carl Jung called "ideological possession."[93]

The crusading spirit has led many US Christians to identify policies on health and workplace safety as essentially religious in their importance. When we deal with possible unionization or workplace health and safety issues such as masking during a pandemic as *essentially* religious, are we not treating our economy or our own autonomy as our God?[94] Poor people, whom the Christian church once characterized as *in loco Dei*, are seen as problems, or not seen at all, by many contemporary Christians. "The market ideology declares that to be a widow, orphan, or immigrant—or to be unemployed—is a self-inflicted wound. It's your fault."[95] But our current economic system was not made by God like rocks and trees. It was made by flawed, chaotic human beings. The fact that we cannot effectively even *suspend* unnecessary economic activity and share with others for a short period of time in favor of the common good, the fact that we are willing to endanger our elders and the weakest among us not out of absolute material destitution but from fear of a slowing of the gears of economic growth, suggests that the economy rules our choices, not God.[96]

In this book, I will turn to Christian thinkers who dare to say they don't have all the answers but present a different way of viewing Christian duty than what is described above. I will draw from a variety of

---

91. Slavoj Žižek makes this point a lot. See *Year of Dreaming Dangerously* for good examples.

92. As Eric Voegelin puts it, "immanentizing the eschaton" (*New Science of Politics*).

93. See L. Johnson, *Ideological Possession*.

94. As Yanis Varoufakis often argues, capitalism is a chosen economy. See for instance, Varoufakis, "Economics without Capitalism."

95. Block et al., *Other Kingdom*, 39.

96. Senator Robert P. Casey Jr. said in his opening statement at the hearing before the Special Committee on Aging, March 18, 2021, "We all know that older adults have suffered the brunt of this pandemic, accounting for 81 percent of all deaths. A tragedy within the broader tragedy of this pandemic has taken place in our Nation's long-term care setting, where more than 178,000—more than 178,000—residents and workers combined have died from COVID-19." Despite this, not only did many people continue to dispute the reality of the pandemic, but many of those people were the grandchildren of the 81 percent, i.e., those under thirty. See Vasilopoulos et al., "Factors Underlying Denial."

ressourcement thinkers and theologians, including David Schindler, D. C. Schindler, and Larry Chapp.[97] I will draw on other spiritual resources from thinkers as diverse as Wendell Berry, Walter Brueggemann, Jacques Ellul, Jürgen Moltmann, Charles Taylor, and Brian Zahnd.[98] I will also be relying on the deposit of Catholic social teaching that bears on my topic.[99] This list does not reflect a unified theology, and these thinkers certainly would not all agree on politics. They take different approaches to God, Jesus, the human soul, metaphysical evil, and questions of community. But they are all asking what life would be like if the Christian God were truly at the center of our lives. For Zahnd, as well as many Christian anarchists, this amounts to proclaiming that Jesus is King, and not the US government, economy, or military, a proclamation that at the beginning of Zahnd's reconversion lost him about half his congregation.[100]

What would a genuinely Christian community look like? If Christians started consistently living their faith rather than just writing checks and getting involved in politics, I suspect they would begin to create communities that would be so attractive that there would be no need to proselytize. For those who are already doing some of this, such as working a food pantry or acting as a court-appointed special advocate, imagine if being a Christian in action were your full-time occupation. The more members of a Christian community could do for each other, the less government in all its many meanings would be needed (including, most likely, court-appointed special advocates), and the less wasteful consumption would occur. As a result, people's lives would be less impacted by government bureaucracy, corporate manipulation, and mammon worship. Arguably, at a certain point, they could drop the profit motive and even monetary income itself (to do this perfectly, they would already have to be beyond a money economy). If all this could somehow happen, they would be freer from overarching human power, but they would all have to deal with each other with less escape.[101] They would

97. See, for instance, David Schindler, *Heart of the World*; D. C. Schindler, *Politics of the Real*; Chapp, *Confession of Catholic Worker*.

98. Here is a suggested book for each of them: Berry, *Life Is a Miracle*; Brueggemann, *Prophetic Imagination*; Ellul, *Anarchy and Christianity*; Moltmann, *Crucified God*; Taylor, *Secular Age*.

99. See Kwasniewski, *Catholic Social Teaching*. I draw especially from Leo XIII, *Rerum Novarum*; Pius XI, *Quadregesimo Anno*; John Paul II, *Laborem Exercens*; John Paul II, *Centesimus Annus*; Francis, *Laudato Si'*.

100. Zahnd, *Postcards from Babylon*.

101. Famously, capitalism hides its social relations behind things; or more

have to learn how to really love, because otherwise they would never be able to consistently cooperate. The price of living Christianity would be ... other people, from whom you could not escape.[102]

Full Christian community was the original vision of the Catholic Worker movement, though much of that movement now has been reduced to radically committed forms of charitable work. In this book, the Catholic Worker movement and its original instigators, Peter Maurin and Dorothy Day, will be a source of inspiration for a different vision of Christian praxis.[103]

Many US Christians have been trained to think that living beyond the profit motive is somehow inextricably tied up with evil and oppression, a belief that keeps people from even dreaming about truly changing human practices for the better. It would take a collective decision for, say, a church or other group to abandon that thinking and head off in the direction of a stronger community. As they assessed their resources and began to rely on each other, members might at first trust each other enough to pool more of their resources and ask each other first for their needs before working more, or going to the government, a therapist, an assisted living center, childcare center, grocery store, or Internet-mediated supply chain. Being self-contained would not be the goal. Isolating and removing the Christian community from the rest of the world was never part of Jesus's agenda, though there have been times when it seemed necessary.[104]

An economic system such as ours must keep growing all the time to prevent death and suffering from lack of food and shelter, not to mention suicide.[105] In 2019–20, some people thought that this fact was enough to prove that we needed to ignore the pandemic and just get back to work. Of course, some thought that COVID-19 was not even real, but most people who wanted to work through the contagion without any restrictions were

---

specifically, the relations among people take on the fantastic form of a "relation between things" (Marx, *Capital*, 1:54). This is a major source of alienation according to Marx.

102. Sartre famously wrote, "Hell is—other people!" (*No Exit*, 54).

103. McKanan, *Catholic Worker after Dorothy*.

104. One can see the monasteries of the early Middle Ages as enacting this strategy. Rod Dreher argues that now is perhaps one of those times in which Christians must sequester themselves from the rest of the world in order to preserve the faith (*Benedict Option*). While I sympathize with the fear this argument is built on, I will disagree in this book that the Benedict option is the best option.

105. This is something President Trump repeatedly pointed out, but not in the name of any sort of economic change.

simply afraid of the very real economic consequences if they did not. They were afraid to the point that they protested mask wearing as detrimental to business because they thought masks kept customers away. Often tying their mask and vaccine stances to their Christian faith, their horizon of liberty had shrunk until being "anti-mask" in their Facebook comments, not wearing a mask, or wearing a mask wrongly became seen as bold and defiant acts of Christian protest and resistance. What does this say about the true state of either Christianity or freedom?

Many US Christians during this time misunderstood the origins of their loss of freedom, and their questioning of authority missed the mark. Truly, their freedom had already been greatly diminished because of the overwhelming influence of corporate money over their work, government, and places of worship, and it was not going to bounce back based on their attitudes towards masks or even their stockpiling of guns. The insurrection at the US Capitol on January 6, 2021, made it clear that some people were either capable of, or didn't much mind, the use of deadly force to assert absolute control over their bodies, gun ownership, and support for Donald Trump as Christian principles. This represents a setback for Christianity, whose definition and scope at this point need another articulation. It is my hope that this book will at least point some readers in that direction.

Political Psychology

Political and economic insights stemming from theology are usefully supplemented by certain strains of psychology, which can explain the mechanisms by which people move from faith in a transcendent God to a secular faith or "ideological possession." Political psychology as a discipline is a curative for the tendency of most modern psychology to focus responsibility, and often blame, exclusively on the individual or, at most, the family unit. Focusing on the individual ignores the material and cultural pressures that bear on individuals and families and have a large role to play in causing psychological problems. This approach lets the material and cultural causes of mental illness fester, and when they are not addressed, the results can be upticks in violent crime, drug and alcohol abuse, and perhaps most significant for our purposes, various forms of religious and political extremism.[106]

106. Fisher, *Capitalist Realism*.

The psychological mechanisms of extremism were the subject of my last book, which had its foundations in the political psychology of Carl Jung. Jung was a twentieth-century psychologist who argued that modern empiricism and rationalism, and the subsequent waning belief in anything transcendent, created a painful sense of alienation.[107] He argued that to avoid that pain, human beings would either transfer to themselves godlike importance (psychic inflation), or they would transfer godlike qualities to political ideologies, nation-states, or dangerous charismatic leaders (mass psychosis). Jung blamed mass psychosis for the catastrophes of World War I and World War II. It is a process that "snowballs" because people are social creatures and, when those around them seem to all agree, they shut down critical thought and move into the realm of pure emotion and instinct.

Jung argued that real religion was superior to ideology when it came to supporting people's mental health. Real as opposed to secular faith retains the idea of something greater and beyond human understanding or powers. Real religion, in which the transcendent being was perceived as truly above normal human capacities and understandings and not controllable by man, kept a person's psyche in its proper place. Only if people kept seriously in mind that they were limited and flawed human beings who did not possess godlike powers and wisdom would their psyches be safe from either extreme narcissism or the lure of political extremism. Seen in this light, today's Christian right's obsession with political power and the figure of Donald Trump as a sort of savior is a symptom of mass psychosis, a self-reinforcing and highly political mass movement that leads to heightened displays of loyalty, belonging, and aggression in the pursuit of gaining and keeping political power.

Jung's suggestion that we might be psychologically healthier with authentic religion, indeed that we might be better off accepting a certain amount of mystery, awe, and ritual, is unacceptable to modern secularists. But we must keep in mind that Jung was grappling with the immediate and unprecedented phenomenon of fascism, Nazism, and totalitarian communism in the twentieth century. Remembering that will help even the most secularly minded reader see why Jung endorsed proper religion as a cure. In his essay "After the Catastrophe" he wrote that the first cause of the political extremism of his time was urbanization during and

---

107. L. Johnson, *Ideological Possession*.

after the Industrial Revolution. The second cause was the rise of the large modern state, made necessary by the subsequent massification of people.

> Thanks to industrialization, large portions of the population were up-rooted and were herded together in large centres. This new form of existence—with its mass psychology and social dependence on the fluctuations of markets and wages—produced an individual who was unstable, insecure, and suggestible. He was aware that his life depended on boards of directors and captains of industry, and he supposed, rightly or wrongly, that they were chiefly motivated by financial interests. He knew that, no matter how conscientiously he worked, he could still fall victim at any moment to economic changes which were utterly beyond his control.[108]

Many people working and living closely together in urban industrialized settings created a "herd" mentality, according to Jung. "Mass man" felt insignificant and anonymous in the crowd.[109] At the same time, people felt the "other life" of transcendent faith slipping from their grasp. Factory and office work reduced people's sense of freedom and agency in their workplace and social environments, and with less agency came the sense that they had less moral responsibility. Jung pointed out that working for wages, rather than working for subsistence (self- and family sufficiency), was inherently precarious and heightened people's anxiety accordingly. In a preindustrial setting, a rural person's livelihood might have been affected by a natural disaster, protection from which he could at least appeal to God. In the postindustrial urban environment, workers were affected by the faceless and seemingly godless "market." Jung's observations on individual and family precarity within the new capitalist system resonated with Marx's view almost a century earlier that capitalism had "resolved personal worth into exchange value, and in place of the numberless indefeasible chartered freedoms, has set up that single, unconscionable freedom—Free Trade."[110] Marx, however, was not unhappy about the development, because he saw it as a necessary stage in the path towards communism.

Jung also understood that the growth of government that culminated in the "welfare state" was a necessary evil that grew up alongside and supported the capitalist market economy. In his view, it too encouraged

---

108. Jung, "Psychology of the Unconscious," 71.
109. Similar observations were made by Ortega y Gasset, *Revolt of the Masses*.
110. Marx and Engels, *Communist Manifesto*, 76.

a mass mentality. He wrote, "The steady growth of the Welfare State is no doubt a very fine thing from one point of view, but from another it is a doubtful blessing, as it robs people of their individual responsibility and turns them into infants and sheep."[111] The state's aggressive extension in the late twentieth and twenty-first centuries into the economy generally and in regulating, planning, and organizing many areas of life, such as banking and finance, economic development, farming and food, education and health care, all in the name of human welfare and a certain type of consumer "freedom," only makes Jung's observations more relevant.[112] This extension has been overseen by both Republican and Democratic administrations in the US, even though the ideological rhetoric of the two parties has always differed fairly dramatically. It has happened in tandem with, and in support of, the neoliberal economic changes that will be discussed at length in this book.

The rural/urban political division in the United States is one very noticeable result of those changes, and it has only gotten worse over the decades. The twentieth century witnessed the virtual destruction of the independent diversified family farm, and with it, small towns and small businesses, rural places of worship, cultural practices, and traditions. In the 1970s, Wendell Berry foresaw the consequences of this great social and economic upheaval, comparing what had happened to rural communities to the prior fate of Native Americans—the "conquerors" bringing a seemingly ineluctable destructive commercial growth:

> Time after time, in place after place, these conquerors have fragmented and demolished traditional communities, the beginnings of domestic cultures. They have always said that what they destroyed was outdated, provincial, and contemptible. And with alarming frequency they have been believed and trusted by their victims, especially when their victims were other white people.[113]

Along with Berry, political philosophers Eric Voegelin, Christopher Lasch, and Charles Taylor, among others, basically agree with Jung's psychological insights at least in this one respect: when social and cultural

---

111. Jung, "After the Catastrophe," 201.
112. This is how W. Brown characterizes neoliberalism in *Undoing the Demos*.
113. Berry, *Unsettling of America*, 6.

dislocation takes place, the resulting pain and alienation can cause political upheaval, including mass extremism.[114]

In another context, we find the same devastating dynamics in twentieth- and twenty-first-century urban areas in which "urban renewal," economic development schemes, and freeways have destroyed long-established neighborhoods in the name of progress. In historical order, first came the urban renewal projects of the mid-twentieth century that caused such anger among disrupted African American communities that riots were the result; the riots led to the "flight" of millions of whites, followed by more disruption to urban neighborhoods caused by freeway construction to accommodate dislocated white suburban commuters. This process has been likened to "root shock." Just as plants uprooted from their soil wither and die, communities' stress of losing material and social foundations is tremendous.[115]

If alienation and root shock are the cause of various social disturbances from urban race riots to white right-wing militia movements, then our focus should not be on the inability of some people to understand "the other," or learn science, or care about the environment, as though the main problem is their intellectual and/or moral failings. Our focus should instead be on fixing the material and cultural deprivations caused by dislocation and alienation in both rural and urban places. For instance, if we want coal miners in West Virginia to support green energy and the politics necessary to achieve it, we should treat them as important to society's overall health, making sure they have meaningful work to do, proper education, and health care, etc. We should not harangue them for their ignorance or moral failures, tell them to figure out how to retool on their own, or ask them to leave West Virginia for another job. If we do, we are proving that we are part of mass psychosis, not part of the cure. Interestingly, attempting to address the causes of the problem rather than the results coincides with the Christian values of love and forgiveness that many Americans profess in church. Thus, we complete the Jungian insight at the beginning of this section that lived real religion is the preventative for mass psychosis.

This book will attempt not only to diagnose our current malaise but to point towards a cure, which as indicated by some of the streams I've discussed here, I believe must partly come from changes in our material

---

114. Voegelin, *New Science of Politics*; Lasch, *Revolt of the Elites*; Taylor, *Secular Age*.
115. Fullilove, *Root Shock*.

circumstances. But there is not, nor has there ever been for long, enough political will to make this happen via reason alone. If I simply argue that people need to understand the origins of our current social and political disruptions to stop them, I would be falling into the same trap as those who blame others for just not respecting science or some other source of rational authority. Obviously, spiritual and psychological deficits lie in the way of contemplating meaningful change. Any solution to our long-festering divisions and our general decline must include a reassessment of the meaning and place of faith and its relationship to politics.

2

Unsettling 1: Leaving the Farm

THE PROCESS I AM about to describe through the story of Harold and Bonnie Bailey, and the fictional Ward and June Cleaver, is the story Wendell Berry tells in so many of his books, both nonfiction and fiction. The chief among those books is *The Unsettling of America: Culture and Agriculture*. There is no substitute for reading this book yourself, but among the insights of *Unsettling* is that once people are forcibly displaced from the location that they have occupied, lived, and worked on for generations, it is not only their location and occupations that change. With displacement comes the destruction of the local culture that supported practices that kept people alive, healthy, socially supported, and economically resilient.

Psychologist Glenn Swogger used the term "dislocation" instead of "displacement" for this phenomenon, and in doing so, widened the aperture of the concept. Using a term used by Charles Taylor in much the same way, he argued that we are inherently *embedded* creatures. It is our nature:

> We are born helpless to care for ourselves, and hence dependent on others. We are born speechless, which we acquire from others. The language that we learn to speak describes a specific world: family, clan, tribe (distinguishing us from other families and tribes). Our values, our social understandings, our sense of the world are soaked up with our mother's milk, by interactions with other close siblings and family members, and by the communities and localities in which we live. We see ourselves

as individuals—and we are—but we are individuals formed and stamped with the characteristics of a specific social matrix, with its characteristics, its peculiarities, and its adaptive and not-so-adaptive habits of thought and action.[1]

Swogger called the result of both voluntary and involuntary removal from our social matrix "dislocation." The development from feudalism into modernity traced by authors like Carl Jung, Leo Strauss, Charles Taylor, and David Schindler, who will be featured in chapter 4, was a process of dislocation and disembedding of Europeans from their social contexts. Dislocations have increased exponentially for those Europeans and their descendants since the fourteenth century, due to rapid changes in technology, transport, and economic arrangements. According to Swogger, "Such changes include immigration, exile, war, family breakdown, rapid social change, social and economic turmoil, changes in our perception of our future, and our changing position in our social network as we age."[2] As inherently socially embedded creatures, dislocations can easily damage and threaten our humanity. The Scientific and Industrial Revolutions were triggers for the acceleration of change, and now we have arrived at a time when people can credibly talk about the possibility of "the singularity," a point of no return in which our technology moves completely beyond our control and becomes an autonomous guiding force on the planet, changing human life in unpredictable and profound ways.[3]

Human beings are now constantly confronted with dislocation, so much so that most have never experienced, and cannot even imagine, the embedded existence most people have lived throughout human history.[4] With "dislocation" comes the destruction of traditional culture, or what Edmund Burke referred to as the "social fabric."[5] Burke argued

---

1. Swogger, "Apocalyptic Evil and Dislocation," 2. Swogger's manuscript on dislocation was bequeathed to me in 2021 after years of conversation about his projects and mine, because we were both interested in political psychology. It is my intention to eventually work through his unpublished material, build on it when necessary, and publish it as a book.

2. Swogger, "Apocalyptic Evil and Dislocation," 5.

3. See Shanahan, *Technological Singularity*.

4. I will deal with Charles Taylor's concept of embeddedness more in ch. 4, but his *Secular Age* is an excellent attempt to gain some knowledge of what the embedded and "enchanted" frame of mind must have been like for most people. See also Dyer, *Making a Living*.

5. Burke uses the term "fabric" five times in *Reflections on the Revolution*. For

that once the fabric is torn, that piece of cloth could never be whole again. People could try to repair it, but it would be different and weaker than before. As Charles Taylor knew about the destruction of the feudal "enchanted" world, it is impossible to recreate a culture once lost. Burke thought, for that very reason, that people in positions of power, as well as people who would protest and even fight for radical change, should step back and respect the value of preserving long-standing cultures. Rather than continual reinvention of ourselves, our livelihoods, politics, and environment, Burke counseled incremental reforms that incorporated as much as was good in previous traditions and lifeways, even if it meant keeping some of the bad.[6]

For Burke, stability was that important to human survival and happiness. This was not the mentality of the "get big or get out" trend that hit American farmers starting in the 1950s. Berry is not shy about calling that trend a part of capitalism, and pointing out that the juggernaut of capitalism has been the demise, not only of local agriculture but local culture. He argues in *The Unsettling of America* that the two go hand in hand: "Let me emphasize that I am not talking about an evil that is merely contemporary or 'modern,' but one that is as old in America as the white man's presence here. It is an intention that was organized here almost from the start."[7]

Of course, the most violent impact on Native Americans was from proximity to settlers (i.e., unfamiliar diseases, weapons, and substances), and settlers' efforts to remove them from any territory they wanted to occupy.[8] But there was another, less straightforward way

---

instance, comparing the English Revolution of 1642 and the Restoration with the French Revolution, he wrote, "At both those periods the nation had lost the bond of union in their ancient edifice; they did not, however, dissolve the whole fabric" (*Reflections on the Revolution*, 19).

6. However, as with everything, one cannot say that Burke was simply or always an advocate of incrementalism or "gradualism." As William F. Byrne writes, "There is definitely an element of truth to this. Burke falls very much within the British gradualist tradition and can in fact be seen as one of the great articulators of this tradition. However, this interpretation is still somewhat problematic since it is not consistently supported by Burke's own political record. As a member of Parliament, he often took positions that are difficult to characterize as representing slow or incremental change. As will be shown, on some occasions Burke opposed even relatively modest changes, but at other times he supported changes that would have been quite dramatic" (Byrne, *Edmund Burke*, 17).

7. Berry, *Unsettling of America*, 7.

8. For an up-to-date analysis of the influence of new pathogens on indigenous peoples in the Americas, see Collen et al., "Immunogenetic Impact."

in which the Europeans affected the long-term trajectory of Native American cultures. Quoting Bernard DeVoto's *The Course of Empire*, Berry references "a constantly expanding market," which "expanded and integrated the industrial systems of Europe" into the new American economy. The European goods sold in the Americas, "tools, cloth, weapons, ornaments, novelties and alcohol," impacted Native American life severely. On the one hand, for those Native Americans lucky enough to survive, the means of mere survival became easier with new tools and goods. On the other hand, as a result, entire *cultures* continued to change rapidly, impacting the roles of men and women in tribal life, their standards of right and wrong, and the relative value of honor. The Indians developed "commercial values," and "became more mobile," to the extent that they attempted to join in the settlers' way of life. The result for Native American *culture* was "cataclysmic."[9] From a rudimentary but stable way of life revolving around seasons of the year and long-standing relationships, beliefs, and customs, to transience and constant forced adaptation, the fabric of Indian cultures frayed. Though they would survive, they would never be the same.

Berry treated DeVoto's analysis at some length because "he is so clearly describing a revolution that did not stop with the subjugation of the Indians but went on to impose substantially the same catastrophe upon the small farms and the farm communities, upon the shops of small local tradesmen of all sorts, upon the workshops of independent craftsmen, and upon the households of citizens. It is a revolution that is still going on."[10] That is, the culture-destroying aspect of the rapid, never-ending change implicit in the impending market imperatives of capitalism did not just impact the Native Americans or other indigenous people around the world. After establishing the supremacy of the white settlers, the same capitalist dynamics tore apart the settlers' own local cultures, and a similar dynamic went to work in successive waves of immigrants that came to the country looking for a fresh start. As Berry puts it:

> It is a revolution that is still going on. The economy is still substantially that of the fur trade, still based on the same general kinds of commercial items: technology, weapons, ornaments, novelties, and drugs. The one great difference is that by now the revolution has deprived the mass of consumers of any independent access to the staples of life: clothing, shelter, food, even

---

9. Berry, *Unsettling of America*, 7. See DeVoto, *Course of Empire*.
10. Berry, *Unsettling of America*, 8.

water. Air remains the only necessity that the average user can still get for himself, and the revolution has imposed a heavy tax on that by way of pollution. Commercial conquest is far more thorough and final than military defeat.[11]

In all cases, capitalism profoundly affected family dynamics and structures, rearranging the roles of men and women continuously, creating ever-increasing transience, and forcing constant retooling and adaptation. Berry is talking about the destruction of rural American culture, but really all human culture, in the solvent of (now) globalizing capitalism. This is what Zygmunt Bauman calls "liquid modernity."[12] Berry's point? What goes around comes around.

Novelist V. S. Naipul captured the ongoing losses of people around the world due to the dislocations of liquid modernity. His character Santosh starts life as a cook for a businessman in Bombay, sleeping on the pavement at night with his friends. But he is taken by his employer to live permanently in Washington, DC, supposedly a step up in both prestige and material well-being. Of his prior life in Bombay, Santosh says, paradoxically:

> I was so happy in Bombay. I was respected. I had a certain position. I worked for an important man. Some of us . . . lived on the street. The others were people who came to that bit of pavement to sleep. Respectable people; we didn't encourage riff-raff. . . . On the pavement we read newspapers, played cards, told stories and smoked. Except of course during the monsoon, I preferred to sleep on the pavement with my friends.[13]

Next, Santosh reflects on his life since moving to Washington:

> I was a free man. I could do anything I wanted . . . I could run away, hang myself, surrender, confess, hide. It didn't matter what I did, because I was alone. And I didn't know what I wanted to do . . . I found there was nothing to enjoy. . . . All that my freedom has brought me is the knowledge that I have a face

---

11. Berry, *Unsettling of America*, 8. Wendell Berry's new book is part memoir and part reflection, especially on the experience of Blacks in the South and racial prejudice: *Need to Be Whole*.

12. Bauman argues that we are in a novel phase of modernity, in which (borrowing from Marx) everything solid melts and everything sacred is profaned, social networks disintegrate, and collective action confronts paralyzing fluidity (*Liquid Modernity*).

13. Naipaul, "One Out of Many," 25.

and a body, that I must feed this body and clothe this body for a certain number of years. Then it will be over.[14]

We are all, albeit more slowly and with more material excess along the way, experiencing the same culture-destroying storm that hit the indigenous peoples of the Americas and that destroyed Santosh. Will we do something about it, or simply continue to adapt until we hit a state that does not seem quite human? There are people on both sides of the answer to that question, of course. In fact, there is an entire school of thought, established in the 1990s, advocating for moving beyond human limitations in a much more thoroughgoing way than we have already done. Transhumanists promote a future in which people are more intimately integrated with the machine than they are now. The transhumanist future is within our reach. We could use genetic engineering and implants to enhance our cognitive and physical strength and our longevity. We could wake up in the morning with the Internet in our field of vision. We could soon have an AI so powerful as to govern our lives more efficiently and rationally than we could ourselves, and we could no doubt colonize Mars or live and work in giant satellite villages orbiting the earth.[15] In other words, we could largely reinvent ourselves and become "post-human."[16] The transhumanist dream, it seems to me, is a desperate accelerationist vision.[17] It is an attempt to deal with the fact that we have already altered ourselves irreparably and are changing our conditions and ourselves more rapidly all the time. The transhumanists' gambit is that we can make good on this late-stage human development by going all the way to the conclusion rather than pulling back or changing the conclusion to something more human.

---

14. Naipaul, "One Out of Many," 58, 61. Gratitude to Glenn Swogger for featuring this short story in his unpublished manuscript on dislocation ("Apocalyptic Evil and Dislocation," 6).

15. These are not idle fantasies, but the aspirations of billionaire entrepreneurs Elon Musk (X–Twitter, Tesla) and Jeff Bezos (Amazon). For Musk's vision to colonize Mars, see SpaceX, "Mars & Beyond"; for Jeff Bezos's idea to create orbiting stations where people can work and live and things can be made, see https://www.blueorigin.com/about-blue.

16. So much has been written about the transhumanist vision, but here are a few recent contributions that will give the reader the basic landscape of this possible future: Hofkirchner and Kreowski, *Transhumanism*; Tumilty and Battle-Fisher, *Transhumanism*; Pilsch, *Transhumanism*.

17. See P. Gordon, "Left Accelerationism."

My primary reason for preferring humanity over the transhumanist option is my faith that God created the world and human beings and that it is wrong to attempt to alter his work to the point of obliterating its very nature. However, to appeal to a more worldly and pragmatic principle, it has certainly not been proven that our attempts since the Industrial Revolution to improve mankind's situation have made people *happier* or even *healthier* in the process. The US was at an all-time high in suicides as of 2022, at almost fifty thousand.[18] As I'll discuss more later in this chapter, farmers are among the citizens more likely to commit suicide. For them, technology has not helped them to be happier but has increased the pressure to get big or get out.

Get Big or Get Out

An ice storm struck the Bailey farm in the early morning of January 2, 1993, and a fire broke out somewhere in the dairy barn.[19] The Baileys never did figure out if the two were even related. Harold and Bonnie (Bonnie passed in February 2022) lived down the road and helped manage the farm with Harold's mother, who lived on site. Somehow the cows got out of the barn—Harold doesn't remember how—but in the freezing rain they now had to be housed somewhere else, and quickly. Before the fire trucks even arrived from Manhattan, Kansas, neighbors and family friends from as far away as Junction City descended on the farm to do what they could. They came with trucks and trailers, and in a now violent snowstorm, they rounded up and transported the Bailey cows to nearby Kansas State University's agricultural college. K-State professors and staff rallied quickly to house the cattle in the university barns for free, making sure each of them was identified as property of the Baileys',

---

18. "The latest provisional estimates for suicide deaths in the United States in 2022," according to the Centers for Disease Control on August 10, 2023: "After declining in 2019 and 2020, suicide deaths increased approximately 5% in the United States in 2021. The provisional estimates released today indicate that suicide deaths further increased in 2022, rising from 48,183 deaths in 2021 to an estimated 49,449 deaths in 2022, an increase of approximately 2.6%. However, two groups did see a decline in numbers, American Indian and Alaska Native people (down 6.1%) and people 10–24 years old (down 8.4%)" (CDC Newsroom, "Provisional Suicide Deaths").

19. The following information about Harold and Bonnie Bailey and the dairy barn fire that they experienced is from an interview that I conducted with them in 2019, in cooperation with undergraduate researchers Natalie Jabben and Erica Beebe, who transcribed the interview and helped construct the interview questions.

for safe return. The university staff milked them and even kept their milk separate from that of the university's cows, so the Baileys would not lose the money to be gained from its sale.

In telling me the story of the fire that consumed part of his inheritance, perhaps the part he loved the most, Harold did not sound sad. He put the emphasis on the help he received from others, not on mourning the loss of his property. He described his community—his neighbors, the friends from Junction City, and the people at K-State—as his extended family. It was a family that was there for him, his wife, and his mother when they needed it the most. He reflected on how it had changed his perspective about who he was—it was when he fully realized that he was deeply embedded in a community that supported him all along. "When I look back, I thought I was independent. I didn't worry about anything. I just took care of myself and my family. But the neighbors, they were really close. We were closer to our neighbors than some people in town who live closer [physically] to their neighbors, because back then your lives revolved around your community."

As that statement suggests, somehow Harold grew up feeling both independent and very *interdependent* with his neighbors. When he really needed help, he was not surprised that it just showed up unasked for. Throughout his life, if they really needed something, he knew his neighbors would be there for him. But the Baileys are living in a pocket of a fading system of neighborly relations based on long-time and even generational occupancy of land. Rural areas in the US have been vacated by families like the Baileys, who had occupied the land for generations. These areas, and the fewer people who are left to live in them, now often revolve around industries like large beef cattle operations, huge commodity crop farms, and meat-packing plants or prisons. Harold and Bonnie's world displays an unimaginable level of community closeness compared to what many people in rural areas experience today.

Most Americans don't live in towns in which their families have stayed grounded in the same land and work for generations. Most Americans also live with far more racial and cultural diversity, with all the attendant difficulties and prejudices that always seem to challenge people's ability to trust and cooperate with each other.[20] On average, Americans also seem to have become more emotionally isolated over time in a way that the Baileys have not. Many of us are more content than the Baileys

---

20. Barcus and Simmons, "Ethnic Restructuring."

to suffer on our own rather than to rely on anyone else, including our nuclear and extended families. If we can't make it on our own, we'd rather rely on state aid, insurance, or lawsuit money than to call on our family and friends for *real material help* (as opposed to occasional emotional support) when we are in need.[21] We have lost something very important in the process of progress, something the Baileys still had.

Sitting beside her husband as their dogs ran circles around the couch, Bonnie recognized that way back then, just as now, there is a balance to be had between individual autonomy and community concern and cooperation. She knew that neighbors could become intrusive or "nosey." But she felt as though her neighbors struck the right balance between ready availability and nosiness. She remarked that she and Harold "knew that if [their neighbors] had a problem we would go help. Most of the time we stayed out of everybody's business unless we knew they needed something." Harold agreed and described the situation with neighborly help as a part of an unspoken code. There was no need to make explicit agreements or arrangements with neighbors, and no need for government supervision or enactment of the community code. "It was just that way. Your neighbor over here broke his leg, and we the neighborhood all got together and plowed his wheat field," he said with a smile.

Bonnie and Harold described a situation of trust among people living near each other that represents one of the greatest virtues of a healthy community anywhere, but needed in rural and small-town life in the US, where help from officials may be harder to access. What they remembered enough to talk about at length was not emotional trust among neighbors, even though that was almost necessarily the case, since the neighbors were willing to come to their aid in an ice storm. They talked instead about material trust in the handling and sharing of things, and trust in the trading of labor. In the Baileys' environs, people didn't often lock their doors, and neighbors sometimes came onto their property to borrow a tool or a can of gasoline, even if no one was at home. Harold confirmed that his neighbors shared tools freely, and Bonnie said that if no one was at home a neighbor could still just go into the Bailey shop for a tool, "since they knew where it was." They could locate Harold's hammer or vice grips because there had been enough visiting and working together over the years that they knew how Harold organized his shop.

---

21. See Klinenberg, *Going Solo*.

They would "borrow them and then bring them back," she remarked in passing, as though this was not a remarkable thing.

These days, Americans find that they can put their emotional trust in just about anything—including the anonymous QAnon believer on the other side of a Twitter feed, or an Instagram "catfish."[22] But a growing percentage of couples either married or in serious relationships involving shared property and expenses do not trust each other enough to rely on a joint bank account.[23] When it comes to our neighbors, how many of us would keep our toolshed (or its high-tech equivalent) unlocked? If our Bluetooth speaker or tablet goes missing from our car, how many of us can assume a neighbor borrowed it and will bring it back? How many of us would be just fine if a neighbor did indeed just come over and borrow our lawn mower without asking? While you are trying to conjure a situation in which you would feel just fine about any neighborly incursion onto your property, think of how different life was in the local culture that embraced the Baileys.

After the fire, Harold and Bonnie hung on to their farm past the demise of their dairy business. They still raised cattle and hay, but they had to get out of the business of producing their own milk. They weren't making substantial profits before the fire because they were finding it harder and harder to compete with the new larger dairy operations, and they could not rebuild and compete with those operations after the fire. Harold was the only sibling in his family who had decided to stay on the family farm, and none of his children opted to stay and take up the occupation after him. Harold's siblings pursued careers in the professional world, and Harold's children and presumably his grandchildren did the same, because they really couldn't see their future in farming the family land. When Harold can no longer manage the farm, it will probably cease to be a farm altogether or the land will become a part of a larger farming operation.

Though it did not work out for the Baileys', some farmers' children even now would like to work the land but do not have the option to do so. Listening to Harold and Bonnie talk about the trajectory of "bigger"

---

22. Catfishers are instigators of fraudulent online romances for the sake of profit, or sometimes just to toy with their victims (Campbell and Parker, "Catfish").

23. According to a survey of 2,404 US adults conducted online between Dec. 2021 and Jan. 2022, "Those most likely to keep their money apart from their partners include millennials (69% have at least some separate accounts), followed by Gen Zers (64%), Gen Xers (52%) and boomers (51%)" ("Financial Infidelity Poll," in Segal, "32% of Coupled U.S. Adults," para. 4).

farming and their inability to keep up with the "bigger and better" trend reminded me of a student who attended my Environmental Political Thought class a few years back. As she sat across from me one day discussing some of the ways agriculture had changed over the years, she got tears in her eyes. Her parents had told her they could afford to have only one child work with them with the aim of taking over the family business when they retired. The profits from their farm could not support more family members. They told her she had to do something else, and this was obviously a huge disappointment to her. To soften the blow, her parents encouraged her to still be in the food business and sent her to college to study grain sciences. With that degree, she would be able to work in office and factory settings, which may sound good to some, but her heart was obviously most content working outdoors on her family's farm. She had tears in her eyes because my class had finally explained to her why her parents could make no other decision. She now understood the larger dynamics at work that meant that she could not live out her life the way her parents had. Now she could see why there was more money by far in processing, packaging, and marketing grain than in growing it. As Michael Pollan puts it in *The Omnivore's Dilemma*:

> In many ways breakfast cereal is the prototypical processed food: four cents' worth of commodity corn (or some other equally cheap grain) transformed into four dollars' worth of processed food. What an alchemy! Yet it is performed straightforwardly enough: by taking several of the output streams issuing from a wet mill (corn meal, corn starch, corn sweetener, as well as a handful of tinier chemical fractions) and then assembling them into an attractively novel form. Further value is added in the form of color and taste, then branding and packaging. Oh yes, and vitamins and minerals, which are added to give the product a sheen of healthfulness and to replace the nutrients that are lost whenever whole foods are processed. On the strength of this alchemy the cereals group generates higher profits for General Mills than any other division. Since the raw materials in processed foods are so abundant and cheap (ADM and Cargill will gladly sell them to all comers) protecting whatever is special about the value you add to them is imperative.[24]

By the time that student went to college, the food-adjacent professional managerial route offered by my university's Department of Grain

---

24. Pollan, *Omnivore's Dilemma*, 93.

Sciences was not an *option* for her and many other students; it was a tearful *necessity*. What had happened to make Harold and Bonnie's experience impossible for their children and for my student? At one point in American history, leaving the farm *had* felt more like an option and a very attractive one at that. The dynamics of our economy that made it such an attractive option were behind the great changes in our agricultural system that had necessitated the Baileys' withdrawal from the dairy business and my student's exile in the food processing and marketing industry. Next, I want to look at some ways in which Christian Americans have reacted to dislocations and disruptions in their way of life. Often, their responses have focused more on culture-level changes, which are seen as products of bad choices, than on economic changes, which are taken more like forces of nature than products of human choice. I will be arguing that the two are related and that often economic change makes for cultural change, and sometimes it goes the other way. But for now, I want to examine two Christian reactions to what is perceived as alarming cultural disintegration.

To Retreat or Not to Retreat: The Benedict Option

Because of evangelical Christians' relative importance on the US political scene, most Americans are aware of the social and political positions and impact that Evangelicals have on the political life of the United States. There are conservative Evangelicals and those who are "deconstructing" or even becoming "exvangelicals," and there is an increasing argument between the two as to which direction Christianity ought to take. I will be addressing these positions and impacts in chapter 7. But here I want to dwell on the Catholic world, which also provides examples of how people can react in different ways to disruptive change. Among many Catholics, there is a level of dismay at many of the changes that have taken place in our culture, especially in the last half century, that is like that of conservative Evangelicals. And among Catholics, there is an argument as to whether the proper response to what they perceive as cultural crisis is to retreat and preserve, or to advance and reestablish Christian orthodoxy, to take the "Benedict option" or go with St. Francis into a new and active orthodoxy.[25]

[25]. The Benedict option is described below. The Francis option is the choice to advance rather than retreat. The Francis option references St. Francis. Tom Hoopes makes the comparison this way: "St. Benedict preserved the light of Christ by building

UNSETTLING 1: LEAVING THE FARM

"The Benedict option" may be a familiar phrase because it is the title of a well-known book, a proposal by Rod Dreher for Christians, many of whom feel like they're dealing with constant, rapid, and disturbing cultural changes that have shaken them to their moral and spiritual foundations. Dreher urges Christians to give up on their futile quest to change the larger US culture, which he considers hopelessly corrupt. Instead, he urges disaffected Christians to create a separate culture of their own. Just as the Benedictine monks did in the Middle Ages, Dreher hopes that today's serious Christians will preserve the faith through dark times of moral and cultural decadence, preserving Christianity's unique values and practices so that they will be available for the larger society when the time is again right.[26]

Dreher, like many other American Christians, places a heavy emphasis on the decline in sexual morality as the most glaring sign of cultural decadence. From his perspective, moral decay is evinced most clearly by an increase in divorce and broken homes, promiscuity, same-sex relationships, and abortions. But Dreher does not put these issues, so troubling to conservative Christians, into the economic, technological, and political contexts that spurred them to begin with.[27] Because it does not take a longer view, *The Benedict Option* comes across as a product of fear and despair more than a product of hope. And at least for some critics, Dreher, intentionally or not, merely fosters nostalgia for a bygone era in which everyone and everything Christian was in its place.

Nostalgia is sometimes experienced as orthodoxy. Dreher, a convert to the Eastern Orthodox Church but read by many Christians, including many Catholics, who strive for orthodoxy, is part of the broad "traditionalist" movement, a subculture of Christians who participate in our identitarian cultural trends through the intense pursuit of correct theology and social opinion. Dreher's earlier book's title is indicative of the larger traditionalist subculture of which he is a part: *Crunchy Cons: How Birkenstocked Burkeans, Gun-Loving Organic Gardeners, Evangelical Free-Range Farmers, Hip Homeschooling Mamas, Right-Wing Nature*

---

a shelter for it to grow into a roaring fire and inviting people to gather around its warmth; St. Francis preserved the light by kindling small flames everywhere" (Hoopes, "Francis Option," para. 10).

26. Dreher, *Benedict Option*.

27. This is a point that is rarely made, because most people who read him are dissatisfied with the mild criticism he does level at capitalism, or the lack of economic analysis does not even occur to them. See Gilger, "What Rod Dreher Gets Right."

Lovers, and Their Diverse Tribe of Countercultural Conservatives Plan to Save America (or At Least the Republican Party).²⁸ The traditionalist movement is highly critical of (classical) liberalism, and includes "trad-Catholics" along with newly minted Eastern and Russian Orthodox converts like Dreher.

There are so many types of Catholic traditionalists, and there are so many subgroups within these types, that anything like a complete account of them would take an entire book. There are sedevacantists, who believe that the current pope, and often many past popes, do not legitimately hold the chair of St. Peter. There are integralists who seek the reunification of church and state beyond a liberal order. There are traditionalists who are faithful to the church but nonetheless very critical of church reforms. They seek out the Tridentine (Latin) Mass, either believing that it alone is valid or that it is manifestly superior to the postconciliar vernacular Mass. There are Opus Dei Catholics who remain within the fold but differ profoundly especially with the current pope because of their thoroughgoing moral, political, and economic conservatism, and do not mind issuing scathing criticism towards the pope and those who agree with him. And there are many more positions and groups in between. Most of these groups are contentious but otherwise harmless, but some of them are more radical.²⁹ The fact that there are so many groups and positions within traditionalism speaks to the reality of a massive disturbance in our material, psychic, and spiritual worlds.

Reactions and reactionaries come to the fore in response to something real that is extremely hard to deal with. But while calling for retreat into an older way of living and believing and advising Christians to wait and bear witness in a decadent world is an understandable way to cope with what seems insurmountable, others from within the traditionalist spectrum have taken a stance that is opposed to the reactionary tendency inherent in the Benedict option. These other, more "Francis option" Catholics are dismayed by the rapid changes in our culture, but they also call attention to corruption and abuse in our economic and political lives. For want of a better title, we will call them "new traditionalists." The new

---

28. Dreher, *Crunchy Cons*.

29. A source for understanding the difference between Catholic traditionalists and radical fridge groups that can be dangerous is Dave Armstrong's *Mass Movements*. Although it takes sides (on the part of traditionalists), Stuart Chessman's *Faith of Our Fathers* surveys the territory quite well. For a less up to date, but more objective take, see Cuneo, *Smoke of Satan*.

traditionalists push back against the desire to retreat and engage in moral puritanism. I will briefly use the work of Sean Domencic, Larry Chapp, and Marc Barnes to describe this interventionist position.

Though he has recently moved on, Domencic's Tradistae website and blog aimed at encouraging other traditionalist Catholics to become new and better traditionalists. He urged them not only to a greater practice of traditional Catholic faith ways, but to join the Catholic Worker movement and seek to run Catholic Worker farms and houses of hospitality, something that is arguably hewing closely to teachings of the magisterium on social matters but is not perceived as traditional or orthodox.[30] Attempting to live his life in a way that honored his principles, Domencic helped run the Holy Family Catholic Worker House in Lancaster, Pennsylvania, which lasted a little over two years, a period that Domencic says is about average for a Catholic Worker house.[31] The Tradistae website, founded in 2017, is still available when access is requested, but these days Domencic contributes to a similarly oriented journal and website called *New Polity*.[32] In 2021, he signed the "New Traditionalist Manifesto," which he authored along with Gaudium et Spes 22 blogger and YouTuber Dr. Larry Chapp and *New Polity* editor Marc Barnes.[33]

Larry Chapp's recent book, *Confession of a Catholic Worker*, speaks eloquently to the desire among some Catholics to get serious about their faith, to move away from the politicization of hot-button issues and toward attempts to live out their faith in an authentic and consistent manner. For Chapp, the problem for faith starts with the modern turn, a point of view I will examine more thoroughly in chapter 4. The liberal "bourgeois spirit," for Chapp, the writers at *New Polity*, and others, has taken over not only our economy but our mental landscape, circumscribing our choices and making truly different economic and social choices seem impossible. But unlike Dreher, Chapp does not take the

---

30. The Catholic Worker movement has long been a countercultural movement within not only Catholicism but among certain Protestants, agnostics, and even atheists who agree on choosing what the Church calls the preferential option for the poor, and who are attracted to the anarchistic approach of Dorothy Day and Peter Maurin, cofounders of the movement, which primarily utilizes direct action rather than politics and lobbying, though the movement takes part in much political protesting. More on this movement in ch. 7.

31. See my interview of Domencic with cohost Spencer Hess (Johnson and Hess, "Tolstoy Injection").

32. See https://tradistae.com/; https://newpolity.com/.

33. See Barnes et al., "Manifesto of New Traditionalism."

Benedict option but the Francis option, the life of intellectual engagement with the world and direct Christian action. Chapp runs a modest Catholic Worker farm and engages his fellow Catholics and prospective Catholics with dialogue that is honest about the failings of the church (such as the pedophile scandal, and the church's tendency not to teach the faithful Catholic social doctrine or the proper understanding of the Eucharist) while remaining faithful to the postconciliar church.[34] As part of the "Communio" *ressourcement* movement within Christianity, Chapp leans heavily on the theology of Hans Urs von Balthasar and Joseph Ratzinger.[35] Of Balthasar, Chapp writes:

> Hans Urs Von Balthasar, in a small but important book called *Razing the Bastions* (published in 1952), was also ringing the alarm bell and took the Church to task for her "head in the sand" approach to modernity. The refusal of the Church to address the unique challenges posed to the faith by the revolution in thought was tantamount to a betrayal of the Gospel mandate to evangelize the world and a nullification of the internal logic of the Incarnation; a logic that compels the Church to "go to the depths" of the human condition in an act of solidarity with sinners in order to lift them up into Christ and transform their darkness into his light.[36]

Chapp, and those associated with the Communio school of thought generally, view the church's call to holiness, especially as it applies to the laity to live it out in action, as the only way to make "the church credible to the world" again. Chapp calls upon the laity to "step forward and take their proper role as witnesses in the world to the light of Christ," which means (as we'll see in later chapters) more than churchgoing and charitable giving. It means things like starting or participating in endeavors like Catholic Worker houses of hospitality and farms. He agrees with Balthasar that the church on its own is now

---

34. *Postconciliar* means after the Second Vatican Council of 1962–1965, which changed the ways in which Catholics worshiped; most importantly, it allowed for and encouraged the use of native languages rather than Latin, though it did not prohibit the use of Latin in Masses. Nevertheless, within a decade the Latin Mass was almost eliminated in many jurisdictions, and the subcultural battle began concerning attachments to this traditional expression. To this day, Pope Francis is still struggling to know exactly what to do with Catholics who still want to attend the Tridentine Mass. While he did not prohibit it, he ruled that priests wishing to use the old rite must ask permission of their bishops.

35. Joseph Ratzinger was the future (now former) Pope Benedict XVI.

36. Chapp, *Confession of Catholic Worker*, 73.

too hidebound, defensive, and bureaucratic to be able to do the job, so the impetus must come from the laity.[37]

While Barnes and *New Polity* still focus quite a bit on individual moral issues, they give a lot of attention to themes that would resonate with Domencic and Chapp. These include a thoroughgoing critique of liberalism that stops a bit short of full utilization of Marxian economics but does tap deeply into Catholic social teachings. For instance, in his article "Liberalism as Heresy," Barnes argues that liberalism is characterized by the belief "that man has the natural law for himself; that he has a secular, 'public morality' and a god-free space of freedom from which he then, in a subsequent move, *decides* to be religious; that he lives, moves and breathes in a world God created for him—but from which God is bracketed. Liberalism takes its ultimate form in Deism, wherein God starts the great mechanism of existence, and then departs from it, like a cosmic CEO who, having outsourced all his tasks to a management machine, retires to a life of income-collection and yacht design."[38] Because of this, for instance, Barnes and his colleagues question whether or not Christians should plan for retirement using 401(k) accounts instead of investing in local land and businesses. They teach that earning money via interest is usury and should not be practiced.[39]

Domencic, Chapp, Barnes, and others advocating for a *new* traditionalism are interesting because, among other things, they attempt to straddle orthodoxy (as adherence to church teachings and the authority of the magisterium) and an affection for certain traditional forms and practices in Catholicism. They do this by insisting that following all the authoritative teachings of the church, including the reforms of the Second Vatican Council (notoriously criticized by conservatives for bringing modernism into the church), and the much-maligned social encyclicals of the church that uphold workers' rights and condemn exploitation of people and the environment are—rightly understood—the ultimate source of tradition *and* orthodoxy. Vatican II allows, they argue, for much traditional practice and a purer understanding of Christian faith, both of which have been blocked by modernists in the church. Therefore, they call for *ressourcement*, a way of doing theology

---

37. Chapp, *Confession of Catholic Worker*, 73–74.
38. Barnes, "Liberalism as Heresy," para. 10; emphasis original.
39. Barnes and Imam, "Evils of Interest." The two did a complete series on money issues, with episodes on topics like tithing and the meaning of poverty.

that reexamines the old sources of orthodox faith as well as more recent sources such as *Gaudium et Spes*.

There was a concerted effort in Tradistae, and there is a concerted effort in Larry Chapp's work and in *New Polity*, to consistently advocate for and live out the entirety of the Catholic doctrine embodied in various papal encyclicals and other teachings of the magisterium, not just those having to do with sexual morality, and especially those having to do with the economy. In some cases, that effort sits alongside a strong attachment to the Latin Mass and other cultural trappings of traditional Catholicism.

Domencic disavowed traditionalism because, in its real-life manifestations, it could not be untangled from unsavory and unpleasant political reactionaries, the Catholic equivalents of evangelical Christian nationalists. Domencic wrote, "I had already encountered Catholic Social Teaching, and had assumed that this was 'part of the deal' when one rejects modernity and returns to tradition. Over the years, I had a hundred rude awakenings: widespread reactionary conservatism, pockets of virulent racism, misogyny, and antisemitism, and a view of the Church, which was not so much pure as *puny*, not so much sacred as *scared*."[40] The final push came in the form of Pope Francis's apostolic letter *Traditiones Custodes*, which made clear that those who considered the new vernacular Masses illegitimate were out of line with the church.[41] Domencic decided to be faithful to the church and not the traditionalist ideal of the church, at which point many traditionalists saw his group as "communists."[42] Whether the world of simplicity, truth, beauty, and faith that traditionalists long for ever existed is an open question that they have expended a great deal of effort to answer.[43] But what is certain is that their longing for a better world has a strong pull on people's emotions. Most of their efforts to achieve a retrenchment in

---

40. Domencic, "Trad No More," para. 3.
41. Domencic, "Trad No More," para. 6.
42. Domencic, "Trad No More," para. 3.

43. See for instance, A. Jones, *Before Church and State*, in which Jones traverses the "Sacramental Kingdom of St. Louis IX" of the thirteenth century, to prove that at least one time during the Middle Ages, there was no hard and fast distinction between church and state because, Willard argues, there was no modern distinction between secular and religious. The entire book is a work of nostalgia. Willard, who is associated with *New Polity*, gets Charles Taylor's analysis of secularity in *A Secular Age* fundamentally wrong, not seeing the aspect of Taylor's argument for transferred or distorted enchantment in government, ideologies, economy, etc. *New Polity*'s William Cavanaugh coincidentally makes the same mistake (Cavanaugh, "Enchantment").

Catholic tradition could be seen as therapeutic but not transformative, because they are not truly orthodox and faithful, as Domencic discovered. Instead, traditionalists in real life are most often simply sucked into America's overall obsession with various culture wars.

Why would traditional Catholics call other Catholics who are also trying to live faithfully "communists"? We live in a society in which thoughts and deeds are not necessarily distinguished, in which attitudes and aspirations are often considered acts, with the full force and power of "making change" or "changing the world." Our highly commercialized economic system heavily influences us to "brand" even our religious and moral ideas and "market" our answers on websites and social media. This commercialized therapeutic approach lacks direct political power, but it has tremendous indirect political and economic power, because it sells the feeling of opposition, protest, involvement, good works, etc., in a way that does not seriously oppose the overall economy. Because of this, traditionalism has largely become yet another identity-focused substitute for real faith and meaning, not that much different from the various other identity pursuits ardent traditionalists dislike, such as gender fluidity. While this de facto therapy holds no political power of its own, it serves the interests of the powerful political-economic-military complex because it diverts a tremendous amount of energy away from meaningful action that could upset the status quo, action as straightforward as union organizing and strikes. The most glaring example of the political impact of this therapeutic culture is the withdrawal of the Democratic Party from class-based politics, an issue I will discuss at more length later in this book.[44]

T. J. Jackson Lears has explained the power of the therapeutic aspect of our economy quite well in his book *No Place of Grace*. With Madison Avenue's emphasis on selling lifestyles, aesthetics, and meaning itself, our reality has been deeply affected by the idea of therapeutic acts, made more necessary in order to obscure the conflict between our economy and our basic humanity. The values that would naturally flow from a proper understanding of human nature, such as the goodness of rest and belief in a transcendent reality whose existence argues against the mere consumption of products and experiences, are lost on us. Lears writes:

---

44. Democrats have largely abandoned support for labor organizing in favor of unapologetically supporting corporate capitalism while engaging in the symbolic rhetoric of identity politics to still appear to be "liberal." See Hedges, *Death of Liberal Class*; Lasch, *Culture of Narcissism*.

> From the therapeutic view, well-being is no longer a matter of morality but of physical and psychic health. And health is often defined in terms of spurious "normality," smooth adjustment, ceaseless "growth," and peace of mind. The insoluble conflicts in psyche and society fall away. Whether it assumes psychic scarcity or psychic abundance, the therapeutic worldview is both a symptom and a source of the continuing evasive banality in modern culture.[45]

So, one way to view the traditionalist who insists on the Latin Mass and tends to see houses of hospitality as "communist" is not only as a product of retreat, and a certain kind of despair, but also as engaging in the larger identitarian therapeutic culture. For many Americans seeking this kind of solace, but who are not as inclined to philosophy and theology as many Catholic traditionalists, there is still an unspoken longing for a previously healthy and simpler religion and culture, somewhere in an American golden age.[46] In that lost era, gender wasn't even a concept, and men and women got married and raised a few children who would be materially better off than their parents. In this better world, the average person could rise to the middle class through hard work alone, and attain a nice house surrounded by a "white picket fence." These blessed people could live out their days unmolested by anxiety, financial worries, or existential dread, all while being wholesome Christians. Most Americans would not identify themselves as traditionalists. In the larger American culture, however, there are many people who sense that we are missing something and, like their more theologically and ideologically inclined counterparts, long for some ideal culture from somewhere in the receding past. They, too, tend to fall back into a nostalgia that might look different, but is largely driven by similar longings for simplicity, truth, beauty, and faith.

Pop Culture Retreat: The Cleaver Option

For older Americans, some TV shows from their youth exude the simpler and better way of life that seemed to recede on the horizon like the setting

---

45. Lears, *No Place of Grace*, 303.

46. In the past year, 2022, I have had the occasion to spend time around at least three people who were dying and in hospice or hospice-like care. Each of them was addicted to *Gunsmoke*, the old TV show, which was both literally and morally black and white.

sun as they became teenagers and young adults. By the time the 1970s arrived, with the drug culture, US involvement in the Vietnam War, inflation, recession, and rising crime, shows like *The Andy Griffith Show*, *Gunsmoke*, and *Father Knows Best* were remembered by boomers as escapes from the madness, faithfully watched in endless reruns on evenings when things just got to be too much. Many boomers still relish these shows today. The reruns of one of these, *Leave It to Beaver*, are currently streaming on Peacock TV. This show featured Ward and June Cleaver, a married couple who lived in a domestic paradise with their sons Beaver and Wally. Ward and June were, figuratively, part of what made the US such a dangerous and culturally fragmented place that some American Christians have more recently sounded the call of retreat into neo-Benedictine monasticism.[47] More on that in the next section of this chapter. But, for the moment, indulge me while I explore the significance of this iconic TV series from another angle—not nostalgic, but economic.

Leave It to Beaver ran from 1957 to 1963. As such, it is for many older Americans a substantial influence on their understanding of the ideal family, one they might have rebelled against in the '70s as hippies, but which they retained in the back of their minds until many of them either became yuppy Reagan-style conservatives in the 1980s or just moved on with the rest of their lives. The Cleavers lived so well that it was enviable. They owned a two-story house with a nice backyard in the suburban town of Mayfield, somewhere in the Midwest. It wasn't just their obvious material fortune that made the Cleavers' way of life so mesmerizing. It was their *lifestyle*, itself a new concept that came into the American consciousness in the 1950s. One gets the sense from watching *Leave It to Beaver* that the Cleavers had a lot of leisure time, even though Ward obviously made good money for which he presumably had to work. Ward and June were upwardly mobile middle-class people, but they lived a life of leisure. For fun, Ward and June might occasionally visit friends for a cocktail party or go to the country club.

Ward was played by real-life lay Methodist minister Hugh Beaumont. Ward's backstory was perhaps influenced by Beaumont's own experience, and at any rate, it is instructive for understanding the cultural importance of *Leave It to Beaver*. A member of America's "Greatest Generation," Ward was the son of a farmer. He served in WWII as an engineer. The show makes it very clear that Ward didn't see any action

---

47. An important work in understanding the cultural significance and impact of *Leave It to Beaver* along these lines is Michael B. Kassel's dissertation, "Mass Culture."

during the war and was not to be counted as some kind of war hero. After the war, he attended college (probably on the GI Bill) and majored in philosophy. He left the family farm for military service and then college, never to return, and as a result he would make a lot more money than his father did.[48]

While Ward was in college he met June, a woman who outranked him on the socioeconomic scale, the only kind likely to be sent to college before "women's liberation." June was the daughter of clearly upper-class parents, and the perfect complement for a professional man on the rise. There is some suggestion that June's parents were not happy with her choice at first, as if she'd married down by choosing a man who was going to have to work for a living. But June had married into the new rising class, the professional managerial class that was going to lead the way to unprecedented American prosperity. The message was, in the 1950s an ambitious woman's criteria for status and upward mobility were changing, and a lower-class man who wanted to work hard could rise and even marry such a woman.

After college, Ward landed a job in marketing for a Midwest branch of a firm that seemed to be headquartered in New York City. Based on how he dressed and lived, Ward's income was enough to provide a very nice life for his family, but not so nice that June could have a live-in housekeeper and nanny. While he worked, she remained quite happily at home, living the life of the ideal American housewife. She was always well dressed, and her makeup and hair were impeccable. Her life revolved around her sons, husband, and friends. This household economy of male breadwinner and female housewife sounds at the same time historically anomalous and old-fashioned, but many Christians idealize it today. A closer look at Ward and June's marriage makes them seem a little less traditionally ideal. True, they played their marital gender roles in a relatively traditional manner, but the Cleavers aggressively pushed societal norms in parenting. It was Ward who almost always dealt out the life lesson of the episode to his two sons, but June usually had a lot to say about what that lesson ought to be about. Still, wasn't theirs a primarily traditional family?

Not really. There were several groundbreaking nontraditional themes in *Leave It to Beaver*, themes that indicated deep changes happening in the Cleaver generation, changes in Americans' material and

---

48. Tokar, "Beaver's Hero."

cultural lives. In a radical departure from the norms of the time, *Leave It to Beaver* was one of the first major child-centric US TV shows, indicating the massive shift in family priorities that came with suburban living. The suburbs represented a new, rootless way of life that got its start in the 1950s. With that new way of life came new kinds of children, children without a material purpose, at least until they graduated high school, and sometimes only after they graduated from college. Dr. Benjamin Spock's famous book, *Baby and Child Care*, which came out in 1946, paved the way for the kind of parenting done by the Cleavers. With Dr. Spock's intervention, US parents now could do their jobs with social, biological, and psychological science expertise at their fingertips. They no longer needed to rely on their instincts and on the hard-won experience of their elders. The Cleavers were emblematic of the first generation of Americans to get used to the idea that the expert knew better than the common man about even the most mundane operations of life.[49]

According to Judy Kutulas, "The Depression and World War II blurred American memories of 'normal' family life, even as they induced intense longing for stability. The Cold War introduced a new set of social expectations: family was to be a secure, consumerist, conformist bulwark against Communism."[50] With this in mind, we can see *Leave It to Beaver* as a therapeutic TV show of sorts, designed to help people think about their place in our new economy, with the inevitable changes that it would bring. Its explicit mission was to teach American adults and children proper behavior in their new familial roles in the professional managerial class. This modern expert view of the family came with a new sensitivity to the special and separate mental and emotional world of children.[51] In a rural and agricultural setting, children were considered assets to the job of caring for the family's needs. They could learn how to grow plants, how to tend animals, how to cook and do other things to keep the family running. In the suburbs, with professional fathers and stay-at-home mothers, children became projects for parents to handle and juggle. How to raise children to become responsible adults without the aid of necessary work and real responsibilities was the question of the day, and Ward and June used their episodes to teach American parents to take on that

---

49. Lasch, in *Revolt of the Elites*, devotes much attention to the ceding of authority to experts in all areas, threatening not only personal and family agency but also the efficacy of democratic citizenship.

50. Kutulas, "Who Rules the Roost," 49.

51. Lillico, "Television as Popular Culture"; Spock, *Baby and Child Care*.

challenge with humor, forbearance, and a new intensity about all stages of education, from kindergarten to college.

The life Ward Cleaver made for himself and his family was remarkably different from that on his father's farm. With less time outdoors, less manual labor, and much more family leisure time, the Cleavers lived a historically strange existence free of physical hardship (and for the most part even physical work) and with an abundance of material comforts. They enjoyed a home with more than one bathroom, a fact that the show seemed to revel in, with episodes featuring the boys making a mess in their parents' special bathroom—one time even allowing a dirty bum to bathe in their bathtub! Instead of helping out with the daily tasks of providing for the family directly, Ward worked all day at his desk job, while June did what reproductive work was still to be done in the house by cooking and cleaning, though she at least sometimes had a house maid for that.[52] One gets the sense, again, that June's work in the home is more of a lifestyle choice than a necessity, chosen for its pleasantness and higher meaning for her and her family.

Wally and Beaver, elder and younger respectively, were also unusual characters by historical standards. They were almost entirely freed from working to sustain their family, and instead, their lives revolved around attendance in public school, encounters with girls, movies and games, and running around town engaging in hijinks. The lessons Wally and Beaver were given by their parents and by life were not about how nature worked and how to fix things, but rather how to get along with other people and how to develop the honest bourgeois virtues necessary for them to go to college and be like their dad. They had to be reminded, occasionally, that the reason to study in school was to get into college, because they preferred to live life as a lark. In the Cleaver picture of American suburbia, children like Wally and Beaver could be out running around after school with little concern that they would get abducted or molested. In Mayfield, neighbors still existed who kept an eye out for children taking their larks too far. This sense of neighborhood security left Ward and June free to read the newspaper together on the couch or plan a party. They had the leisure also to continually foster romance through attention to their appearance and the time to make lighthearted banter with each other.

---

52. Abbott, "Mother's Helper."

UNSETTLING 1: LEAVING THE FARM

Of course, *Leave It to Beaver* depicted an ideal 1950s middle-class family, not necessarily the reality for many families, even if they were living in suburbia and striving to be happy like the Cleavers. The Cleavers are a representation of a cultural ideal of the late 1950s and early 1960s. However, Ward's trajectory from farming and manual labor as a way of life to a professional desk job was a reality for ever-growing numbers of people in America, and it is that reality that necessitated the Cleaver option, a way of rethinking what a family should be about: less work, more play, consumer pleasures, and aspirations for ever more leisure and material abundance. Upward mobility became the expectation, and consumerism became the way that mobility was measured.

Visually, *Leave It to Beaver* epitomized the consumer ideal of the 1950s, and this was tied up with real-world changing roles for parents and children. Kutulas observes, "In real life, dad's centrality to the family was slipping away as the family became more of a consumer entity (mom's specialty) and as dad worked longer hours and learned to fit into a corporate culture. On television, though, dad was always around, the impeccable reflection of the new ideal."[53] In fact, everything and everyone was mostly ideal. Everything and everyone in the show was, for instance, clean and neat. Tidiness was enough of a factor that the boys' occasional dirtiness was a theme in the show—they tried to escape taking baths (again, showing the bathrooms) using numerous ruses. Sometimes they managed to squeak by a little dusty, which they considered a major triumph. A clean-cut young man looked destined for college and a professional career. Reflecting the reality of what it took to achieve middle-class luxury, the show made it clear that Ward and June both had college degrees and expected their kids to do the same. The message the show wanted to deliver to American viewers who wanted that lifestyle was that college was the ticket to upward mobility and that "dirty jobs" were not desirable.[54]

The Cleavers' consumer mentality was made possible by a large single-earner professional income and a housewife whose main job was purchasing.[55] Indeed, the housewife became the family's chief consumer, and

---

53. Kutulas, "Who Rules the Roost," 51.

54. Hence the irony years later when *Dirty Jobs* entered the entertainment scene to give Americans access to their longing for physicality—a way to reflect on their own growing incapacity to fix anything outside of their area of specialization. See Rowe, *Dirty Jobs*.

55. Allison Hawn observes this in her thesis and asks if we are still aiming advertising at updated June Cleavers in "Escaping June Cleaver."

much advertisement was aimed in her direction from the 1950s on. In this new system, the Junes of the world, with their newly expansive shopping habits, were necessary to keep the Wards employed and upwardly mobile. Along with the price-decreasing effects of mass production, the income of the new professional class made a material lifestyle possible that was previously accessible only to the few wealthy. But most of what was generated by Ward in the way of marketing, and then consumed by June, was not *necessary* for anyone. Like the Cleavers, more and more people would now make a living on unnecessary, ginned-up products. The Cleaver level of material consumption and comfort was a wholly historically unprecedented situation for "average people," not traditional, and necessarily morally corrupting (with extra money comes more opportunities to choose wrongly). Neither one of their labors created anything new in a material sense, and their economic activity, while normalized today, had a strange self-cannibalizing unreality to it.

There are many *Leave It to Beaver* episodes that celebrate the Cleavers' consumerism, but in season 1, episode 32, "Beaver's Old Friend," we see a nice example of the looming throwaway culture that became a necessity if the American economy was going to continue to grow at an ever-increasing rate. In this episode, Ward, Wally, and the Beaver are working in the garage, their mission to throw out everything that they don't use anymore. When Ward comes back into the kitchen briefly to consult with June, he opines with a smile that even though they threw out everything in the garage that was "worthless," it looked like there was still as much junk in the garage as before. To this, June replies wistfully, "Well, don't worry dear, someday we'll move and leave it all behind us."[56]

The Cleavers were in their second house, and one can imagine that this was their first family garage cleanup in the new place. Garage cleanups remind us that people now get attached to many useless things because of how they make them feel; we might call them sentimental items. Beaver's teddy bear was one such item. Given to him by his aunt, it was among the junk that Ward and Wally threw out in the garage cleanup, and the Beaver was embarrassed to admit he wanted to keep the bear as a memento from his childhood. Ward and Wally were unaware of the Beaver's sentimentality about his bear, even though Ward had a similar fleeting emotional moment about a shot put ball he no longer used. After the trash got taken away, Beaver had regrets and ran after the garbage

---

56. Tokar, "Beaver's Old Friend."

truck. After some adventures and some cooperation from the garbage man, Beaver rescued his bear. But, in a not too surprising twist, his parents eventually persuaded him to give it away to a kid who needed it more. As any modern middle-class family knows, charity is giving other people your junk. To make sure the lesson about not hanging onto possessions was thoroughly learned, the necessity of throwing things away was reinforced a bit later in the same show. Wally came home complaining of having to eat a lot of a neighbor's leftover tiny club sandwiches. Ward asked June why Agnes Haskell would give tiny party sandwiches to growing boys, and June snidely replied, "Well, you know Agnes, I suppose she didn't want to throw them away." Clearly, a classier hostess would have dumped the food in the trash.

So, what do we have here? Do we have in the Cleavers an icon of traditional family values? Not unless family values include the soft overturning of traditional male and female roles, a lot of consumer materialism, endless jockeying for social position, and conscientious, principled waste. The Cleaver option represented radical and rapid changes taking place in the American way of life and value system. Previous generations would have thought the child-centric household as strange as they would find ridiculous the idea of a therapeutic TV show teaching parents how to parent. Who would take that seriously? To do a job in marketing (a profession that ramped up in the '50s) Ward had to get a college degree, a qualification that previously would have seemed as absurd as the job itself. It may be surprising to us that Ward got a marketing job with a philosophy degree. Today, things are more absurd—he would need a four-year degree (at least) just in marketing!

Just like their mother, the Cleaver kids didn't have to work. For the first time ever, they got to live most of their childhood in leisure, grudgingly learning at school and much more enthusiastically having fun. Even though they had become largely financial burdens on their parents, and a job to raise due to their relative idleness, the children had become the very center of the familial universe, doted upon and worried about constantly. In the Cleavers' world, unlike their predecessors, so much junk accumulated that they had to routinely throw things out, and June measured her family's status against the neighbors partly based on how much her family could waste.

In one generation, Ward went from a frugal rural life to a sophisticated professional middle-class suburban life, and his body got a whole new work environment. That environment was low on physicality and high on human relationships and creativity. It no longer really mattered if Ward was physically strong—it was all about his smarts and ability to sell himself. Though he did much less labor, owned next to no land, and was not a merchant or business owner, his income put him at or near the top of the new, growing professional managerial middle class. June did very little work at all and could spend most of the day looking beautiful, being empathetic, and spending money. Such a life didn't exist for almost all women except the wealthiest even a few decades before. Most women have always had to work, because there *was* no luxury middle class.[57] They had to work hard physically to maintain their home, and often had to labor in fields or factories, as well as in kitchens. And, of course, outside of the abnormal Cleaver blip of the 1950s and 1960s upper middle class, women continued and continue to work to strive for or be in that middle class. But now, out of misplaced nostalgia for the Cleaver option, traditionalist Christians long for the times when women could choose to stay at home. In sum, Ward Cleaver's trajectory is American economy-driven cultural upheaval in a nutshell. And this upheaval, even when experienced voluntarily and with enjoyment, is still "dislocation" and "disembedding."

Does the *Leave It to Beaver* picture seem altogether traditional and wholesome now?

Rethinking the "Green Revolution"

Harold Bailey's and Ward Cleaver's families represent the kind of large shift in occupation and values to which conservative Christians, like Catholic traditionalists, are reacting. To understand the trade-offs correctly, we need to take a step back and examine more closely why and how we moved from sustainable diversified farming to industrial farming and an international food chain. What was going on that made Harold Bailey unable to restart his dairy business and made Ward Cleaver eagerly leave his family's farm for city living? Yes, they were brought about through capitalism, but were these changes necessary due to the workings of a free, self-moving, and autonomous market? And what, materially, did we lose by taking the Cleaver option?

In the Bailey example we saw that in the past, families relied more on each other and the people near them and, for their food, on local

---

57. Kessler-Harris, *Women Have Always Worked*.

farms and businesses. Many families engaged in subsistence farming and gardening because it made economic sense. In *subsistence* farming, the crops planted and animals raised were primarily for the benefit of the family and only secondarily for sale. This way of farming predominated for millennia all around the world but is now considered undesirable by political and economic leaders almost everywhere in the world. Yet only recently, i.e., since the mid-twentieth century, has our society accepted that it is superior to grow large commodity crops like corn and wheat on vast acres of land to make into processed food and nonfood items for export.

Norman Borlaug is the man most responsible for initiating what has come to be known as the "green revolution" that saved an estimated billion people or more from starvation in the mid-twentieth century. Borlaug, who had a BA in forestry and a PhD in plant pathology and genetics, originally worked for Dupont, and during WWII worked on projects as varied as finding an adhesive not susceptible to saltwater corrosion and developing DDT to curb malaria. After the war, however, Borlaug devoted much of his remaining career to research and development of new wheat crop varieties to combat world hunger, with significant funding from the Rockefeller Foundation. Borlaug's career was both heroic and tragic—an example of how good intentions and a faith in science can create new, often unanticipated problems.

When Borlaug's team pioneered the engineering of wheat and other crops for maximum drought and disease resistance in the early 1960s, the main motivation was to end hunger in developing countries like Mexico, India, and Pakistan. A secondary consideration was to grow wealth by allowing farmers anywhere to sell more of their product on the open market. In just a few decades, his genetic innovations powered vast increases in yields in the US and in developing countries, and Borlaug was given a Nobel Peace Prize and other honors for his significant contribution to agricultural knowledge. The benefits of Borlaug's green revolution did not come without costs, however. Borlaug anticipated at least one of the potential costs when he noted in his acceptance speech that the additional production should be seen as buying time, perhaps as much as thirty years, so that people could use more technology to curb population growth. He was aware that increasing food supplies would not only decrease hunger but increase population, and he warned that the right way to think of the green revolution was that it bought human beings time in the race to end the population explosion.[58] The implication was what Cochrane would recognize as the "technological treadmill." One innovation would solve a problem but lead to more problems. Those problems would then be solved by additional technological innovations, etc.[59]

In addition to the perils that Borlaug warned against, because his newly minted intensive agricultural techniques made use of less fertile lands and squeezed more energy from them, they necessitated a reliance on artificial petroleum-based nitrogen fertilizers. Not only would this not help the basic soil fertility problem, which can be solved only by adding biomass back into the soil, but it meant that more fossil fuels would be pumped and used to make these fertilizers, contributing to pollution and climate change. More intensive farming also drove increasing use of heavy machinery in cultivation and harvesting, also contributing to pollution and climate change. Over time, these more intensive farming techniques also had social and political ramifications. They encouraged the consolidation of farmland into fewer hands as wealthier farmers, with the money to buy bigger and better machinery and artificial fertilizers, could buy up and farm more land with less help.[60] At the top of the list of prices humanity has paid for Borlaug's green revolution are the losses of livelihood for many farmers, their subsequent dislocation (think the Baileys and the Cleavers), and the loss of national security and independence when it comes to food.

In addition to social dislocation and political disruption, loss of national security is an aspect of these industrializing developments that often gets overlooked. For most of human history, willingly reducing control over a country's food supply would have been seen as an unthinkable strategic mistake. Adopting the globalized food chain leaves every country involved more vulnerable to other countries' intentions and economic situations. Currently, that kind of interdependence seems normal, but that does not make it truly desirable, despite the (now falsified) argument that more economic interdependence would guarantee

---

58. Borlaug said, "There can be no permanent progress in the battle against hunger until the agencies that fight for increased food production and those that fight for population control unite in a common effort. Fighting alone, they may win temporary skirmishes, but united they can win a decisive and lasting victory to provide food and other amenities of a progressive civilization for the benefit of all mankind" ("Acceptance Speech," para. 6).

59. See Cochrane and Wilcox, *Economics of American Agriculture*.

60. See Goswami, "Farmland Consolidation."

peace.⁶¹ People have known the perils involved with not being food independent for a long time. The potential consequences of losing control of national food production are evident in the Irish example from the 1840s, an example everyone learns about in school. England had encouraged the growing and export of wheat from Ireland as a cash crop, a move that primarily benefited English investors, and not the Irish. That left the Irish population with a problem: How could they engage in commodity crop farming for trade, and still grow enough to feed themselves, since they couldn't afford to do that mainly with imports? To devote what arable land was suitable for wheat, they needed to grow food for themselves on the remaining relatively poor soil. They needed food with enough calories and nutrition to keep them healthy so they could produce the commodity crop of wheat for trade. The potato, an import from the New World and previously unknown in Ireland, was discovered to grow well in the poor Irish soil. The Irish settled on a single high-yielding potato variety to get their required calories. This potato variety quickly became the Irish staple crop, a food they ate every day, like many people eat bread or rice.⁶²

Predictably, the Irish population grew due to the seemingly plentiful supply of cheap potato calories. But the people's poverty enforced a reliance on the crop for life itself, putting them in a situation of extreme precarity, which perhaps wasn't felt until something happened that was beyond their control. When a rotting blight destroyed the potato crops for several years in a row, the Irish poor had nothing to fall back on. Inspired both by the profit motive and liberal ideology that said that making the market freer would increase profits, England continued to export Irish wheat instead of encouraging the Irish to move back to more diversified farming. They also repealed the "corn laws" (corn was a generic name for grain at that time) that fixed wheat prices, with the idea that the Irish would be able to sell their grain more readily on the open market. They hoped that the profits would be enough for the Irish to import the food they needed to keep going, but the low prices they received for their wheat on the open market made that impossible.⁶³

61. A classic of international relations that deals with the impact of economic interdependence and discusses how the spread of liberal economic relations is a possible catalyst for peace is Keohane and Nye, *Power and Interdependence*.

62. See Nally, "That Coming Storm"; see also Donnelly, *Great Irish Potato Famine*.

63. Nally writes, "In other words, 'food aid' had the twin ulterior motives of encouraging a market-led economy as well as instigating the dietary regeneration of Ireland by

The result was a famine so deep and prolonged that approximately one million Irish people died from starvation or malnutrition. During this period, the Irish population declined by 25 percent due to death and mass migration to the United States and other countries (an immigration problem for the US that made for considerable anti-Irish prejudice and persecution). This was a disaster that could have been averted simply by allowing national agriculture to naturally evolve to feed the Irish people with crops that grew well in the area.

Even now, there are many places in the world where smaller communities of subsistence farmers and adjacent craftspeople and/or small businesses are still intact and growing food for themselves and nearby customers. In fact, "two-thirds of the world's agricultural workers are still using manual techniques."[64] And, only 2 to 3 percent of the world's farmers use motorized equipment, but many more use some inputs associated with Borlaug's green revolution, such as fertilizers or insecticides.[65] According to the Foundation on Future Farming, one third of the human population lives from agriculture. Small farmers, fishermen, and hunters still produce most of the food human beings consume.[66] And according to the UN's Food and Agricultural Organization 2014 report on the state of agriculture and family farming, over 90 percent of farms are family farms relying on family labor. Seventy to eighty percent of farmland is controlled by these small producers, and they produce more than 80 percent of the world's food.[67]

When traditional family farming is disrupted anywhere in the world, voluntarily or involuntarily, people are subject to dislocation. What Cochrane called the "technological treadmill" can take over not only the land but cultures and ways of life. The treadmill is

> based on technological advances achieved through mechanization, plant breeding for high-yielding varieties, the use of agrochemicals and genetic engineering, etc. With increasing external inputs, the unit costs of production are declining and

---

weaning the population from the barbarous (and unprofitable) potato crop. As noted earlier, the dietary regimes within Irish workhouses were also directed toward the same end. In this sense, 'food aid' was a cornerstone of colonial biopolitics" ("That Coming Storm," 729).

64. Sourisseau, *Family Farming*, 22.
65. Sourisseau, *Family Farming*, 22–25.
66. See Global Agriculture, "Industrial Agriculture."
67. Food and Agriculture Organization of the United Nations, *State of Food*, 2.

the productivity per worker is increasing. Production is growing and producer prices are falling. The only businesses that can survive on the market are those that remain one step ahead of their competitors by investing in rationalization and expansion, or those with locational advantages. If others catch up with them, another round begins. An end to this treadmill is not in sight: The more global the market, the higher the speed and the more incalculable the game becomes for each.[68]

Some countries have no doubt learned from mistakes like the English mishandling of Irish agriculture that led to the potato famine or the decimation of rural life in the US corn belt, and are resisting the "get big or get out" trend. In India, farming is still the primary source of income for almost 60 percent of the population. Not long ago, Indian subsistence farmers and small farm businesses showed that they were still numerous enough to mount a serious yearlong protest. Largely ignored by the US press, they literally occupied and held for months areas all over the country but especially in and near the capital of New Delhi. More remarkably, these protests took place during and despite the COVID-19 pandemic. Unbelievably, the farmers were successful. As an article in *Commonweal* notes, "After more than a year of nonviolent demonstrations, the country's farmers succeeded in forcing the repeal of three laws that would have deregulated India's agriculture sector and allowed major agribusiness conglomerates to buy up massive tracts of farmland."[69]

Prime Minister Narendra Modi succumbed to the protestors' demands in December 2021, probably concerned about his chances in upcoming elections. He announced the repeal of three laws that had passed a little over a year earlier. These laws had been designed to remove the restrictions, regulations, guarantees, and subsidies that kept in place the ingredients for the independence of farming families. The laws worked against Indian national self-sufficiency in favor of dependency on the global marketplace. The laws Modi wanted to implement would have accelerated the consolidation of family-owned farmland into the hands of fewer, larger, and richer landowners and corporate interests. Modi wanted India to fully join the fray of international competition in agricultural products

---

68. "The Agricultural Treadmill," in Global Agriculture, "Industrial Agriculture"; from a summary of the International Assessment of Agricultural Knowledge, Science and Technology for Development (IAASTD) conducted between 2005 and 2007 and initiated by the World Bank.

69. McGowan, "Modi Backs Down," para. 1.

and to take advantage of international markets, a process very similar to what happened in the United States in the twentieth century.

Hard hit by these changes in government policies that made it very difficult for them to compete and make a profit, Indian farmers committed suicide at a rate that exceeded the suicides of American farmers during a similar "green revolution" period in the US. "In 2019, more than 10,000 people in the agricultural sector ended their own lives," CNN reported as it announced the partial victory of the Indian farmer protesters over the state's attempt to favor industrial agriculture and run them out of business.[70]

The lesson of the Indian example, as well as agricultural history in the US, is that government policy is crucial both ways—laws and regulations either support the maintenance of a more equal distribution of land and more of a reliance on local production, or they support the concentration of land in the hands of fewer people and the reliance on the global food chain. This trend continues at an ever more rapid pace.[71] Most US farms are still owned by families, but there are far fewer farms than there were in the 1950s, and most that remain are monoculture productions. These farms are set up to mass-produce a certain commodity crop or animal and must be able to afford the "specialized machinery, software and proprietary inputs such as seed, fertilizer and pesticide systems that lock farmers into their production choices and make it extraordinarily difficult to independently innovate." And, alarmingly, "Four percent of farms produce 50% of US agricultural products."[72]

Everywhere we look, despite the interests of farming families and communities, local business owners and their employees, government officials at every level in the US and of both parties consistently choose laws and regulations that eliminate small and medium-sized local property owners in favor of a corporate, anonymous, and global system that benefits shareholders more than farmers, their families, communities, or consumers. With the shift away from rural life has come an equally massive shift to urban living for a growing percentage of the world's people. Like my student, and the Baileys' kids, many people have given up and left the family business of farming because the occupation has become inherently unprofitable. Farming is no longer highly respected in a culture where people view desk jobs as superior. To put it another

---

70. Mitra and Mogul, "Indian Farmers Forced Modi," para. 17.
71. Hudson and Laingen, *American Farms, American Food*, 11.
72. Hanschu and Johnson, "Economic and Psychological Origins," 32.

way, our culture long ago decided it was better to be Ward Cleaver than Cleaver's dad.

There are many other issues related to the trend towards large-scale farming, but what causes American farmers to commit suicide at an alarming rate is this cultural diminishment, and the fact that they go year after year struggling to make a profit and hang onto their farms when competing with industrial-scale commodity farming that has been greatly encouraged and subsidized by their government. Farmers make up a very small percentage of the US population, but they are responsible for 80 percent of what the nation eats. The US does import a lot of fruits and vegetables but is essentially self-sufficient when it comes to meat and dairy. Of course, to avoid malnutrition, a steady diet of fruits and vegetables is needed, so the US has a serious vulnerability in its food supply. To get fruits and vegetables that are safe and delivered at the peak of their freshness and nutrition, they need to travel short distances and be consumed not long after they're harvested. Local and regional farmers who grow fruits and vegetables on diversified farms are the obvious answer to this fundamental national need. But somehow, their importance to the country's well-being is not translating into anything like prosperity for most who try to supply this need. Suicides happen—especially among men—when they lose their grandparents' farm, when they cannot deal with their debt, when they can't keep up with "get big or get out" competition, when they can't afford to "level up" to larger equipment, and when they can't find the mental and physical health services to help them cope.[73]

> Industrialized farming is related to lower relative incomes; greater income inequality; higher unemployment and poverty rates; lower total employment generated locally; decreases in local retail trade and diversity of retail firms; declines in population size; increases in crime and civil suits; increases in teenage pregnancies; higher rates of stress and other psychological problems; fading of community organizations and lower rates of participation in community social life; decline in churches and public services; deterioration of water, soil, and air quality; and an abundance of environmental-quality and chemical-related health problems.[74] Also, communities located near industrial

---

73. See Reed and Claunch, "Risk for Depressive Symptoms," for a comprehensive review of evidence on suicide among farmers.

74. See Blanchette, *Porkopolis*; Smithers et al., "Dynamics of Family Farming."

farms experience less democratic decision-making, as agribusiness interests dominate local politics.[75]

As alluded to earlier, many Democrats as well as Republicans in the United States have enthusiastically approved of the free market "bigger is better" trend in farming and in many other areas of our economy. They have promoted "bigger" not only in agriculture but in business. At the local level, this means city fathers using eminent domain law to move small businesses out of downtowns and replace them with big-box stores. Why does this strange contradiction exist between what these city fathers often say they value and the laws and policies they enact? The answer is complicated, but their seeming hypocrisy is at least partly a cultural-ideological artifact—a lag between what they feel and believe in their hearts, and the reality of what they are doing (and feel compelled to do).

Ironically, people who still try to live more materially self-sufficient lives by being downwardly mobile (think tiny homes or communal living), or who simply make a point to buy local agricultural products when possible, are immediately perceived as ideologically left wing by their critics. It is true that the terms "local" and "organic" have been used by progressives in the US to gain social credit without any serious move to support either "trend" with government policies and funds. It is also true that the original advocates of organic agriculture tended to be "hippies," and hippies protested capitalism and war back in the 1960s. But most of those same hippies, later, stepped into jobs like everyone else and largely got about the business of leading "normal" lives. Most of them did not cling to radical activism or the leftist convictions they had in their youths.[76] Their subsequent tendencies towards "socially conscious" and "green" consumerism have not helped more people live a simpler, more locally oriented way of life, even if they somehow influence people to pollute slightly less.

As I have just implied, most US progressives are not leftists. They are ardent capitalists, like Nancy Pelosi.[77] But since the rural Midwest America's "conservative" majority is pro-capitalist, the small, diversified farming that is idealized by progressives as "green" is seen by those conservatives

---

75. Hanschu and Johnson, "Economic and Psychological Origins," 32–33.

76. Gurvis, *Flower Children*.

77. In 2017, answering an NYU student who said that most millennials no longer supported the system of capitalism, Nancy Pelosi responded, "I thank you for your question. But I have to say, we're capitalist—and that's just the way it is" (Marans, "Nancy Pelosi's Comments," para. 7).

as socialism through the back door. They commit the error of "guilt by association." Many organic farmers are aggrieved that they have to sell more kitsch than substance to folks who want to feel good about what they buy (because, by and large, "green" consumers really don't want to pay what local food is worth, and still buy only a small proportion of their food locally).[78] The irony is that most local farmers make most of their money on tours, jam, and pies, rather than on their actual agricultural products. Many of them love their work and find life's meaning in it, but they must devote much of their time to what amounts to agritourism: lodging, festivals, crafts, and—yes—marketing. They are all keenly aware that the only way they can stay afloat is to make farming a hobby and the "farm idea" the main product. They then surrender to reality and get second and third jobs to support their farming hobby.

To the extent they keep going despite the odds, they are responding to some of the most radical and jarring events in social and economic history through their choices. It is beyond ironic that this group and their economic activity should be seen by the wider American culture as too radical. Small organic farmers are going against the grain of everything US culture currently considers normal, but they are trying to obtain a semblance of what was considered normal less than one hundred years ago. If anything, that makes them conservatives.

---

78. To learn all about this irony, read Salatin, *Folks, This Ain't Normal*.

3

Unsettling 2: Nonstop Change

THE UNITED STATES HAS had more than its share of odd developments and unrest in the past few years. By the time this book is published we may be nearing or even past the 2024 presidential election. No matter which way it goes, there is no denying that the situation is unusual and that it has been, at least since Donald Trump began to gain political credibility and momentum, and then eventually win the White House in 2016. Chapter 5 will cover the Trump phenomenon in more depth, by looking at some of his key speeches prior to and in the days after his 2016 election. But for now, it is enough to note that there has been an upswing in phenomena that are harbingers of political unsettling in any regime: more unusual, demagogic candidates, more violent mass demonstrations, more mass shootings, and car rammings, etc. It would not be a surprise if more of this type of thing happened during 2024 and beyond, regardless of who wins the election. As of this writing, states are disputing whether Donald Trump should even be allowed on their ballots, due to his having violated the Fourteenth Amendment prohibition against inciting an insurrection in 2020.

Despite how unsettling some of our leaders' and their followers' words and actions have been, the reason this book focuses on the longer view in many of its chapters is because only by stepping back and refusing to point fingers can we hope to solve the problems that have caused such dissatisfaction and fear. Taking the longer view makes it possible to reimagine even extremists as at least partly responding to conditions beyond them, *just like political extremists and rebels do in other parts of the world*. Indeed, to not see the more systemic causes of the right-wing resurgence and general unrest in the United States is to engage in a strange type of prejudice. If we assume that a country as "advanced" as the US could never produce a mass disturbance leading to the type of radical and violent movements and mass murder events so common in the rest of the world (such as separatism/irredentism, neo-fascism/tribalism/ethno-nationalism, fundamentalist religious extremism, and various forms of racism) we are engaging in the fantasy of American exceptionalism.[1]

Systemic problems abound in the United States, and these can and do cause disturbances, just as they do in other places. These problems are shared by people living in rural *and* urban areas. The following sections will explore, first, the phenomenon of accelerating automation and how it influences our social existence. Next, I will focus on the red parts of the US, which are often crucial to the national food supply, and continue to undergo profound environmental, economic, and cultural changes.[2] The goal is to reveal what lies below the surface that is ultimately responsible for the political divisions that continue to discourage meaningful cooperation.

We have experienced, in a relatively short span of human history, a vast and socially traumatic acceleration of economic and technological change. Wendell Berry blames it for the "forcible displacement of millions of people." If that seems like an extreme statement, remember that this comes from one of our most beloved citizens, one often admired by localist conservatives. Wendell Berry is not a Maoist revolutionary—he's a farmer and poet from Kentucky. So, how can he justify making that statement? He explains:

> I remember, during the fifties, the outrage with which our political leaders spoke of the forced removal of the populations of villages in communist countries. I also remember that at the same time, in Washington, the word on farming was "Get big or get out"—a policy which is still in effect, and which has taken an enormous toll. The only difference is that of method: the force used by the communists was military; with us, it has been economic—a "free market" in which the freest were the richest.

1. Berry, *Unsettling of America*, is again the inspiration for this chapter's title.
2. Some of the books in recent years on these problems include Blanchette, *Porkopolis*; Wuthnow, *Left Behind*; Neel, *Hinterland*; and Jerolmack, *Up to Heaven*.

The attitudes are equally cruel, and I believe that the results will prove equally damaging, not just to the concerns and values of the human spirit, but to the practicalities of survival.[3]

In the spirit of Wendell Berry, and particularly his most well-known prose work, *The Unsettling of America*, let's examine a key ingredient that led to an unnoticed and ongoing mass migration.

Automation

Capitalism has created an ever-accelerating amount of automation, which has resulted in many good things. As a result of automation, we can produce things more quickly, uniformly, and cheaply. Producers can reduce labor costs, and one of the positive results of reducing the cost of labor has been increasing consumer access to many goods.[4] But we must understand that automation is *inherently socially destabilizing*. It constantly knocks people out of work, including people in the second half of their working lives, and makes them shift and retool, and pay for it. It also makes some people far richer than others, causing resentment.[5] Capitalist labor often does not allow people to experience themselves as the true authors of their production, or to see their fellow workers as members of a cooperative community (rather, they see them as competitors). It does not encourage people to see the social relations and personal worth that go into the products they buy. And the way in which they work, live, and supply their needs with commodities obscures from view the natural world from which all our products originated. Marx frequently referred to the alienation or estrangement of man from his labor, from himself as a species, and from nature, and was capable of stating that man was a spiritual being whose life, as such, had become animalistic under capitalism.[6] For instance, in *Estranged Labor*, he

---

3. Berry, *Unsettling of America*, 45.

4. In ch. 15 of the first volume of *Capital*, titled "Machinery and Large Scale Industry," Marx writes: "Like every other instrument for increasing the productivity of labour, machinery is intended to cheapen commodities and, by shortening the part of the working day in which the worker works for himself, to lengthen the other part, the part he gives to the capitalist for nothing. The machine is a means for producing surplus-value" (1:492).

5. Goda, "Global Concentration of Wealth."

6. In "Estranged Labor," Marx references human beings' spiritual nature five times: "Just as plants, animals, stones, air, light, etc., constitute theoretically a part of human consciousness, partly as objects of natural science, partly as objects of art—his spiritual

wrote: "Nature is man's inorganic body—nature, that is, insofar as it is not itself human body. Man lives on nature . . . with which he must remain in continuous interchange if he is not to die. That man's physical and spiritual life is linked to nature means simply that nature is linked to itself, for man is a part of nature."[7]

Why is it so difficult to acknowledge the alienation from others, from our very human nature, and from physical nature, as well as the loss of personal and family security that came along with capitalist development? First, it's difficult because the experience of this change has been generational. Like the frog that eventually boils in slowly heating water, we have a hard time noticing that we are being cooked. This train wreck has been going on for over two hundred years with an accelerating rate of change in the way we make things and distribute them, the way we work, and the way we think of and interact with our families. The big winners when it comes to material benefits have been the owners—and sometimes the creators—of the technological innovations that have transformed our lives. The relative losers (though many have certainly made gains from the days of no electricity and indoor plumbing) have been the middle and lower middle classes and the poor all over the world, both in rural areas and in cities, who now work mainly for others, rather than themselves, and are often "one paycheck away" from a frightening vulnerability.

In addition, just in the past few decades, we have had to deal with being seemingly always available even when we are not at work, providing free labor in the form of clicks, likes, providing free content in ad revenue–generating machines like Facebook, and coping with "surveillance capitalism," where our time, habits, and movements are often tracked, measured, and monetized both at work and in the rest of our lives.[8] These changes have meant that everyone regardless of whether they are rich or poor has lost ground in basic security and meaningful quality of life, though these losses may not be easy to detect. Sloterdijk characterizes

---

inorganic nature, spiritual nourishment which he must first prepare to make palatable and digestible—so also in the realm of practice they constitute a part of human life and human activity" (4). "That man's physical and spiritual life is linked to nature means simply that nature is linked to itself, for man is a part of nature" (5). "[Estranged labor turns] man's species-being, both nature and his spiritual species-property, into a being alien to him, into a means of his individual existence. It estranges from man his own body, as well as external nature and his spiritual aspect, his human aspect" (6).

7. Marx, "Estranged Labor," 5.
8. Zuboff, *Age of Surveillance Capitalism*.

our age as one of "infinite mobilization," one that feels less and less about achieving some grand vision or the culmination of progress, and more and more like one is on an escalator or wheel, always in motion but going nowhere ultimately good:

> Sure, we continue to advance, but not upward—that is the quintessence of post-progressive reflections on the relationship between mind and time—and this confirms that pre-modern spirits are also to be found in the post-modern hustle and bustle for whom the wheel of fortune makes far more sense as a symbol for historic time than a ladder of progress. . . . What has really emerged in the course of the experiment is precisely that it is by no means certain that a later knowledge is the better one.[9]

To really see how capitalism brings relative prosperity only at the expense of our feeling less materially or emotionally secure, often anxious, empty, and lost, we must take some large steps back and get an even more sweeping and comprehensive view of what has happened to us, remembering that we are, among other things, creatures. We comprise a physical species that, like all other species, has limits as to how fast it can adapt to changes in the environment. When change happens too fast, sometimes species become extinct, and sometimes a few who are more capable of rapid and radical change survive and move the species to a new level. Either way, for almost all species, too much rapid change produces anxiety, suffering, and even death. For humans, arguably, this process is made worse by the fact that we are more conscious, and therefore capable of a much deeper fear and anxiety, than any other creatures on the planet.[10] Berry explains that we take those fears and anxieties, at least partly caused by our feelings of helplessness as we automate and specialize our way into incompetence, into our role as consumers and voters:

> In our time the rule among consumers has been to spend money recklessly. People whose governing habit is the relinquishment of power, competence, and responsibility, and whose characteristic suffering is the anxiety of futility, make excellent spenders. They are the ideal consumers. By inducing in them little panics of boredom, powerlessness, sexual failure, mortality, paranoia,

---

9. Sloterdijk, *Infinite Mobilization*, 123. See Varoufakis, *Technofeudalism*.

10. Nietzsche's writings are perhaps the most eloquent accounts of this human vulnerability and its consequences. See Nietzsche, *Genealogy of Morality*; and Nietzsche, *Advantage and Disadvantage*.

they can be made to buy (or vote for) virtually anything that is "attractively packaged."[11]

Another source of anxiety, having to do with the imperative to be efficient in the making or acquiring of our goods and services, is a sense of ever-accelerating time. We are conscious of the changes in our perception of time and the way in which our current time consciousness affects our minds, our work, our entire existence. Bauman explains our experience of time as "the emancipation of time from space," the unhinging of our consciousness of time from the seasons of the year, and the distances between places and things.[12] We tend to believe that we are somehow set apart, capable of overcoming sheer instinct and the physical challenges imposed by nature as well as those imposed by our own technological innovations. At the same time, we sense most acutely in our experience of our own families that we are being continuously left behind. Of the contemporary working man, Berry observes, "He wishes that he had been born sooner, or later. He does not know why his children are the way they are. He does not understand what they say."[13]

How many of us come to parenthood thinking that we will experience something timeless, the regeneration of life and the passing on of family traditions and values, only to feel alienated from our own children, perhaps irreparably, even if we continue to have a loving relationship with them? This alienation stems at least in part from the acceleration of cultural change due to the acceleration of technological change. Like the parent who hardly recognizes his children, we understand what is happening to us at least enough to feel it, if only dimly and partially, and the frustration of not knowing how to handle the changes continually coming our way can lead to irrational and self-destructive tendencies, not to mention scapegoating and conspiracy theory building. Theologian Stanley Hauerwas has argued that this syndrome, in the context of our current moment of populist nationalism and the reaction to it in the United States, reveals:

> an even deeper pathology—namely, the profound sense of unease that many Americans have about their lives. That unease often takes the form of resentment against elites, but, even more troubling, it funds the prejudice against minority groups as well

---

11. Berry, *Unsettling of America*, 26–27.
12. Bauman, *Liquid Modernity*, 113.
13. Berry, *Unsettling of America*, 23.

as immigrants. Resentment is another word for the unease that seems to grip many good, middle-class—mostly white—people. These are people who have worked hard all their lives yet find they are no better off than when they started. They deeply resent what they interpret as the special treatment some receive in an effort to right the wrongs of the past.[14]

I would add to Hauerwas's statement only an emphasis on the first part. The resentment he refers to goes beyond the racial level to a deep suspicion of "elites" generally, elites who seem to—and do—live in a different world than most Americans of any color. It is a world in which people imagine that the wealthy and powerful do not feel the precarity, anxiety, and emptiness that the rest of us feel. Their lack of pain, moreover, is perceived to be bought at the price of everyone else's pain.[15] What racial animus exists among the many who feel this pain tends to get filtered through the sense that powerful elites are imposing an unfair agenda that supports politically favored ethnic groups more than their own. What is the "deep story" that corresponds to this typical conspiratorial response to hardship? Hochschild found in her sojourn into the Louisiana bayou country that the deep story of "white, Christian, older, right-leaning Louisianans . . . was a response to a real squeeze. On the one hand, the national ideal and promise at the brow of the hill was the American Dream—which is to say *progress*. On the other hand, it had become hard to progress."[16]

But what is the real "hardship" people in the US are experiencing in a world in which fewer and fewer of them engage in hard physical labor compared with their ancestors a couple of generations ago? How can a life like that add up to the anxiety, emptiness, and precarity I've been describing? Finding the answers to these questions necessitates more historical background than Berry provided in *The Unsettling of America*. It requires a trip across an ocean. By examining the moment in which capitalism began, I believe it is possible to see more clearly the true impact of that economic system on human life. The ever more rapid economic and technical change that we now seem "used to" (but

---

14. Hauerwas, "Good Life," para. 9.

15. Ruben Andersson tells the tale of globalized separation and exclusion into "green zones" and "red zones" (*No Go World*).

16. Hochschild, *Strangers in Their Own Land*, 187; emphasis original. Hochschild describes the motivation for these responses as the "deep story" or "feels as if" story of people on the right.

we are not) began in a particular place and time—England in the seventeenth century. In a relatively short span of time, this change ended the feudal system that had been in place for over one thousand years, an incident that is inherently destabilizing.

Enclosure

It started in the countryside. English nobles had long held power over the peasants who lived on and farmed their land holdings, but they had done so in the context of a reciprocal relationship that allowed them to use lands in common and reap the fruits of their estates while allowing the peasants who lived on them to survive. Generations of peasants fed, housed, and maintained themselves on the same land with similar arrangements, passing down their homes, equipment, and knowledge from father to son, mother to daughter. It was not a system of equality, but it was a system of *relative* stability and security, unless of course it was temporarily disrupted by a disaster like war or plague. Simon Fairlie writes:

> Private ownership of land, and in particular absolute private ownership, is a modern idea, only a few hundred years old. The idea that one man could possess all rights to one stretch of land to the exclusion of everybody else was outside the comprehension of most tribespeople, or indeed of medieval peasants. The king, or the Lord of the Manor, might have owned an estate in one sense of the word, but the peasant enjoyed all sorts of so-called "usufructuary" rights which enabled him, or her, to graze stock, cut wood or peat, draw water or grow crops, on various plots of land at specified times of year.[17]

Although the exact starting time of enclosure in England is disputed, it is generally thought that enclosure of farmlands and forests slowly took place from the fourteenth to the nineteenth centuries. As early as the fourteenth century, English nobles began to take open fields previously used in common for farming, hunting, foraging, and fishing, and to use their own lands with a stricter idea of private property in mind, enclosing them, i.e., prohibiting others from entering. The result was often riots, trespassing, and other acts of disobedience.[18] In the early

---

17. Fairlie, "Short History of Enclosure," 19.

18. An example of the crown's reaction to unrest caused by enclosures: England and Wales, "Proclamacion."

sixteenth century, Thomas More, in *Utopia*, described the situation as sheep devouring men:

> Fields, houses, towns, everything goes down their throats. To put it more plainly, in those parts of the kingdom where the finest, and so the most expensive wool is produced, the nobles and gentlemen, not to mention several saintly abbots, have grown dissatisfied with the income that their predecessors got out of their estates. They're no longer content to lead lazy, comfortable lives, which do no good to society—they must actively do it harm, by enclosing all the land they can for pasture, and leaving one for cultivation. They're even tearing down houses and demolishing whole towns—except, of course, for the churches, which they preserve for use as sheepfolds. As though they didn't waste enough of your soil already on their coverts and game-preserves, these kind souls have started destroying all traces of human habitation, and turning every scrap of farmland into a wilderness.[19]

Around the dawn of the seventeenth century, the English nobility began to find that they could make more money by renting their land to others, namely tenant farmers, rather than taking ownership of the sheep themselves or the larger commodity crop farming that was developing. The attraction to this new way of enrichment no doubt had to do with advancements in shipping that made international trade easier, ramping up the demand for wool and other commodities. As Ellen Wood points out, it also had to do with the early centralization of the English state and monarchy, which left the nobility with less real power, and thus less ability to extract taxes and assistance directly over the people in their areas. Also, land in England had become more concentrated over time, with fewer but larger landholders. "What they lacked in 'extra-economic' powers of surplus extraction they more than made up for by their increasing 'economic' powers."[20] The dynamics at work led to the development of a market in which competition was experienced as an imperative for survival rather than a choice, and it is this element, market imperatives, that marks the emergence of capitalism: "There was, in effect, a market in leases, in which prospective tenants had to compete. Where security of tenure depended on the ability to pay the going rent, uncompetitive production could mean outright loss

---

19. More, *Utopia*, 46–47.
20. Wood, "Agrarian Origins of Capitalism," 15.

of land. To meet economic rents in a situation where other potential tenants were competing for the same leases, tenants were compelled to produce cost-effectively, on penalty of dispossession."[21]

Prior to the founding of the Church of England, the Catholic Church's position on the issue of enclosure under the reign of Henry VIII, championed by the king's chancellor and the church's Cardinal Wolsey, was for the common farmer. As chancellor, Wolsey appointed a commission that began to charge those who enclosed their lands against peasant farmers, threatening them with fines if they did not level their fences and allow prior practices to resume. However, after a strong start, Wolsey's attention turned to other matters when he was appointed papal legate by Leo X in 1518. The forces of enclosure resumed.[22] After Henry's famous split from the Catholic Church, the new Church of England spawned a variety of responses, but no unified policy or teaching, to the agricultural changes underway. Some, like Pastor John Moore, expressed grave moral concerns over the process of enclosure due to its impact on the lives of the poor. Moore's pamphlet, "The Crying Sin of England, of Not Caring for the Poor" (1653), "insists upon the morality of stewardship," whereas Pastor Joseph Lee responded with "a moralized justification for improvement" in his "Considerations Concerning the Common Fields and Inclosures" (1654).[23] In other words, pastors were dueling over the same questions that are still raised about capitalism today: Are the technological, material, and economic improvements that benefit some more than others still better for all in the long run, or should Christians resist such changes as not obviously good for the poor?

Under these conditions of economic imperatives and moral confusion, the lords completed the long process of driving peasants from their intergenerational holdings, homes, and possessions. Along the way, there had been a series of peasant revolts and uprisings, movements that strove to regain access to the land that had fed the people through farming, hunting, and fishing.[24] Treated like criminals if they tried to squat somewhere and live off the land, they were driven by necessity into cities, which grew quicker than adjustments could be made. There, they might find work in the homes of the wealthy, work in the emerging factory system, engage in petty theft and prostitution, or starve. In the cities, from Thomas More's

21. Wood, "Agrarian Origins of Capitalism," 20.
22. Kines, "Reaction to Enclosure," 20–21.
23. McRae, *God Speed the Plough*, 76–77.
24. Martin, *Feudalism to Capitalism*.

time through the nineteenth century, vagrancy and homelessness were made crimes punishable by various draconian measures such as legally enforced slavery, imprisonment, corporal punishment, and even death.[25] Marx characterized the historical trajectory this way:

> The process of forcible expropriation of the people received a new and terrible impulse in the sixteenth century from the Reformation, and the consequent colossal spoliation of church property. The Catholic church was, at the time of the Reformation, the feudal proprietor of a great part of the soil of England. The dissolution of the monasteries, etc., hurled their inmates into the proletariat. The estates of the church were to a large extent given away to rapacious royal favourites, or sold at a nominal price to speculating farmers and townsmen, who drove out the old-established hereditary sub-tenants in great numbers, and threw their holdings together.[26]

And here, Marx describes the treatment of those who committed the crime of being unemployed after being forcibly removed from their ancestral lands:

> Hence at the end of the fifteenth and during the whole of the sixteenth centuries, a bloody legislation against vagabondage was enforced throughout Western Europe....
>
> Henry VIII, 1530: Beggars who are old and incapable of working receive a beggar's license. On the other hand, whipping and imprisonment for sturdy vagabonds. They are to be tied to the cart-tail and whipped until the blood streams from their bodies, then they are to swear on oath to go back to their birthplace or to where they have lived the last three years and to "put themselves to labour." What grim irony! . . . [Some time later,] the previous statute is repeated, but strengthened with new clauses. For the second arrest for vagabondage the whipping is to be repeated and half the ear sliced off; but for the third relapse the offender is to be executed as a hardened criminal and enemy of the commonweal.
>
> Edward VI: A statute of the first year of his reign, 1547,* ordains that if anyone refuses to work, he shall be condemned as a slave to the person who has denounced him as an idler. The master shall feed his slave on bread and water, weak broth and such refuse meat as he thinks fit. He has the right to force him to

---

25. Marx, *Capital*, 1:881–82. Marx's entire section on "So-Called Primitive Accumulation" is excellent for a detailed account of enclosure in England.

26. Marx, *Capital*, 1:72.

do any work, no matter how disgusting, with whip and chains. If the slave is absent for a fortnight, he is condemned to slavery for life and is to be branded on forehead or back with the letter S; if he runs away three times, he is to be executed as a felon.[27]

Thus, lords turned into landlords, with the help of the government. Renting their land to tenants, rather than peasants on generational common ground supplying them with service and products, became their chief investment vehicle. Some of their tenants managed to grow the food needed by people in the cities. But whether raising sheep and commodities like wheat for exports or farming for urban consumption, these tenants and their landlords initiated a new kind of market. In this market, landlords were always looking for tenants who could pay the highest rent, and tenants were always looking for ways to eliminate competition from other potential tenants by using their own leverage and finance to control rentable land and squeezing out their competitors. Over time, those tenants who controlled considerable land got more; those who had little lost what they had.

This change in how agricultural land was used was the actual beginning of the capitalist system, not urbanization or the introduction of factories. Capitalism is characterized by the way in which actors are forced by the dynamics of the system to behave competitively in certain predictable ways. The new market in rents and agricultural commodities was the beginning of capitalism because most economic actors in the system acted based on *imperatives*, not choices. For the average worker, the chief imperative was to eat and buy the things necessary to survive. For the average owner or renter, the imperative was to do what was necessary to compete with other owners or renters to not be put out of business. To do this, the average owner or renter had to continually reduce production costs to maximize profits and to gain (literally) ground and market share.[28]

The account above indicates that it is a mistake to think that capitalism is defined as a system of private property. Private property existed long before capitalism, even in ancient times. Likewise, capitalism is not to be equated with markets, or the ancient Greeks and Romans would have been advanced capitalists. Capitalism isn't about the emergence of factories. It is not even defined by factory production. Organized, factorylike

---

27. Marx, *Capital*, 1:896–97.
28. Wood, *Origin of Capitalism*, 97.

labor for wages sometimes took place in the medieval era. Capitalism is set apart from other economic systems by the fact that, once involved, people are not free to decide not to compete, or even in many cases how to compete, because they have nothing to fall back on—no land of their own, no way to produce for themselves the means of staying alive. In a way, we can say that with the inception of capitalism, people traded the imperatives of nature, which set limits to how to grow and gather or hunt their own food, and replaced them with more abstract imperatives. Capitalism's imperatives are abstract but nevertheless incredibly real and unavoidable. As we will see better in chapter 5, Milton Friedman was incorrect to say that people in the capitalist system are "free to choose," unless the choice of starvation and homelessness is a valid option.[29] But capitalism creates the illusion of the freedom to choose if people have enough income to buy their means of subsistence.

The factory system emerged from the new landlord-tenant agrarian reality characterized by market imperatives. All the people who were no longer "necessary" on the estates of the wealthy, all who were forced to leave the land that had fed them and given their families shelter for centuries, now became a vast, vulnerable workforce that became the fuel for urban manufacturing as it took off. As Wood puts it, "Without a productive agricultural sector that could sustain a large non-agricultural workforce, the world's first industrial capitalism would have been unlikely to emerge. Without England's agrarian capitalism, there would have been no dispossessed mass obliged to sell its labor-power for a wage. Without that dispossessed non-agrarian workforce, there would have been no mass consumer market for the cheap everyday goods—such as food and textiles—that drove the process of industrialization in England."[30] Former "peasants," now "workers," could not supply their own basic needs on their own anymore. They were literally at the mercy of urban businesses to pay them enough money to buy the things they formerly supplied themselves without money—food, water, housing, clothing, cooking, and heating fuel. That is, these former peasants became materially much less free, much less independent, and more dependent on power brokers and an economic system that was not built so much to support them as to work them for the bare minimum to keep them coming back.

29. *Free to Choose* was the name of a PBS series originally airing in 1980 and featuring the economic philosophy of Milton Friedman. It will be discussed at more length in ch. 5.

30. Wood, *Origin of Capitalism*, 142.

UNSETTLING 2: NONSTOP CHANGE

Since the Industrial Revolution, the owners that matter most have been those who control the technology of increasing automation. However, as globalization has advanced, that has begun to change. The emerging dominant owner class specializes in the "information asymmetry business" and has been called the "vectoralist" class.[31] Vectoralists do not own factories or stores. Instead, they wield their vast computing and organizational power to use the factories, warehouses, stores, manpower, and expertise of others to sell their products and services. They control the means of production and distribution through contracts; they do not need to own them. This benefits them as they are not burdened by the liabilities of direct operational ownership. Tyson, for instance, is a largely vectoral business. It does not own the thousands of farms that grow its chickens, cows, and pigs. It contracts with these farms, providing all the inputs (for instance, the chickens, feed, medications, shipping, etc.) and dictating the exact way the animals should be raised. If something goes wrong in growing the chickens, the responsibility for dealing with the losses falls on the farmer.[32] Another example of a vectoralist enterprise would be Airbnb. It does not own the homes and apartments its customers rent. While it does provide some insurance for the owners of properties, most of the risk of the physical assets lies with the owners. The fact that vectoralists don't own the factories, farms, cars, and homes they use to make money means that they escape having to deal with all the liabilities of property ownership such as upkeep, paying for accidents, dealing with labor issues, etc.[33]

The Human Cost

Automation has made hard physical labor a thing of the past for many people in the West, but it has also led to the loss of jobs, uncertain retirements, and the transformation of how we work in ways both positive and negative. Work is often physically and intellectually easier due

---

31. Wark, *Capital Is Dead*, 45. Wark finds this effect so pronounced that she even wonders if we've entered a postcapitalist phase in which owners of the vector rule over the relatively stuck owners of capital.

32. As Tyson says on its website, "We have been working with poultry farmers on a contractual basis since the late 1940s. We supply the birds and feed, as well as technical expertise, while the poultry farmer provides the labor, housing and utilities to support the birds" (Tyson Foods, "Feeding the World").

33. See Birch, *Assetization*.

to automation. But because of that, it may lower our physical fitness, and is more likely to be boring and unfulfilling. Berry's description of the personality that tends to result from all this is harsh, but instructive: "From morning to night he does not touch anything that he has produced himself, in which he can take pride. For all his leisure and recreation, he feels bad, he looks bad, he is overweight, his health is poor. His air, water, and food are all known to contain poisons. There is a fair chance that he will die of suffocation. He suspects that his love life is not as fulfilling as other people's."[34]

Because of our increased ability to monitor work pace and performance, our work is often psychologically stressful. All these observations apply to blue-collar and white-collar jobs alike. The globalized economy has greatly increased the pool of labor that corporations can draw from. It also has led to a decline in real wages and opportunities in developed countries, especially for those without advanced technical skills.[35] The rise of the "gig economy" has led to more employers treating employees as independent contractors, responsible for their own health care and retirement planning. These same workers, now made completely responsible for their security or lack thereof, are preyed upon by an economy that thrives on unnecessary spending by creating unnecessary desires. People are encouraged through advertising to buy things for emotional reasons, often on credit. The increased anxiety and depression caused by all these stressors has led some to be cynical towards their jobs.[36] Millennials and younger generations see a future with fewer opportunities than their parents.[37]

Twenty years ago, the Social Security Administration compared the average household debt in the US in 1995 and 2004. They found "a significant rise in median debt, from $19,697 in 1995 to $40,300 in 2004, and mean debt, from $58,124 in 1995 to $97,363 in 2004."[38] Debt had increased across the board, but most concerning was an increase in near-retiree debt from 79.8 to 82.7 percent. Since 2004, American household debt has continued to increase, with one small dip around

---

34. Berry, *Unsettling of America*, 22–23.
35. Piketty, *Capital in Twenty-First Century*.
36. Crary, *24/7*; Briggs, *Cauldron of Anxiety*.
37. Aaronson and Mazumder, "Intergenerational Economic Mobility"; J. Brown, *Millennials and Retirement*.
38. Anguelov and Tamborini, "Retiring in Debt," below table 2.

2012, and is now at an all-time high.[39] Americans owe more credit card debt than ever before, and interest rates were on the rise through 2023 due to Federal Reserve policy to curb inflation, making it harder for people to pay off their debt.[40] The average student loan debt is actually not that high, but this kind of debt can be crippling for those who went all in to get an expensive degree. According to an article in *Forbes*, "People carry their education debt well into middle-age and beyond. Borrowers ages 35 to 49 owe more than $620 billion in student loans. This cohort has the highest number of borrowers who owe more than $100,000 in loans. Even retirees feel the pressure from student loans; there are 2.4 million borrowers aged 62 or older that owe $98 billion in student loans."[41] Perhaps the most alarming trend is that older people have not paid off, but accumulated more debt, and they often die with substantial financial obligations that either eliminate or greatly reduce what assets they can pass on to their children.

The problem of little to no assets to leave to heirs is so common that we forget that inheritance is one of the main ways out of intergenerational poverty, and surely one of the reasons so many millennials and younger people are worried about their futures. To make us forget that inheritance can lift people out of precarity, liberal economic ideology diminishes the desirability of inheritance, shaming young people who might hope for some help from their family's estate, and encouraging parents to spend it all because they "earned it."[42] As Fessler and Schürz state, "Inheritance fundamentally violates the meritocratic justice principle of society,"[43] meaning, of course, that it violates the principles of *liberal* society. Inheritance violates the liberal expectation that everyone will be self-made and earn his merit and privileges completely on his own, an expectation that does not reflect historical reality. But this guilt

39. Center for Microeconomic Data, "Household Debt and Credit Report."

40. Lewis, "Credit Card Debt."

41. "Federal Student Loans by Age," in Hahn and Tarver, "2024 Student Loan Debt," para. 2.

42. "Another growing issue is financial independence, the Edelman report found: 85% of parents said they value autonomy, but 4 in 10 are still supporting their adult children financially. 'As parents, we are struggling with how to support our kids,' said Jason Van de Loo, head of wealth planning and marketing at Edelman Financial Engines. At the same time, views of inherited wealth are changing, Hirshman noted. Parents may feel less inclined to pass on large sums of money, she said. The mentality is 'I earned this and so should you' (Dickler, "Boomers Have More Wealth," paras. 11–13).

43. Fessler and Schürz, "Inheritance."

and hand-wringing about inheritance is a problem only for the middle class and below. As a result, *their* wealth is drained by either high debt, high living, eldercare, or simply the strong conviction that each person should make it on her own. Each of these sources of wealth depletion could be mitigated by parents and children making different choices, for instance choosing to aid each other and pool resources as more families used to do. To cooperate and pool resources, and especially to reap the benefit of inheriting real property, the fundamental choice would have to be relinquishing the ability to move anywhere at any time for better economic prospects.[44] But our individualistic culture makes those choices seem not only less lucrative but wrong. Meanwhile, the wealthy have so much money that they can maintain their "dignity" in old age and leave their heirs with a massive inheritance. "The top 1% received 35% of all wealth transfers, and the top 20% received 84%. In other words, wealth transfers are about as unequal among recipients as their household net worth."[45]

A common reason for spending down the family wealth, which belies liberal ideology, is to not "burden the children" while the parents are still alive but needing help. Angel observes, "Study after study shows that most elderly middle-class parents do not want to be a burden to their children and do not want to encumber their children's lives."[46] To not encumber the children means to not ask them to participate in caring for their parents. This, in turn, means seeking eldercare and assisted living, which are both expensive options. These options precipitate a spend-down of family assets until nothing remains and Medicare or Medicaid takes over. This move does remove the burden of direct care or overseeing care from the children, but it also leaves them to run their own race of accumulating assets to avoid penury and pain in their old age. While sometimes assisted living is the right answer, or nursing home care is the only option due to children literally not having the psychological and/or physical means to render care, parents and children often make this decision for reasons of false notions of independence. They aspire to be unhindered and to "keep their options open." However, the reality is we

---

44. Real property is most valuable intergenerationally if it is not sold upon death, but is transferred to another family member, who then does not have to work most of his life to pay off a house. The price (and benefit) is relative stability, rather than continual dislocation.

45. Wolff, "Why Piketty is Wrong."

46. Angel, *Inheritance in Contemporary America*, 53.

never live in a situation in which all our options are open. Instead, we trade one set of constraints for another when we opt for outsourcing family care. This often helps the engine of capitalism more than it helps members of a family, because the inherited wealth lost in the care-for-hire option can be a source of inequality, but it is just as likely to be the source of upward mobility.

Government's Contribution

As we have seen with the US and India examples, economic globalization often increases the gross domestic product (GDP) of countries, but it decreases their economic stability, particularly through the loss of local subsistence agriculture. Combined with the loss of the commons, more people have experienced constant anxiety about how to supply themselves, and inequality has increased, making for more resentment.[47] This growing sense of frustration has coincided with increased migration into the US and other relatively wealthy countries by people willing to do the jobs that American citizens don't want, like working in meat-packing plants and harvesting fruits and vegetables.[48] A misplaced anger towards foreigners has grown as more pressure has been put on cultural and community resources. Arlie Hochschild, in *Strangers in Their Own Land*, writes about the resentment of white working-class Louisianans from Bayou d'Inde, which is dominated by the oil and chemical industries. The Bayou area has seen its fishing waters and general environment ruined by pollution, reducing property values to such a low that people can't sell their property and leave. These workers, she wrote, felt like newer arrivals were "cutting in line," taking advantage of jobs and government benefits when they had not been trying as long as their more embedded neighbors. The reality is that their employers in the chemical and oil refinery businesses made decisions that were harmful to their employment prospects, their health, their fishing and hunting areas, and their property values. The state of Louisiana chose to support the chemical, oil,

---

47. Piketty, *Capital in Twenty-First Century*. The United Nations states that while inequality across countries has declined in the past few decades, inequality within countries, particularly developed countries, is on the rise (Department of Economic and Social Affairs, *World Social Report 2020*).

48. Tyburski, "Curse or Cure?"

and gas industries rather than their employees, giving the industries lots of tax breaks and incentives and peeling back regulation.[49]

How did this happen? As the example above indicates, the short answer is, federal and state-level political leaders made decisions that encouraged the development of large corporate businesses over diversified local and regional businesses. Why would they do that? The most common response to that question usually entails an argument about how corporate campaign contributions unduly influence American politics, but that argument is at best only partly correct. It is true that, especially since Citizens United v. FEC (2008),[50] corporate contributions have skyrocketed via PAC and interest group spending. Perhaps partly from a fear of what would happen to them if they did not compete with their rivals by giving generously, corporations have found ways to supply massive amounts of money to political campaigns at every level of the US government.[51] Sometimes these contributions are made because they reflect the politics of the CEOs and board members, regardless of shareholder views (shareholders are largely not informed and are unaware of corporate campaign contributions through PACs or other means).[52] But many post-2008 studies show that there is little measurable influence and real advantage gained by specific corporations against their rivals.[53] This does not mean, however, that corporations don't form PACS and donate, because their CEOs and boards of directors *believe* such activity will influence US politics. And it is harder to argue that these contributions have no influence on legislators and leaders at every level if we ask whether they produce a bias in lawmakers in favor of corporate business generally, as opposed to privately held medium and small businesses. In other words, the effect may very well be to simply produce a pro-corporate environment. As we will see below, there's a lot of evidence that US politicians of both parties have long favored corporate businesses at the expense of medium and small private businesses.

Another response to the above question is less common and has to do with international relations and power politics. Since Alexander Hamilton won the ideological battle with Jefferson in favor of a

49. Hochschild, *Strangers in Their Own Land*, 25–38.

50. See Federal Election Commission, "Citizens United v. FEC," for more information.

51. Eismeier and Pollock, *Business, Money*.

52. Lund and Strine, "Corporate Political Spending."

53. Fowler et al., "Quid Pro Quo?"

commercial republic, but especially since WWI, national leaders have had to concern themselves with the projection of US power around the world to gain and then maintain US superpower status. Corporate business is a superior source of national economic and political power because it can be much more easily projected abroad.[54] The very nature of corporate legal structure is to be essentially stateless, capable of locating and relocating, contracting, and making deals in various places to suit current conditions, while avoiding regulations and penalties in any place. As Mander described them, "Corporations exist beyond time and space. As we have seen they are legal creations that only exist on paper. They do not die a natural death; they outlive their own creators. And they have no commitment to locale, employees, or neighbors. This makes the modern corporation entirely different from the baker or grocer of previous years who survived by cultivating intimacy with the neighbors. Having no morality, no commitment to place, and no physical nature (a factory someplace, while being a physical entity, is not the corporation), a corporation can relocate all its operations to another place at the first sign of inconvenience: demanding employees, higher taxes, restrictive environmental laws."[55] All of these attributes make globalized corporations an inviting tool of US foreign policy.

How can corporate power be seen as a source of American power? As Joseph Nye explained in 1990:

> The dictionary tells us that power means an ability to do things and control others, to get others to do what they otherwise would not. Because the ability to control others is often associated with the possession of certain resources, politicians and diplomats commonly define power as the possession of population, territory, natural resources, economic size, military forces, and political stability.... Today, however, the definition of power is losing its emphasis on military force and conquest that marked earlier eras. The factors of technology, education, and economic growth are becoming more significant in international power, while geography, population, and raw materials are becoming somewhat less important.[56]

The new significance of "soft power," as Nye calls it, meant that no government could afford to think of transnational corporations as "just

---

54. Mander, *Absence of the Sacred*, especially ch. 7.
55. Mander, *Absence of the Sacred*, 133–34.
56. Nye, "Soft Power," 154.

business." In 1990, the US was headquarters to 34 percent of the top multinational corporations. In 2021, the US was home to 33 percent of the top multinationals, with Japan (a firm US ally) coming in second with 12 percent, and China in third place with 10 percent.[57]

The US maintenance of this dominance vis-à-vis China and other potential rivals is of supreme importance to the US government. However, wielding this kind of soft power is getting more and more difficult, especially in the age of powerful computing and the Internet, the age of true "vectoral power" that gives corporations maximum flexibility to maneuver on the global stage. In this world, what we see is a struggle between global corporations and governments for who will use who. Both try to control the other, and both experience successes and failures as they try.[58] In general, multinationals work to suppress and evade labor unionization and environmental and other forms of regulation, along with taxation.[59] Governments are relatively at a disadvantage, and must compete with other governments to create a corporate-friendly low-tax, low-regulation environment.[60] It gets even more complicated when we consider that countries pursue various foreign investment strategies, partly to guarantee a good rate of return for their people and partly to influence the power of particular corporations or countries.[61]

Perhaps with both of those factors in mind, over time, US political leaders made sure that labor unions did not impede corporate business. Contrary to those who mainly blame President Reagan for ruining US labor unions, the blue-collar union movement in the US began to weaken around the same time as small farms and businesses were challenged by the US government's decision to prioritize corporate production and engagement in global markets. As we have learned already, in the 1930s and 1940s, with the enactment of the Wagner Act (1935), we got a "system predicated on two main considerations—workers and unions should neither hinder the promotion of labor peace nor stymie demands from the corporate sector for a legal environment favoring economic expansion. By 1947 . . . even National Labor Relations Board (NLRB) arbitrators expected union leaders and workers to 'lie down like good dogs.' Deprived of the ability to sustain the grassroots militancy that had

57. Davies, "US MNCs." See Clegg and Hollinshead, "Politicization."
58. Bartley, "Transnational Corporations."
59. Garcia-Bernardo and Tørsløv, "Multinational Corporations."
60. See, for instance, the example of Ireland (Cotter, "Inside How Ireland").
61. Milan et al., "Rise of Transnational."

forced the State to reckon with it in the first place, the labor movement found itself enmeshed in a web of legal rules and institutional constraints that put it on a road of secular stagnation and decline." That means, again contrary to popular expectations, it was New Deal liberalism whose "collective bargaining law and practice articulated an ideology that legitimated employer domination in the workplace."[62]

With labor unions defanged completely in the 1970s and '80s and nation-states competing for which one could provide the most corporate-friendly environment, the imperatives of international competition consistently took priority over the well-being of any country's farmers and workers. In the United States, the force of that international competition became palpable for many workers beyond the farming sector. "By the 1970's the expansion of the world economy in countries like Germany and Japan that had benefited from US postwar aid and protection had begun to affect the domestic economy. US manufacturers were having a difficult time competing with foreign manufactured goods, leading to a drop-off in blue collar jobs in the US and reductions in wages, benefits, and job security for those who remained."[63] That has been the story of American labor ever since. While low taxes and fewer regulations on corporate activities have been promoted by both Democratic and Republican administrations, the general trend continues. Cheaper labor costs abroad lure many corporations abroad. Our politicians talk about the importance of thriving local businesses and a strong middle class, but the talk does not yield results. Shareholders benefit regardless of where corporations locate their operations, and the gap between the wealthy and the precariously employed continues to grow.

> In agriculture, the Nixon administration made a conscious decision, articulated by Agricultural Secretary Earl Butz, to provide subsidies and supports to large-scale monoculture commodity crop farming. It was not long before ethanol was mandated by many states as a prop for the giant corn farms that dominate the American Midwest, creating what Sautter and colleagues call "a fool's paradise." These events precipitated the demise of the diversified family farm, and small-town businesses and communities began to languish.[64]

---

62. Vinel, "Christopher Tomlins' *The State*," 178.
63. Hanschu and Johnson, "Economic and Psychological Origins," 27.
64. Hanschu and Johnson, "Economic and Psychological Origins," 27.

Beginning in 2005, city commissions began to use eminent domain law to confiscate small business properties.[65] Then Republicans started to pass ironically named "right to work" laws, which helped large businesses to avoid paying higher union wages and become even more competitive. In other words, Reagan's anti-union moves were not "the first huge offensive in a war that corporate America has been waging on this country's middle class ever since."[66] Both Republicans and Democrats had become free traders. In his aptly named book *Revolt of the Elites*, Christopher Lasch captured progressives' shift from substance to style better than anyone else:

> The current catchwords—diversity, compassion, empowerment, entitlement—express the wistful hope that deep divisions in American society can be bridged by goodwill and sanitized speech. We are called on to recognize that all minorities are entitled to respect not by virtue of their achievements but by virtue of their sufferings in the past. Compassionate attention, we are told, will somehow raise their opinion of themselves; banning racial epithets and other forms of hateful speech will do wonders for their morale. In our preoccupation with words, we have lost sight of the tough realities that cannot be softened simply by flattering people's self-image. What does it profit the residents of the South Bronx to enforce speech codes at elite universities?

Most workers will not profit from speech codes. Their jobs often come with no real security, and they never really own most large items like cars and homes. Many of them fall into the category Guy Standing calls the "precariat." Precarity is not just for store clerks and fast-food employees. This is because fewer and fewer jobs provide real security and the benefits to ensure a decent retirement even for many people solidly in the middle class and above. Now, all workers are dependent upon the ups and downs of globalized economic cycles. The precariat is huge.[67] Because its members lack real property and live on unpredictable wages, they are easy to exploit. They come from many industries and lack a sense of shared experience, which makes organizing them almost impossible. Workers are encouraged to see themselves as responsible for their precarity. Individual responsibility is a bedrock value

---

65. Kelo v. City of New London, 545 U.S. 469 (2005).
66. Schwarz, "Murder," para. 5.
67. Standing, *Precariat*, 13–14.

of American ideology.⁶⁸ Despite the independence they are supposed to feel, in their gut they feel (rightly) vulnerable. They often cannot afford what they work to produce and sell and are one paycheck away from losing everything. Surely, all of this is at least part of the reason much of the country has gone "red."

Red and Blue

People tend to realize that part of the problem is indeed the rural/urban division created by the trends just discussed, but they do not realize that this problem was, as I have argued, literally centuries in the making, and it has continued to accelerate in our day. The United States serves as a good focal point, but the effects are widespread and include massive displacement.⁶⁹ Again, we need to realize that America is no exception. Like the rest of the world, it has experienced *much* unsettling, from the migration of European settlers displacing Native Americans, to the importation of slaves and the integration of African Americans into the social landscape, to the various waves of immigrants. Behind each of these dislocations and disruptions has been constant technological and economic change. Wendell Berry puts it this way:

> But we know . . . that these intentions have been almost systematically overthrown. Generation after generation, those who intended to remain and prosper where they were have been dispossessed and driven out, or subverted and exploited where they were, by those who were carrying out some version of the search for El Dorado. Time after time, in place after place, these conquerors have fragmented and demolished traditional communities, the beginnings of domestic cultures. They have always said that what they destroyed was outdated, provincial, and contemptible. And with alarming frequency they have been believed and trusted by their victims, especially when their victims were other white people.
>
> If there is any law that has been consistently operative in American history, it is that the members of any *established* people or group or community sooner or later become "redskins"—that is, they become the designated victims of an utterly ruthless, officially sanctioned and subsidized exploitation.⁷⁰

---

68. Standing, *Precariat*, 25.
69. Fullilove, *Root Shock*, 5.
70. Berry, *Unsettling of America*, 6; emphasis original.

In contrast to European development, the US changed in less than 250 years. In terms of human history, urbanization in the US has happened in the blink of an eye. The migration from rural to urban areas that Berry is thinking of above, and which I have discussed in this and the previous chapter, was forced by the market.[71] Market imperatives were shaped by the dynamics of accelerating capitalism, and by economic policy changes born in a stew of liberal ideology and the desire for global power. The current red/blue division in interests is the immediate, but not the deepest, source of the sharp political conflicts we have experienced in the first quarter of the twenty-first century.[72] The deepest source of all this is dislocation, justified and fueled by liberal ideology, with its concomitant spiritual devastation and its ultimate fruit of global corporate capitalism.

"'Root shock" is defined as "the traumatic stress reaction to the destruction of all or part of one's emotional ecosystem."[73] It deprives people of "social, emotional, and financial resources," but its victims are told that each step they take to respond to dislocation, such as getting more education, or moving to a more urban area, is voluntary and actually positive.[74] The same phenomenon "at the community level fractures communal bonds, literally ripping apart the social fabric."[75] The emphasis is on their freedom of choice in adaptation, but their lived reality speaks to a lack of choice, producing cognitive dissonance. Many do not seem to be adapting all that well. They get depressed; do drugs; drink too much; or get addicted to porn, video games, and more. Some are attracted to mainstream American Christianity and learn to seek individual salvation as a solution (more on that later). But the problem does not come from the spirit, even though it becomes a spiritual problem. It comes instead from long-term economic and social disruptions. For those who can't or don't want to chase an addiction or adopt a religion, venting on social media is always an option.

But the most attractive and addictive social phenomenon of all is ideology. Vulnerable people become attracted to violent mass movements, a process I detailed at length in *Ideological Possession and the*

71. J. MacDonald et al., *Three Decades*.

72. K. Johnson and Lichter, "Rural Depopulation"; McGranahan and Beale, "Understanding Rural Population Loss."

73. Fullilove, *Root Shock*, 11.

74. Fullilove, *Root Shock*, 14.

75. Hanschu and Johnson, "Economic and Psychological Origins," 30.

Rise of the New Right. But why do people become attracted to ideological (and politically charged religious) extremism rather than seeking solace and stability in orthodox religion? If Jung is right, it is because genuine religion is no longer available to them. Both Islamic extremism and the rise of the New Right/populist politics in the US and around the globe are consequences of the economic dislocation and cultural disruptions caused by globalized capitalism. Right-wing identity movements in the United States are part of a global trend.[76]

Globalized capitalism shifts work to wherever labor is cheapest. It alienates people from each other by making it impossible to pin down who is responsible. It pits men against women; college educated against noncollege educated; white against Asian, Hispanic, and Black. Worst of all, it has created changes in weather and climate that have sparked new problems in parts of the world already hard pressed to make ends meet, which has encouraged more illegal immigrants and asylum seekers, adding to the tension and paranoia.[77] The last thing Americans will blame for all of this is capitalism itself and their participation in it, because they have been taught that capitalism is a neutral system that benefits us all and punishes only the lazy and immoral.

Let me be even more plain. We will not blame ourselves for worshiping mammon, but we can and will find common cause in blaming Jews, Africans, Asians, or Hispanics, or this or that political party, or this or that famous personage or wealthy individual. These are our scapegoats. We do this, not because we are morally bad, but because (as Jung taught us) we are psychologically predisposed to project our own darkness, our shadow, onto others to cope with our own culpability and our fears and anxieties. Speaking of the tendency to scapegoat, and referencing the circumstantial unity between Pilate and Herod, Brian Zahnd writes: "This kind of satanic unity is the glue of civilization; harmony is achieved through blame, accusation, and scapegoating, leading to communal violence that is condoned as necessary, just, and even sacred. This is how Cain built the first city—the Bible's theological telling of the origin of human civilization. But on Good Friday the

---

76. Brazilian president Jair Bolsonaro, Turkey's Recep Tayyip Erdoğan, the rise of Marine Le Pen in France are just some examples.

77. Burzyński et al. state, "Assuming constant migration laws and policies, we predict that CC will increase the number of working-age migrants of all types by 45–97 million over the remainder of the 21st century. Adding dependent children, this means an approximate total of 100–200 million climate migrants" ("Climate Change, Inequality," 1192).

whole foundational system of accusation and violence reaches a hellish crescendo in the crucifixion of Jesus."[78]

Most people express their rage at scapegoats while sitting on their couches, instead of engaging in violence. But we are seeing now that the added fuel of online participation can and does sometimes inspire mass shootings and riots. Such spasms of violence do not lead to solutions to our problems any more than virtual expressions of discontent. They do not represent reasoned, concerted action but rather raw, uncontrolled emotions. And, these days, when people instead try to engage in reasoned, collective action, the results are most often toothless performative protests, such as those we see most outside of abortion clinics, nuclear power plants, and munitions depots. Such protests are, again, ways of venting, but at a more sophisticated level. They do less damage, and if anything, they have even less effect than their violent counterparts. It seems impossible, now, to have meaningful collective action that brings lasting positive change. In a time in which all human resources, including the great "grand narrative" ideologies, seem to be bankrupt, it is reasonable to remain open to the possibility that we are not capable, on our own, of fixing our problems and finding ways past our divisions. It makes sense, hopefully, to ask the question, what has gone wrong spiritually?

---

78. Zahnd, "Good Friday."

4

Secular v. Sacred

In previous chapters, I discussed historic and current trends and events that help explain why we should care about economically driven dislocation and its social and political effects. But while the economy plays a huge role in the damaging demographic shifts and political changes that have taken place over more recent decades, materialistic arguments cannot explain everything. It seems to be a rule of political theory that one must find the heart of our problems either in materialism or in culture, but not in both. However, the truth betrays the rule—economics and culture are both causal forces, and both influence the other. Here I want to make the argument that the damage caused by globalized capitalist markets and the dislocation and alienation they have caused have their origins in a preceding "modern" turn that took place *centuries ago*. I will suggest that this way of being and thinking, which developed alongside, and interacted with, emerging technologies and economic arrangements, also helped create the problematic world in which we now live. Ours is a world that *feels like* the "end of history," a world in which the abstract domination of capital seems like the only possible reality, a reality that we must all serve of necessity, as if it were God himself.[1] But prior to the ascendency of mammon, God was more real.

---

1. Francis Fukuyama, though he has since reconsidered, treated the globalization of liberal democracy and capitalism not only as triumphant but responsible for a near future of peace and prosperity (*End of History*). See also Fisher, *Capitalist Realism*.

For many people, the first half of the twentieth century *also* seemed like the end of history. World War I, World War II, the Holocaust, the atomic bombings of Hiroshima and Nagasaki, and the disastrous failures of Bolshevism in Stalinist totalitarianism and Mao Zedong thought in China revealed the modern tendency to technologically accelerated catastrophic destruction and ideologically driven mass movements. Our man-made predicaments became so obvious that they spawned the philosophies of existentialism, realist theory in international relations, fictional literatures of futuristic doom, and a fracturing and confusion of aesthetic sensibilities in art.[2] The implications of the mass destruction and the obvious evils of the twentieth century drove many people to atheism, due to their inability to conceive of a God who cared.[3] But as early as the sixteenth century in Europe there were shifts in thinking and belief that prepared the way for those modern events and for the situational and rebellious atheism that became a moral standard in the twentieth century, particularly of the educated classes. I am referring to the long march towards secularity, with its origins in Europe. Even though in the second half of the twentieth century we saw something of an economic and political rebound (and a growing faith in the power of liberal democracy and capitalism obscured our moribund spiritual condition), a centuries-in-the-making functional atheism had begun to crystallize well before these catastrophic events.[4] This atheism remains with us today, and it shapes our perceptions and reactions to society, politics, economics, and our environment, whether we are conscious of it or not.

The loss of religious faith due to major historical developments in European thought and practice started in events you probably learned about in high school, such as the Scientific Revolution, Renaissance, Protestant Reformation, the consolidation of nation-states, the Enlightenment, and the Industrial Revolution. These events have of course been discussed by many thinkers. Their influence on the catastrophes of the twentieth century has not been lost on anyone who is a student of intellectual history. Despite many important philosophical and religious differences among the thinkers I will feature in this chapter, there is a common

---

2. Rosenthal describes the feeling of despair in *Mourning Modernism*.

3. Weinberg voices this feeling as well as many others in *Dreams of Final Theory*.

4. Leo Strauss refers to something similar when he uses the term "political atheism." He writes, "Political atheism is a distinctly modern phenomenon. No pre-modern atheist doubted that social life required belief in, and worship of, God or gods" (*Natural Right*, 169).

focus on an important shift in the consciousness of people in the modern era (in and around the sixteenth century and forward), and particularly in the modern European scene. Scholars differ on exactly when this shift happened and what its most important elements were. Nevertheless, they all observe a modern turn away from religious belief, community, and the common good in favor of a secular outlook and the primacy of individual self-interest and worldly welfare. After the turn, it was obvious that something more than technological innovations or new economic practices had changed, and this change was of huge importance for how modern people organized themselves and interacted with their environments. Carl Jung, Leo Strauss, D. C. Schindler, and Charles Taylor all help us get a better grasp on the nature and impact of this shift. They are helpful for filling in the larger picture precisely because none of them focus *primarily* on economic causation. All four of them attempt to pinpoint what it means to be "modern" by looking at noneconomic factors such as psychology, ideas and ideologies, religion, and culture. Each adds his insight to the bigger picture I have already started to describe.

Scholars often speak past each other due to lack of exposure to other schools of thought, or because prejudices were formed against those other schools early on in graduate training. In general, Catholic and other Christian scholars, for instance, do not engage with Strauss, who is too secular, too Jewish, or too conservative. Christian scholars engage more with Taylor, but often only superficially, because their scholarship still prioritizes biblical argumentation over philosophy. Generally, they have not engaged with Strauss.[5] If the point is to persuade people in a way that may change the social and material conditions of the world, intellectual insularity and lack of reach become real obstacles to solving problems. I hope that by putting all these thinkers together in the same chapter, readers can tell how much agreement there is among them, how their differences all add something valuable to our understanding, and how much one can gain by learning from more than one school of thought. Put into dialogue with each other, they can offer valuable insights into our suffering today.

---

5. Or, they have engaged only to argue. See Havers, "Straussian-Thomistic Quarrel."

Carl Jung

Jung's contribution is unique because, though a psychologist, Jung deals with the role of religion very seriously in a way that his mentor and later nemesis Freud did not. This won him a mixed reputation as a thinker who dealt too much in "mysticism," a scholar who was often not scientific enough for contemporary sensibilities. As Grant Maxwell notes, Freud dismissed Jung for refusing, ultimately, to be his acolyte and choosing to delve into what Freud thought were arcane spiritual/religious matters, and much of the scholarly community followed Freud.[6] However, this criticism of Jung is largely a prejudice born of the very secularism that I am examining. Maxwell argues that Jung's view is perhaps hampered by the fact that he primarily sees religion in psychological terms, and not necessarily as an ontological reality (Jung typically suspends judgment). But even if this is entirely true, Jung's insights are intriguing enough to encourage us to gain what we can from his theories and observations.

Jung discussed at length the alienation from society and nature felt by many in the nineteenth-century Romantic movement, which was reacting to industrialization. He argued that this alienation was born in the Enlightenment, especially in a new functional atheism stemming from the embrace of science, empiricism, and rationalism.[7] The scientific view tended to erode traditional ways of life, because (as Edmund Burke also pointed out) most traditions could not be justified with "reason" alone.[8] Rationalism and skepticism towards tradition damaged people's experience of religious faith. As traditional cultural and religious institutions began to fracture, Jung argued, psychic forces previously channeled through religion were rechanneled, producing a growing number of neuroses in individuals, and mass psychoses in society and politics.[9] In mass psychoses, people acted collectively, without

---

6. See Maxwell, "Widening of Consciousness."

7. Jung, *Modern Man*, 145.

8. As Lauren Hall remarks, "Burke's suspicion of purely rationalistic approaches to rights stems from his belief that rights are rooted in human nature, which is both rational and passionate, as well as both social and individualistic. A purely rationalistic approach to rights fails, on Burke's account, because the abstract rights of the revolutionaries are devoid of emotional attachment, and thus unsafe for direct application to social life" ("Rights and the Heart," 610).

9. Eugene McCarraher employs the concept of mis-enchantment, the pouring of those psychic forces/religious attachments into the market/consumer/entertainment in *Enchantments of Mammon*.

conscious judgment, effectively worshiping charismatic leaders and making religions out of political ideologies.[10]

In Jung's view, the development of twentieth-century ideologies like Nazism and totalitarian communism did not happen because individuals were not reasonable or were morally bad. They literally resulted from misplaced religious faith.[11] And, Jung could see the connection between this loss of faith and economic and political change. In fact, he argued that the triggers for the catastrophes of World War I and World War II were the dislocating and disintegrating effects of urbanization, wage labor, and massification. Jung saw the deep cause of such catastrophes as a type of spiritual death, the denial of the religious expression of the archetypal forces that lay in everyone's psyche. He saw the trigger for extreme mass action as a response to the alienation caused by dislocation or "root shock." What was it about industrialization and mass organization of human behavior generally, such as expanding cities and popular armies, that alienated people to this extent? Jung argued that mechanized and routine work, and increasingly urban lifestyles abstracted from nature and normal social life, created a "herd" mentality. As more people crowded into cities and experienced their often isolating and depersonalizing effects, their sense of individual moral responsibility weakened. This promoted a moral problem of immense significance: diffused responsibility.[12] The most well-known example of diffused responsibility is the case of Adolf Eichmann, a bureaucrat who ordered the transportation of thousands of Jews to extermination camps. While

10. Jung described this mass psychosis as "the communism of a primitive tribe where everybody is subject to the autocratic rule of a chief or an oligarchy" ("Undiscovered Self," 250).

11. Eric Voegelin makes a similar point about the development of destructive mass ideologies in the twentieth century, prominently communism and fascism. He goes so far as to describe the emergence of these movements as like the creation of the golem in Jewish mythology, the Frankenstein creature of man produced by man. Though Voegelin refers to Gnosticism as the source of the modern golem and reminds us that gnostic movements have been around since at least the Axial age, they increased in number and intensity with Christianity, a religion that asked people to believe in an invisible and inscrutable God. The invisible God of pure logos or love called forth efforts to find some foothold, or formula, to balance the equation of human and godly power. The gnostic foothold gained creates a false sense of human control, and as the world became harder to deal with, the effort to create the formulae of control only intensified. Voegelin sees modern secular mass movements as essentially gnostic (*Science, Politics and Gnosticism*, 53–54).

12. For more on "diffused responsibility," an important concept for understanding modern catastrophes, see Balfour et al., *Unmasking Administrative Evil*.

on trial in Jerusalem, Eichmann pleaded with the court that he was just doing his job.[13] Arguably, the Eichmann mentality is now the norm for most people, whose work occurs in industrial or bureaucratic settings whose processes they cannot fully understand or control.

Jung argued that people who lived in rural areas tended to be more settled. They were more likely to be attached to a place, and to have intact families.[14] If they worked on farms, were craftsmen, or were engaged in small local businesses, they would more easily retain a sense of agency and responsibility, because it would be easier for them to see and feel their impact in their smaller world. Because of this, so long as they had enough people to form a functional community, Jung believed that people in small towns were stronger than those in cities. As opportunities to continue this agrarian way of life dwindled, however, a cultural clash was in the making between the growing number of people who lived in cities and the decreasing number of rural people whose way of life was being erased and whose way of thinking was considered by the larger urbanized society to be retrograde.

Jung observed that wage labor was precarious in ways that rural subsistence labor was not. Wages could be withdrawn by an employer for any reason, and the most likely reason would be a downturn in market forces beyond anyone's control. It was true that in rural settings people were constantly dealing with "acts of God" or forces of nature. But the actions of nature's God were often seen by traditional peoples as coming from a divine (not human) source, a source that was perceived as having reason and actively supporting a moral order. They existed in a spiritual framework in which natural challenges could be explained and coped with. A religious framework allowed people an appropriate response to hard times (prayer, repentance, praise, and worship), and it offered continual hope for the future, because God was seen as ultimately in charge. By contrast, an urban worker's prospects were profoundly affected, not so much by the direct natural forces of a transcendent God, but by the faceless and entirely human "they."[15] In short, Jung argued that God was harder to find and experience in urban settings where people were buffered to a great extent from the natural world, and without access to what

---

13. Arendt, *Eichmann in Jerusalem*.

14. Jung, "After the Catastrophe"; Jung, "Psychology of the Consciousness," 71.

15. With climate change and weather effects, more and more city dwellers are beginning to get a taste of the ultimately inescapable power of nature beyond human control, a nature that people must cooperate with to tame.

he would consider a psychologically healthy religion. Thus, urbanites were more susceptible to ideological extremism.[16]

Post-World War II, to the extent that governments intervened in the economy, and as we have seen they most certainly did, they did so not in the interest of individuals, families, or groups but rather with abstract technological progress and economic growth in mind. Governments thus became sources of further alienation rather than sources of a sense of belonging and purpose. In Jung's theory, the means of dealing in a healthy way with this alienation would involve cooperating with and harnessing the interior archetypal forces of the human psyche in a process Jung called *individuation*. Individuation could be obtained either by practicing a living, psychologically healthy religion, *or* by undergoing Jungian psychoanalysis. It involved recognizing the power of the archetypal forces, both good and bad, that existed in our unconscious psyches, instead of projecting those forces onto "others" using political ideologies.[17]

Dealing with the tendency in modernity to scapegoat others as stand-ins for metaphysical evil, Charles Taylor refers to what Jung is talking about here simply as "good religion," arguing that for human beings "the religious dimension is inescapable" and that "there is only the choice between good and bad religion."[18] A good religion, for Taylor, would achieve "the belief in transcendent reality . . . and the connected aspiration to a transformation which goes beyond ordinary human flourishing . . . and it would lead to the true ability to love and forgive instead of scapegoat."[19]

In Jung's view, psychologically healthy religion allowed people a chance to "individuate" by perceiving the forces of good and evil as beyond (or bigger than) themselves, but also in relationship with themselves, a relationship that could allow a proper level of humility and proportion. A person practicing "good religion" or becoming individuated would not identify their own conscious egos with absolute good or their enemies with absolute evil. That is, an individuated person, whether made so by psychoanalysis or religion, would not suffer from either psychological inflation (I am God, and everything revolves around me) or mass psychosis/ideological possession (we are good, and they are the devil who must be

16. Jung, "Psychology of the Consciousness," 71.
17. Jung, *Jung on Christianity*, 78.
18. Taylor, *Secular Age*, 708.
19. Taylor, *Secular Age*, 510.

eliminated to make way for heaven). In modernity, science, technology, capitalism, communism, and fascism were too often made into secular religions that fed on the tendency to psychological inflation. They were received by people not as tools to be used within a larger transcendent and moral framework, but as gods to be followed. Jung wrote that "when the collective dominants of human life fall into decay . . . there is bound to be a considerable number of individuals who are possessed by archetypes of a numinous nature that force their way to the surface to form new dominants. This state of possession shows itself almost without exception in the fact that the possessed identify themselves with the archetypal contents of their unconscious, and, because they do not realize that the role which is being thrust upon them is the effect of new contents still to be understood, they exemplify these concretely in their own lives, thus becoming prophets and reformers."[20]

Jung taught that the two human types that result from ideological possession are the pathological egoist and the ideological crusader. Unfortunately, we see both in abundance today. The psychological egoist uses her resources to give herself pleasure and seeks relationships to "validate" and "gratify" herself; the ideological crusader uses his resources to "save the world" from the enemy and seeks relationships primarily to enjoy the collective "participation mystique"[21] of being on the same team. Hopefully the reader can see how these types can and do combine. Suffice it to say that such people are strongly attracted to both products and movements that stimulate tribal feelings of belonging. This is why modern advertisers use the word "community" so much when talking about their customers. Eugene McCarraher argues that as traditional religious faith has waned, people have become enchanted by "Mammon" and its currently dominant form—the commodity.[22] In his view, as well as Jung's, the psychic/spiritual alienation and the economic exploitation many people experience are related. The dislocation and environmental damage of capitalism and communism have contributed to spiritual impoverishment and psychological stress.[23] This creates ideological polarity and extremism in an unhelpful feedback loop. The diminishment of traditional religious

---

20. Jung, *Jung on Christianity*, 210.

21. Jung, *Collected Works*, 37.

22. McCarraher, *Enchantments of Mammon*; W. Brown, *Undoing the Demos*; Foucault, *Birth of Biopolitics*.

23. Bauman, "From Pilgrim to Tourist"; Giddens, *Modernity and Self-Identity*.

faith means that people lose yet another source of worldly stability and security in the face of that existential threat.

Leo Strauss

For Leo Strauss, change happened because of new political practices and ideas, instead of new practices and ideas trailing economic change. Most of his work concentrated on the political and social impact of major thinkers who established new categories of political thought. A large part of the modern shift, for Strauss, was the publicly proclaimed distinction, best voiced by Machiavelli in the early sixteenth century, between justice (or morality) and politics. Machiavelli overturned the older idealist philosophy of the ancient Greeks, which had been taken up and transformed by the Catholic Church. That older philosophy found its standards in ideal forms and in teleology, and its aim was not mere individual survival but the flourishing of human beings as social, intellectual, and spiritual beings within the best community possible. With Machiavelli, the focus shifted from the higher aim of living the good life as social and spiritual beings to lower, and much more achievable, worldly goals—namely the safety, survival, and material well-being of individuals seen as inherently antisocial. Machiavelli set the tone for the modern thinking by treating the church as a worldly institution whose influence on human behavior could be useful, or not, depending on how it was managed by rulers. He established the basis of the modern European rejection of both ancient idealism and genuine Judeo Christianity.[24]

Strauss worked to contrast classical or ancient with modern political thought, building a strong argument for the moral and political superiority of the ancients. He did this despite ancient philosophy's undemocratic teaching that some were more suited to rule than others. Understanding ancient idealism well, understanding why modern thinkers like Machiavelli rejected key elements of ancient thought, and understanding the harmful consequences of modern realism were all key to explaining why the twentieth century was a century of crisis and destruction. Strauss believed this upheaval was ultimately the result of modernity's positivism and nihilism.[25] Machiavelli, Strauss wrote, argued that "there is something fundamentally wrong with an approach to politics which

24. Strauss, *Thoughts on Machiavelli*.
25. Strauss, "What is Political Philosophy?"

culminates in a utopia, in the description of a best regime whose actualization is highly improbable. Let us then cease to take our bearings by virtue, the highest objective which a society might choose; let us begin to take our bearings by the objectives which are actually pursued by all societies."[26] Machiavelli rejected the substance of morality, treating it as conventional, rather than a natural or transcendent truth. This is why Strauss could argue that Karl Marx's ideas in some ways followed from Machiavelli's: Marx too believed that morality was a social (economically driven) construct. With Machiavelli, in the sixteenth century, the intellectual rug was pulled out from under not only morality and religion, but the larger concept of truth itself. Machiavelli started something that would end in the full embrace of nihilism.[27]

Inspired by the achievements of pagan Rome, Machiavelli sought to find a formula to incentivize, and if need be, compel people to obey and produce within a unified nation-state. He rejected the idea that there was a natural superiority to be found in those who had previously held authority, such as aristocrats or priests. Instead, he could see that there was real power, and even a certain earthy wisdom, in the lower classes. This power, if harnessed, could lead to the consolidation and growth of the nation-state, if the people could be trusted and trained to bear arms and fight wars. This new focus on the people and the hope of more national political and economic power if they could become ordered and organized led Machiavelli to conceive of a new agreement, if not yet a contract, between the people and their governments. In his view, the best government was a republic.[28] But in a principality, the smart prince

---

26. Strauss, *What Is Political Philosophy*, 41.

27. Adi Armon writes, "Marx rejects Plato's ideal doctrine or any other attempt to transcend the limits of human reason or creation. He therefore rejects the tension between 'Jerusalem' and 'Athens,' the two cornerstones of the West according to Strauss. Strauss's Marx tries to change man completely and to solve all of his problems through societal means, abolishing private property, conquering nature through technology. In his lecture 'Why We Remain Jews' (1962), Strauss claimed that the Jews are the proof of the impossibility of redemption. He saw the Marxist vision as a dangerous fantasy of a universal, global, and free society that radicalizes modernity and aspires for salvation. Marx's ideal man is nothing more than the 'last man': the manifestation of human decay, the abolition of the noble and of politics, and the abstraction of man" ("Leo Strauss Reading," 40).

28. Machiavelli's *Discourses on Livy* were written around the same time as his more famous work, *The Prince*. The *Discourses* is a full-throated argument for the superiority of republican government and a guidebook on how to establish and maintain one. See also G. Bock et al., *Machiavelli and Republicanism*. On the nature of Machiavelli's republic, see Warner, "Friendless Republic."

would give the people good government, and the people would give their princely benefactor their loyalty, and the state their very lives.[29] Not surprisingly, it was out of this new realization of the power of common people that liberal social contract thinking emerged.

According to Strauss, seventeenth-century English philosopher Thomas Hobbes saw the danger of Machiavelli's argument that morality was nothing more than a man-made construct, and so he sought to reestablish a basis for reasoning about justice and morality by proposing a state of nature scenario in which the desire for self-preservation is paramount, and in that extreme situation natural rights are found.[30] He agreed with Machiavelli that "traditional political philosophy aimed too high" because it demanded that people become truly just in their inner character. He agreed that there was no natural superiority or authority that people could simply acknowledge and obey. So how should we get people to be just? According to Strauss, Hobbes "demanded that natural right be derived from the beginnings" of what it meant to be human in a scientific sense. This meant taking as primary "the elementary wants or urges, which effectively determine all men most of the time," and rejecting man's telos or perfection as the standard.[31]

For Hobbes, it was obvious that most people were motivated by selfishness most of the time, and carrying this assumption into the state of nature meant that all human beings had a natural right to their self-preservation. The motivator that Machiavelli preferred, the glory of princes (and by extension, their people), gave way to simple human equality in fear—for Hobbes, everyone should remember that everyone else was a moral threat unless government and law intervened. In Strauss's view, then, Hobbes went "lower" because he did not aim at excellence (rejecting even Machiavellian princely glory) but emphasized mere survival, and by extrapolation, that "the good is fundamentally identical with the pleasant."[32] Hence Hobbes, with his social contract that justifies absolute monarchy in the name of personal survival, erases even the ghost of a transcendent moral value (such as God, glory, and honor, all of which he thought drove people to irrational violence) in favor of brute human

29. Foucault sees the full implications of this shift in his concept of biopolitics (*Birth of Biopolitics*).
30. Strauss, *Natural Right and History*, 191.
31. Strauss, *Political Philosophy of Hobbes*, 48.
32. Strauss, *Natural Right and History*, 169. See also Strauss, *Political Philosophy of Hobbes*.

force, which is inherently amoral. The emphasis on the popular will as the only legitimate source of power remains in Hobbes, even though disguised in an argument for absolutism.[33]

Only a generation after Hobbes, according to Strauss, English philosopher John Locke went lower still. For Strauss, "lowness" consisted in giving up on the project of knowing what is good, beautiful, and true, and instead following the path of self-interested agreement on the lowest common denominator. Lockean liberalism is built upon sand, in Strauss's view. With Hobbes, the purpose of government and even of life had come to mean baseline survival, and hopefully the room to build up some property through contract enforcement. Locke simply doubled down on the low aims of the liberal social contract. Locke "realized that what man primarily needs for his self-preservation is less a gun than food, or more generally, property. Thus the desire for self-preservation turns into the desire for property, for acquisition, and the right to self-preservation becomes the right to unlimited acquisition." Through Locke's economism, "we can say that Machiavelli's discovery or invention of the need for an immoral or amoral substitute for morality, became victorious through Locke's discovery or invention that that substitute is acquisitiveness."[34] Straussian scholar Martin Diamond, applying this general argument to the American regime, remarked on the price paid for the material growth that developed from the compromises of liberalism: "But the cost must be recognized, precisely in order to continue to enjoy the blessings. Again in comparison with the pre-modern perspective, that cost is the solid but low foundation of American political life."[35] Given all this, perhaps it should go without saying, but obviously Strauss did not think that capitalism was the great civilizer and savior, as some of his later followers would argue.[36]

---

33. Hobbes's argument for absolutism is peculiarly modern. Indeed, the argument can be made that absolutism did not exist as an idea prior to the Hobbesian formulation, anticipating the consolidation of the nation-state and the centralization of political power that can be obtained only in an era of expanding communications capabilities and military power and organization. See Hobbes, *Leviathan*.

34. Strauss, *What Is Political Philosophy*, 49.

35. Diamond, "Ethics and Politics," 59.

36. The Claremont Institute, influenced by the Straussian school, took this turn, but it is not clear that Strauss would have approved. See https://www.claremont.org/ and https://claremontreviewofbooks.com/. Catholic neoconservatives also took this turn. Some prominent neocon Catholics include Richard John Neuhaus, Michael Novak, Fr. Robert Sirico, and George Weigel.

Strauss went on to trace the development of modern thought through thinkers like Rousseau, Kant, Hegel, Marx, and Nietzsche. However, for Strauss, the seeds of modern nihilism were sown with Machiavelli in the sixteenth century with the fundamental rejection of moral truth, either in religion or philosophy, in favor of an amoral realism. Key to its full development was the realization in French philosopher Jean-Jacques Rousseau that, if human behavior hinged on man-made constructs like the social contract, laws, and law enforcement, and not God's will and/or natural law, then social engineering was possible.[37]

From the modern perspective, idealism, and Christianity in particular, had created nothing but disappointment and endless conflict, conflict about ephemeral ideas and beliefs. From the modern perspective, this was not only a waste of time and mental effort, but a serious moral mistake. Even morally speaking, it was better to deemphasize "the Truth," and emphasize the low and practical concerns that everyone could agree on, such as self-preservation, comfort, equality, freedom, and universal human rights. Through modern social engineering as envisioned from Machiavelli to Rousseau, the aspiration was that we could obtain a much greater degree of agreement and cooperation and end our senseless conflicts. Thus, with the modern turn, the "ideal" was lowered and recreated as a man-made scheme for molding people into a social machine. Man was now seen as "almost infinitely malleable," and therefore "almost infinitely perfectible."[38]

Strauss detected a great contradiction in such modern positivism. Without establishing what was good or just first, modern thinkers made claims about what they *thought* society ought to be like, with no real or substantive basis for making their claims other than their own preferences and feelings, or those of the majority. What Alasdair MacIntyre called "emotivism" was at work here, and as he argued, emotivism was essentially groundless.[39] Strauss simply called it "relativism," and identified these developments with full-blown societal nihilism, the kind championed by Friedrich Nietzsche.[40] Nihilism, the acknowledgment that there was no transcendent "Truth," but only "truths" as defined by individuals

---

37. Strauss sorts through what message Rousseau really believed in—the radical doubt of the goodness of reason and science or the upholding of their goodness within the bounds of morality ("Intention of Rousseau," 462).

38. Strauss, *Natural Right and History*, 271.

39. MacIntyre, *After Virtue*.

40. Strauss, *Rebirth*, 13–26.

and groups, meant that those who had the most power could, in effect, dictate the social "truth." This meant there was no need for justifying the use of raw, naked, and absolute power to achieve whichever societal vision the strong happened to prefer. Catherine and Michael Zuckert sum up Strauss's argument like this:

> Strauss came to see that this crisis, in both its philosophical and its political aspects, derived from modern philosophy's great act of rebellion against classical philosophy and biblical religion. The founders of modernity, thinkers like Machiavelli, Hobbes, and Spinoza, set mankind on a path that, via an almost inexorable dialectic, produced the end of philosophy and the "last man" as announced and diagnosed by Nietzsche. If modernity was at the bottom of the problem, then, Strauss concluded, the proper response was a retreat or a return to premodernity.[41]

The Zuckerts read Strauss's argument to call for a return to premodernity, or even a "retreat" into the past. If they are right, Strauss's project is doomed from the start. There is no going back to an ideal past because, as Charles Taylor has demonstrated, the ancient and medieval mind, in which all things were experienced within an enchanted frame, is not something we can recreate at will. However, if Strauss's project is to get us to see the utility of establishing moral ideals based on reasoning about what it means to be human, his project is not necessarily dead. Strauss's project does not have to entail a retreat or adoption of previous ways of being and thinking. If human nature is partly the result of historical trends in technology, economics, and culture, that does not have to mean that humans are "infinitely malleable" and nihilism inevitable. This is a false dichotomy. Catholic scholar D. C. Schindler can pick up where Strauss left off because he can see human nature as having some fixed characteristics but also as being strongly influenced by historical trends, and he wraps all of this up into a still-unfolding account of living Christianity. But first, we need to incorporate the ideas of Canadian philosopher, Charles Taylor, as a bridge.

Charles Taylor

For Taylor, whose major work *A Secular Age* focuses on developments in religion and their social ramifications, the decisive shift that changed

41. Zuckert and Zuckert, *Truth about Leo Strauss*, 36.

everything occurred in and around the time of the Protestant Reformation in the sixteenth century. The Reformation period was, according to Taylor, characterized by a move from religious "enchantment" to "disenchantment," from the "porous self" to the "buffered self," and from humans who were socially "embedded" to a great "disembedding." How does Taylor think these changes happened? The unsettling answer he gives is that they happened largely by chance—or, at least, they were not inevitable, nor were they planned.

According to Taylor, until the Reformation, people experienced themselves as "porous." This means that their experience of life was characterized by being constantly aware of and penetrable by external spiritual forces. Taylor is specifically looking at Western developments. He argues that for people living in medieval Europe, God, angels, demons, and spirits of all kinds were constant, palpable presences, not just in overtly religious settings like churches but in everyday life and even in people's experience of time.[42] Belief in God was not seen as an option but as a given, so being on the right side of God was really the only protection from the dark forces that threatened people's lives and souls. The sharp distinctions we now make between "the immanent and the transcendent, the natural and the supernatural" did not exist in the minds of these medieval people.[43]

The enchanted world of medieval Christendom contained three features. First, Taylor writes, "the natural world they lived in ... testified to divine purpose and action" not only because it seemed divinely designed, but because "the great events in this natural order, storms, droughts, floods, plagues, as well as years of exceptional fertility and flourishing, were seen as acts of God."[44] Second, "God was also implicated in the very existence of society ... the life of the various associations which made up society, parishes, boroughs, guilds, and so on, were interwoven with ritual and worship. ... One could not but encounter God everywhere."[45] Third, in a spirit-charged world, atheism was almost inconceivable.[46] Spirits, demons, holy relics, along with the God-filled force of storms and floods, were all

42. Taylor, *Secular Age*, 3.
43. Taylor, *Secular Age*, 13–14.
44. This first feature should remind us of Jung's observation that people who used to live more closely to the land could more easily perceive themselves as encountering God ("Psychology of the Consciousness," 71).
45. Taylor, *Secular Age*, 25.
46. Taylor, *Secular Age*, 26.

experienced as spiritually "other," i.e., external to and directly interacting with people, not as wholly or partly subjective interior experiences, concepts, and feelings as they may be experienced now.[47]

Along with this porous experience came a kind of social embeddedness, Taylor argues. People experienced themselves as inherently social, part of a given larger group, not chosen or optional, from which they naturally expected aid and counsel. With enchantment and the porous self, Taylor argues, "it was not just that the spiritual forces which impinged on me often emanated from people around me, e.g., the spell cast by my enemy, or the protection afforded by a candle which has been blessed in the parish church. Much more fundamental, these forces often impinged on us as a society, and were defended against by us as a society."[48] Because people were of necessity "in this together," any disagreement about how to handle the dangers lurking in the world was seen as a serious, even life-threatening event. Social cohesion was at a premium, and thus "heretics" were monstrous and frightening. This explains the extreme intolerance that often came to the surface in medieval times and through the Reformation period, such as burning "witches" at the stake and putting moral malefactors in stocks for public display.[49] As Taylor points out, it's very hard for us to imagine how important it was for everyone to stay in line—it was perceived as absolutely a matter of social survival.

However, Taylor argues that alongside enchantment and social embeddedness, throughout the medieval period there were movements within Catholicism that encouraged "a more intense, inward, devotional life" not only for monks and nuns, but literate and motivated laypeople too. For instance, the quest for union with the Godhead expressed by Meister Eckhart, or the desire for inner purity and spiritual relationship detailed by Thomas à Kempis, appealed to the aspirations of some laypeople who wanted to get closer to God and to live a truly meritorious religious life.[50] Most of the common people continued to rely on the clergy to create a spiritual bridge between them and God. They relied on the prayers and works of the priests, monks, and sisters

---

47. This description also would be familiar to Jung, who described people's experience of archetypal forces breaking through into consciousness in the same way—they were perceived as bigger and other than their conscious egos (Jung, *Archetypes and Collective Unconscious*).

48. Taylor, *Secular Age*, 42.

49. Crane, *Witches, Wife Beaters, Whores*.

50. See Magill, "Turn Away the World."

to stand in for them and gain merit for them in God's eyes. This was why supporting the church was so important. But through exhortations of some holy men and women, the emphasis sometimes turned towards the ideal of holiness for laypeople (and implicitly, for a diminishment of the need for a "bridge").[51] Taylor writes, "People were seeing a more personal religious life, wanting a new kind of prayer, want[ing] to read and meditate [on] the Bible themselves."[52]

This popular puritanical impulse waxed and waned throughout the medieval period, long before the Protestant Reformation, and coexisted with more traditional understandings of the role of religious and lay commitments.[53] The motive for these movements, whether puritanical, gnostic, or both, was a desire for a more authentic holiness without the accretions of customs and institutions blocking at least some people's aspirations to climb higher in their relationship to God. Some of these movements were seen as heretical by the church, perhaps because they inadvertently threatened her authority. For instance, Eckhart, whom Carl Jung considered a Christian gnostic, was charged with heresy by the church, but died before he could be judged.[54] Some of these movements offended others in the clergy by being overly critical of church practices that seemed a bit too much like magic.

None of these purity movements necessarily had to lead either to a split with the Catholic church or secularism. But, as history moved closer to the Reformation, these views, which were simultaneously critical of the laypeople and of the church for being insufficiently pure, increased. Those seeking a truer, deeper, and more holy existence began

---

51. In modern times this line of thought expressed itself in Vatican II's "the universal call to holiness." See Paul VI, *Lumen Gentium*.

52. Taylor, *Secular Age*, 70.

53. There is convergence between Taylor's observation that these puritanical impulses were always there, but became more prevalent over time, and Eric Voegelin's insistence that Gnosticism has always existed parallel with true philosophy and religion, but that it ramped up with the advent of Christianity and became even more dominant in modern times via secularization. Voegelin writes, "In the period of secularization leaders could not be presented as God-possessed paracletes. By the end of the eighteenth century a new symbol, that of the 'superman,' begins to take the place of the old sectarian categories" (*Science, Politics and Gnosticism*, 72).

54. Carl Jung writes, "The world-embracing spirit of Meister Eckhart knew, without discursive knowledge, the primordial mystical experience of India as well as of the Gnostics and was itself the finest flower on the tree of the 'Free Spirit' that flourished at the beginning of the eleventh century. Well might the writings of this Master be buried for six hundred years, for 'his time was not yet come.' Only in the nineteenth century did he find a public at all capable of appreciating the grandeur of his mind" (*Aion*, 194).

to see others' ways of dealing with God, and especially the church's rituals and formulae, as shallow, materialistic, even superstitious.[55] Over time, a new spiritual ideal opened for more people, and a spiritual lay elite emerged that began to see traditional church-centric piety as less worthy. This of course created social divisions, but notice that these divisions, to the extent they started to exist, emerged not because of the Scientific Revolution or due to Enlightenment atheistic reason, but from a deep desire to become closer to God.

If the impulse to purity had been present for a long time, and was not inherently secular in nature, what happened in and around the time of the Reformation that tipped the scales towards eventual disenchantment, the buffering of the self, and the subsequent "great disembedding" of modern liberal society? According to Taylor, the typical answer entails a "subtraction story." This story, present to a certain extent in Jung, but clearly in the account of Max Weber, explains the march towards secularity as an inevitable by-product of growing knowledge.[56] According to this narrative, secularity stemmed from scientific and technical discoveries that one by one discounted spiritual explanations for physical phenomenon, and "has led to the disenchantment of the world has also undercut the claims of any viewpoint, including the viewpoint of science, to have ultimate meaning and value."[57] For instance, when Galileo proved that the planets revolved around the sun, not the sun and planets around earth, his discovery dislodged the church's understanding of the centrality of human beings in creation. From this "subtraction story" point of view, as science advanced, religious beliefs would automatically become more and more difficult to take seriously. However, for Taylor, secularity came from the very opposite direction. Tragically (at least if one holds the spiritual life dear), secularity emerged as the accidental by-product of the very quest for spiritual inner depth and purity and, at a certain point, it led to the Reformation. The Reformation, itself born in the quest to bring a new level of holiness to religious and laypeople alike, *accidentally* gave birth to insights that led to secularism.[58]

55. Taylor mentions some particularly disturbing practices such as "employing the Host as a love charm," and "having a Mass for the dead said for a living person, in order to hasten his demise" (*Secular Age*, 72).

56. Weber, "Science as a Vocation."

57. Main, "In a Secular Age," 279.

58. Bradley Gregory also argued that secularization got its start in an unintended way, from the attempts of Catholic thinkers such as William of Ockham and Duns Scotus to conceptualize God as a part of the known and knowable universe, and not

We have already contemplated the first step in this process without knowing it. The movements toward a purer inner life for all, which had flickered on and off throughout the medieval period, gained strength over time. Because not everyone was either literate or highly motivated towards religious purity, this created a wedge between those who sought greater spiritual depths and ordinary people. Those who were more dedicated began to think of themselves as better than others, and on a quest to bring those others along, especially laypeople. Before the Reformation, these purity movements had proposed a "reversal of the field of fear," from fear of evil spirits and the church's "white magic" to a fear solely of God.[59] They proposed that getting closer to God would protect a person better than all the lesser maneuvers people were encouraged to perform.

The Protestant Reformation, then, began not as a split from the Catholic Church but as a quest to bring original principles and purity back to the clergy and to extend that purity to the laypeople, as the "priesthood of all believers." The sale of indulgences, which inspired Luther to write his Ninety-Five Theses, was from this perspective simply another, and admittedly even cruder, bridge that some in the clergy, with their special connection with God, were at that time offering the less spiritually adept laity. For laity taking the offer, money represented something valuable (their work) that they gave up to obtain this exemption from time in purgatory for themselves or their loved ones. Luther wanted the church and the laypeople to return to a greater holiness through a universal fear and dependence upon God's mercy alone.[60] He argued for not relying upon human works like obtaining indulgences (which from this perspective could be seen as a type of false magic) but on God's grace, and human faith alone, aided by that grace.[61] In general, "Reformers rejected medieval Catholicism, with its monastic orders and ideas about condign and congruent merit. The path of the saint or the monk was seen to be humanly impossible and even idolatrous in its quest for purity. The magisterial reformers such as Luther and Calvin,

---

incomprehensible. With this turn towards empiricism, something we also see later in the theological thoughts of Thomas Hobbes, the march of scientific knowledge eventually seemed to disprove God's very existence. Gregory goes on to connect the subsequent encroaching secularity with materialism, liberalism, and capitalism (*Unintended Reformation*, 318).

59. Taylor, *Secular Age*, 74.
60. Luther, *Treatise on Good Works*.
61. Luther, "95 Theses."

and much later others such as John Wesley, insisted that God and not human codes or human actions redeem human beings."[62]

Luther had no intention of encouraging people to split from the Church when he nailed his Ninety-Five Theses, originally in Latin, to the Wittenberg church doors. He aimed his views at the scholarly and clerical community that could potentially read and dispute his theses. Unintentionally, though, Luther had tapped into an increasingly numerous lay audience, one that had been building for hundreds of years; was recently troubled by the seeming corruption of certain church authorities; including the pope; and was seeking leadership. The potential audience for Luther's ideas had grown, due to technological developments, as more people became literate and engaged in commerce. These publicly minded people were more capable of learning and perhaps needed more assurances of their salvation.[63] As Taylor explains, "Luther was touching on *the* neuralgic issue of his day, the central concern and fear, which dominated so much lay piety, and drove the whole indulgences racket, the issue of judgment, damnation, salvation. In raising his standard on this issue, Luther was onto something which could move masses of people, unlike the humanist critique of mass piety, or the rejection of the sacred."[64] That is, the people who followed Luther and other Reformers into an eventual and unanticipated split with the church were pursuing their (increasingly personal) salvation and piety, and definitely not secularization, a concept they could scarcely yet imagine.

As social embeddedness was lost, with the emergence of spiritual elites and then with the splitting of whole sects from the Catholic Church as the Reformation took off, social disorder increased, posing its own challenges. If not the church but individuals—in direct communication with the Holy Spirit—determined their own beliefs about God and religion, further disembedding was inevitable. As people began to experience themselves as individuals first, no doubt encouraged by increasingly diverse commercial activities that coaxed some and forced others off their ancestral lands, they naturally experienced life as more separate or "buffered." They also began to think of themselves as qualified to assess

---

62. Schweiker, "Humanism," 137.

63. B. Gregory, *Unintended Reformation*, 195. And, perhaps too cynically, they might be interested in lowering their spiritual "taxes," since "faith alone" with no middleman is inherently free.

64. Taylor, *Secular Age*, 75.

and solve social, economic, and political problems as well, without the need for any spiritual or aristocratic authorities above them.

One early development in response to the possible social chaos that could be caused by this rising individualism and self-confidence was the emergence of what Taylor calls the "police state." This political phenomenon emerged within Protestant Christianity to take an equality of holiness to all, and it inadvertently moved society even closer to secularity. The goal of the "police state" (think the Massachusetts Puritans, Calvin's Geneva, or Oliver Cromwell's England) was to make people better Christians who could bridge the divide between God and man without the church's bridging magic. They would make people better Christians through enforcing external moral behavior via heavy worldly penalties.[65] These negative views about the world are coupled with "the belief that salvation from the evil of the world is possible," through a "historical process." To be clear: despite their insistence that salvation comes through grace alone, Protestant Christians showed through their actions (according to Voegelin's criteria for gnosticism generally), that they believed this historical process toward moral purity and reconciliation with God was "possible through man's own effort," and that holy men and women must "seek out the prescription" that would yield that change. That is, they would seek out the *gnosis*, or knowledge (such as the art of governance) necessary to create the conditions for man to change.[66]

According to Taylor, the aim of the Protestant "police state" during the Reformation period is "good social order; in which there is always a religious component, but which is never exclusively defined in religious terms. The situation of the poor and of mendicants undergoes a reevaluation. They begin to lose their evangelical aura, are less seen as occasions of charity, and more as social problems which need to be dealt with. They are dealt with by being organized, taken in hand, disciplined, sometimes

---

65. Taylor, *Secular Age*, 86. Moral purity was an aim that most people could imagine attaining, and hence it was more attractive than the spiritual purity and depth that might have attracted a subset of people in earlier iterations of purity movements. Voegelin would see these Protestant Christian movements as fundamentally gnostic. He identifies Gnosticism as the belief that the world is fundamentally disordered, "a prison from which [man] wants to escape" (*Science, Politics & Gnosticism*, 8).

66. Voegelin, *Science, Politics and Gnosticism*, 64–65. For Voegelin, the alternative to Christian Gnosticism and puritanism is orthodox Christianity, which believes "that the world throughout history will remain as it is and that man's salvational fulfillment is brought about through grace in death." Voegelin also anticipates Taylor in tracing the effects of gnosticism post-secularization as expressed in Hegelianism, Marxism, and Nazism (*Science, Politics and Gnosticism*, 9).

semi-incarcerated."[67] This was a tragic and dangerous development not only because of the massive suffering caused by religious fanatics, but because through these attempts, Protestant leaders discovered that governments could influence human behavior and even thoughts in extremely powerful ways. A government that could aspire to enforcing the correct beliefs and attitudes towards God, including godly "sober and productive" behavior, could also aspire towards nonreligious or even sacrilegious social engineering at all kinds of levels.[68] Eventually, the same methods that were used to produce good Puritan citizens were unmoored from their religious goals completely, and used by increasingly powerful states to create social, political, and economic orders of their own making.

As Strauss explained in the mid-twentieth century, Machiavelli was an early proponent of secular social engineering, and it was not long before proto-liberal and liberal thinkers after him took up the challenge to create a secular social contract as a means of saving us from the tyranny and conflicts that come from using government power to make people good Christians. Protestants had uncovered the power of seeing human nature as infinitely malleable, and introduced the context for the errant thought that we might not need God to make people better. Thinkers like Hobbes and Locke emerged, and liberal governments overtook earlier aristocratic forms of government as the next form of power that promised, but did not deliver, peace, harmony, and prosperity.[69] Enlightenment and later positivist and historicist thinkers taught that human nature was highly malleable as a product of historical evolution. If human thoughts and behavior are largely defined by our environment, then we cannot really speak of a permanent "human nature," and many questions must be excluded—questions like what is good and what is evil, and what is life for?[70] In fact, philosophy itself becomes impossible. Voegelin goes so far (unlike Strauss) as to see in this rejection of the philosophic frame of mind, which he describes as disposed to the existence of truth and a natural moral order, modern man's self-conscious revolt against

---

67. Taylor, *Secular Age*, 86. Taylor goes on to describe these attempts at reform as activist, uniformizing, homogenizing, and rationalizing, all the elements necessary for a modern socially engineered state.

68. Taylor, *Secular Age*, 86.

69. Many Christian academics have tried to prove that liberal political and economic arrangements are inherently Christian in nature and, indeed, represent the true will of God. See, for instance, K. Cooper, *Thomas Hobbes*.

70. Voegelin, *Science, Politics and Gnosticism*, 19–20. Strauss and Voegelin have similar critiques of the modern turn towards positivism and historicism.

God. Ideological man closes the door to the most important questions of existence, proclaiming that they cannot even be asked, and creating closed-loop or self-referential systems.

For the modern buffered self, there was a clear line of demarcation between the individual's world and wherever God resided. Disenchantment, and the emergence of the buffered self, led to a great social disembedding, which was very much aided by the development of liberal political and economic philosophy. People began to lose the feeling of oneness with others based on their common experience of a spiritualized nature and community, and began to experience themselves as isolated, autonomous, self-interested individuals. These atomistic individuals were buffered from whatever now lay beyond themselves, not only God but each other, and this gave them both a great sense of power, and as Tocqueville pointed out in his commentary on America, also made them into ideal social lemmings. In countries like America, where liberal democracy is entrenched, "while the majority is in doubt, one talks; but when it has been irrevocably pronounced, everyone is silent, and friends and enemies alike seem to make for its bandwagon."[71]

While Tocqueville could see that democratic conformism threatened the convictions of true religion by literally penetrating the soul and pushing out any unequivocal commitments, he did not fully anticipate the results of the combination of liberalism and religion.[72] Religion became subjective, based on individual interior thoughts and opinions, whereas it had been previously experienced as an objective shared reality. The multiplicity of religious positions continued to expand as their actual reach into people's interior domains continued to shrink. Taylor argues that disenchantment and social disembedding meant permanent doubt about religion, and this doubt led to an endless quest for meaningful identity, including the proliferation of various religious sects and spiritualities (and we might add now, the extension of identity-seeking into areas that traditional/conservative religionists tend to abhor such as gender, sexuality, race, and ethnicity). It created a hunger that cannot be filled, and an endless reservoir of resentment and division to stoke conflicts.

---

71. Tocqueville, *Democracy in America*, 254–55. See L. Johnson, *Honor in America?*
72. Tocqueville, *Democracy in America*, 255.

D. C. Schindler

For Catholic scholar D. C. Schindler, the major shift in thought and practice that we have been dwelling on in this chapter is found in Western society's embrace of liberalism sometime in the seventeenth century as one of the fruits of the Protestant Reformation. Schindler writes, "The very essence of liberalism is the rejection, not of 'Christian faith,' but specifically of the Catholic Church, insofar as the Catholic Church is the actual presence of Christianity in history, or in other words insofar as it is the faith as having to come to bear on concrete human existence, embodied in the world."[73] Even though it is church-centric, Schindler's view has a lot in common with Strauss's contention that modern political thought, and especially liberal thought and practice, loosens its grasp on truth and absolute moral standards and rejects the idea of the state as a shaper of human character. Schindler's critique of the liberal God of "pure potentiality," which I will discuss at more length below, describes the modern rejection of authority in favor of moral relativism. Moral authority, whose former foundation rested on a transcendent reality, was diminished in favor of what Strauss would characterize as individual subjectivity, or for that matter, what Alasdair MacIntyre would describe as "emotivism."[74] All three thought that something happened in the modern turn that put "authority" back on the individual and his or her subjective and emotional "affective" choice, rather than on an objective universal source, i.e., God.[75]

Schindler starts his explanation by saying, "The rejection of the Church that constitutes the reality of liberalism cannot occur without first having been made theoretically possible in a reconceiving of the nature of God. The political need presupposes a metaphysical/theological 'event,' namely, a shift in the most basic horizon of understanding."[76] In his view, the "reconceiving of the nature of God" began in the late medieval period with the emergence of nominalism, particularly the theology of William of Ockham. The nominalist position held that universal categories, such as those developed by Plato and Aristotle, were simply

---

73. D. C. Schindler, *Politics of the Real*, 18–19.

74. MacIntyre, *After Virtue*.

75. Affect theory is a general category that emerged in the twentieth century and is indicative of this turn. For an overview of affect theory in its different disciplinary manifestations, see Gregg and Seigworth, *Affect Theory Reader*.

76. D. C. Schindler, *Politics of the Real*, 23.

intellectual constructs that had no reality in themselves. For Ockham, what this meant was that God alone was universal, and his will alone was the source of all other meanings.[77] Ockham's God of pure, unlimited potential could rearrange space and time according to his pleasure, so that any categories (even natural laws) that humans thought they discerned as universal were in reality contingent on God's will, and thus not in their very essence always and everywhere true.[78]

In the nominalist framework, God "has in fact revealed himself in this particular way, namely, supremely in the incarnation of Christ, but he could have revealed himself in an infinite number of ways, or even not at all. This amounts to saying that the actual revelation we have received is not decisive, it does not in fact disclose anything essential about God. It is thus evacuated of any ontological density at a single blow."[79] If the actual revelation about God that we have received is not definitive, then surely the historical manifestation of God on earth as defined by the Catholic Church is not definitive and authoritative. This position opened new horizons of possibility for people deciding how to think about the relationship of church (and other religious institutions) and state.

One can see how this shift in thinking about God and nature could lead to a change in expectations regarding human beliefs about God. It paved the way for the Protestant Reformation and its proliferation of Christian sects, and for the later liberal reaction to the competition among Christian sects—namely, that the various disagreements among them were matters (as Locke put it) of indifference.[80] Indifferent things do not bear on the essence of God or the Christian faith. With this change, over time the essence of faith became nothing other than belief in the abstract God of pure potentiality, not the historical God of the incarnate Christ. Tradition, which relies on historical particularities, faded more and more into the background as merely aesthetic, and largely irrelevant.

For generations now, most of Western society has viewed the liberal God, the God of pure potential but nothing in particular, as the only rational concept of God, this despite all the readings of Old Testament Scripture in church services. The liberal God is everything to everyone, the God of "moralistic therapeutic deism," an idea that promotes a flaccid

77. Gaidenko, "Medieval Nominalism."

78. Jeffrey E. Brower outlines the tension between nominalism and Aquinas's natural law universalism in "Aquinas on the Problem."

79. D. C. Schindler, *Politics of the Real*, 25.

80. Locke, *Letter Concerning Toleration*, 233–34.

tolerance drained of all real conviction, and thus any genuine motivation to act rather than simply talk about "godly business," or "social justice."[81] But Schindler states that younger generations are much more comfortable raising "astonishingly bold" questions about liberalism. They ask, for instance, whether liberalism is the best and last system of government and economics. What we must remember is that this boldness is built on decades if not centuries of intellectuals asking exactly those questions much more boldly, certainly from eighteenth-century Romantics like William Blake to contemporary philosophers like Charles Taylor and beyond. Those intellectual currents are now getting more popular attention because of the new trend that questions liberal shibboleths, but still only among the public cognoscenti and certain elements in academia.[82]

Schindler's contribution, building on the insights of his father and other core Communio founders, lies in his insight that "it is a matter of straightforward historical fact that what defines liberalism in its origins is a rejection of Christianity, specifically in the form of the Catholic Church, at least in its actual historical condition in the Middle Ages. The basic question is whether this rejection actually served to bring out the deepest truths of the Gospel regarding individual freedom and dignity, which coincides with a recognition that Christianity was never meant to be a political entity, or whether this rejection of the Church is a repudiation of Christianity simply, a repudiation one might go on either to celebrate or lament."[83] Whereas most US conservatives today believe that

---

81. "Neither a nice, pleasant spirituality (God-as-therapist) or secularized justice-as-faith (God as activist-in-chief) are the robust, multi-faceted deity represented in the Bible and Christian history" (Haluza-DeLay, "Say No," para. 7).

82. What is getting more popular attention lately is the gut-level rejection of liberalism embodied in global, popular right-wing nationalism, a rejection largely uninformed by any of those intellectual currents. Right-wing nationalism, and the religious traditionalism that often accompanies it, are informative of our future. Very little communication occurs between the intellectual critics of modernity and popular right-wing influencers, but they are both reacting to the same thing. Without that communication, popular reactions will always be wrongheaded and largely destructive. In other words, our intellectuals have not provided any degree of leadership for the public. They are too busy publishing articles and books behind a prohibitive paywall.

83. D. C. Schindler, *Politics of the Real*, 6–7. "The thesis we will propose is the following: at the theological core of liberalism is the most radical rejection of Christianity possible, because it posits and enacts an undoing of the very thing that defines Christianity, that makes Christianity Christian, namely, the Incarnation of the Son of God, which is an 'extension' of God, so to speak, into time and space, through an assumption of nature in its deepest reality, an extension-through-assumption that aims ultimately to embrace the whole of reality: the cosmic liturgy" (8).

liberalism (as exemplified in the American founding) is the expression of Christianity par excellence because it was somehow biblically based and done by faithful Christians, the truth is closer to what Schindler is saying here. Liberalism represents the rejection of God, and historically, the rejection of the Christian religion, at the very least in its historical expression in the Catholic Church, but even in its Protestant expressions.[84] Liberalism is the rejection of any authority higher than that of individual human beings who make self-interested decisions and temporary agreements to keep the peace and enforce a variety of contracts. It is as simple as that. But let us follow Schindler's thread.

Schindler argues that Christianity was meant to be a political, that is, a public and social thing, not just a product of individual choice and various private contractual agreements (which, we must admit, is how we look at our choice of religious institutions today). It was meant to have a public expression not just in individual deeds or collective voluntarism, but in a highly organized way, in a universal church that is more like a family than a contract, and which has an organic relationship to a likewise Christian state. "As John Milbank has recently put it, 'Christianity cannot be sufficiently "incarnated" in a fashion that is essential to the work of salvation unless it is in some fashion or other politically "established."'"[85] The church developed through history, incorporating the traditions of the Jews, Greeks, and Romans. Schindler argues that this history must be considered a genuine part of the Christian story, not a tragic mistake, as Christian anarchists would have it.[86] From the Jews, the church received its foundation, its biblical basis in the Old Testament and in Christ's incarnational presence and teachings. From the Greeks, the church received the accretion of philosophic wisdom leading to her understanding of natural law, which allowed her to articulate clear moral positions on human matters. From the Romans, she inherited the "aspiration to gather all the peoples of the world into a harmonious whole, made secure by enduring legal institutions that were not subject to the vicissitudes of natural passions or cultural differences."[87]

---

84. All three of these books by me deal in part with this aspect of liberalism: Bagby, *Thomas Hobbes*; Bagby, *Hobbes's Leviathan*; L. Johnson, *Locke and Rousseau*.

85. D. C. Schindler, *Politics of the Real*, 184.

86. For a great explanation and defense of Christian anarchism, see Christoyannopoulos, *Christian Anarchism*.

87. D. C. Schindler, *Politics of the Real*, 11.

These historical developments led to the institution of the Roman Catholic Church in its current form, which Schindler takes to be not a random historical contingency that could have developed differently or not at all (a view in line with the idea of God as pure potentiality but with no trajectory or will in particular), but a working out of God's intentions in history. The nominalist/liberal view with which Schindler disagrees sees a God with no essential worldly and permanent identity. Embracing that nominalist/liberal view means that we can walk back from any historical development in Judeo Christianity as a matter of "indifference," as not essential to our faith in God.[88] Logically that would mean that we were free to not only reject the history of Roman Catholicism but the history of the early Christians and the ancient Hebrews. We know that Christians who want to reject Catholicism also tend to wholeheartedly embrace the history, as they understand it, of the early Christians and the ancient Hebrews. But this seems arbitrary.

Schindler's point is well taken that the Judeo-Christian God doesn't mean much if we do not take his historical presence in the world as indicative of his eternal nature. Indeed, the very incarnation of Christ, as Schindler points out, is the foremost indicator that God's identity is wrapped up in particularities within human time and space. If this is true, then God must be viewed not as pure potentiality but in the historical expression in which he has manifested himself. And, if that is the case, it would also mean that we are not free to reject natural law or other moral teachings of the Catholic Church, including her social teachings, which are typically underrated or ignored by Catholics.

Schindler argues that things change dramatically once we let go of the liberal framework and rediscover the Judeo-Christian God and natural law. Among the things that change is our sense of ownership of our bodies and property. In the liberal view *consistently applied*, our bodies are our first absolute property, to be used (and hence defined) in any way we desire.[89] Property is obtained as an extension of our ownership of our

---

88. David Schindler, D. C. Schindler's father, points out that the "ontological Pelagianism and nominalism undergirding the Western consumerist style of life" (David Schindler, "Communio Ecclesiology and Liberalism," 776). See David Schindler, *Heart of the World*.

89. John Locke, in his *Second Treatise of Government*, ruled out only suicide, as a desire for life is what the rest of his theory is based upon. He called upon not only logic but the idea that God gave us our lives and so only God could take them away. But beyond this one caveat Locke had nothing to say about how we used our bodies or about how we used our property, the extension of our bodies through our labor or

bodies, through our labor, and it is absolutely ours to do with as we please. That is, our body is private (ours to control), and our acquired property is likewise private. From this liberal perspective it is no wonder that people get angry when the state says that our business, house, or the products we sell are ours to do with what we wish (which is more rhetoric than reality), but also says that our sexuality (such as our choice of with whom to have sex, how to present our gender and sexuality, or to obtain sex reassignment) can be regulated by the community. Contemporary conservatives often call to end the liberties people take with their bodies, a call that is in contradiction with their own liberal and capitalist principles of individual liberty and ownership. The call to sexual order through law is essentially illiberal and runs contrary to the capitalist impulse to stimulate differences, which leads to our redoubled efforts to possess what we want and express ourselves as we please.

Natural law thinking presupposes a God who is the ultimate owner of creation, whose will defines the purposes and uses of that creation. If this is so, then property can never be seen as an absolute right, or fully private to the individual. Schindler employs a reading of Hegel to advocate for a different position on property, but he also employs the earlier medieval view that simply reflects the natural law perspective on property. His conclusion is that "rather than being essentially a privatizing of the public, property is most basically a kind of making public the private, even as it includes taking in a reality into the existence of the self. Through the acquisition of property, the person 'real-izes' himself and manifests his otherwise merely inward being, making himself available in a new way to others and a significant agent in the common life of the whole."[90]

The medieval fisc existed with the assumption that, ultimately, the king "owned" everything, and that he "owned" it analogously with God's loving ownership of creation. Human ownership with this set of assumptions amounts to something like responsibility, a "binding of the self to some reality in the world, a reality that remains in the (commonly available) world as a thing even as owned by the self."[91] One's property

---

investment. Locke needed a prohibition against suicide or his argument concerning liberty would fall apart—we could not enslave ourselves to another because to do so was to put our lives in their hands. See "Of Slavery," in Locke, *Two Treatises of Government*, 109–21.

90. D. C. Schindler, *Politics of the Real*, 154.
91. D. C. Schindler, *Politics of the Real*, 156.

becomes an extension of oneself into the world, a public declaration of responsibility for a particular place or thing. What this responsibility should entail is defined by the property itself—what it will take to keep it in good shape, to improve it by assuring its full natural potential as defined by its end or purpose, as further defined by its Creator. In other words, the standards for how to treat property are not defined by an individual "owner" but by the property itself, because that property is already imbued with God's natural laws. If we viewed our bodies in this way, we would do everything we could to be fit, healthy, and at a reasonable weight. If we viewed our real property in this way, we would develop it to enrich the soil and enhance its health, beauty, and productivity. A quick walk through a mall or drive across town will reveal how we think of our responsibility for our bodies and real property.

Schindler rejects the liberal definition of freedom as the license of the individual to do as he or she pleases without interference. Rejecting liberal modernism's notion of freedom as license in favor of freedom as submission to God's sovereignty and truth, Schindler observes that if there is one true God, and he is the Christian God, then to be free means to be in consensual harmony with God's reality, not to be able to do whatever we please even if it harms us or God's creation. The latter is like self-abuse or slavery to sin, and is seen from this perspective as disordered.[92] Schindler gives an example of how license can be seen as slavery: "We have what any sane person looking in from the outside would view as a cancerous pursuit of science as technology, essentially untethered to any concern for the common good or for man's eschatological end, a pursuit that, through the momentum of its accumulating financially-driven force, in turn tends to drive our now-empty politics."[93] People who pursue technological ends without considering the moral claims that nature and human nature make upon their actions are engaged in idolatry. They are enslaved to what Jacques Ellul referred to as *technique*.[94] They have mistaken technology as an end, worshiping it as a false god. No one enthralled to a false god can be thought of as free.

Schindler goes one step further because of his theory that the Catholic Church is the true incarnational presence of God in the world. He argues that full freedom entails living within a system in which the society and state are in unity with the church and the historic traditions

---

92. D. C. Schindler, *Politics of the Real*, 180.
93. D. C. Schindler, *Politics of the Real*, 189.
94. Ellul, *Technological Society*.

of the Jews, the Greeks, and the Romans.[95] This claim is tied up with his account of authority as emanating from a knowledge of the good, an argument that stems from Greek philosophy, as taken up by the church, especially by Aquinas. If the rest of his argument is correct, including the part that has to do with the superior knowledge of the Catholic Church, which comes from Christ's institution in Peter and the church's threefold tradition, then it stands to reason that the church is a source of *authority*, whereas the liberal state (artificially separated from the church) has no authority, but only coercive power. In Schindler's view, both church and state should continue to exist, and they should cooperate with each other, but if we are looking for guidance as to what to legislate and what to enforce, the authoritative guidance would come from the church. Ideally, the transformed state, a state that is not separate from nor subordinated to the church but is in alliance with the church, would share authority with the church in a way that the liberal state cannot.[96]

For Schindler's vision to happen in full would require nothing less than a very specific and thoroughgoing transformation of our society. We would have to experience mass conversion to a particular form of Christianity, a more serious form, and one that recognized the authority of the Catholic Church. It would have to be such a thoroughgoing conversion that most if not all our officials were influenced if not guided by the church's moral and social teachings. They would have to be informed, not in the cherry-picking fashion that even our Catholic elected officials now display, but in a serious, mature way that expressed knowledge of the good. Society would have to reject its atomistic individualism. We would have to reject the immense power of corporate businesses to operate with license, to treat their property and other people's property as mere utilities, and to sell us anything they want, no matter how harmful

---

95. D. C. Schindler, *Politics of the Real*, 185–88.

96. For this argument, see for instance D. C. Schindler, *Politics of the Real*, 224–25. Schindler takes inspiration on this point from the scholarship of Andrew Willard Jones. In *Before Church and State*, Jones uses the kingdom of St. Louis to represent perhaps the best example in history of this type of cooperation between church and state, with the church as an overarching moral authority but with a complicated and largely unplanned division of labor that resembles a family or friendship more than a social contract. Jones takes great pains to prove his point. In my view, he is not entirely convincing in the case study of the book, but his vision of the proper relationship between church and state still presents an alternative to either the separation of church and state or its opposite, theocracy/integralism. Schindler's critique of liberalism is indebted to John Milbank's work and vice versa. For a good introduction to Milbank's criticism, see Milbank and Pabst, *Politics of Virtue*.

to us and our environment. Most difficult of all, we would have to have a radicalized laity such as Pope Francis calls for in *Laudato Si'*. They would have to be willing to reject consumerism and the aspiration of never-ending economic growth, and engage in de facto revolutionary struggle to organize and reconstitute society. What Schindler is asking of people is nothing less than a full-scale rejection of their way of life—a rejection of all the influences on them from the inception of liberalism and capitalism—and the taking up of a new life that revolves around things higher and more important than themselves.

The potential for theoretical incoherence is here. Schindler has asked us to accept that the Catholic Church is the incarnational presence of God on earth, that it thus has authority, and that the nature of that authority is filtered through the long history of the Jews, the Greeks, and the Romans. But he is asking us to treat as completely wrong and foreign all the modern liberal revolutions, including the English Revolutions of 1642 and 1688, the American Revolution, the French Revolution, and the various European republican revolts of 1848, and the social and economic ideas and practices that emanated from those events, including socialism. He is asking us to reject bourgeois society, even though from bourgeois society has come the most powerful and extensive empire the world has ever seen, more powerful than that of the Jews, the Greeks, or the Romans at the height of their powers. The bourgeois empire's intellectual and technical influences are built upon the other traditions Schindler holds dear (not to mention an unparalleled exploitation of natural and human resources), and stem, according to his own argument, from a branch of Christianity that was originally seeking to purify the Catholic Church of corruption and error.[97]

This is not to say that Schindler's ideal is incorrect, but it is to suggest that the historical approach he takes to establish it is a potential Achilles' heel. Not only is it possible that he is incorrect if just one of the historical influences on the church can be seen as illegitimate and hence not authentically Christian, but there is no clear reason to accept all these other influences, two of them pagan, but reject bourgeois civilization's influence as entirely illegitimate. On what basis should we choose which historical influences to accept and which to reject? And, if we reject the most recent one, are we committing the error of thinking we can somehow "go back" to a previous way of life, a life

97. They were also built on an unparalleled exploitation of natural and human resources.

that Taylor finds impossible for us to even fully access? Isn't consciously choosing to "go back" the kind of ahistorical maneuver Schindler normally would identify as modern?[98] In other words, has Schindler really understood that modern society is now a part of the "real," which must be moved through to be superseded?

Conclusion

Karl Marx and Friedrich Engels understood the community-destroying nature of liberal individualism, and observed in the nineteenth century that capitalism "resolved personal worth into exchange value, and in place of the numberless indefeasible chartered freedoms, has set up that single, unconscionable freedom—Free Trade."[99] Exploring the ideas of four thinkers who would not call themselves Marxists, but who would all agree with Marx and Engels on the above assessment of liberalism and capitalism, even though they would disagree profoundly on the goodness of these developments, will again impress upon the reader how thoroughgoing, powerful, and diverse the critique of modernity has actually been, and how many resources we really have for understanding our situation. The thinkers chosen for this chapter are major representatives of schools of thought that tackle modernity and liberalism from different standpoints but whose work, if combined, is even more powerful.

Carl Jung argued that the Scientific Revolution created obstacles for the healthy expression of unconscious collective symbols. Healthy religion allowed people a framework in which to contemplate good and evil, and to understand that they were neither gods nor mere matter. The need for belief in a transcendent power which cannot be controlled by human beings is universal, in Jung's view. As faith began to recede, people tended to project the self- or God archetype onto worldly leaders and systems, creating new secular religions. Jung, along with Aleksandr Solzhenitsyn, could see this dynamic not only in Soviet communism and Nazi Germany, but in modern liberal states whose power over people's

---

98. Nietzsche argued that in the modern age, when it was no longer possible to fully believe as people did during and prior to the Middle Ages, what was left was using history to create essentially artificial "horizons" for people to live under, people who could not stand the awareness of no meaning like the Overman could (*Advantage and Disadvantage*). Is this what Schindler is doing—creating artificial "horizons" to save us from a degrading and nihilistic culture?

99. Marx and Engels, *Communist Manifesto*, 76.

lives continued to grow. All this intervention was done in the name of a political and economic system that promised a certain "freedom" but resulted in soft totalitarianism.[100] Jung thought that, after realizing this dynamic, authentic religion (along with psychoanalysis) could be viewed, perhaps even promoted, as a better alternative to the worship of ideologues, governments, and corporate power.

Strauss argued that the modern turn moved us away from the pursuit of the good, and the goal of governing with a correct understanding of natural right, and towards a moral relativism that crippled human nature. The modern turn moved us from a concept of human beings as social animals who flourished only under the guidance of good leaders and laws, to artificially isolated individuals who defined the good life for themselves and often wallowed in base hedonism for want of any better goal. Strauss's chief contribution is to recognize the nihilism inherent in modern politics, a nihilism that can be liberal but is also a prerequisite for totalitarianism. If the only thing that determines what is right and just is power (whether in the form of guns, money, or numbers), you have moral relativism, and a vacuum of authority waiting to be filled by a tyrant or demagogue.[101] Strauss was not hoping that we would move back into the ancient frame of mind, but that we could become aware of the deeply flawed nature of our current forms of government so as to not trust them too much or think of them too highly. To see liberal democracy through a Straussian lens is, at the most, to see a deeply flawed "best practicable regime" whose weaknesses and tendencies to turn towards totalitarianism need to be soberly understood.

Charles Taylor sees the modern problem coming from the loss of the Christian acknowledgment of human fallibility. He too points to the time of the Protestant Reformation for the origin of the problem, but he sees the Reformation as the latest of many attempts throughout the Middle Ages to return the Catholic Church to its origins, and Christians to their purest selves. Indeed, for Taylor, it was not scientific advancements that led to the eventual doubts and retreats from religious faith, but precisely the pious desire to not rely on the church's "white magic" for salvation. One unintended consequence of this attempt to become more holy was separation from the church and its traditions. Another unintended consequence (combined with escalating technological

---

100. Sheldon Wolin referred to this as "inverted totalitarianism" (*Democracy Incorporated*). Paul Rahe uses the term "soft despotism" (*Soft Despotism*).

101. Porter, "Interpretations of Nazi Totalitarianism."

developments) was a historically rapid disembedding of people from their social and cultural identities. Out of all this came the adoption of a new individualism. The quest for holiness ultimately stimulated advances in social engineering. At first pursued for the sake of making people more godly, social engineering eventually became unmoored from religion and became a powerful tool in the hands of modern governments. This was a major source of disenchantment. As social embeddedness was lost, social chaos increased. If individuals could communicate directly with God and determine their own beliefs, the practical results of disembedding and conflict were inevitable.

Schindler's unique contribution is to make a more positive argument, and to make it specifically for the Catholic Church. He spends a great deal of time diagnosing the problem, and in doing so he covers some of the same territory as Jung, Strauss, and Taylor, though using different language and a different set of sources. But unlike our three other thinkers, Schindler is also building a case for a new order, one in which the church regains her cultural influence over society and government. While Schindler is not arguing for integralism, he is nonetheless arguing for a great increase in church authority in people's lives, both directly and indirectly. While we may find his goals impossible, or we may even be afraid of the practical results of moves in their direction, we also ought to respect Schindler for being the rare thinker willing to put forward a positive ideal with enough clarity and substance to be critiqued. Schindler's vision of the dual cooperative authority of church and state in a thoroughly Catholic society serves, if nothing else, to show us how very differently we live and think, and how far we would have to go, to get into a different, more social, and collectively spiritual social embedding.

How do we mesh these insights with the contents of chapters 1–3? As I argued in those earlier chapters, as the US moved away from agrarian life, traditional means of independence were destroyed, and spiritual resources such as churches and civic/service organizations shrunk in influence. Contrary to what many in the United States are told, this decline was not just the fault of "big government," the "nanny state," or "cultural Marxism."[102] Instead, I hope that this chapter shows that the ultimate origins of this decline are deeper and much longer in the making. They come from changes in feudal Christianity, the Scientific Revolution, Protestant

---

102. Anyone who uses the term "cultural Marxism" has never read Marx, or they would know that Marx thought of culture as epiphenomenal, trailing economics, and having no particular importance on its own.

Reformation, the Enlightenment, and the urbanizing, industrializing, and globalizing processes of capitalist development. As much as I admire D. C. Schindler's attempt to propose a solution in a reinvigorated and politically relevant Catholic Church, it is likely that, practically speaking, we do not have this option. We probably cannot responsibly choose to simply reject all of liberalism because it negates faith. Whichever solution we arrive at must deal with the fact of all these losses but deal with that fact in a way that acknowledges the changes in human thought and arrangements that have occurred since modernity.

5

Ideological Strong-Arming: Free to Choose

IDEOLOGICAL STRONG-ARMING IS MY term for a type of social, psychological, and spiritual coercion that leaves people feeling as though there are no options other than their current way of life within the existing system. It is a kind of subtle bullying. I will argue that the promotion of "free market" capitalism constitutes a form of strong-arming so powerful that almost the entire ideological spectrum of the United States has adopted it. All human beings are social creatures and must have a story to give them context, explanations, and purpose. Whereas the free-market story first attracted those who could flex their entrepreneurial muscles and succeed, it now also expresses the worldview and hopes of people who are increasingly on the economic outs (the "precariat" I introduced in a previous chapter). The story is so strong, and so attached to their desire for self-reliance, that it obscures the reality of their precarity. It identifies them as "red" people, whose anger is aimed at the "blue" people, "socialists" who want to destroy their morality, culture, and economy. The "blue people," meanwhile, participate in the same story in reverse—the "fascists" are out to destroy their country.

I will argue that, contrary to the free-market narrative, the US economy is highly socialized already, and the moral and cultural damage that the US right wing complains about has been done largely by that economy, with a lot of cooperation by red and blue people alike.

Republicans and Democrats have supported a type of government that, in financial and regulatory terms, has long supported big agriculture and big business at the expense of small farms and businesses. There is no turning back the clock to a time when the government was not heavily involved in our markets. Therefore, the question should not be whether we want socialism, but whether we can organize our already socialized economy for the majority.

The Democratic Party has proven itself to be unequipped to fully understand and deal with the problems of the poor and middle class, not to mention the food and environmental problems outlined in the preceding chapters. Ideally, the Democrats would be attuned to those who are economically and culturally marginalized, but this chapter will argue that they have, for quite some time, also been strong-armed by free-market ideology. While understandable, the progressive tendency to think in terms of individual identities and rights, along with the tendency to dismiss religious people and ideas from the outset, prevents contemporary US progressives from being able to address the concerns and needs of the poor and working classes, adding to the intransigent nature of the red–blue divide. Indeed, progressives have largely joined right liberals in their efforts to strong-arm the losers in the economic game into silence. But before getting into the theme of the betrayal of American progressives, we need to remember how the free-market ideology was first introduced to the public.

Free to Choose

In 1951, future Nobel Prize–winning University of Chicago economist Milton Friedman used the term *neoliberalism* to define a resurgent ideological faith in free-market capitalism. He was aware that the Great Depression and FDR's New Deal programs had led Americans to lose their trust in laissez-faire economics and to believe that business needed a strong government to regulate it, to control it, to employ people when necessary, and to support certain enterprises like farming with subsidies. New Deal work programs created an incredible amount of public infrastructure that helped the American economy grow, but that infrastructure is now around ninety years old, and crumbling. In 1951, people were just beginning to reap the benefits of all those public works, and many of them could directly thank the government for their family's survival during the Great Depression. There was still a great deal of fear, driven by the experience of the depression and WWII, but this fear stood alongside a growing optimism born of surging prosperity—those were the Cleaver years.

Because the story he wanted to tell had to deal with people's past and future, their vision of what life was and what it should become, Milton Friedman knew he had to address and even create feelings, not just facts. This is why he adopted explicitly religious language in his early writings on neoliberalism, instead of just sticking to the facts. He spoke of Americans who appreciated the New Deal programs because they benefited from them as adopting a faith in "collectivism." During the Cold War, Friedman saw a way to turn their feelings in another direction, to break them away from their supposed false religion. So, he painted social welfare programs and business regulations with the same broad brush as the hated Soviet communism. Repeatedly speaking in terms of "beliefs" and "faith," Friedman notably promoted himself as a kind of prophet. "Collectivism," he intimated, was a misguided religious belief, while "individualism" and "neo-liberalism" represented true faith. In his own words:

> Until a few years ago, there was a widespread—if naive—faith among even the intellectual classes that nationalization would replace production for profit with production for use, whatever these catchwords may mean; that centralized planning would replace unplanned chaos with efficient coordination; that it was only necessary to give the State more power in order to solve the supposed paradox of poverty in the midst of plenty and to prevent the "selfish interests" from exploiting the working masses; and that because socialists favoured peace and international amity, socialism would in some unspecified way further these goals. The experience of the last few years has shaken if not shattered these naive beliefs.

He added, "We have a new faith to offer; it behooves us to make it clear to one and all what that faith is."[1]

Friedman had found a formula for a mild form of strong-arming. Everyone wants to feel like they understand events; no one wants to be "naive." This rhetorical strategy perhaps worked with a few of the people who happened upon what he wrote in 1951, but Friedman would have to work a lot harder to get the attention of the wider public.

---

1. Friedman, "Neoliberalism and Its Prospects," 2.

Almost thirty years later, in 1980, PBS ran a documentary series hosted by Friedman called *Free to Choose*, which followed the arguments of his book *Capitalism and Freedom* (1962). The series was a vehicle for its author and his faith in the free market, and it marked the beginning of a stronger push, using mass media, to change the culture in the direction of neoliberal economics and politics. Friedman was one of the first mass-market multimedia public intellectuals in the realm of economics. Unlike many academics, he was not content to write books in a comfortable office. He was a fierce advocate for what he believed, and he had learned how to put himself forward in an appealing way to communicate effectively to the public. The series, the culmination of three decades of efforts to promote neoliberal ideology, covered the argument for why political liberty and economic freedom worked together, how the free market made production efficient, lowered costs, and sent goods and services to where they were needed.[2] He explained how government regulations inhibited this natural ordering of the marketplace, and how politics in effect sullied the impersonal process with ulterior motives, like using lobbying and campaign contributions to get government regulation unfavorable to competition.

Friedman argued against the prevailing theory that the Great Depression was caused by a failure of capitalism. Many people believed that capitalism was saved by the government programs in FDR's New Deal because capitalism would not work well without guardrails and redistribution. They became convinced that the government needed to be involved not just in regulating the money supply but also in continual regulation of the market, as well as welfare spending. Now with extraordinary access to the attentive public through a taxpayer subsidized PBS program, Friedman argued that they were mistaken. He explained his theory that the 1929 stock market crash and the Great Depression were caused by the recently created Federal Reserve's decision to "throttle the monetary system" by not supplying the money that it had on hand to

---

2. Friedman expressed the general ideology this way: "The experience of the last few years has shaken if not shattered these naive beliefs. It has become abundantly clear that nationalization solves no fundamental economic problems; that centralized economic planning is consistent with its own brand of chaos and disorganization; and that centralized planning may raise far greater barriers to free international intercourse than unregulated capitalism ever did. Equally important, the growing power of the State has brought widespread recognition of the extent to which centralized economic control is likely to endanger individual freedom and liberty" ("Neoliberalism and Its Prospects," 2).

ease anxieties during a bank run.[3] He argued that Keynesian-inspired welfare spending did not get the US past the depression or effectively address the problem of poverty. Instead, it created waste and bloated government bureaucracies that took resources away from those who could use them to stimulate the economy and make more jobs. It hampered economic growth by taking resources from productive elements in society and sidelining it in less productive outlets. What was needed, he argued, was an unfettered market instead, one that would encourage economic growth and the creation of new and higher paying jobs. This unfettered market would, however, need to be supported and managed by active government manipulation of the money supply, including bank bailouts when necessary. Kotsko explains that the seeming contradiction is surmountable. Friedman was not promoting a laissez-faire economy, but a financially managed economy:

> Under a hypothetically pure laissez-faire regime, bailouts would indeed be off-limits, but as Friedman had pointed out already in 1951, a simple return to that model is neither possible nor desirable. A generalized bailout of all major players—one that neither picks winners nor asserts direct government control over any of the individual firms—is the only possible response to a failure in the all-important financial sector, which serves as the market of markets under neoliberalism. Far from a contradiction, a financial sector bailout is precisely the duty of the neoliberal state as ultimate guarantor of market structures, which helps to explain the fact that every neoliberal regime has resorted to such tactics in the face of financial crises.[4]

Friedman argued that the free market within the context of proper monetary policy would produce more equality among people than redistribution could, although he thought that it was not possible to guarantee equality of anything but opportunity. Some inequality was a necessary ingredient in a dynamic and growing economy. Such an economy would lift everyone up, though at different levels. In the same TV series, Friedman attempted to demonstrate this by suggesting reforms

---

3. Interestingly Friedman starts the episode on the market crash and the Great Depression by recounting that the New York Bank of the United States was run by and served many Jewish businessmen, and when this bank began to fail, anti-Semitism was one of the reasons other banks and the Federal Reserve did not automatically move to back its deposits. I doubt such honesty about the disastrous effects of prejudice would be allowed today.

4. Kotsko, *Neoliberalism's Demons*, 21.

in education policy, arguing for parental choice and the use of vouchers for privately run schools instead of government-run schools. He also argued against consumer protection laws. The market could better sort out which products were good for people and which were not, whereas government regulation always favored some businesses at the expense of others, for political reasons. Unions and government laws protecting workers were also not necessary, he argued. Market competition for the best workers would automatically raise wages and benefits as well as raise the pool of talented labor. In the last two episodes of his PBS series, Friedman argued against the US Federal Reserve printing more money to stimulate the economy.

Like other free-market thinkers such as Ludwig von Mises and Friedrich Hayek, Friedman was motivated by anti-conservative radicalism.[5] His way of thinking about laissez-faire economics, as being opposed to conservatism, may seem counterintuitive to Americans because they are used to thinking of Friedman-style economics as "conservative." But that is only because at a certain point, Keynesian-inspired Democrats adopted the term "liberal" as their own, and US conservatives dropped the term "liberal" to identify themselves. Thus, and mainly in the United States, "conservative" came to mean what in most other countries is a classical liberal, and "liberal" was taken over by New Deal Democrats. As Alan Brinkley explains, "Nothing . . . so irritated many conservatives of the 1930's and 1940's as the New Deal's appropriation of the word 'liberal.' The real liberals, they insisted, were the enemies of New Deal statism, the defenders of individual rights against the 'social engineering' and 'paternalism' of the Left."[6]

To understand how strange this reversal of terminology really was, we can turn to von Mises, one of the leading lights of the neoliberal school of thought, who explained in *The Anti-Capitalist Mentality* how antithetical his ideas were to true conservatism:

> Conservatism is contrary to the very nature of human acting. But it has always been the cherished program of the many, of the inert who dully resist every attempt to improve their own conditions which the minority of the alert initiate. In employing the term *reactionary*, one mostly refers only to the

---

5. Both of these authors were prolific. For good examples that illustrate the case, see von Mises, *Omnipotent Government*; von Mises, *Interventionism*; Hayek, *Road to Serfdom*.

6. Brinkley, "Problem of American Conservatism," 416.

aristocrats and priests who called their parties conservative. Yet the outstanding examples of the reactionary spirit were provided by other groups: by the guilds of artisans blocking entrance into their field to newcomers; by the farmers asking for tariff protection, subsidies and "parity prices"; by the wage earners hostile to technological improvements and fostering featherbedding and similar practices.[7]

Eugene McCarraher explains why Friedman continued to use the term "liberal" to describe his free-market positions despite the terminology prevalent in the United States: "Lamenting that 'liberalism' had been stolen and corrupted by Keynesian enthusiasts for activist government, Friedman continued to use the term because, in his view, 'conservatism' was 'not a satisfactory alternative.' Indeed, the belligerent Friedman maintained, just as 'the nineteenth-century liberal was a radical ... so too must be his modern heir.'"[8]

Given his rejection of the instinctive tendency of people towards stability and conservative ways of thinking and being, Friedman perhaps more than anyone else understood that the ultimate rhetorical trick would be to make people think that what is radical is conservative and traditional. Conversely, it would truly be a feat to make them think that any longing for stability and control over their fate represented a destabilizing, radical position. This revaluation of values was something Friedman was now able to accomplish. Friedman's message to the American public via PBS brought von Mises–style radicalism to them in a palatable format, with a strong dose of appealing anti-communism. He communicated an emotion-infused conviction that America was winning the Cold War because her capitalist economic system did not stifle competition and creativity. Since Soviet communism destroyed human freedom, the supposed opposite of communism—capitalism—would of course guarantee human freedom. The public support for the change in economic imaginaries Friedman proposed had begun to build in the 1950s during a time of increasing prosperity, the golden age of the head-of-household family exemplified by the Cleavers. By the 1980s the public was much more receptive, especially as the US began to move out of the latest recession and history headed towards the fall of the Berlin Wall.

Friedman and other neoliberal advocates were not incorrect about the pernicious effects of big, bureaucratic government. Government

7. Von Mises, *Anti-Capitalistic Mentality*, 64–65.
8. McCarraher, *Enchantments of Mammon*, 590.

bureaucracies are often inefficient and do not always achieve their intended goals. Often, they are politicized and used by various economic interests to favor their agendas over others. Bureaucracies can operate at cross purposes, and they can perpetuate problems like systemic racism and racial divisions that already exist.[9] Competition can lead to new innovations and better results. Oftentimes people do make better decisions about their needs and how to pursue them than the government could make, because they understand their own circumstances better than remote bureaucrats can.[10] However, I hope I've made it clear that Friedman's ideas swung dramatically in the opposite direction, towards a radical reduction in government intervention in people's lives. His popularity was tied up with a moment in time—from the Cold War between the US and the Soviet Union to the end of the Cold War and the seeming triumph of Western-style liberal democracy and capitalism.[11] His ideas were couched in the mythic story of capitalism v. communism. These categories were equated with freedom v. unfreedom, good v. evil. He was proposing, rather explicitly, a secular religion. The popularity of neoliberal ideas such as those in *Free to Choose* rose as people thought more in terms of this mythic narrative as the defining one for their nation. It wasn't so much that neoliberal economics represented timeless truths (though it presented itself as doing just that). Rather, it represented the opposite of the despised, atheistic communist failure. US, capitalism, freedom, and God—good; USSR, communism, slavery, and godlessness—bad.

---

9. B. Green, *Smart Enough City*, especially chs. 4–5.

10. A volume edited by Harrison, *Globalization and Poverty*, provides solid evidence for the relative gains for many poor people in global trade competition and covers the drawbacks. What is not addressed is the loss of independence, both personal and national, in the mix. When food security is seen as a matter of family/community and national security, the waters are muddied. Texas A&M agriculture and agricultural economics professors Edwin Price, Naureen Fatema, and Abdul Saboor Rahmany provide evidence that US national security is threatened by global food insecurity due to its threats to the global economy of which the US is a part. They assume the answer is to further develop the competitiveness of developing countries (Price et al., *Global Food Security*). For the case for some protection against global competition to preserve the independence of peoples around the world, especially in farming, see Kloppenburg, *First the Seed*. Kloppenburg argues for preserving biodiversity on farms and maintaining crops and practices suited for the immediate environment by resisting reliance on genetic engineering. See also J. Cooper et al., *Agricultural Biodiversity*.

11. Freedman, *Chicago Fundamentalism Ideology*. See especially 197–280.

Ideological Strong-Arming

Ironically, as we have seen, both neoliberalism and collectivism were explicitly presented by Milton Friedman as religious faiths, and he made no attempt to bring the Judeo-Christian God to bear on either side. Indeed, Friedman was an agnostic with very little interest in traditional religion. As his friend Rev. Robert Sirico said on Friedman's passing, "Milton Friedman was not an avowed advocate of the unity of economics and religious faith. We had our differences on questions of religion to be sure, specifically on the notion that liberty needs to be oriented to truth to insure its proper use. Friedman was a true Enlightenment disciple and feared that truth claims could lead to coercion."[12] Any reference to real religion was, in Friedman's strategy, better not said, as those who heard his message and found it appealing could make that connection for themselves if they so desired.

This storyline that made free-market capitalism the moral equivalent of Christian faith was so attractive partly because of America's preexisting "city on a hill" civil religion.[13] It reflected America's notions about its providential place in world history, inspired by the ultimate battle of good v. evil conveyed in the Bible. It piggybacked on simple categories already in the ether that everyone knew and could understand. Most importantly, with all our attention focused on what we were not—godless communists who hated freedom and competition—we were free to not think about what we were turning into—godless materialists whose social organization (big business, big government) also impeded the freedom to choose. For instance, the freedom to choose to be a homemaker rather than to get a job was impeded. Filling in the blanks to square capitalism with Christianity is how the improbable combination of support for unfettered capitalism (which, as we have seen, decimated rural life, split up families, and automated out of existence previously venerated professions, especially farming and the trades, and destabilized Christian moral foundations) became such a powerful emotional force in American rhetoric. Logically, it never made a lot of sense. Emotionally, it made absolute sense, in the same way Stockholm syndrome allows prisoners to admire their captors.

---

12. Sirico, "Milton Friedman," para. 13.

13. Van Engen traces the "city on a hill" image from its emergence in a seventeenth-century sermon by John Winthrop to an image of American exceptionalism (*City on a Hill*). See also Gamble, *In Search of City*.

Eugene McCarraher's massive *The Enchantments of Mammon: How Capitalism Became the Religion of Modernity*, has a special place for the Friedman faith in its discussion of what has come to be known as capitalist realism. A term coined by Mark Fisher, *capitalist realism* conveys the same sense of ineluctability and futility that political realism conveys: our current capitalist order is the way it is, and any attempt to change it is foolhardy. In the name of such realism, all objections are to cease and any ideas for a different way of life are to be scoffed at. "Conveyed in a flippant rhetoric of historical determinism—'inexorable,' 'irresistible,' 'irreversible,'—these and other auguries of market predestination were volleys in what David Graeber has called a 'war on the imagination': a blitzkrieg against utopian speculation, a mission to sabotage the capacity to even dream of a world beyond capitalism."[14] Any pain caused by the current system was to be suffered as preferable to the pain inflicted by trying to resist it. Therefore, all the precarity, dislocation, and humiliation caused by automation and globalization, all the loss of wealth caused by reduced real wages and benefits and increasing costs of "retooling," are just what is normal, and we can only do worse. As McCarraher puts it, "These assaults on the livelihood and dignity of workers have been justified as painful but necessary steps on the interminable road of Progress, guided by infallible market forces to which we owe homage and genuflection."[15]

Friedman's theory made people feel smarter, and made other people second-guess themselves if they did not agree with the growing chorus of believers. His realistic view of human nature asserted that every human being is motivated by self-interest, and to think otherwise is simply to be naive. It valorized the tendency people already have to be selfish, to not want to help others. In fact, the message was, you'll help others most effectively by focusing single-mindedly on helping yourself. It also appealed by treating the market as an autonomous force whose "logic" was objective and, if not unduly hindered, would act of its own accord to solve social problems as disparate as racism, poverty, poor education, and pollution. This meant that to solve our dilemmas we needed to concentrate only on getting out of the market's way and seeking our own good. Perhaps most powerfully, Friedman's message

---

14. McCarraher, *Enchantments of Mammon*, 665.
15. McCarraher, *Enchantments of Mammon*, 664.

appealed to those who wanted to be identified with "good" and not with "evil," that is, almost everyone.

There is nothing that acts more powerfully on people's minds and has more staying power than religion. Adam Kotsko senses the power of this yearning in the guise of politics: "In the neoliberal worldview, we live in a world full of isolated individuals who yearn to express their freedom through participation in market competition, and the best thing to do is to set up policies that effectively create a world full of isolated individuals who yearn to express their freedom through participation in market competition. From this perspective, neoliberalism is arguably the most coherent and self-reinforcing political theology ever devised."[16] Neoliberalism, Kotsko argues, affirms that everyone is morally free to choose. Therefore, they have only themselves to blame if they make a choice that is bad for their bottom line, destructive to themselves or others, or harmful to the environment. Smart people make smart choices that are in their long-term self-interest, and if we all did this, according to the faith, we would have a good society.

Kotsko demonstrates how close this narrative is to a common reading of the biblical account of the fall and the ongoing role of the devil in humanity's propensity to sin. The original fall from grace was precipitated by Satan's free choice to rebel against God. Due to Satan's temptation, humanity fell from grace in the garden of Eden. Now, people continue to fall by choosing to follow Satan's lead. Kotsko is describing a very commonsense, biblical reading of divine punishment for sinful behavior, and this reading often leads naturally to people blaming their own sinfulness for their misfortunes. "Has a disaster struck? That was God's way of chastising you for being insufficiently faithful. Has the kingdom been invaded, and the population shipped to a foreign land? Far from showing that God has been defeated, it is all part of God's plan to purify the people of Israel and ultimately restore them to the promised land."[17] The biblical narrative, Kotsko explains, was indeed vulgarized to justify political and economic oppression, especially in societies that were prosperous and powerful.[18] In a refrain that has echoed throughout Christian history,

---

16. Kotsko, "Neoliberalism's Demons," 500. See also Kotsko, *Neoliberalism's Demons*.

17. Kotsko, "Neoliberalism's Demons," 501.

18. "Persecution of heretics was not at its peak when Christian hegemony over Europe was weakest, but on the contrary when it had most thoroughly saturated the culture. Persecution of Jews did not follow the familiar pattern of trying to find a proxy target for venting frustration in the wake of a crisis, but intensified precisely when

the sin of dominating and enslaving others was cast upon the victims, who served as scapegoats. Kotsko writes about the various demonizing persecutions in Christian history:

> Witches and heretics were tortured until they "freely" offered confessions for which they were then executed. Jews were isolated from mainstream society and then persecuted for being isolated from mainstream society. Native Americans, who had obviously never heard of Jesus before the Spanish showed up, were viewed as being obligated to accept Christianity and then conquered as "retaliation" for rejecting the Gospel. All of the victims were in the same negative sweet spot of freedom as the devil—just free enough to be blameworthy, but not free enough to exercise meaningful agency. They were free enough to be punishable, but not free enough to change their situation, nor even to legitimately resist.[19]

So, the biblical narrative affirms human freedom, which is a valuable contribution to our modern world, but it also lends itself to the distorted curse of scapegoating. It can easily be hijacked for affixing absolute blame to the victims within systems of domination. Kotsko argues that, secularized, this way of thinking has come to offer a thoroughly worldly theodicy, a justification of the neoliberal God of the market, with its inscrutable, seemingly impartial, and always just mechanisms. In the Friedmanian belief system, as subjects free to choose at every moment, if we fail in the free-market arena and find ourselves poor, unsatisfied, in debt, unhealthy, etc., we must fully become our own scapegoat, because we were "free to choose," and apparently, we chose badly. This is even though, much like Eve and Adam, neoliberal individuals are not 100 percent responsible for their economic "failures" because they did not choose the context in which they are operating in the first place.

Wendy Brown calls the neoliberal strategy of scapegoating the losers in the game "responsiblization."[20] Though she does not make the

---

and where the medieval paradigm was most dominant and confident—above all in the newly reunified Spain, which expelled all Jews in 1492, the same year that Columbus 'discovered' the Native American populations who would be relentlessly demonized and enslaved in the coming centuries. Much the same could be said for the persecution of witches, where panic reached a fever pitch toward the end of the medieval period, which is to say, exactly when our progressive instincts would lead us to expect more proto-modern and enlightened views" (Kotsko, "Neoliberalism's Demons," 505).

19. Kotsko, "Neoliberalism's Demons," 505.
20. W. Brown, *Undoing the Demos*.

theological connections that Kotsko does, she effectively describes how this secular political theology of neoliberal logic has unfolded into other areas of our lives in a totalizing fashion reminiscent of strong religion. In fact, she describes the marketization of all areas of life, and the spillage of the sin and blame mentality into them. We as responsiblized individuals have only ourselves to blame if we can't find a job or afford something we need, and if we fall into depression, can't find a mate, or get divorced, can't find friends, become addicted to drugs or alcohol, become obese, contract heart disease, or any number of other contemporary ills that stem from our capitalist consumer economy.[21]

Brown argues that the neoliberal economy is different in kind from mere capitalism. It rules us not just through the normal means of manipulating government and laws but in a totalitarian fashion, through managing the way we think.[22] In fact, she argues that neoliberalism has eclipsed capitalism because the relationship between governments and corporations is so tight as to function as a managed economy, not an autonomous freewheeling system of individuals.[23] Neoliberalism ironically ensures that governments stay big and constantly intrude in our economic decisions. In what I've earlier called a rhetorical trick, it does all this while promoting an ideology of small government. At the same time, politicians continually work to privatize public services, putting more and more social responsibility solely on individuals. While it sends the message that we are competing on an even playing field and are thus responsible if we fail, government's subsidies, tax abatements, rules, and

---

21. Brown finds misshapen sources of identity within the mess created by the neoliberal economy in her latest book and points to: "deterritorializing demographic flows; the disintegration from within and invasion from without of family and community as (relatively) autonomous sites of social production and identification; consumer capitalism's marketing discourse in which individual (and subindividual) desires are produced, commodified, and mobilized as identities; and disciplinary productions of a fantastic array of behavior-based identities ranging from recovering alcoholic professionals to unrepentant 'crack mothers'" (W. Brown, *States of Injury*, 58).

22. On that latter point, Brown is not alone. She has intellectual precursors, some acknowledged in the book and some not. Among them are Ellul, *Technological Society*; Hedges, *Death of Liberal Class*; Klein, *Shock Doctrine*; Wolin, *Democracy Incorporated*.

23. Brown writes, "The state loses even its guise of universality as it becomes ever more transparently invested in particular economic interests, political ends, and social formations—as it transmogrifies from a relatively minimalist, 'night watchman' state to a heavily bureaucratized, managerial, fiscally enormous, and highly interventionist welfare-warfare state, a transformation occasioned by the combined imperatives of capital and the auto-proliferating characteristics of bureaucracy" (W. Brown, *States of Injury*, 57–58).

regulations enable business competition mainly in ways that favor large corporations and large corporate farms.[24]

Perhaps most significantly, neoliberal logic has invaded religion and education, the two areas that are about shaping souls and characters. Churches have come to present themselves, and to think of themselves, as some kind of business. They count the number of attendees and the amount of the contributions, and success is defined as the rate of growth. They discuss how to make sure that their church "brand" is resonating.[25] Universities count how many students they have, their rate of postgraduation employment, and their starting salaries. Faculty count the impact factors for their scholarly articles, calculated largely by counting others' citations of their work, rather than their real-world impact. Schools see students as clients, whose approval ratings they work to improve, even if this strategy waters down what they offer.[26] Given this reality, it should not be a surprise that the neoliberal juggernaut has affected our view of democratic citizenship profoundly.

Ronald Reagan and Margaret Thatcher promised that the average citizen would be empowered by freeing the market. Government was simply in the way, holding back ingenuity and entrepreneurship. While big government has not solved the poverty problem, it still very much exists, and has become even more intrusive in our lives. Small government and free enterprise have not actually been obtained despite decades of neoliberal reforms such as tax cuts and other incentives for business growth. Neoliberals have not, therefore, solved poverty, crime, and other social ills as they promised back in the Friedman/Reagan/Thatcher days. At the same time, through the neoliberalization of our upbringing (now largely institutionalized) and formal education (now largely instrumentalized), these changes in our culture have almost destroyed our ability to be informed citizens with enough knowledge of history and ideas to

---

24. The American Enterprise Institute's (AEI) two-volume publication *Agricultural Policy in Disarray* covers this territory particularly well when it comes to agriculture. Though the book comes from the ideological point of view embraced by the AEI, which tends to be very pro-laissez-faire economics, the data and facts discussed in the volumes leave little doubt that the government's priorities have shaped the sector in ways that favor large mono crop and concentrated animal farming over small and medium and diversified farming. See V. Smith et al., *Agricultural Policy*.

25. Kenneson and Street, *Selling Out the Church*.

26. A new edited volume fights back against this trend, arguing from every angle that the business/marketing model in higher education is destroying the very heart of education, the liberal arts. See Bilbro et al., *Liberating Arts*.

understand what has happened. Our economy has harmed the environment to the point where we must cope with increasing catastrophic weather events and the increasing loss of arable land to feed ourselves. It has made our "essential workers" less free economically, politically, and spiritually. Alarmingly, we are now living in a world in which corporate control (think Google, Meta) dominates our lives much as Reagan and Thatcher feared big government would do.[27]

To reiterate my main point, we have become capitalist realists so completely and for so long, despite the harm, because we have been strong-armed into a false faith. It is a faith that if we keep taking the damage inflicted by the current system, and keep accepting responsibility for failures, we can continue to overcome and eventually enter paradise. The ultimate outcome (as Voegelin would say, the "immanentized eschaton" or the future paradise on earth) will be a rational and good society in which all our economic and social ills will be cured.[28] One cannot use logic and evidence against a deeply ingrained religion. No number of facts will prevail against a strong faith, especially a faith that claims that it has all the facts and logic on its side, and that in effect gaslights you: if you don't see it, you are part of the evil force somehow assaulting the world. Not that long ago, universities were not seen as arms of corporate economic interests, and places of worship were not alienating entrepreneurial competitors for attendance and dollars.[29] But the world has changed dramatically and, as usual, there is a huge psychological lag between the reality of rapid transformation and people's conceptions of what life is all about. Most people are willing to accept the responsiblizing that Kotsko and Brown refer to, to keep their deeply ingrained civil faith intact, rather than face the daunting reality that it is not going to somehow save us. Most people do not realize that they have, in the process, slowly traded the faith of their fathers for what Eugene McCarraher calls the religion of "Mammon."[30]

In the typical American social milieu, to not approve of neoliberal capitalism is to be crazy or evil—an immoral cartoon-character

---

27. *Technofeudalism* is the current term for the tendency of information corporations to silently rule our lives and invade our privacy on a scale never imagined. See Geddes, "Meet Your New Overlords"; Kotkin, *Coming of Neo-Feudalism*; Yanis Varoufakis has picked up on the concept in his upcoming book, *Technofeudalism*.

28. The term comes from Voegelin, *New Science of Politics*.

29. Seybold, "Struggle against Corporate Takeover."

30. McCarraher, *Enchantments of Mammon*.

communist, a sort of social pariah or sociopath. This is the social pressure of ideological strong-arming. On the right, powerful, well-funded organizations, media sources, and public movements are angrily lined up against educators from K–PhD.[31] The aim is to smear these scapegoats with the label of "cultural Marxist" for promoting cultural and moral change they don't like.[32] On the progressive end of the spectrum, cheerleaders for free-market capitalism, like CNN's Fareed Zakaria, see people who do not believe as just needing more education.[33] This right-wing strategy, as well as the selective funding, and sometimes the outright defunding, of the humanities and social sciences at public schools and universities, has worked.[34] Under these conditions, who but truly brave souls, or people at elite private schools with plenty of endowment money, would now openly disagree with the American civil religion of free-market capitalism? And we must acknowledge that the volume and tenor of strong-arming has only increased as the decades have passed.

31. Turning Point USA is probably the most prominent example among many organizations whose main mission seems to be to complain, blame, and target institutions and individuals for blame. Turning Point USA keeps a professor watch list (https://www.professorwatchlist.org/). The Freedom Foundation targets teachers and teachers' unions (https://www.freedomfoundation.com/category/teachers-unions/). Big money funds these groups and lines the pockets of those who comply with speaking fees, research money, junkets, and more. The currently notorious example of Supreme Court Justice Clarence Thomas reads like someone thoroughly corrupted by this kind of money, over a lifetime.

32. This is the famous maneuver of right-wing Prof. Jordan Peterson, who uses the term "postmodern neo-Marxism" as well (Lynn, "Cultural Marxism").

33. Zakaria is well known for his centrism and his seeming inability to be defined on the ideological spectrum, but he is a consistent and unabashed supporter of capitalism. Responding to statements by Mitt Romney in 2012 about the importance of culture on a country's economic performance, Zakaria opined, "Had Romney spent more time reading Milton Friedman, he would have realized that historically the key driver for economic growth has been the adoption of capitalism and its related institutions and policies across diverse cultures" ("Capitalism, Not Culture," para. 5).

34. A study conducted in 2007 found that true Marxist orientation was rare in US academia, and became rarer the younger the professors were. Overall, only 3 percent of academics identified as Marxists. In the humanities, the percentage was 5 percent, and in the social sciences, the percentage was just under 18 percent. This reflects the reality that almost all US academics are liberals, either tending progressive to moderate (the majority) or on the conservative end (the minority). The left-right spectrum in the US is almost entirely liberal, a point I hope I made sufficiently earlier in this book. This means that hardly any professors in the US want anything more radical than Sanders's style of economics, which is still capitalist with a much larger welfare state. The typical left-leaning professor of today is hardly any different from the Tip O'Neill democrat of old. See Gross and Simmons, "Social and Political Views"; Gross and Simmons, *Professors and Their Politics*.

IDEOLOGICAL STRONG-ARMING: FREE TO CHOOSE

If you watch Friedman's PBS series and then listen to an old Rush Limbaugh radio show, you will already notice a difference in tenor. Friedman comes across as very genial and kind, and he patiently offers what he considers common sense. Limbaugh is not as nice; he is bitingly sarcastic. In the 1970s and 1980s, Limbaugh offered a first glimpse of what came to be known as "infotainment," because his political commentary was laced with jokes and parodies.[35] Limbaugh made mockery a center point of his communications strategy, and when he wasn't mocking his "liberal" opponents, he was working himself up into angry, indignant rants against them.[36] Friedman focused primarily on a positive faith, what could be gained by allowing the gods of the free market to operate largely unhindered, and appealed to our better angels on matters of human equality. Limbaugh focused primarily on the negative, offering his listeners an identity that can be summed up as "we are not them." Limbaugh and future commentators, including popular conservative luminaries like Glenn Beck, worked on people's emotions, their suffering, and their fears, particularly their fear of being on the social outside, of being associated with "them."[37]

The meteoric rise of Limbaugh and Glenn Beck came in the same decade that Ronald Reagan served his two presidential terms. But unlike Reagan, they did not sound as much like Friedman as they did contemporary conspiracy theorist Alex Jones and others like him who emerged more prominently in the '90s (Jones attained his first radio show in 1996, but soon enough moved to the Internet because he refused to conform to the station's standards, and *Infowars* was born).[38] While figures like Fox News personalities Sean Hannity and Tucker Carlson straddled the line between old and new sensibilities, the twenty-first century also saw figures such as Steve Bannon, Richard Spencer, and Nick Fuentes rise to prominence, all mainly on the Internet.[39] They avoided broadcasting

---

35. Matthews, "Infotainment."

36. You can find an archive of Limbaugh's shows and information about his many books at https://podcasts.apple.com/us/podcast/rush-limbaugh-timeless-wisdom/id1155318497.

37. You can find Glenn Beck's shows and information about his books and other communications at https://www.glennbeck.com.

38. See https://www.infowars.com/.

39. Steve Bannon is now hard to find on the Internet, except for stories of his indictment, sentencing, etc. For a good introduction to his activities, see J. Green, *Devil's Bargain*. Original alt-right leader and Unite the Right rally instigator Richard Spencer has largely been deplatformed. Nick Fuentes pops up on Twitter (X) occasionally but is largely deplatformed. See Rogers, "Deplatforming."

standards by going online, and ditched any concern for social niceties, openly discussing white nationalism, "race realism," race wars, anti-immigration, civil war and secession, anti-woman "incel" identities, etc.[40] I doubt Milton Friedman would recognize these men as descending from the same lineage as himself, but in some ways they do indeed stem from his stock. The through line is liberalism—individual freedom and autonomy, and the fear, loathing, and suspicion of big government. There is also a strange common optimism: if we can just get a few obstacles out of our way, human beings operating in an unhindered state can live peacefully and prosperously with little guidance. Unlike older liberals like Friedman and Reagan, what needs to get out of the way for the newer commentators includes not just big government (now the "deep state") but racial minorities, feminists, queers, and transsexuals.[41] But, it must be noted that there was some (subtler) blaming of all these groups even from the start among the followers of Friedman-style neoliberalism. And current right-wing leaders continue to need people to blame for getting in the way of everything good and decent because the improvements promised by Friedman and Reagan, the improvements average voters continue to be promised, never materialized.

Every right-wing opinion leader I have mentioned convinced people to support them by telling them that they had obviously good solutions to our problems, *and that anyone who disagreed was either stupid or evil.* This is, ironically, also the historic strategy of the real-world Marxist leaders in countries where communism became totalitarianism. In other words, the extreme right and left use similar strategies of social, psychological, and spiritual strong-arming to get people to agree and go along with their programs. Why is it, then, that the right-wing version has become more pronounced in the United States in the past few decades? And why did many Americans remain vulnerable to it long after it proved that it could not deliver the goods it promised?

Abandonment from the Left and Its Consequences

As we will see in more detail in the next chapter, right-wing ideological strong-arming has had a major impact on American Christians' understanding of their own faith, and much of that has to do with their

40. For a solid account of these dimensions of online idea-mongering, see Nagle, *Kill All Normies.*

41. Bloom and Moskalenko, *Pastels and Pedophiles.*

perception that the family is under siege from culturally liberalizing movements such as LGBTQ rights. However, in his book *Haven in a Heartless World*, Christopher Lasch told a better story than this misguided right-wing ideological faith: the story of capitalist socialization and its catastrophic impact on the family. Originally published in the 1970s, *Haven in a Heartless World* demonstrated that the crisis of the family began not in the hippie years but in the nineteenth century, or even earlier. Describing the quick and massive changes that have taken place in just a few short centuries of capitalist growth, Lasch writes, "The history of modern society . . . is the assertion of social control over activities once left to individuals or their families."[42] He is referring to the fact that the Industrial Revolution effectively removed production from the family household, which usually meant the extended family, and "collectivized it" in factories. When people responded to the demands of the new mode of production by moving to cities, sometimes far away, extended families broke apart. Scientific human management was later developed to design and control mass-production settings in ways to lessen mistakes and increase productivity, but also to smooth over worker dissatisfaction. Spurred on by the success of factory-management systems, and especially by the increasing employment and independence of women, the social managerial spirit went further to intrude on our private lives, filling in for the increasingly fragmented and de-skilled family.

As the economy developed, the business of "commodity propaganda" (advertising) became more and more sophisticated, and aimed at the new chief consumers in the modern family—women (and, secondarily, their now relatively emancipated children). Lasch called the development of collective labor and the managerial intrusion into the family the *socialization of production* and the *socialization of reproduction*. Increasing collectivization/bureaucratization of work and life created people who needed experts. While they did their factory or office job, other people were busy supplying what they no longer could—including the very essentials of life—food, fuel, shelter, clothing, transportation, etc. This is why Marx remarked that no sooner had the worker been paid than he was beset by capitalists to take it all from him.[43] Eventually, the

42. Lasch, *Haven in Heartless World*, xx.

43. "No sooner is the exploitation of the labourer by the manufacturer, so far, at an end, that he receives his wages in cash, than he is set upon by the other portions of the bourgeoisie, the landlord, the shopkeeper, the pawnbroker" (Marx and Engels, *Communist Manifesto*, 80).

nexus between government and corporate management was complete, with government aiding corporate growth via increased social welfare programs of all kinds, along with enormous amounts of corporate welfare from the municipal all the way to the international level, in the name of providing jobs to the people. These developments, Lasch wrote, made people increasingly dependent upon experts, managers, professionals, employed by corporations and the state, eroding their capacity for independent thought and self-help.[44] It is no wonder that people came to feel like bureaucracies of all kinds were beyond their comprehension or control, and grew to resent them.

Though economic developments yielded relatively better living in a material sense for many, the price has literally been the blowing up of the family, extended family, and community experienced by people for centuries. This is the true, deep cause of the fragmentation of the family, not cultural challenges like the coming out of the LGBTQ community, which happened far later. As an example of what I am trying to get at: capitalist development led to more female independence, and eventually to feminists' demand for complete political equality. But as women in the workplace increased, real wages lowered for men and women, and divorce rates and solo living increased.[45] Now, both partners in a marriage usually need to work at least full-time and sometimes more to live a middle-class way of life. Their children are in day care centers, and their parents are spending the family inheritance on "assisted living" to get impersonal care. Everyone is too dependent on industrial food and other accoutrements of life, with all the damage to our environment all that commerce causes.

My argument is not that we should regret female equality, but equality is much more than the equal right to get a full-time job or equal pay. Capitalism naturally exploited the impulse toward liberation and used it to expand. Male and female liberation should not have to come at the price of the destruction of so many habits, institutions, and mores that were sources of stability and happiness for all of us. But it has, and we should not consider this "liberation" and this "equality" good enough. Again, the social changes I've mentioned were not caused by cultural challenges from gays or "cultural Marxists." They were direct by-products of capitalist expansion. We have been experiencing higher divorce rates,

---

44. Lasch, *Haven in Heartless World*, xxi.
45. D. MacDonald and Dildar, "Married Women's Economic Independence."

falling birth rates, the continual upturning of moral norms, and radical changes in the roles of men and women, since the latter half of the nineteenth century.[46] Eventually seen as crises at least by some, these are among the reasons the neoliberal imaginary, so useful for making people believe that they are being moved by inevitable economic and social forces they cannot hope to control, is slipping. As always, that slippage is happening in a messy and less than optimal way.

After believing in the Friedman religion for decades, more and more people are finally beginning to lose faith, and to think in sometimes frightening alternative frameworks. The current reality is an odd mixture of many who still believe in neoliberalism and a growing number of people willing to openly resonate with populism, hyper-masculinity, ethno-nationalism, religious traditionalism, socialism, and authoritarianism. These emerging positions are spread over age brackets, with even older Americans moving from pure neoliberal ideology to the Trumpian nationalist position and/or into the zone of conspiracy theories like QAnon.[47] The MAGA movement had its strongest support by far in the white segment of the US population, but it did pick up more diverse support than prior, more neoliberal Republican candidates have mustered. Indeed, Trump picked up support among Blacks and Hispanics between his 2016 victory and his 2020 defeat. As Texan Mateo Mokarzel, a Hispanic man of forty, told the BBC about why he voted for Trump for the first time in 2020, "He really delivered on his anti-globalisation policy," he said. "Neoliberal expansion has really hurt both Mexico and the US, and when you have family that live there, and you can see how it's hurt people living, their jobs, their wages, it really has increased the narco-war, and this is one of the things Trump came in saying—'hey, we're going to tear apart these trade deals'—and then he actually did it. That was for me the first sign that he actually meant some of the things he was saying."[48]

Trump's official rhetoric expressed the tendency within the American electorate that sensed that neoliberalism had not benefited them in the long run, and who were doubting it would ever do so. *The Salt Lake*

---

46. Lasch, *Haven in Heartless World*, 8.

47. Tanner Mirrlees, "Trump and the Alt-Right," in Perry et al., *Right-Wing Extremism*, 77. The average age of rioters at the January 6 insurrection at the Capital was forty-two (Jensen, "Link," para. 2). I am aware that people differ as to how nationalistic Trump's policy was, but his rhetoric was a repudiation of many neoliberal positions.

48. Nagesh, "U.S. Election 2020," para. 11.

Tribune summarized this sentiment from a state whose majority support for Trump has been solid:

> First, neoliberal policies fostered globalization. Globalization, together with new technologies, produced both winners and losers. The winners were primarily multinational corporations and consumers. Multinational corporations gained from lower production costs, stemming from outsourcing jobs to China and elsewhere. Consumers gained from lower prices. The losers were primarily blue-collar workers, those who built the goods now produced elsewhere or produced by new technologies. Trump won by convincing blue-collar workers and other economically disadvantaged voters that he could return those jobs to the United States. Second, many Trump supporters felt a sense of economic injustice. They resented policies imposed on them by the urban elites, policies that benefited urbanites but hurt those living in rural areas who depended on the land for their livelihood. They saw the system as rigged. Environmental policies and government control of public lands made it more difficult for ranchers, farmers and miners to earn a living. Marginalized and without any allegiance to neoliberalism, they sought to reverse policies of the urban elites. Third, neoliberalism failed to address rising inequality in income and wealth, the result of the very policies that neoliberalism supported. Free trade, corporate tax cuts, deregulation, financialization and so on benefited corporations, consumers and the more affluent. Their failure to compensate blue-collar workers and those in rural areas evoked a populist countermovement with two distinct versions: Progressive populism (Bernie Sanders, Elizabeth Warren, et al.) and reactionary populism (Trump).[49]

Candidate Trump's campaign announcement speech in 2015 was an immediate indication of his intended audience. Within just a few sentences of beginning his speech, he had signaled that he would stop China from having an unfair trade advantage over the United States:

> Our country is in serious trouble. We don't have victories anymore. We used to have victories, but we don't have them. When was the last time anybody saw us beating, let's say, China in a trade deal? They kill us. I beat China all the time. All the time. When did we beat Japan at anything? They send their cars over by the millions, and what do we do? When was the last time you saw a Chevrolet in Tokyo? It doesn't exist, folks. They beat

---

49. Seidelman and Watkins, "Trump Meant the End," paras. 3–5.

us all the time. When do we beat Mexico at the border? They're laughing at us, at our stupidity. And now they are beating us economically. They are not our friends, believe me. But they're killing us economically. The U.S. has become a dumping ground for everybody else's problems.[50]

Trump's early focus was on international politics, and particularly the idea that China and many other countries had taken American jobs due to corrupt politicians in America who thought more about their stock portfolios than their constituents' livelihoods. His critique of American military capabilities and domestic infrastructure ("our bridges, our railroads, our airports") depicted a country lurching toward ultra-corruption and decrepitude. He called out the other Republican candidates for not acknowledging the loss of American jobs and productivity, and not criticizing our trade competitors for their unfair practices. He did say he was a "free trader," but he immediately also said that the problem with free trade is that workers needed "a really talented negotiator to negotiate for [them]." The problem, he argued, was that other countries were refusing American goods so they could protect their own workforce, putting up tariffs and other trade barriers to create an unfair playing field. He called out Ford for planning a large auto manufacturing plant in Mexico. He promised that one of the first things he'd do was tell the president of Ford that every car that came across the border would be taxed at 35 percent. Despite his remark about free trade, many of the economic strategies he talked about amounted to protectionism. He repeatedly called out political leaders for being in the pocket of multinational corporations. He also appealed to patriotism, particularly caring for veterans, whom he said the country had abandoned. To rally retired workers to his side, he defended Social Security against the threat of cuts. And he argued that we needed someone who could take the "American brand and make it great again."

These themes were repeated in his 2017 inaugural address, the "American carnage" speech. Near the beginning of this speech, Trump proclaimed that Washington elites had scooped up benefits for themselves that were not shared with the people. Politicians continued to thrive while "jobs left and the factories closed."[51] He repeatedly contrasted Washington elitism with the struggles of ordinary people. "Mothers

50. Donald Trump, in *Time* Staff, "Donald Trump's Presidential Announcement," paras. 5–8.
51. Trump, "Inaugural Address," para. 9.

and children trapped in poverty in our inner cities, rusted out factories, scattered like tombstones across the landscape of our nation, an education system flush with cash, but which leaves our young and beautiful students deprived of all knowledge, and the crime, and the gangs, and the drugs that have stolen too many lives and robbed our country of so much unrealized potential."[52]

The way Trump saw it, the Washington elites did not mind that those jobs went overseas, leaving American workers behind. The elites, as shareholders in globalized corporations, would benefit from rising stock prices and dividends. This is what was meant by "the wealth of our middle class has been ripped from their homes and then redistributed all across the world."[53] Rhetoric like this is how he tapped into the deep resentment and disappointment felt by so many. Notice that Trump did not point the finger of blame at Hispanics, Blacks, or any other group in the United States, and not even directly at other countries, but at power elites whose main motivation was to make excessive profits. The narrative that Trump was primarily a racist of some kind was not supported by the formal speeches he gave at the beginning of his career as a presidential contender and winner. Indeed, he called for unity and made the point that it did not matter if one was black, brown, or white because "we all bleed the same red blood of patriots."[54] He did not even come across as a xenophobe, just an assiduous negotiator. Evoking the "city on a hill" trope, he did seem to be some kind of Christian, reminding people that they were not just protected by their military and police (though they were) but also by God. Judging by what he said in his most important communications, his politics seemed mildly nationalistic, more than a little protectionist, and extremely populist.

At least as the voters learned about him through his speeches, tweets, and other image-making efforts, Trump was and is more conservative than most recent Republicans have been. This is simply because he does not apply the neoliberal solution to every problem. Trump was and is a populist candidate. He is proud of being a billionaire, but rhetorically, he ironically uses his experience in the real estate and business worlds to prove his point that wealthy people don't pay taxes and politicians are influenced by big money. He calls out the government elites who allow this bilking of taxpayers because their profits are not affected, and he pits

52. Trump, "Inaugural Address," para. 24.
53. Trump, "Inaugural Address," para. 34.
54. Trump, "Inaugural Address," para. 66.

their interests against the regular folks. In his attitude towards ordinary Americans, he thinks in terms of home and away, us and not-us, and not in the globalist way in which borders, cultures, and nationalities are considered ideational and fluid. This makes him a kind of nationalist, and, because of all this, he is a protectionist. For our purposes, the debate about whether he acted on behalf of the common people or benefited the corporate elites is not relevant; it is enough to ask what people *thought* they were going to get when voting for him.

By the time Trump gave his first State of the Union Address, the speech sounded much more like a typical Republican presidential address. It did not start out with any talk about elites taking their money overseas or even bare-knuckle negotiations with other countries to bring back American jobs. Instead, Trump gave plenty of space near the beginning to the beneficial effects of the latest tax cuts. However, he did give one paragraph to the subject of trade further down in his remarks, saying, "Many car companies are now building and expanding plants in the United States—something we have not seen for decades. Chrysler is moving a major plant from Mexico to Michigan; Toyota and Mazda are opening up a plant in Alabama. Soon, plants will be opening up all over the country. This is all news Americans are unaccustomed to hearing—for many years, companies and jobs were only leaving us. But now they are coming back."[55] He referenced the "unfair trade deals" America had been in for decades that "shipped away our companies." He proclaimed that the "era of economic surrender was over," and that from now on, only fair and reciprocal trade deals that protected American jobs and intellectual property would be made.[56] He also reprised another theme from earlier speeches, proclaiming, "As we rebuild our industries, it is also time to rebuild our crumbling infrastructure."[57]

As with many populist leaders of the past who, having gotten a taste of power, became more and more paranoid, so did Trump. By the time he gave his speech to the rally goers at the inauguration of Joe Biden on January 6, 2020, Trump's speech was front-loaded with resentment against the news media elites, the "fake news," his political enemies, and his own vice president, whom he considered at that moment to be of dubious personal loyalty. It was filled with cultural symbolism instead of class-based economics—fear that statues and monuments would be

55. Trump, "State of the Union," para. 22.
56. Trump, "State of the Union," para. 26.
57. Trump, "State of the Union," para. 28.

torn down, how democracy was being stolen, how the news media were propagandists.[58] And when he eventually turned to his record after four years of the presidency, he again brought up conventional Republican talking points: taxes and regulations had been cut, the military had been beefed up, and a new military branch had been created, the Space Force. He discussed helping veterans receive timely health care. Then, after more grousing about losing the election due to alleged fraud, he found his way momentarily back to China and stolen jobs, via an argument he had engaged in with congressional Republicans about how much COVID relief money to send individual taxpayers.

> You know, "We don't want to give $2,000 to people. We want to give them $600." Oh, great. How does that play politically? Pretty good? And this has nothing to do with politics, but how does it play politically? China destroyed these people. We didn't destroy. China destroyed them, totally destroyed them. We want to give them $600, and they just wouldn't change. I said give them $2,000, we'll pay it back. We'll pay it back fast. You already owe 26 trillion, give them a couple of bucks. Let them live. Give them a couple of bucks. And some of the people here disagree with me on that, but I just say, "Look, you've got to let people live."[59]

Amid frequent refrains of suspicion about his election, Trump noted that America's far-flung military empire was unduly costing soldiers their lives.

> I brought a lot of our soldiers home. . . . They're in countries that nobody even knows the name, nobody knows where they are. They're dying. They're great, but they're dying. They're losing their arms, their legs, their face. I brought them back home, largely back home. Afghanistan, Iraq. Remember, I used to say in the old days: "Don't go into Iraq. But if you go in, keep the oil." We didn't keep the oil. So stupid. So stupid these people. And Iraq has billions and billions of dollars now in the bank. And what did we do? We did get nothing. We never get—but we do, actually. We kept the oil here. We kept—we did good.

He spoke of building the border wall between the US and Mexico, which he implied was well under way, if not completely built. But more

---

58. This is the Republican equivalent of the Democratic move towards identity politics issues.

59. Jacobo, "What Trump Told Supporters," paras. 70–72.

than three quarters of the speech was devoted to assertions of voter fraud and the treachery of various enemies. Trump's urgings to negate what he depicted as massive election corruption was the main thing his supporters heard, and then, while he slipped back to the White House, some of the rally goers not only made their way to the Capitol but violently invaded the halls of Congress, causing representatives and senators to run for their lives.

The reason I have dwelled on the content of three major speeches by Trump is that I want the reader to focus on something other than the many sideshows of the Trump presidency. If the question is what attracted voters to Trump in the first place, and why did many continue to support him even after the January 6 debacle, the answer lies, I believe, in what he said on the campaign trail for the 2106 election, and in his inaugural address. I have not mentioned Trump's tweets, which the media obsessed about ad nauseam for over five years. From the beginning, Trump's own personality, his own psychological and spiritual problems, mixed with his message, causing most detractors to lose focus and to engage in nothing but feelings-based criticisms of the most indefensible part of Trump's leadership, his lack of self-control augmented by social media. But what was it about Donald Trump that made people suddenly throw their support behind such an unlikely presidential candidate? I think that the answer is, his message and his uncouth personality appeal deeply to many who in the past would have been considered exclusive Democratic turf. Only by giving this charitable reading can we begin to understand what happened, and what is continuing to happen, in the divided politics of the moment.

To recap, Trump's official rhetoric resonated with the following themes that apparently appealed to large segments of the US electorate in 2016 and beyond:

- A suspicion that the Friedmanian neoliberal faith had not served most Americans economically or culturally or had served economic elites far more
- The sense that many Americans had lost employment and/or had to retool at their own expense because their jobs had been downgraded to lower pay and less security, gone overseas, or been automated out of existence
- Fear that American infrastructure and resources were being hollowed out because of a lack of concern for US-based industry

- A weariness of being lectured by urbane, cultural elites in the news and entertainment media who constantly insinuated that most Americans were ignorant, and their troubles were deserved (why Trump's in-your-face, uncouth persona was enjoyed by his supporters)
- A deep suspicion that large corporations did not care about average Americans and were willing to benefit China and other countries at their expense
- Fear that American companies providing good jobs were going to continue to lose ground and that the US government was not working to stop it
- Suspicion that US political elites like those in Congress were corrupt, taking corporate donations to do their bidding, and did not really care for the people they represented
- Fear that the American military was being asked to occupy and fight in areas of the world the US had no real business being in, but was there to safeguard the interests of global economic elites
- The desire to bring US troops back home from these unnecessary foreign adventures, and giving ill-used veterans the support they were due
- Suspicion that political and economic elites did not respect and were derisive of middle-American cultural values, including Christian values

Many of these themes might have, at a different time and coming from a different person, been embraced by Bernie Sanders–style Democrats, or even people further to the left. Certainly an underlying reason, much discussed by scholars but largely ignored by the media and thus most progressives, that voters have gravitated towards Republicans starting at least with the first presidency of Ronald Reagan, is that the Democratic Party has for decades now adopted neoliberal positions and has indeed abandoned, and exuded an elitist disdain for, Americans concerned about these kinds of issues.[60] Thomas Frank, in his aptly named *Listen, Liberal*, which was written before Donald Trump won the White House, wrote this about the Democratic Party: "'Failure' is admittedly a harsh word, but what else are we to call it when the left party in a system

---

60. See Wuthnow, *Left Behind*; Frank, *What's the Matter*.

chooses to confront an epic economic breakdown by talking hopefully about entrepreneurship and innovation? When the party of professionals repeatedly falls for bad, self-serving ideas like bank deregulation, the 'creative class,' and empowerment through bank loans? When the party of the common man basically allows aristocracy to return?"[61]

Much of the disdain of progressives for the working class has come disguised in culture-war speech and behavior that has elicited right-liberal critiques of "wokeness" or "political correctness" and "cancel culture." Democrats have retreated into identity politics. But why? Identity politics thrives alongside what Christopher Lasch calls our "culture of narcissism," and it thrives particularly well among the new managerial elites who, as many members of the precariat suspect, owe their positions less to raw talent than to gatekeeping degrees and interpersonal skills and relationships.[62] Writing of his observations about the environment in which many of them work, Lasch observed, "I was struck by evidence, presented in several studies of business corporations, to the effect that professional advancement had come to depend less on craftsmanship or loyalty to the firm than on 'visibility,' 'momentum,' personal charm, and impression management. The dense interpersonal environment of modern bureaucracy appeared to elicit and reward a narcissistic response—an anxious concern with the impression one made on others, a tendency to treat others as a mirror of the self."[63] In this environment, it stands to reason that gazing at self, and contemplating oneself through others' eyes, would become a top priority. Conversations with people in this category amount to listening to a monologue about their identity, or their search for it, and often such conversations include the easy-to-reach-for secular categories of sex, gender, sexual orientation, religion, race, and lifestyle values. Finding oneself is easier if that self can be slotted into preexisting physical or mental categories. But perhaps because these categories never get to the spiritual roots of the problem with our entire way of living, alienated from nature and from God, these unintentional narcissists continue, despite their efforts to find themselves, to suffer from feelings of emptiness and inauthenticity.[64] Finding meaning outside of themselves at a spiritual level would eliminate the void they feel, but that type of transformation is not encouraged. This is because

61. Frank, Listen, Liberal, 255–56.
62. Eirenreich, Fear of Falling.
63. Lasch, Culture of Narcissism, 283.
64. Lasch, Culture of Narcissism, 284.

narcissistic personality traits are perfect for the preservation of the neoliberal consumerist economy. Traits such as "a certain protective shallowness, a fear of binding commitments, a willingness to pull up roots whenever the need arose, a desire to keep one's options open, a dislike of depending on anyone, an incapacity for loyalty or gratitude" are exactly what you want in a perpetual consumer.[65]

As Marxist theorist Slavoj Žižek puts it, "Western political correctness ('wokeness') has displaced class struggle, producing a liberal elite that claims to protect threatened racial and sexual minorities to divert attention from its members' own economic and political power. At the same time, this lie allows alt-right populists to present themselves as defenders of 'real' people against corporate and 'deep state' elites, even though they, too, occupy positions at the commanding heights of economic and political power."[66]

The underlying reason for this Democratic shift towards identity politics is economic. As globalization began to ramp up and US workers began to feel the sting, Democrat leaders were either largely impotent to stop it, or as Žižek (and Trump) suggests, did not want to stop it because it benefited them financially. Democrats became convinced of the neoliberal notion that the workers' painful precarity and dislocation were inevitable and even morally necessary to move society forward. The Democratic Party, realizing that it did not have the political will to engage in protectionism, or to argue for socialism to redistribute corporate profits, retreated into cultural issues to appeal to urban voters, especially the professional class, as "progressives." Largely, Republicans also played the game of holding on to their rank and file, middle-America working-class and rural people alongside rural elites, with hot-button cultural issues that provoked continuing feuds with their counterparts, while at the same time pursuing basically the same neoliberal policies as Democrats. Both parties partly created and certainly have taken advantage of our "culture of narcissism," in which they have retreated from "civic spirit" or thinking about the common good, in favor of their own good. That is, until Donald Trump came along and, for a moment, long-pent-up popular frustration with America's economic priorities mixed with the more familiar brew of culture-war issues, and surfaced like the tip of an iceberg in the Republican sea.

---

65. Lasch, *Culture of Narcissism*, 285.
66. Žižek, "'Woke' Left and Alt-Right," para. 10.

Lasch presciently took note of the Democrats' identity-politics maneuver in his book *The Revolt of the Elites and the Betrayal of Democracy* in 1995:

> The industrial working class, once the mainstay of the socialist movement, has become a pitiful remnant of itself. The hope that "new social movements" would take its place in the struggle against capitalism, which briefly sustained the left in the late seventies and early eighties, has come to nothing. Not only do the new social movements—feminism, gay rights, welfare rights, agitation against racial discrimination—have nothing in common, but their only coherent demand aims at inclusion in the dominant structures rather than at a revolutionary transformation of social relations.
>
> It is not just that the masses have lost interest in revolution; their political interests are demonstrably more conservative than those of their self-appointed spokesmen and would-be liberators. It is the working and lower middle classes, after all, that favor limits on abortion, cling to the two-parent family as a source of stability in a turbulent world, resist experiments with "alternative lifestyles," and harbor deep reservations about affirmative action and other ventures in large-scale social engineering. More to Ortega's point, they have a more highly developed sense of limits than their betters. They understand, as their betters do not, that there are inherent limits on human control over the course of social development, over nature and the body, over the tragic elements in human life and history.[67]

Lasch characterizes the new progressive's disdain for the vulgar masses as "hygienic." This kind of Democrat was and is more about making sure our environment is smoke- and tobacco-free, and that our speech does not hurt others' feelings, than about making sure working people are protected from precarity. "Middle-American" values have come to be seen by these hygienic progressives as obstacles to progress, as "retrograde," "unfashionable," and "provincial." They indeed act like cultural elites and look down upon the popular culture of the masses as low and stupefied. But Lasch insists that these would-be progressives have lost track of the fact that a "crisis of the middle class" is ongoing, as fewer Americans benefit from the huge profits that have propelled the opulent lifestyles of many of those lecturing them on manners. While the professional and managerial elites that represent the upper middle class, which Lasch

---

67. Lasch, *Revolt of the Elites*, 28.

characterizes as the upper 20 percent of income earners, pull away from the now downwardly mobile middle class and below, a values and lifestyle chasm grows, and an entrenched elite has formed with less social mixing and intermarriage than ever before in US history.

Lasch noted of these, "A more salient fact is that the market in which the new elites operate is now international in scope. . . . They have more in common with their counterparts in Brussels or Hong Kong than with the masses of Americans not yet plugged into the network of global communications." The new managerial elite is insidiously meritocratic, resting on "the fiction that its power rests on intelligence alone." This description, Lasch argues, represented quite well the priorities and attitudes of the Bill Clinton administration. If we keep this in mind, it may be easier to understand why Hillary Clinton's comments about the "basket of deplorables" in her own run for the White House was received like the typical progressive insult towards ordinary Americans that it indeed was.[68]

As this new Democratic elite adopted the neoliberal faith and pushed justifications of meritocracy, they began their own campaign of strong-arming. Meritocracy, Lasch argued, extolled the idea that anyone had the opportunity to advance, and if they did not, it was their fault. This, it turns out, is a very similar message to the Friedmanian faith more explicitly held by the US right. This attitude cut the progressive elites off mentally from people in the middle class and below, making it ever more likely that they would "exercise power irresponsibly, precisely because they recognize so few obligations to their predecessors or to the communities they profess to lead."[69] As educational reforms allowed the top performers of the lower classes to escape to the managerial elite, and for the children of elites to receive what they needed to continue their family legacies, true inherited class positioning became more and more likely. Think about who is most able to take advantage of public schools' gifted programs, tuition vouchers, advanced placement courses, and leisure and competitive after-school opportunities, and you will begin to understand Lasch's argument. Even public institutions like schools emphasized more and more the separation of the intellectual and creative elites from everyone else. This further aggravated the problem of a cosmopolitan class that did not feel any kinship with

---

68. Rielly, "Hillary Clinton's 'Basket.'"
69. Lasch, *Revolt of the Elites*, 35.

its fellow citizens, and no real concern for the well-being of any nation within existing borders, even their own. It goes without saying that this progressive elitism does not coincide with Christian values any more than right-wing nationalism does.

Considering the abandonment of the precariat from the left, Trump's popularity with large segments of the US population is more understandable. It had to do with his pro-precariat, pro-family positions, which went along with his personal style, and which was decidedly not like that of the progressive elites. Early on, he signaled that he was not another neoliberal believer, that indeed he was a radical outsider capable of thinking along the lines of protectionism and redistribution. Some of his positions could even be characterized as leftist (his insistence that people needed to make a living, that they needed jobs that paid well, that the government ought to manipulate the economy to work for them, and that they sometimes deserved a handout). At the same time his views validated the sense of many people that their way of life and their values were constantly being insulted by a cosmopolitan elite in the news media, in entertainment circles, and from educators. This is why Trump could come across as uncouth, and have a track record of relative immorality, but still resonate with people when he talked about God and Christianity. He was, and is (even now, under indictment), the champion of people who feel disrespected, who feel like they have been "left behind."[70] Because he is their champion, they support him not so much because he perfectly embodies all their preferred qualities but because he represents their values and qualities in the public arena anyway. And he does all of this with a significant thumb in the eye of the overly genteel and progressive cultural elites. If this is all true, then a charismatic leftist who could sympathize with popular culture and Christian values might also have resonated at some point as the tension was building, but that type of leftist is nowhere to be found.

Conclusion

We have seen that neoliberal theory provides a narrative about the US economy that isn't true, but that expresses the hopes and fears of the precariat in a quasi-religious way. First, it tells us what we long to hear. Yes, we should desire the common good, but the best way to achieve the

---

70. Wuthnow, *Left Behind*.

common good is to be selfish. If we are selfish, and we trust the system to act on our behalf, the impersonal mechanisms of the free market will take care of others' welfare much as God takes care of nature. In addition to the allure of this quasi-religion and the pressure it puts on us to conform, there is also the powerful promise of complete autonomy, complete independence from others, and even from the transcendent God we cannot control. The unspoken attraction is that through our cooperation with the system, we can make grand changes to our way of life without that God (or with him simply cheering on from the sidelines as we approach the economic singularity).

In this way, the neoliberal faith gives us extraordinary hope, but at the same time, the story comes with teeth—a great deal of strong-arming. If we are not experiencing all that the faith promises, we are told that we as individuals have made bad choices (we have sinned) and simply need to try again. Preachers of this economic faith also tell us that all we need is the commitment to stay the course and sacrifice as necessary in the short term, trusting that the system will ultimately work towards everyone's benefit. The hope of that heavenly promise of a future of full prosperity, the economic eschaton, should justify the compromises and suffering entailed. Finally, this secular religion tells us to blame ourselves and others if we fail. Because we can blame only ourselves, we fear that others will blame us as well, and we will lose their cooperation, friendship, kinship, and perhaps even our employment. So attached are Americans to the pride and the allure of total self-reliance, and so fearful are Americans that their failures are their fault and that others will abandon them because of those failures (chief among them, the failure to believe), that there seems to be no escape. Through neoliberalism we may escape the need for God himself, but we cannot escape the need for capitalism.

The populist/nationalist turn has happened, at least in part, because the precarity, dislocation, and fragmentation caused by rapid economic changes have made people especially vulnerable to radical political messages, especially those that appeal to their strong need to belong and to change things. Those drawn off into these paths have made attempts, albeit feeble and misshapen, to break free from neoliberal ideological strong-arming. The pain and disruption caused by increasing automation and the off-shoring of previously secure jobs have encouraged the creation of new types of communities not based on place and driven by frustration. Human beings are social by nature. We understand ourselves largely by our relationships with others. The need for real, meaningful relationships has not changed, but now it is not being fulfilled in the normal ways it has been for most of human history. Our previously firm familial relationships (father, mother, son, daughter, aunt, uncle, grandfather, grandmother, neighbor, and friend) necessarily mean much less than they used to in our world of constant disembedding and dislocation. Our world has produced a social void that too often goes unanswered, and that void has pushed some people beyond the acceptable political horizon into groups that have served to foster their radicalization. It has driven others to suicide.

The haphazard and unproductive ideological detour of those who have struggled to cut themselves loose from the neoliberal religion has led many people down a dark path on which they cannot see clearly what is obvious in the light of day. Liberalism and capitalism have had much to do with the rapid and destructive cultural change that these new radicals instinctively mistrust and rebel against. It is an irony of modern Western life that people most often do not make the connection between our economic system and the various cultural and moral choices we make. For example, the categories of "male" and "female" are now considered by many to be matters of personal expression on a spectrum, not biology. This is considered a problem for the right, while it is a positive development for those on the progressive left. But, as these two sides bounce off each other in the ideological ping-pong match that is American politics, nobody seems to see the impact of consumer capitalism on our ideas of personal freedom and choice. If everything else in our lives is optional, fluid, and transient, if we are indeed "free to choose," why would we stop choosing at some biological dividing line?[71] Similarly, why would we be surprised if women thought they should be free to choose, without moral complications or regulatory restraints, what to do with their pregnant bodies? What part of liberal/capitalist logic upholds any restraint on our choices? The logic of the market works best when we keep all our options

---

71. In a cruel twist, the right currently sees the seeming increase in trans people as itself the threat to Western cultural stability rather than an inevitable development given the values implicit in their own economic and political systems. Trans people are not the problem; they are simply trying to find their identity, purpose, and fulfillment from discovering who they are in a hostile society that has abandoned them to their own devices. They are doing it in a more profound and personally challenging way than the middle-aged straight man whose identity crisis destroys his marriage as he buys the sports car and has the sad affair that he thinks will make him happy. It must be said that a man who fully transitions is a braver soul than the much more typical straight man who abandons his family due to his midlife crisis. And both may be motivated by the same quest for individual authenticity and fulfillment.

open. It is particularly frustrating to hear from those on the right who think of themselves as traditionalists how much they think these expressions of personal choice threaten our social stability. Their economic faith comprises the very shifting tectonic plates that have created social fault lines and earthquakes so vast they appear normal and acceptable, rather than disastrous. American right liberals, and their progressive cousins, cannot see the proverbial forest for the trees.

From this perspective, the increased interest in gender expressions *and* the growing right-wing interest in ethnic identities have their origins in the free-market "free to choose" ideology. But they are also reactions to that ideology, attempting to create domains that are not entirely dominated by market logic, such as gender and ethnic performance, including art forms. These often very creative domains nonetheless largely get recycled back into market logic, because expression itself is constantly co-opted by capitalists looking to sell expression and belonging. In a weak insurrection against neoliberalism, all these people on the American left and right are looking for some home, sense of purpose, belonging, and community beyond the liberal frame. But political/ideological/ethnic/gender/religious communities, on the left or right, can never substitute for the glue that holds human societies together: friendships, family, loving relationships based on trust and reciprocity, and a relationship with God. Such relationships have never been easy. They take a lot of work to establish and maintain. But in a world like ours, real relationships are both nearly impossible and necessary if we hope to step back from our current impasse.

In our world, most of the alternatives to these attempts at strong identity (choosing one's gender or fully expressing one's ethnic or religious identity even through excluding others) are thin by comparison. Being a member of a consuming community (such as Thrive Market, Minecraft, Starbucks, Lululemon, Genesis Fitness, Yoga with Adriene) gives people a very fleeting sense of belonging. It certainly has sold a lot of supplements, games, coffee, and workout clothes—the opportunities to purchase community feelings are endless—but it is apparently wearing thin with some, and others cannot afford to buy the feeling. Belonging to a political or social movement that is not just about consuming provides a thicker sense of belonging, because there is an ingredient of shared values. Belonging to an online movement in which people feel some semblance of fellowship as they digest content and discuss together is a much thicker relationship than that experienced by others who mainly consume and won't even take the time to have such conversations. It is already an act of relative daring.

In our postmodern environment, political ideology and its expressions in movements like ethno-nationalism and nonbinary gender identity are powerful options for people trying to find a home and a sense of meaning. These expressions are not, in the final analysis, in themselves going to overturn the liberal system, but they are stronger expressions of a deep dissatisfaction that has the potential to unsettle it. They hold the potential for positive change and deeply negative change, depending on how they are shaped and channeled by those who lead. But despite all this unsettling, and the strong signal of support for a populist turn in Donald Trump's improbable election, US Republicans and Democrats have continued to cling to neoliberal capitalism as though its operations are like forces of nature, with partisan differences only on the finer points. Both still agree that free-market capitalism is the economic ideal, though they support policies that distort the market. They agree that market imperatives are like natural laws whose impacts can be blunted, but which cannot ultimately be disobeyed. They do not address the underlying reasons for our cultural problems. Instead, they keep promoting a false faith and engaging in ideological strong-arming. This leads to increasing tensions and vulnerabilities as they continue to ignore our grave environmental, social, and cultural challenges.

6

Religious Strong-Arming

In July of 2021, thousands of people gathered at the geographical center of the United States, in Lebanon, Kansas, for a Prayer at the Heart of America rally. The first thing shown on the screen in the recording of this event was not a prayer to Jesus but a song of praise to America on her 245th anniversary, a video featuring patriotic images like waving flags, smiling blond women, and the word "America" embedded with the Stars and Stripes. This was followed by a child's voice saying the pledge of allegiance, along with images of cowboys riding horses. Then the video began to showcase America's international involvement with photos of aid workers and American soldiers, while a male narrator praised the US for protecting the world, "making it safe not only for us but for others." He also praised its leadership in medicine and in industry. America's commercial goods, including Disneyland, the narrator said, "have circled the earth." He then launched into biblical imagery, stating that the European settlers of America "drew an immediate parallel to the promised land of the Bible."

After the video finished, the camera panned onstage. There was no visible cross or other Christian symbol on screen. Instead, the US and other national flags were shown. Then, a variety of speakers got up to deliver prayers. The stated mission was to "reconsecrate the nation to God." To do this, P. Douglas Small, organizer of the event, said, "We are going back to the ancient prayers and covenants from the very beginning of this nation." Going back to ancient times (actually, modern times, around three hundred years ago at the most) was a theme of the event, as the speakers tried to tie their reconsecration of America to what they considered to be the sacred Christian covenants the first European settlers brought to North America's shores. Small spoke to the crowd about what had gone wrong with the country. He mentioned three things: 9/11, the 2008 financial crisis, and churches being shut down during the COVID quarantine. Interestingly, the moral issues of abortion, homosexuality, gender identity, and "communism" were absent from his remarks. He cited arguably the most famous classical liberal philosopher, John Locke: "On the video that we're about to show you, John Locke said that when parties, nations cannot agree and they cannot come to terms, their only recourse is to make an appeal in the courtroom of heaven asking for God's intervention."[1]

And thus, a liberal philosopher of toleration, whose actual thoughts on Christian faith were far from orthodox,[2] a philosopher whom D. C. Schindler would argue was a major proponent of liberal secularism (in Schindler's view the ultimate negation of God), was invoked as an authority for the participants' own "appeal to heaven."[3] God, the speaker argued, worked through the signers of the US Constitution. Forty-five minutes into the live stream, still no picture of Jesus had appeared, but more flags, soldiers, pickup trucks, and blond women had. At the end of the long day, participants lined up with prayer requests, which were burned in street barrels in an "offering by fire."[4]

This event, though relatively benign in its impact, represents the spiritual transference many American Christians make onto their nation-state, and it is part of the religious strong-arming that has pushed many Christians, for economic, social, and spiritual reasons of which they are perhaps only dimly aware, to accept and promote religious and political ideas at which they would never arrive on their own. This strong-arming abets political and commercial forces that flourish best

---

1. From the transcript of Projectpray's video, "Prayer at the Heart," 36:39. I capitalized "God" and added two commas, but otherwise this is a direct quote from the transcript, which exists due to the automated speech recognition of YouTube. John Locke was never mentioned on the video that came after this remark.

2. "The Source and Solution to Religious Conflict," in L. Johnson, *Locke and Rousseau*, 83–106.

3. Locke and revolutionary Americans used the phrase "appeal to heaven" as a stand-in for taking matters into their own hands, i.e., revolution, though it wasn't clear if Small knew this (Kang, "Appeal to Heaven").

4. Slezak, "Faithful Head," para. 5.

when people are stuck in an endless loop of political-ideological conflict. The type of Christianity on display, which is all about the individual receiving grace and forgiveness through his or her direct relationship with God, is a perfect accompaniment to a political ideology, shared by both Republicans and Democrats in the US, that promotes the "everyone must buy everything for themselves" economy. As Dr. Jordan Peterson recently tweeted (in response to Pope Francis's call to fight poverty), "There is nothing Christian about #SocialJustice. Redemptive salvation is a matter of the individual soul" (Mar. 2, 2023).[5]

At the Lebanon rally, as the speakers prayed that America and their various states would be reconsecrated to God, they focused on the political and geographic entities to which they belonged rather than what they themselves could do. The emphasis was put on changing the way the states and nation were governed, and how Christians were handled by their politicians, as though the only way to fix the world's problems were to fix the government. Hardly any time was given to how churches govern themselves, what their mission should be, how they should deal with their memberships, and what they owed to themselves and others.

If Jesus was most important, the source of Truth itself, why wasn't he front and center in Lebanon, Kansas? Why did the crosses that made it onto the site remain outside the tent?[6] Why all the imagery of cowboys and soldiers and flags, but a noticeable lack of Christ, the disciples, the cross? Was this Christianity? Yes and no. This was the peculiar American brand of Christianity, one that propagated a civil religion of American patriotism.[7] But to not understand the *difference* between religion and politics, to conflate the two in a strong civil religion, leads to grave moral errors.[8] Brian Zahnd, a self-described deconstructed evangelical minister, admits to sitting on his couch, eating pizza, and drinking a Coke, enjoying video footage of the US attack on Iraq in the wake of 9/11. Years later, he asked himself, what kind of Christian watches the destruction of people, land, and vital infrastructure as though it were entertainment?[9] Luckily, God sought Zahnd out for another, fuller conversion, and he has been

---

5. If we didn't already know that Peterson is anti-Catholic and pro-Protestant, we see some good evidence here.

6. There were three wooden crosses elsewhere on the property of the gathering where people could pray.

7. On America's civil religion, see Hewell, *Worship beyond Nationalism*.

8. I am referring to making a distinction between religion and politics here; I am not touching on the relationship between "church and state."

9. Zahnd, *Farewell to Mars*, 2.

trying his best to bring Evangelicals from "water to wine" ever since.[10] But despite the efforts of Zahnd and other Christian leaders who are having second thoughts, or never were on board the American civil religion, millions of Americans are convinced that to be a Christian one must be an American patriot, and a patriot of a certain sort.

Nothing expresses this American Christian imperative better than the American Patriot's Bible. On the cover is an American flag, the Declaration of Independence, pilgrims, and George Washington in prayer. On the spine, we find the Statue of Liberty. On the back cover there is a picture of the Iwo Jima US Marine Corps war memorial and a quote from Ronald Reagan. The Reagan quote at least refers to the Bible, where we can find "the answers to all the problems that mankind has ever known." There are no crosses, pictures of Jesus, or pictures of any stories or teachings from the Bible on the jacket. The Bible's publisher, Thomas Nelson, was acquired by Harper Collins in 2012. On the company's website, one reviewer for this Bible opines, "One of the BEST hardcover study bibles I've ever bought! Learning SO much about our founding fathers!"[11] The Bible's readers will learn about economics too. According to the Bible's editor, "Ingrained deep within the American spirit is the willingness and the desire to give an honest day's work for an honest day's pay. This independent spirit has no desire to simply exist on handouts from government or to depend on the generosity of others. It is this same independent spirit that has allowed America to create the greatest and strongest economy in the history of the world."[12]

---

10. For Zahnd's views on the use of military power and the value of warfare post–second conversion, see his classic *Farewell to Mars*.

11. For reviews, see https://faithgateway.com/products/the-nkjv-american-patriots-bible-hardcover-the-word-of-god-and-the-shaping-of-america?variant=34351515664520. In the Bible's "National Work Ethic" section, only one quote from Thessalonians is cited in support (Lee, *American Patriot's Bible*, "The Seven Principles of the Judeo-Christian Ethic," unnumbered front page, para. 6, pull quote), though the section says the work ethic runs throughout the Bible. "The Seven Principles of the Judeo-Christian Ethic," as listed in the front pages, are: the dignity of human life, the traditional monogamous marriage, a national work ethic, the right to a God-centered education, the Abrahamic covenant, common decency, and our personal accountability to God. Though the term and the concept "Judeo Christianity" go back further than the short life of America, and their principles are disputed by serious Jewish and Christian theologians, this rendition of the Judeo-Christian ethic assumes a Protestant emphasis on work, bourgeois virtues, and sexual morality. For a thorough review of the disputed origins and meaning of the term "Judeo-Christian ethic," see Nathan and Topolski, *Judeo-Christian Tradition?*

12. Lee, *American Patriot's Bible*, "The Seven Principles of the Judeo-Christian Ethic," unnumbered front page, para. 5.

The American Patriot's Bible emphasizes the same strong, dominating American economy as the rally in Lebanon. We have already seen how economic history laid the groundwork for the type of alienation that led people to become angry enough to seek out an ideological god, but now we must look at exactly what goes on at the spiritual level when people take this turn. Why and how do some Americans start mixing Christianity and ideology, forming a religion that often downplays Christ's teachings in favor of patriotism, economics, and liberal individualism? Though this chapter is focusing mainly on the right-wing manifestation of Christianity because of its current impact on American politics, we may as well ask, why and how do other American Christians get their faith caught up in being (often superficially) critical of patriotism, money, and liberal individualism? Why and how do these politicized Christians, right and left, persist over the course of a lifetime, such that some of their most ardent and vocal representatives are people over fifty?[13] The short answer is, in a world where people have been stripped of all organic forms of association—nuclear family, extended family, meaningful family life and provisions, local community, meaningfully human work—they are desperate for belonging, meaning, and purpose in and through a locally embedded church community. Churches present themselves as ideal, strong communities. But, too often, once in the door, individuals looking for a home are subjected to social, commercial, and spiritual pressures to agree and conform if they want to continue to receive a semblance of community, no matter how thin. Below I'll examine the cross these people find themselves on, in a phenomenon I'll call "religious strong-arming."

Strong-Arming

There is something very powerful inside the human psyche that needs to belong, and which readily submits to those who act as though they know what they're doing. We can think of the recent case, unrelated

---

13. A 2015 Gallup Poll revealed the tendency for highly conservative Christians to be over fifty. Frank Newport, Gallup senior scientist, stated that the data from interviews with 17,845 Republicans revealed that "religiosity is related to age, and the data show that the more a candidate narrows his or her focus down to highly religious and conservative Republicans, the more that candidate will be talking to an older audience. Ideology is also related to age, with conservatives significantly older than moderate/liberals" (Newport, "How Many," para. 7).

to religion but still powerfully proving the point, of a father who was able to move into his daughter's dorm, live there for months, and go on to manipulate, sexually and psychologically abuse, enslave, and rob her and several of her roommates, in what can only be described as a personality cult.[14] Of course the notorious Milgram obedience study (1961) and the Stanford prison experiment (1971) also spring to mind as classic examples that show that most people cannot stick to their own convictions when confronted with authority figures who tell them to do things they otherwise would never do, like shock people with electricity to the point of death.[15] This tendency to obey the would-be authority is a major explanatory factor in the strong-arming engaged in by some religious and political leaders. But the topic of this section is religious strong-arming, and in the case of religious strong-arming, what we have is the perfect storm of motivations. We have already learned that ideological mass movements work like secular religions—they tap into the deep religious impulse in human beings, an impulse that wants to connect with something higher and better than themselves. What about when religions act like ideological mass movements?

A friend tells me about a woman in her early twenties who lives out in the country with her husband and her son, a toddler. Her husband is a fundamentalist, and she is surrounded by a family that generally believes the same as he does. She also believes, having been raised by parents with very similar views. Among the beliefs that these people hold dear is the necessity of godly male leadership in the family. In this kind of family, women need to obey their husbands. They are generally supposed to stay at home and be mothers and homemakers. My friend says her cousin is being abused. She's been physically assaulted by her husband and generally worn down by his incessant demands for submission. She wants to leave because she has come to believe that her son is also not safe in their household. And so, my friend asks if she can stay at my house while she sorts things out, gets into the welfare system, gets counseling, and so on. I have a basement apartment that has the basics for separate living. Because I feel not only bad for this woman, but also some solidarity with her, I readily say yes.

It takes a while for her to get to my house. A couple of members of her family, who do not believe that a woman should stay in an abusive

14. Sgueglia and Almasy, "Father."
15. See Balfour et al., *Unmasking Administrative Evil*, "Compliance, Technical Rationality, and Administrative Evil," 23–38.

marriage, must figure out how to get her out of her house when her husband is gone. This takes time, planning, and negotiations with her. They also must figure out how to take some basic supplies for her toddler, and clothes for her. Most importantly they must arrange for someone, preferably a male someone, to stay with her in the apartment at least for a few days in case the husband figures out where she is and comes to get her.

We're all ready and, with very little notice, she arrives. I help her and her son get their stuff in and show her around, letting her know how some things work in the apartment. She's so young! She's quiet and just matter-of-factly settles in and attends to her son. I let her know that if she needs anything, she should just ask. For the next few days, someone is there with her, and I mainly watch for anything unusual. Then he leaves. I interact with her a bit more—going downstairs to visit. She asks me how to use the Internet TV. I show her and make guest accounts. She lets me know she's never been "allowed" to watch the shows from those services. When I'm upstairs, it sounds like she's mainly letting her son watch kids' shows. About two weeks in, she lets me know that she's sleeping in the walk-in closet with her son, because they prefer it. She's got bedding in my closet and clearly is using it this way. She seems a bit proud when she tells me she's never slept on my bed yet, and probably won't. I tell her she should do whatever she's comfortable with.

About three weeks in, after my friend has lined up counseling and social services for her, there are rumblings of repentance. She says she wants to leave, that she's unhappy not doing anything down there and just hiding out. She lets my friend know she feels like she made the wrong move, that her husband is not so bad, and even expresses some dissatisfaction with my friend for having intervened. When I go down to see her, she tells me that she was probably confused, and that her husband does the things he does because he cares about her and her son. I can see the handwriting on the wall. I've let her know once before that real Christianity doesn't look like this, that I'm confident Jesus does not want abused women and children to stay with their abusers. I tell her that again, and hope that at some other point, my words will come back to her. However, I realize that she's been thoroughly strong-armed by everyone who is important to her—her husband, her parents, his parents, their extended families, their community, and most importantly their pastors. She can't imagine leaving that world—it's the only one she knows. It is her social reality, and to leave it would mean completely reinventing herself, relying on strangers, taking enormous risks, trusting strange impersonal systems, and trusting strangers like me.

She leaves when a friend who supported her exodus comes to collect her. Her husband has promised not to strike back. He says he's willing to go to counseling, though it will probably be Christian counseling. She leaves so abruptly that items are left behind, including an expensive-looking stroller. She's not coming back, and she won't be in touch. If she tries again, she probably won't come here. I regret not spending more time with her. I thought that after all that she'd been through, she probably would like some space, some autonomy to say whom she talked to and when. I remember telling her that she could ask me down, but that I would ask permission before going downstairs, because I wanted her to know what having control over her space felt like. Now I wonder if I should have been more intrusive, to counterbalance what was going on in her head. She was clearly overwhelmed with what little freedom she had. I'll never know if being more friendly and guiding would have been the better move.

This story is far from an isolated incident. This is the most ordinary thing in the world in parts of the country where fundamentalist Christianity holds sway. Among other things, this type of Christianity has given cover to men who are tyrants in their homes. True leadership is not abusive, violent, selective, or emotionally domineering. True leadership is achieved when those who lead have qualities of character that are so obvious to all that others willingly trust them and take their cues from them. "Godly" leadership, however, is wielded by men who have few qualities that would automatically be recognized by spouses or others as authoritative. Because they do not possess authoritative qualities of character, these small men fall back on their mere sex; superficial, selective biblical backing; and the much more substantial backing of the other men in their churches and in their lives. They use the tried-and-true tactics of bullying, gaslighting, and ostracism to maintain their power. This type of intimidation and social pressuring—religious strong-arming—is the opposite of authority. It is what weak men do when all else has failed. And yet we see it, not only in small towns in rural Kansas, but in coastal population centers with megachurches.

Christianity Today broke a story in February 2023 that deeply resonated with my experience with that young woman. Twenty years prior, Grace Community Church, a megachurch in Sun Valley, California, had grossly failed in its responsibility to protect a woman and her children from their abusive husband and father. Eileen Gray went to the church for aid, counsel, and protection from her husband, because he was a danger not only to her but to her children. She also asked the church to find appropriate help and counseling for her husband, because he was also a danger to himself. She expected the aid that any member of a Christian community, perhaps particularly one that prides itself in masculine leadership, ought to expect. Instead, in a reversal of the chivalric values that the church's men would no doubt say they admire, she was bluntly told to suffer her husband's abuse, and to do it for Jesus. The church sided with her husband, and publicly disciplined and humiliated Eileen for not going back to him.[16]

The practice of John MacArthur, who is still the lead pastor, was to literally call out people in the church whom he thought were sinning, during services. Eileen, whose charges of spousal and child abuse were subsequently vindicated in a court of law, was one who was called out for "discipline," which amounted to Protestant excommunication (really ostracism) in front of the congregation. According to Julie Roys, of *The Roys Report*, Gray was publicly shamed twice. The first time MacArthur called her out was in May 2002. "In the months between her shamings, GCC members and staff repeatedly harassed and visited Eileen at home, urging her to obey the elders, according to Eileen and dozens of pages of court documents obtained by *The Roys Report*."[17] The second shaming from MacArthur, who never met with Eileen personally about her problems, was during communion on August 18, 2002.

These are the pastor's words: "I want to mention a sad situation, a person who is unwilling to repent. And the church bears responsibility before God to be the instrument of discipline. . . . This is what the Lord wants. He wants discipline . . . to be put out of the church, to be publicly shamed, to be put away from fellowship. In this case it applies to Eileen Gray."[18] According to Roys, MacArthur explained that Gray had sinned by leaving her husband. She had chosen "'to grant no grace at all, to take the children, to go away, to forsake him.' This, MacArthur emphasized, meant rejecting 'all the instruction and counsel of the

---

16. A video of this incident is on the *Roys Report* page cited below. For another critical perspective on MacArthur's church from a broader point of view on the church's theology concerning women, see Reid, "Unjust Signifying Practices."

17. Roys, "John MacArthur Shamed," para. 20.

18. Roys, "John MacArthur Shamed," para. 3.

RELIGIOUS STRONG-ARMING

elders, all instruction from the Word of God.'"[19] MacArthur then told the congregation to "treat her as an unbeliever"[20] and led the church in singing "Amazing Grace."[21]

Twenty years went by. During that time, Gray's husband was convicted for aggravated child molestation, corporal injury to a child, and child abuse. He was given a sentence of twenty-one years to life in prison, and yet the church apparently never recanted its condemnation of Eileen or reconsidered its ways. So, when her children were all adults, Eileen Gray decided that she would no longer remain silent due to fears of reprisals from the church and spoke to Julie Roys. Then-church elder Hohn Cho, an attorney, was asked by other elders to take another look at the case. But when it was evident to him that the church had done wrong, he found himself on the outs as well. He was asked either to stop talking or to leave the church. Cho decided to leave, and then something both predictable and extremely disturbing started to happen. He began to hear from other people about additional cases, including one that was ongoing in the fall of 2022. If he had had any doubts that the problem was continuing, he was quickly disabused of them.[22]

Christianity Today was able to interview eight women from Grace Community Church who had experienced the same strong-arming. All of them were advised to forgive, stay with, and submit to their husbands, even if they were abusive. In a case very similar to Eileen's, another woman was told by Bill Shannon, a man who served as a counselor for the church, to go back home and submit to her husband. Church elders submitted sworn statements on behalf of her husband, including defending him in an incident that involved him kissing his daughter using his tongue. The woman was cited Bible verses to "believe all things" and forgive "seventy times seven," which in the case of spousal abuse functions as gaslighting and causes the victim to blame themselves for their abusers' actions and their own lack of loving forgiveness. As *Christianity Today* puts it, "In marital counseling, pastors asked wives whether their attitudes contributed to the patterns of violence, anger, and manipulation in their relationships."[23] But this woman, despite being gaslighted repeatedly, was also strong enough to power through

---

19. Roys, "John MacArthur Shamed," para. 4.
20. Roys, "John MacArthur Shamed," para. 5.
21. Roys, "John MacArthur Shamed," para. 7.
22. Shellnutt, "Grace Community Church," para. 5.
23. Shellnutt, "Grace Community Church," para. 53.

the abuse of the church and move on to reach a settlement with her husband, separating from him. Before it was all over, the betrayal of her church caused this woman to doubt the existence of God. After leaving the church, she was able to regain her faith and separate the church's actions from her understanding of God.[24]

The founder and still the leader of Grace Community Church, John MacArthur, is a huge name in conservative Christianity. In fact, according to *Baptist News*, "there is no single pastor who has been more influential on young theological conservatives in the last 50 years than MacArthur. Not Billy Graham. Not Adrian Rogers. Not Charles Stanley. Not John Piper."[25] He is a huge industry, earning a sizable salary, payments for side hustles, book contracts, speaking fees, etc. "MacArthur has been the gold standard for conservative and Reformed theology not only through his preaching but through his books, his commentaries, his study Bible, his podcasts, his videos, his conferences, his public appearances."[26] A variety of sources put MacArthur's net worth at $10–$20 million, but there is no way of knowing for sure what he is worth.[27] MacArthur owns several homes and, we can say at the very least, does not live like an average American.[28]

What causes thousands of people to shut off their critical thinking skills to the point that they would either ignore years of contradictory behavior from their church leaders or endure years of outright abuse from them before they even think of separating from a church and finding someplace else to go? Why wouldn't a good percentage of those thousands of Grace Community Church members be able to see that they had gotten themselves into a cult of personality, and more, an actual self-reinforcing, life-draining, and money-draining cult that could even put some of them in the way of bodily harm? How could

---

24. Grace Community Church's website lists Bill Shannon as a counselor as of March 9, 2023, stating, "Bill has served on staff since 1989, and he is the co-pastor of Anchored, a Sunday morning adult fellowship group. Bill oversees and is actively involved in the biblical counseling ministry—he teaches discipleship counseling and marriage and family classes through Grace Equip and provides formal and informal counseling for church members and regular attenders of Grace Church. He is also a member of the Association of Certified Biblical Counselors (ACBC) where he serves as a fellow" (Grace Church, "Bill Shannon").

25. Wingfield, "John MacArthur," para. 5.

26. Wingfield, "John MacArthur" para. 6.

27. Sam, "John MacArthur Net Worth"; Mercer, "John F. MacArthur"; Stefan, "MacArthur Net Worth."

28. Roys, "Prosperous Lifestyle."

churchgoers sit through communion service hearing other people being called out by their lead pastor and not think that they might be next? Why do people get attracted to this kind of warped strong community and stick with it despite all the warning signs?

For church member Chris Orozco, the moment came in and around 2015, when he realized that MacArthur was preaching politics instead of Christianity and wrote him a letter of objection. As he recapitulated in another letter to MacArthur, this one in 2017 after the Trump election, and after forty years of membership at Grace Community Church: "In your political pronouncements, I did not hear God's word preached, nor did the light of the gospel of salvation shine forth, and Christ was not lifted up or honored, but rather your words lifted up and installed upon your pulpit an ideology and a political party rather than the gospel and Christ as the focal centerpiece. This created a huge stumbling block for me in continuing to sit with peace of heart and soul under the teaching ministry at Grace."[29]

Perhaps the reason that Orozco's realization came only after forty years was that the church had drifted slowly over those years into error, having started out with fresh and good intentions. But also, Orozco points out repeatedly that leaving the church meant huge and lasting losses of relationships, social stability, and personal identity. As he began to realize that he no longer felt at home, and that he was reworking his identity in opposition to the church's pronouncements, Orozco experienced the pain of exile, something like the sense of sorrow and emptiness that comes in the wake of a divorce: "I also began to suffer a great sense of loss—loss for the comfort and confidence I had known and felt within the teaching at Grace, and loss because of the growing separation I experienced from the community at Grace, from the family of believers of which I was once joyously part."[30] So difficult was this process of separating that he did not officially leave the church until September 2020, after the church's now-familiar Trump-inspired politics festered in his consciousness for quite a while, and only after an extraordinary effort in the way of correspondence to try to get MacArthur and other church leaders to see that they were making mistakes.[31]

---

29. Orozco, "Broken Coffee Cup," para. 10.
30. Orozco, "Broken Coffee Cup," para. 11.
31. You can read Chris Orozco's account of all this correspondence ("Letters, Correspondence, & Dialogue").

Chris Orozco is far from alone. Most people who go down the path of highly politicized or extreme Christianity do so because a church has become their entire world. The costs of diverging from the community are very high. Those who decide to disagree or to leave risk alienating their immediate and extended families, losing their friends, even in some cases losing their jobs. In addition, they risk their very identity, their sense of purpose. Because of all of this, there is a very good chance that to leave, they would have to reinvent themselves and start anew, a very frightening prospect that might end badly. This radical dependency is not some sort of ignorance or retrograde choice. It stems from the fundamental fact that human beings are naturally social. They are not simply rational liberal individuals making informed autonomous decisions every step of the way. Quite the contrary, they are not only social, but hierarchical in temperament.[32] Therefore, as hard as we might try to think in egalitarian terms, we humans tend to cede power and responsibility automatically and even instinctively, both to the herd and to those within it who act like they know what they are doing.

This tendency to cede power and authority to the masses and their would-be leaders has been intensified by certain factors in modern times. Alexis de Tocqueville noticed that, ironically, the very drive towards liberal individualism and "equality of conditions" created conformity. The more isolated individuals became from former sources of guidance and meaning (extended family, higher culture, and aristocratic and religious leaders), the more they were required to manufacture their own opinions and mores. But because it was impossible for individuals to come up with all the answers on their own, they looked towards the only source of authority that seemed legitimate in a democracy, the opinion of the masses. The leveling effect of democracy, compounded by the northern commercial character, tended to create people who ceded their judgment to the crowd. The crowd, in turn, and for the same reasons, looked towards experts and opinion leaders for what to think. The result was less, not more, independent reasoning. To counteract these tendencies, Tocqueville wrote, Americans would have to do everything right—provide high-quality education to men and women, foster intermediate civic and religious organizations, and promote true civic virtue. Clearly, the country failed to do any of that very well.

---

32. Robert Michels called this the "iron law of oligarchy" in his book *Political Parties*, originally written in 1911. Aristotle got a jump on Michels by a couple of millennia by reasonably arguing both facts in his *Politics*.

Psychologists who disagreed with each other on almost everything focused on the problem of mass-mindedness from different angles. Gustave Le Bon argued that the critical faculties of mind literally shut off in a crowd, producing a state like hypnotism.[33] Sigmund Freud agreed with Le Bon on the hypnotic quality of mass psychology. Individuals in a mass feel they are safe to act upon libidinal impulses they would otherwise repress, and they are susceptible to aggressive suggestions in this state about how to express those impulses. Freud observed that churches are crowds motivated by a strong love of the father figure, Christ, as well as love for each other. He classified churches and armies as artificial groups, "that is, a certain external force is employed to prevent them from disintegrating and to check alterations in their structure. As a rule, a person is not consulted, or is given no choice, as to whether he wants to enter such a group; any attempt at leaving it is usually met with persecution or with severe punishment or has quite definite conditions attached to it." Freud concluded, "It would appear as though we were on the right road towards an explanation of the principal phenomenon of group psychology: the individuals' lack of freedom in a group. If everyone is bound in two directions by such an intense emotional tie, we shall find no difficulty in attributing to that circumstance the alteration and limitation which have been observed in his personality."[34] As we already know, Carl Jung differed with Freud on the sexual origins of the drive towards mass mentality and leaders who represented "mana personalities." Instead, Jung derived the attraction into mass psychosis from the primitive "participation mystique," i.e., the archaic identification of the various archetypes that make up the self with gods and other external objects, including forces of nature and godlike leaders. In modern times, this primitive tendency came to the fore in mass psychosis, attaching to authoritarian leaders and ideologies.[35]

Meanwhile, José Ortega y Gasset theorized the dominance of the masses in his 1930 classic *The Revolt of the Masses*. He pointed to a change in modern times (through the urbanization I discussed earlier, fueled by capitalism), that concentrated masses of ordinary people into urban areas and then slowly raised the average standard of living so that

---

33. Le Bon, *Crowd*.

34. Freud, *Group Psychology*; see also Freud, *Civilization and Its Discontents*.

35. Jung credits Lucien Lévy-Bruhl with the concept of "participation mystique" (*Psychological Types*, 82).

they could aspire to a comfortable existence and beyond.[36] Because of the psychological effects of population concentration, which is now extended to almost everyone regardless of location in the age of TV, the Internet, and social media, the average man (those who want to be nothing more than they already are) triumphed over the more qualified "minority" (those who strive to take on more and understand better). Ortega argued that liberal democracy was giving way to a kind of "hyperdemocracy" in which the masses were no longer kept in check by rule of law but exerted their force via the pressure of their numbers and, unfortunately, sometimes under the sway of demagogues.[37]

Suffice it to say that scholars from very different political and theoretical perspectives have noted the mob or crowd mentality, now a ubiquitous part of our lives. They all seem to agree that the technological, economic, and social organizational advancements since the nineteenth century have ramped up the prevalence and intensity of mass behavior. Thinkers as different as Carl Jung and Charles Taylor have observed that the rise of modernity was problematic for direct religious experience. People sought religious identification with worldly figures and ideas, maybe more so for those in groups looking for real experience, i.e., evangelical, Pentecostal Christians, etc. In this chapter, I hope I've made it clear that worldly leaders in the guise of pastors and other religious authorities are *the most likely* to easily obtain the enthusiastic and stubborn obedience of many people who long for order and love. Add to all this the type of precarity and insecurity felt by many in our world, described in previous chapters, and it should not be a surprise that people, dislocated and detached from traditional sources of meaning and identity, will "cling to" politicized religious leaders at all costs. These leaders have tapped into the ultimate heady brew of fundamental power, taking millions of people with them.

In comparison with the abusive dorm dad, or the Milgram experiment's white coat–wearing doctors, the pastor of a popular church has even more credibility for a new participant. For those who still are open to faith, the pastor represents the gateway to truly experiencing the transcendent reality people long for. When the pastor starts to take command, pushing those who want to trust that the spiritual life is real and can guide

---

36. Ortega did not focus on capitalism because he thought that throughout human history there had been times of "plenitude" in which people became complacent and decadent.

37. Hoover, "Political Thought."

them, he is dealing with the people most susceptible to being manipulated. Just as the corrupt medieval Catholic Church leaders abused their power to enrich themselves, or recent and contemporary Catholic priests and Boy Scout leaders abused their authority to molest young people in their spheres of influence, today's politicized Christian leaders use the faithful's strong inclination to trust and to obey God's representatives to their own advantage, for fame, money, and power. From the Christian standpoint, what they are doing is morally problematic in the extreme, and increasingly so the more cynically conscious they are of their role as financial, political, and power manipulators. The unfolding history of Fox News's interaction with right-wing religious leaders and the Trump campaign reveals this conscious manipulation for the sake of profit.

It's common knowledge that Fox News is the only news source that is trusted by millions of Americans.[38] Fox News serves as a cultural guide and a major virtue signal for right-leaning Christians, who treat the channel as a matter of faith, unquestioningly. But the Fox News alliance with Christian right pastors is perhaps less well known by those who do not frequently watch the channel. For the many who do primarily watch Fox, it may surprise them to know how much about business this alliance is. For example, Fox has used Dallas megachurch pastor Robert Jeffress, Plano Texas Baptist pastor Jeremiah J. Johnston, and former Catholic priest Jonathan Morris as contributors; and evangelical, fundamentalist, and many Catholic Christians look to them, and to Fox News generally, for their guidance about what to think, not only about politics but about Christianity.[39]

Going all the way back to Glenn Beck's days on Fox News, the agenda of supporting right-wing Christianity and persecuting those who disagree has been a significant subset of Fox News activities.[40] Beck famously declared, much like Jordan Peterson later, that Christianity was not about "social or economic justice," and proceeded to use Fox funds and staffers to go after Rev. Jim Wallace of *Sojourners Magazine*, a left-leaning Christian journal.[41] *Sojourners* is a sort of mirror image of Fox's right-wing politicization of Christianity. But his attack, and many other

---

38. In a recent survey, 61 percent of white Evangelicals stated that they watched Fox News (Burge, "Faith in Numbers," para. 9).

39. Fox News, "Dr. Robert Jeffress"; Fox News, "Jonathan Morris"; Fox News, "Jeremiah J. Johnston."

40. Glenn Beck is a Mormon.

41. Strider, "Fox News Funds Research."

attacks over the years from Fox News personalities against Christian leaders they consider too "woke," is similar in effect to John MacArthur's public shaming of Eileen Gray. The message to Fox News viewership is to stay within the fold, don't question, don't find common ground, because social ostracization and shaming could happen to you too.

In 2023, news came out about the cynical manipulation of Trump supporters by Fox News personalities (who privately did not believe what they were saying about Trump or the 2020 election results). Fox accurately called the election for Biden in 2020 at the appropriate time, but its viewers were in disbelief and grew angry, eliciting a doubling down of Fox's public support for Trump, including much coverage questioning the validity of the election. Fox actively promoted the idea that voter fraud had happened, among other ways, via faulty voting machines. This tactic might have shored up their viewer base. But a lawsuit from Dominion Voting Systems, a company whose voting machines were attacked as flawed, was what brought to the public's attention the comments of Fox personalities who clearly disliked Trump. They knew he had lost the election, contrary to what they said on air.[42] As the *New York Times* reported: "Documents released in recent weeks as part of a $1.6 billion defamation suit against Fox News by Dominion Voting Systems have revealed extraordinary private communications and depositions from the network's star hosts and executives. In those statements, many of them expressed disbelief about President Donald J. Trump's false claims that the 2020 election was stolen from him, even though the network continued to promote many of those lies on the air."[43] Tucker Carlson, on air one of Trump's most ardent supporters on Fox said this about Trump two weeks before Joe Biden's inauguration: "He's a demonic force, a destroyer. But he's not going to destroy us. I've been thinking about this every day for four years."[44]

In these Fox News revelations, we have definitive proof of conscious, cynical manipulation of an audience, including a vast number

---

42. Bauder et al., "Fox, Dominion."

43. Peters and Robertson, "Fox Stars," para. 1 from original article. Paragraph 1 from updated article similarly reads: "Newly disclosed messages and testimony from some of the biggest stars and most senior executives at Fox News revealed that they privately expressed disbelief about President Donald J. Trump's false claims that the 2020 election was stolen from him, even though the network continued to promote many of those lies on the air."

44. Robertson, "5 Times Tucker Carlson," under "On the Aftermath of the Capitol Riots."

of right-leaning Christians, for reasons that were almost entirely profit driven. Fox News wanted to maintain and increase its ratings, and hence its advertising revenue, and it had its influencers put out whatever views and news achieved those ends, with no regard for their viewers' well-being. Influencers like pastor Robert Jeffress and Jonathan Morris repeatedly weighed in to let Fox's Christian viewers know that supporting Trump was the right thing to do. Morris opined on the moral rightness of Trump's border policy in response to the Democrats' calls for more open borders in 2020, going so far as to speak for all US Catholic bishops, indicating that they differed with the pope's position.[45] More recently Jeffress predicted that either Mike Pence or Donald Trump would be well supported by evangelical voters in the 2024 election, but that Trump would most likely be the first evangelical choice.[46]

Figures like Jeffress, Morris, and others like Ralph Reed and Jerry Falwell Jr. work with Fox News routinely to influence politics, and Fox uses them to hold on to its Christian right viewership. What I want to emphasize here is that the people in their crosshairs, whether watching on TV, participating in their social media mystique, or sitting in their pews, are being spiritually strong-armed. The sources of power, psychological and spiritual in nature, that these figures use to influence people and win power are extremely difficult for people to resist, and resistance when it does occur brings instant pain in loss of friends, family, connections, jobs, and identity. Openly saying that Fox News is lying can shatter one's entire social circle. This is the cross that many people endure every day, so enmeshed in it that they are no longer fully responsible for their religious and political decisions.

Strongholds

Still, why can't people stand up to social coercion like this at least when their well-being, and that of their family members, is at stake, or when grave moral lines are clearly crossed? Need I remind the reader of cases of extreme cult influences leading to disasters? The Jim Jones catastrophe in the 1980s, in which over nine hundred cult members either obediently

45. Parke, "Jonathan Morris."
46. "My sense of where we are right now—and I've talked to the former president recently—I think that, eventually, if not immediately, evangelicals will end up coalescing around former President Trump again," Jeffress said (Edson, "Evangelical Vote at Stake," para. 4).

committed mass suicide or were murdered by their fellow Peoples Temple members, is a case in point. Jones's message sounded good enough on the surface. It promoted a communal type of "socialism" and radical racial equality. When interviewed years later, some of Jones's own children and other survivors explained that even when they were told to work long hours and follow Jones wherever he went, they felt good about what they were accomplishing. They wanted to work hard for a goal and ideal bigger than themselves, and they also enjoyed the genuine camaraderie with their fellow members. Yet they were also so thoroughly manipulated by Jones that they not only followed him to Guyana, but willingly gave their lives to show their resolve and dedication to his values.[47]

The phenomenon of cult followers blind to major danger signals is very real. We might think of Jonestown as at the far end of a spectrum in which Grace Community Church stands in the middle. The followers of Rev. John MacArthur share with the Peoples Temple members a lack of critical responses to unethical moves made by leaders in the church. The result at Grace was endangered women and children, not mass suicide. But if we see churches like Grace as on the spectrum of cult behavior, we can avoid casting blame upon people who are better thought of as psychologically and spiritually enmeshed. They are burdened by a phenomenon that has appeared again and again in human history and is capable of overpowering individual human reason and will. In fact, we all accept things as normal and acceptable that, if we really looked at them objectively, would appear as absurd and harmful. Members of churches like Grace (and there are many) are, from a spiritual perspective, enslaved.

One way to understand cultlike behavior that leads to the destruction of health, happiness, and life itself is to apply the concept of "spiritual stronghold." This is a well-known concept in evangelical and Pentecostal circles, but not so well known outside of those circles.[48] According to Beth Moore, strongholds are explained by the apostle Paul in 2 Cor 10:5. She writes, "Basically, a stronghold is any argument or pretension that "sets itself up against the knowledge of God." She continues, "A stronghold is anything that exalts itself in our minds, 'pretending' to be bigger or more powerful than our God. It steals much of our focus and causes us to feel overpowered. Controlled. Mastered."[49] In our day,

---

47. Nicholson and Lopez, "Jonestown."

48. See J. Gordon, *Evangelical Spirituality*; Howard and Albrecht, "Pentecostal Spirituality."

49. For Moore, strongholds are from "the enemy," that is, from Satan (*Praying God's*

in the United States, it is foremost from the religious right that we find the most egregious cases of *spiritual* strong-arming, and it is there that we find the greatest political implications, the type of behavior that indicates a stronghold may be in play. The religious left plays its part as the other side of the echo chamber and may also be a part of that stronghold. When left-leaning Christians, and progressives generally, approach the religious right with disdain and moral condemnation, they only make the situation worse. *And yet they do it repeatedly.* They are, literally, blaming the victim, and not addressing the strongholds.[50]

Progressives of all types, Christian or otherwise, tend to argue that American Christian conservatives simply need to learn about science and history, or give up their nostalgia, or just stop hating. Such arguments miss the mark and help perpetuate their brothers' and sisters' enmeshment in their stronghold. Groups hold together more closely when there is a clear, distinct, and distinctly "evil" other with whom to compare themselves.[51] When the Christian right obsesses about a particular phenomenon like transgender people or guns, they are validated by the instant mirror-image pushback of their counterparts on the left. The outcome: neither side spends time on questions of the deepest and most lasting significance for Christians, such as who God is; what he wants from us; what we should do as individuals, as groups, within churches and beyond, apart from political posturing, lobbying, canvassing, and voting. When neither side deals with these questions, nothing good happens, and the stronghold has triumphed.

Christianity beyond Ideology

I've already touched on the phenomenon of extremism in previous chapters in the context of the economic and psychological origins of extreme political ideologies, the 2016 election of Donald Trump, and

---

Word, 3). Pope Francis would agree with the idea of this, even if he doesn't use the same language. He has spoken of the idolatry involved in thinking that technology and human invention can make the earth and everything in it, including human nature, entirely plastic and manipulable, and that human beings can use their own inventions to escape from any natural predicament they have caused (*Laudato Si'*).

50. While not using the "strongholds" language, Joanna Kaftan explores this phenomenon on the right and left through a content analysis of two Christian publications, the left-leaning *Sojourners* and the right-leaning *Evangelicals*. If anything, Kaftan finds more reactivity and specific politicization in *Sojourners* ("Religious Messages").

51. Helm, "Hate."

the subsequent political instability the country experienced and which culminated in the Capitol insurrection. Here I am addressing the phenomenon of the radicalization of the religious right, of which Christian nationalism is a sort of subcategory, explicitly from the vantage point of Christian faith.[52] *This* section is not aimed primarily at the followers but at the influencers, the people who bear responsibility for wielding their power either without full consideration of its consequences or with outright knowledge of those consequences and a disregard for people's welfare. Somehow, for many of these leaders, from theologians to local pastors, Christianity has become identified with things like hyper-masculinity, exclusively male leadership, self-defense, military power, and strong national borders.[53] For instance, probably the most sadly humorous recent example of the common hyper-masculine mentality comes from House Representative Lauren Boebert (R–Colo), who in 2022 at a Christian conference, remarked, "On Twitter, a lot of the little Twitter trolls, they like to say, 'Oh, Jesus didn't need an AR-15, how many AR-15s do you think Jesus would've had?" She continued, "Well, he didn't have enough to keep his government from killing him."[54]

After quoting Boebert's remark for *The Hill*, reporter Chloe Folmar reminded her readers that "the Christian New Testament teaches that Jesus willingly died on a cross to take the penalty for the sins of those who follow him and that he dissuaded his followers from using violence to try to save him, including one instance in which Jesus rebuked a disciple for cutting off the ear of a soldier who arrested him." While Folmar's

---

52. Various nationalisms can be seen as secular faiths, as I argued in ch. 6. David A. Ritchie reaches a similar conclusion, that nationalism is demonic and offers a false gospel (*Why Do the Nations Rage?*).

53. This type of masculinity is well described in Kristin Du Mez's book *Jesus and John Wayne*. I should note that I disagree with Du Mez's thesis that white Evangelicals have simply made a wrong turn in religion and that this is what has caused the fracturing of the country. Hopefully some of the deeper reasons (economic, psychological, philosophical) for the fracturing have been laid out in previous chapters in an understandable way. This chapter is dealing with the outcome of these deeper reasons. That is, our ideological divisions and their religious manifestations are the ultimate unfolding result of dynamics that go back at least several centuries. Du Mez uses the same title as the song from the Gaither band and does mention that song in her conclusion. She acknowledges that the song does not support the equation of Jesus with John Wayne. The song makes quite a distinction between Jesus and John Wayne, which are depicted as temperamental opposites. One might compare the Gaither band's take on Jesus with Rep. Boebert's mentioned next to see how far many Evangelicals have departed from more biblical notions of Jesus.

54. Folmar, "Boebert," paras. 2–3.

theology is debatable in its assumption that substitutionary atonement is the meaning of Jesus's death on the cross, her take on New Testament teaching is particularly poignant because this is the exact reading of the crucifixion that evangelical and fundamentalist Christians tend to adopt.[55] If Jesus died willingly on the cross as a way to appease God and save people from eternal damnation, as conservative Evangelicals tend to argue, his entire mission would have been nullified if he had taken up arms to prevent his death. Indeed, the entire message of the Gospel would be different if Jesus was either a defender of abusive husbands or a warlike Messiah who vanquished his foes by force. When Jesus arrived, he wasn't recognizable to many of the Jews as the Messiah precisely because he did not purport to be a politically revolutionary figure. Jesus was something different, by all New Testament accounts.

Boebert and opinion leaders like her no doubt struggle with the fact that Jesus died on a cross rather than simply ruling through his awesome power and telling his followers to take up arms. But Boebert's joke about Jesus perhaps needing weapons to protect himself reveals a deep impiety, or at least a lack of concern about the consequences of offending God. In Boebert we have an example of a political leader who inspires many Christians who, at least in this example, are led to treat Jesus in a shockingly light manner. Politicians and religious rhetoricians like Boebert, when cornered, may try to tell us that they were just being humorously ironic, and that we have misunderstood the context.[56] However, at least in Boebert's case, what Christian is so impious in the name of good humor as to blaspheme the essential nature of God? In Boebert we have an example of a political leader who inspires and leads many Christians, whose casual comments unequivocally deny the divinity and mission of Jesus Christ.[57] But many American Christians still cannot see the glaring contradiction because they have been

---

55. As Du Mez puts it: "To be an evangelical, according to the National Association of Evangelicals, is to uphold the Bible as one's ultimate authority, to confess the centrality of Christ's atonement, to believe in a born-again conversion experience, and to actively work to spread this good news and reform society accordingly" (*Jesus and John Wayne*, 5). One could argue that Evangelicals who take the Christian nationalist turn adhere to none of these things in practice, even if they would still say that they do, because other tenets of their faith have been so thoroughly usurped by political ideology and nationalism.

56. Milo Yiannopoulos is the pioneer in this regard, and many have followed suit. See Wilson, "Hiding in Plain Sight."

57. God would need only to will his enemies to stop; he would not need physical weapons to do so.

strong-armed. They are, as I argued in my last book, "ideologically possessed," a category that is psychological in its origins, but which does not preclude the possibility of real spiritual possession. Those who are possessed either psychologically or spiritually cannot free themselves without help. They are literally enslaved to demonic forces, and they will strongly resist any attempt to exorcize their demons.[58]

If we need any more proof that the Christian right option proposed by so many pastors, politicians, and opinion leaders throughout the years constitutes a grave error, we can simply contemplate Christ crucified and find the negation of all their cherished notions—Jesus is obviously not about self-defense, military power, protecting his interests through borders or otherwise, or being a powerful manly man. To think otherwise is to engage in a mythical remaking of Jesus into Zeus. Yet to be an American Christian from the right-liberal perspective is to love the US flag, own guns, lead the family if one is a man, and consistently vote Republican. Whether any or all those things is worthy of doing is beside the point—none of those things is what Jesus cared about. To flip right-wing Christian concerns around so that we can see them more clearly, these leaders signal that anyone who does not vote Republican, thinks that guns should be controlled, or shares full or partial leadership with his spouse cannot be a Christian. That is spiritual strong-arming, designed to keep everyone in the stronghold. It seems that many right-leaning evangelical Christian pastors and theologians are uncomfortable with who Jesus really is. They do not want to engage the biblical Jesus, because that Jesus would ask them to do things, and think things, they are not temperamentally inclined to do or think.

The equation of religious faith with political positions, indeed the subsuming of faith under political beliefs and activity, is a heresy.[59] It is morally akin to the corrupt politicization of the late medieval Catholic Church. The medieval church forgot that political power and wealth were not the targets. And just as we blame the pope and Catholic hierarchy for sometimes leading people astray in medieval times, we should primarily blame the leadership and not the "peasants" in the churches' pews for our current corruption. The reason we do not is because we live in supposedly democratic times wherein every person is supposed to be completely responsible for all their thoughts and decisions all the time.

---

58. L. Johnson, *Ideological Possession*.

59. While this is a strong term, I am not alone in using it to describe this phenomenon. See Leithart, *Between Babel and Beast*, 71, 152.

From this angle, if we allow ourselves to be enmeshed, we have made a mistake, and we are to blame. But we know that this moral individualism is a liberal fiction, and it functions to get the powerful influencers and would-be authorities off the hook.

The heresy that religious right leaders are promoting is a strong form of idolatry. In the Old Testament, we see idolatry sometimes directly, as when the Hebrew people choose to worship false gods in the form of statues. We see it early on in the story of the tower of Babel, in which God destroyed the tower and confused the peoples' languages and dispersed them, because "if now, while they are one people and all have the same language, they have started to do this, nothing they presume to do will be out of their reach" (Gen 11:6). Karl Barth notes that God stopped the building of the tower (by multiplying languages) not because the new technology used to build it was inherently sinful, but because of the people's intent in building it. The intention, as Barth quotes Gen 11:4, is to "make us a name, lest we be scattered abroad upon the face of the whole earth." God knew that the peoples' desire was to reach up to him, not in worship but to make themselves his equals, based, so they thought, on their own efforts. They were full of hubris. Barth writes, "What is brought under this judgment is the care and therefore the arrogance with which unity tried to help and assert and maintain itself, to make itself a name, to play the part of providence in respect of the blessing of unity entrusted to it." The lesson was supposed to be that "everything is in vain, and moves self-evidently to destruction sooner or later, that is enterprise by man with the same intention as this building."[60] Among the Christian right, the risk of heresy comes with hyper-politicization and church empire-building with an intent to develop a purely human power. Their political theology really does not encourage knowledge of God as like Jesus, and its fruit does not reveal trust in God as revealed in the New Testament. In their politics, hope is replaced with ambition, and confidence in God is replaced by trust in an organization, a party, or even one man or woman. Stanley Hauerwas elucidates the difference when he juxtaposes hope with mere optimism, arguing that optimism is hope without truth: "Hope—that is, the person who lives a hopeful life and lives it well—knows the limitations of power. It knows that optimism needs the truth, and that hope is schooled in faith and love. The hopeful life must bend to the demands of truth, or it will, by a paradox as certain as the fact that power

---

60. Barth, *Doctrine of Creation*, 316.

corrupts, lose its hope, become mere optimism, then turn to cynicism, and finally issue in a despairing life."[61]

Hauerwas thinks that it is necessary to take a critical stance towards the liberal order that most American Christians unthinkingly accept, precisely because liberalism is inherently hostile to the very idea of Christian church and values. Referring to the speech by Aleksandr Solzhenitsyn, which warned the West of the consequences of its own faults as the Cold War settled in on the American mind, Hauerwas writes: "We . . . feel puzzled by critiques of our society such as that of Solzhenitsyn. For it is the brunt of his charge that a polity is ultimately judged by the kind of people it produces, and from such a perspective our society can only be found wanting. He suggests that for all the injustice and terror of the Russian and Eastern European societies, they have been through a spiritual training far advanced of the Western experience."[62]

Solzhenitsyn could see that Western society, whose economic and technological progress had vastly outstripped the USSR and whose people were undeniably freer, had spawned "mass living habits, introduced by the revolting invasion of publicity, by TV stupor, and by intolerable music." As Hauerwas points out, the typical Christian response to this critique is to try to separate politics from culture, and then to critique the vulgar and degraded culture that our system tends to produce. Then they deny that there is any connection between that culture and our liberal political and economic philosophy. Solzhenitsyn knew that liberal politics and economics wrongly denied any connection between a country's politics, economics, and its culture and moral values, but like Leo Strauss, he argued for the "classical view."[63] His speech made it clear that there was a connection. Hauerwas explains: "In effect he is suggesting that when freedom becomes an end in itself people lose their ability to make sacrifices for worthy ends. The problem with our society is not that democracy has not worked, but that it has, and the results are less than good." He adds, "The constant desire to have still more things and a still better life and the struggle to obtain them imprints many Western faces with worry and even depression, though it is customary to conceal such feelings."[64]

---

61. Hauerwas, *Christian Existence Today*, 211.
62. Hauerwas, *Community of Character*, 74.
63. Hauerwas, *Community of Character*, 75.
64. Hauerwas, *Community of Character*, 75.

Hauerwas thus refers to the ingredients in strong-arming. The values of Christianity do not naturally align with material largess, needless consumption, gross inequality, and environmental despoiling. Even our own human natures rebel internally against the dynamics of capitalist market imperatives. But we are locked into a stronghold—there seems no way beyond the system as it currently exists. This inherently painful and bewildering situation elicits in us more consumerism as a way of validating the existing order in which we all participate. The momentary rush we can hope for from our consumption, at whatever financial level we can muster, may temporarily block out the deep sense of emptiness that lurks in the background. But ultimately, we cannot escape it, and more and more of us experience the burgeoning psychological ailments of our relatively affluent society—anxiety, depression, addictions, reliance on psychopharmaceuticals to make it through our day, to get to sleep, etc.

To be clear, it is not that Christian political activity is always wrong, or that churches should never be big or use modern technology to reach more people. Nor is it necessary that churches urge their people to go back to the "horse-and-buggy" days. But a politics that validates our existing order often directly contradicts Christianity. The Christian right and left have both taken the path of validating the existing order. The Christian right has veritably equated its own libertarian, nationalist, and pro-capitalist stances with the Christian position, while the left has equated liberal progressivism with the teachings of Jesus. We have seen how much of this is a result of social strong-arming, especially on the right. Cultish churches and movements tend to attract people who are in despair, who are motivated by what Hauerwas would call mere optimism, instead of Christian hope. People in them are fearful of complete social disembedding should they disagree, but they are also entranced by numbers, glamor, and power. Because it can be difficult to tell the difference between hope and optimism, these churches and the people behind them can lead large numbers of people further into the grip of strongholds, promoting and endorsing enthusiastically a way of life that is killing us both physically and spiritually.

We see idolatry whenever people turn away from their special relationship with God and towards the seemingly safer and easier shelter of the imperial state, yielding to its values and priorities. Perhaps the most memorable biblical example of this occurs when the Israelites complain of God's provisions in the wilderness and openly advocate for returning to Egypt, because at least there they would be able to eat. But within the story of their Exodus, at a different register, we see the eternal conflict emerge between the people of God and the idolatry inherent in any empire. Egypt, the great imperial power, is ultimately defeated by Yahweh, who first hardens the hearts of the Egyptians. The Egyptians believe that things will always stay the same and that they will always be in control, but they are proven embarrassingly wrong. In breaking the people of Israel out of slavery, Yahweh does not offer them safety, security, and prosperity, but he does offer them his freedom in a special covenantal relationship of love. As Walter Brueggemann puts it:

> The radical break of Moses and Israel from imperial reality is a two-dimensional break from both the religion of static triumphalism and the politics of oppression and exploitation. Moses dismantled the religion of state triumphalism by exposing the gods and showing that in fact they had no power and are not gods. Thus, the mythical legitimacy of Pharaoh's social world is destroyed, for it is shown that such a regime appeals to sanctions that in fact do not exist. The mythic claims of the empire are ended by the disclosure of *the alternative religion of the freedom of God.*[65]

In the wake of their escape from Egypt, the people of Israel were called to the "intentional formation of a new social community to match the vision of God's freedom." Keep in mind Americans' tendency to nationalism, excessive patriotism, and near adoration of capitalism (the last two traits shared by both right and left liberals), as Brueggemann describes God's freedom like this: "By the middle of the plague cycle Israel has disengaged from the empire, cries no more to it, expects nothing of it, acknowledges it in no way, knows it cannot keep its promises, and knows that nothing is either owed it or expected of it."[66] Unlike the liberated Jews, American Christians largely have not been able to disengage from their empire, or even realize that their country is an imperial power. Like all of us, they far too often get caught up in its dramas, expect it to meet all their needs, and give their precious working lives to its prosperity and power.

Despite the relapses in the wilderness mentioned above, Israel forged new political territory as it gained its independence from Egypt, putting God's leadership at the forefront, not succumbing to the worldly tendency to reduce everything to power and wealth. This lasted, as Brueggemann

65. Brueggemann, *Prophetic Imagination*, 6; emphasis original.
66. Brueggemann, *Prophetic Imagination*, 12.

would have it, for about 250 years, until the reign of King Solomon.[67] One could put the turning point earlier, with God's acquiescence to the Israelites' plea to be like all the other nations and elect a king. This was the end of the rule of the priesthood, and God warned the people that their choice to forgo priestly rule would bring them pain. The first Israelite king was Saul, but Brueggemann argues that there was a steady decline in leadership from Saul to David to Solomon. By the time of Solomon, the corruption caused by the political and economic temptations that came with state power were obvious, including a royal harem, a system of taxation aimed at state control of the tribes, an impersonal bureaucracy, a standing army for the constant projection of power and suppression of dissent, a "fascination with wisdom, which ... represented an attempt to rationalize reality," and "conscripted labor from the villages to support massive building projects."[68] Solomon put power and prosperity, particularly his, first, and tried to subordinate God to his own agenda.

Perhaps Brueggemann's most important insight is that "prophetic faith knows that if a criticism is to be mounted, it must begin in the unfreedom of God, which in turn results in a royal order quite free now to serve its own narrow interests."[69] What he means by this is that legitimate protest stems from the resistance to God's freedom within the human worldly order, which then ought to give rise in faithful people to a protest against that order. God's freedom in this sense is the freedom to have things happen as he wills, a freedom that he willingly allows human beings to stymie with their own free ability to choose to do right or wrong. Most American Christians are urged by their leaders to protest in favor of red or blue ideology, arguing that they are not free to get on with God's business because their political party is not dominant, and the other party is threatening them. In their equation of Christian action with right-wing or progressive liberal politics, American Christians too often attempt to suppress the freedom of God, a freedom to be felt and seen mainly in places where people care far less for security and worldly possessions than either of the two main American political parties do. But the double irony, as we have seen, is that many Christian followers who legitimately are not well served by our current political system, namely people living in decimated rural and inner-city areas, are some of the chief protagonists in this drama.

67. Brueggemann, *Prophetic Imagination*, 7.
68. Brueggemann, *Prophetic Imagination*, 24.
69. Brueggemann, *Prophetic Imagination*, 30.

The Old Testament is said to foretell the coming of Christ and indicate his nature in many places, though Isaiah's prophecy in chapter 53, of the "lamb led to slaughter," is perhaps the most often cited.[70] Throughout his writings, Brian Zahnd teaches that Jesus shows us who God is. The life of Jesus is one that, from beginning to end, was humble, not seeking political or financial power, disregarding both wealth and poverty. Jesus was born of a woman; he chose not to simply materialize in glory. He came into the world not in triumphal heavenly chariots, but as a baby that could not even feed himself. The infant Jesus was born in a cave or barn and slept in a manger (perhaps literally a feeding trough for farm animals), not a fancy inn or palace. He was born on the road, on the way to where his family had to participate in the census ordered by Caesar Augustus (Matt 1:18–24; Luke 1:26–38, 2:1–20). He grew up the son of a carpenter, and submitted to his worldly parents' authority (Luke 2:51). In some apocryphal texts that didn't make it into the official Bible, whose canon was finalized by the church in the Council of Rome in AD 382, Jesus deals aggressively with a few adversaries in his youth. But we have no evidence of Jesus doing so in the biblical canon all Christians accept. It is abundantly clear from the texts we have that Jesus would never harm his enemies.[71] In fact, we see the opposite approach from him throughout the Gospels. When the servant of the high priest gets his ear sliced off by Simon Peter, Jesus performs a miracle and heals him, then allows the Roman soldiers to arrest him. Jesus says, "Put your sword into its scabbard. Shall I not drink the cup that the Father gave me?" (John 18:10–11). He tells stories not just about forgiveness but about extreme charity in attitude (turn the other cheek; he who is without sin, cast the first stone) and in material possessions (give him your cloak also).[72] He spent a lot of

---

70. Most Christians agree that Isa 53 is a prophetic text that presages the life of Christ.

71. The not-so-forgiving child Jesus appears in the gnostic Infancy Gospel of Thomas. For instance, in this Gospel not included in the Bible, we find this account of Jesus's childhood escapades: "But the son of Annas the scribe was standing there with Joseph; and he took a branch of a willow and dispersed the waters which Jesus had gathered together. And when Jesus saw what was done, he was wroth and said unto him: O evil, ungodly, and foolish one, what hurt did the pools and the waters do thee? Behold, now also thou shalt be withered like a tree, and shalt not bear leaves, neither root, nor fruit. And straightway that lad withered up wholly, but Jesus departed and went unto Joseph's house. But the parents of him that was withered took him up, bewailing his youth, and brought him to Joseph, and accused him 'for that thou hast such a child which doeth such deeds'" (James, "Infancy Gospel of Thomas," 3.2).

72. "But I say to you that listen, love your enemies, do good to those who hate you,

time dealing with Jews such as the Pharisees who were very focused on the law and outward morality according to the mores of the day, and he almost always took the opposite position from them. In his seven woes to the scribes and Pharisees, Jesus says: "But woe to you, scribes and Pharisees, hypocrites! For you lock people out of the kingdom of heaven. For you do not go in yourselves, and when others are going in, you stop them. Woe to you, scribes and Pharisees, hypocrites! For you cross sea and land to make a single convert, and you make the new convert twice as much a child of hell as yourselves" (Matt 23:13-15).

Jesus is tempted in the desert with the power to obtain food and water, the ability to call down heavenly might to save him and do his bidding. He is offered all the political power in the world (Matt 4:1-11).[73] The last two temptations sound like the kind of Jesus that many American Christians desire—the powerful, warlike, politically dominant ruler. Jesus suffered both with others (as in when he wept upon hearing Mary and others weeping for her brother Lazarus, who had died [John 11:35]), and he submitted to the Roman authorities and willingly endured torture, humiliation, and a death considered one of the worst and most shameful ways to die.[74] On the cross, he forgave all those involved in his death. The last two people he talked to were two thieves, on his right and left. One spoke to him with faith that he was speaking to God.[75] He spoke to them

---

bless those who curse you, pray for those who abuse you. If anyone strikes you on the cheek, offer the other also; and from anyone who takes away your coat do not withhold even your shirt. Give to everyone who begs from you; and if anyone takes away your goods, do not ask for them again. Do to others as you would have them do to you" (Luke 6:27-31). "They said to him, 'Teacher, this woman was caught in the very act of committing adultery. Now in the law Moses commanded us to stone such women. Now what do you say?' They said this to test him, so that they might have some charge to bring against him. Jesus bent down and wrote with his finger on the ground. When they kept on questioning him, he straightened up and said to them, 'Let anyone among you who is without sin be the first to throw a stone at her.' And once again he bent down and wrote on the ground" (John 8:4-7). "If anyone strikes you on the cheek, offer the other also; and from anyone who takes away your coat do not withhold even your shirt" (Luke 6:29).

73. Most pertinently: "The tempter came and said to him, 'If you are the Son of God, command these stones to become loaves of bread.' But he answered, 'It is written, "One does not live by bread alone, but by every word that comes from the mouth of God."'"

74. "Crucifixion in Roman times was applied mostly to slaves, disgraced soldiers, Christians and foreigners—only very rarely to Roman citizens" (Retief and Cilliers, "History and Pathology," 938).

75. See Hauerwas's meditation on the final words of Jesus (*Cross-Shattered Christ*, 37-48).

as though they were worth his time, promising that the lately faithful one would be with him in heaven that day (Luke 23:39–43). Jesus's strength was not the strength of a Caesar but of an extremely forbearing, self-controlled, loving, and respectful Father.

Did Jesus condemn military service? No, but neither was he about military service or war.[76] Was Jesus ever angry? He certainly was, and not just when he overturned the money changers' tables that were polluting the temple. He was, in my words, often testy. You can feel the frustration with humanity in much of what he says. But this just reveals how much forbearance he demonstrated when he refused to use miraculous might and political power to his advantage. His radical take on forgiveness would lead, in practice, to some things we cannot even imagine happening, like Ukraine surrendering rather than fighting the Russians, even though the Russians attacked first. The fact that we can't imagine Ukrainians or anyone else carrying through fully on Jesus's level of forgiveness and forbearance does not mean that Jesus did not teach these things. All of this is what every Christian knows almost by osmosis if they go to a church where the Bible is read to them in a preordained sequence throughout the year. To know these things is to be burdened by the palpable contradiction between what Christ taught and the practical realities of our lives. To know is to be aware of the serious challenge Jesus's teachings present to much of what we do and say. But if a pastor is selective about which biblical passages he focuses on, it's quite possible to not know all of this, saving us the burden, challenges, and culpability that come from knowing.

For Christians, that the New Testament takes precedence over the Old Testament is axiomatic. Jesus is, for Christians, the fullest representation of God that has ever existed in our world—he is the incarnation of God. This means that Old Testament events and teachings are to be viewed in light of Jesus's life and teachings.[77] When the Old Testament

---

76. "The very first Christian writers, the composers of the gospels, seem not to have been concerned with the issue of the legitimacy of Christian enlistment and participation in warfare. They were uninterested in the salvation of the souls of individual soldiers (echoing Jesus?)" (Iosif, *Early Christian Attitudes*, 305). See Christoyannopoulos, *Christian Anarchism*; Durward and Marsden, *Religion, Conflict*.

77. This statement reflects my own sense of the relationship between the Old and New Testaments, which has been influenced by authors like Brian Zahnd, Bradley Jersak, Walter Brueggemann, etc. There are, in fact, several competing views of the relationship between the Old and the New Testament within evangelical, Catholic, and other Christian schools of thought. See for instance D. Bock, "Evangelicals"; Goldingay, "What Are the Characteristics"; Clifford, "Changing Christian Interpretations"; Nel, "Pentecostals' Reading."

seems to reveal a God that is definitely not like Jesus, Christian theologians deemphasize the Old Testament account one way or another, in favor of the New.[78] But a recent debate in evangelical Christianity about the relationship of Father and Son in the Triune Godhead reveals the underlying unease that some American evangelical theologians have with God being fully identified with the nature of Jesus.[79] In a highbrow but similar error to that of Rep. Boebert's AR-15 comment, theologians Wayne Grudem and Bruce Ware of the Council on Biblical Manhood and Womanhood[80] argue that Jesus is forever subordinate to the Father in the Trinity. For instance, they argue that because of God's "commanding, directing, and sending" Jesus into the world to accomplish his preordained mission, Jesus was always and is inherently inferior to the Father, though he is also coeternal with the Father.[81]

While these types of debates among religious elites about the exact nature and relationship of the three persons of the Godhead have been around as long as Christianity has, what makes Grudem and Ware's argument different is their apparent linking of Christ's subordination with the idea of the goodness of worldly hierarchy (specifically in gender roles) by analogy. But while scholars like Du Mez, who is critical of the sexism of much of evangelical Christianity, focus on Grudem and Ware's mission to justify "complementarianism," or the complimentary but different natures of men and women in sex-based hierarchy, the more startling implication of their position is that Jesus's nature and teachings while on earth are not necessarily a timeless representation of God. If Jesus was eternally submissive to the Father, representing a hierarchical relationship in which God the Father has more authority than the Son, then the Father would not always need to be like Jesus. In fact, God could decide to send Jesus in a different way—perhaps with a different

---

78. See for example, Webb and Oeste, *Bloody, Brutal and Barbaric?*

79. I first encountered this debate from a reference in Du Mez's book *Jesus and John Wayne* and subsequently viewed a debate between Wayne Grudem, Bruce Ware, Thomas McCall, and Keith Yandell on "Relations of Authority and Submission among the Persons of the Godhead," at the Carl F. H. Henry Center for Theological Understanding, Trinity Evangelical Divinity School, Deerfield, Illinois, in 2013. I also read several statements about "complementarianism" on the website of the Council on Biblical Manhood and Womanhood, including Grudem, "Letter." While I think that Du Mez is correct in the motivations of Grudem and Ware, considering that they are representatives of a council strongly supporting traditional gender roles, I hope to argue that the implications of such a politically motivated move are bigger than that.

80. https://cbmw.org/.

81. Grudem, *Systematic Theology*, 250; Ware, *Father, Son, and Holy Spirit*.

teaching and at a different point in history. For ordinary people, the practical implication of all this is not as complicated as the theological arguments. The implication is that the pastor speaking to them can be correct even if Jesus's words in the New Testament contradict what he or she is saying. If God is not necessarily *always* like Jesus, then God *could* send Jesus or the Holy Spirit to endorse the American empire and American nationalists, to teach that all Americans should be armed and ready to defend themselves, or really anything else he wanted. D. C. Schindler, the Catholic scholar critical of liberalism featured in chapter 4, would see the specter of the liberal God of "pure potentiality" in Grudem and Ware's position—the God who can be like Jesus, but like Zeus and Mars too. Zeus and Mars are more relatable gods to people who are attracted to "godly leadership," guns and cowboy hats.

If God can be like Jesus and like Zeus and Mars, then why prioritize learning from Jesus, as Christians insist on doing? If, on the other hand, Grudem and Ware are wrong, and Jesus is the incarnation of the eternal God on earth, his nature perfectly representing God now *and always*, then the crucified and resurrected Jesus as he is conveyed in the New Testament must be our guiding star. The person of Jesus must inform how we think about everything, including not just our "private" lives, but matters of state, nationality, national boundaries, leadership, violence and war, social responsibilities, material possessions and property, economic behavior generally, etc.

Jürgen Moltmann was a German Reformed theologian who knew that God was like Jesus. He was a soldier in Hitler's army but, when he found out about the concentration camps, he surrendered to the British immediately. Spending time in a British prisoner of war camp, he reflected on the horrible predicament of twentieth-century man. He was introduced to the Bible and not long after being imprisoned, he converted. He went on to become one of our greatest modern theologians. Much of Moltmann's work in one way or the other contemplates the situation of people like the Jews at the hands of the Nazis, experiencing the very worst that human beings can do to each other and asking the question, where is God in this? Moltmann's view of Jesus as "the crucified God" is heavily indebted to Martin Luther's discussion of the same. Fully adopting this view of God helped Moltmann reconcile God with human history, and it can help us step back and take in the incomprehensible—a God who suffers, dies, and resurrects because this is his true nature and represents his intentions for human beings and the world. The crucified God loves humanity and the creation he made, and this love entails suffering for it, suffering particularly in solidarity with the lowliest and poorest of the poor. Moltmann writes:

> Now the death of Christ was the death of a political offender. According to the scale of social values of the time, crucifixion was dishonour and shame. If this crucified man has been raised from the dead and exalted to be the Christ of God, then what public opinion holds to be lowliest, what the state has determined to be disgraceful, is changed into what is supreme. In that case, the glory of God does not shine on the crowns of the mighty, but on the face of the crucified Christ. The authority of God is then no longer represented directly by those in high positions, the powerful and the rich, but by the outcast Son of Man, who died between two wretches. The rule and the kingdom of God are no longer reflected in political rule and world kingdoms, but in the service of Christ, who humiliated himself to the point of death on the cross.
>
> The consequence for Christian theology is that it must adopt a critical attitude towards political religions in society and in the churches. The political theology of the cross must liberate the state from the political service of idols and must liberate men from political alienation and loss of rights. It must seek to demythologize state and society. It must prepare for the revolution of all values which is involved in the exaltation of the crucified Christ, in the demolition of relationships of political domination.[82]

If God is characterized by co-suffering love, then "for the crucified Christ, the principle of fellowship is fellowship with those who are different and solidarity with those who have become alien and have been made different. Its power is not friendship, the love for what is similar and beautiful (*philia*), but creative love for what is different, alien and ugly (*agape*)."[83] This is because, according to Christ, in loving what is familiar we do no better than the pagans. But to love that which is alien is to be like God, and that is what Christians are called to be.[84] This means that, truly, Christians are called not to resist people unlike themselves,

---

82. Moltmann, *Crucified God*, 327.
83. Moltmann, *Crucified God*, 28.
84. "For if you love those who love you, what reward do you have? Do not even the tax collectors do the same? And if you greet only your brothers and sisters, what more are you doing than others? Do not even the Gentiles do the same? Be perfect, therefore, as your heavenly Father is perfect" (Matt 5:46–48).

but to love and embrace them, as difficult, uncomfortable, and impractical as that seems. Recently Moltmann, who was ninety-three when interviewed, was asked if there could ever be a "good nationalism," and "he referred to Germany today, and warned that 'the spirits of the past are coming up again.'"[85] But he also expressed hope: the God who loves humanity enough to become one of them, and one at the very bottom, willing to suffer along with the most oppressed, is not one who will look kindly upon nationalistic hostility.

To bring this back to the question at hand, currently, the religious right and Christian nationalists are using threats and coercion to bind Christians together to achieve worldly ends. The religious left is not currently nearly as politically powerful, but we can acknowledge that it also uses social pressure to achieve conformity in its communities as well. Sadly, spiritual strong-arming works well, but is not of God. God has revealed himself as so supportive of human moral freedom that he would suffer with our self-inflicted wounds and even endure a worldly death at our hands, rather than take that freedom away. Even more, his death on the cross guarantees our freedom, and no worldly leader, whether like Jim Jones or John MacArthur, can remove our right to that freedom, even if he effectively blocks our ability to exercise it for a lifetime. The attempts of politicized Christian opinion leaders to create cultlike unity for their own purposes of power and wealth are not of God. The binding agent in their attempts is hurtful, divisive, negative, and violent. It is the opposite of love. Love is the nature of God, and (scarily) love necessarily entails moral freedom. As Block, Brueggemann, and McKnight put it, "If love wins there is no moral binding, and you can't threaten people to act right. There's no retributive capacity, no market discipline to confine or make demands on us."[86]

Beyond the dilemma of right- and left-wing religious politicization, and coercive tactics for political purposes, lies the very question of the freedom of conscience itself. We fear to claim this God-given freedom because within it lies the threat of misuse, of coming to the wrong conclusion, of using our freedom for evil purposes. Yet this freedom appears to be part of our very nature. It is the way God made us, and what makes us human. It is also the reason Christ came into our world the way he did rather than coming armed for battle. Moral freedom is necessary if we are to make a real choice to do the right thing under

---

85. Stanford, "Jürgen Moltmann," para. 15. Moltmann passed on June 3, 2024.
86. Block et al., *An Other Kingdom*, 11.

God's kingship. As Nikolai Berdyaev puts it, "Human nature is rooted in fathomless, pre-existential meonic freedom, and in his struggle for personality, for God's idea in him, man had to fashion consciousness with its limitations to bring light into darkness, and to subject subconscious instincts and strivings to the censorship of consciousness. There is a demonical element in man, for there is in him the fathomless abyss of freedom, and he may prefer that abyss to God."[87]

Conclusion

In our time, the religious right is on the ascendant, not only in America but in many other places in the world. That makes it more important, for the moment, to understand and address the problems on the right. We have previously looked at some of the economic and social/psychological reasons for the activation of the Christian right. Now we have examined the thinking and the behavior on display on the right through the lens of faith. It is far too easy for those not caught up in the religious right movement to condemn its followers as wrongheaded or, if we were once a part of it, to wonder why we only lately came to see its true nature. I hope that this reaction has been complicated, both for the critics and for followers of the Christian right movement. I hope I got these two points across:

First, we need to understand that followers of any movement who become uncritical in their acceptance of leaders' words and actions are caught up in the thrall of psychological and spiritual forces that are strongly rooted in human nature. It is not primarily their fault; they are not necessarily unintelligent, and they don't necessarily have grave character defects that make them far different from other people. We must stop seeing people who become dangerously enmeshed and unable to easily extricate themselves as exceptional. Clearly, based on extensive and well-known historical evidence and psychological research, human beings are often easily strong-armed. Whether we are looking at American patriots at a rally in Kansas; abused women and children struggling to free themselves from men claiming godly leadership; students coerced into sexual slavery; study participants willing to painfully shock others; people following a cult leader all the way to suicide; or just ordinary Christians who accept manipulation, bullying, and thievery, clearly this is a matter of common human nature and not a series of incredible exceptions. We just like to think we are different, but the reality is, we

87. Berdyaev, *Destiny of Man*, 69.

all are susceptible, depending on the trigger. Therefore, the question we should ask is, how can we avoid being strong-armed ourselves, and how can we help others escape these strongholds?

Second, modernity has made people only more vulnerable to abuse and manipulation. We have become more and more dislocated, fragmented, disembedded, disenchanted, and isolated from each other and our environment as we have moved into technocracy and a fully globalized economy. Our information technology (TV, cell phones, the Internet, social media) have made psychological and spiritual manipulation so much easier—it can literally act in a vectoral fashion and spread beyond national borders in the blink of an eye. If the history of Anabaptist leader Jan Van Leiden is any proof, horrifically bloody cults happened in Reformation times too.[88] But what could not happen in the sixteenth century is the lightning-fast and far-reaching spread of cultism in the form of conspiracy theories and nationalistic politics. In this environment, in which everybody can know what is happening on the other side of the country or elsewhere on the globe with incredible speed and remarkable inaccuracy, people become much more easily attracted to mass movements detached from place and their lived reality, and to strong leaders who tell them that they have the truth, that they can fix all things and make us happy again. If we blame anyone, it should be the leaders, not the followers of such movements, especially leaders like John MacArthur and Fox News personalities who cynically manipulate our vulnerabilities. Those who help these popular influencers, the political and theological intellectuals who give them cover, bear perhaps even more responsibility.[89] It is time for these leaders and their enablers to take a step back and, perhaps fearing the God revealed by Jesus in the New Testament, admit they were seduced by power and influence to ride the crest of the popular wave.

---

88. See Hofmann, "Historical Case Study Analysis."

89. I am thinking here of scholars like Grudem and Ware, but it should be noted that John MacArthur is an example of both. He is the ultimate attractive cultish leader. One search of theological literature turns up his ubiquitous and largely positive presence in that realm—there is hardly any mention of controversy related to his church in a search on EBSCO Religion, even now.

7

The Role of Church and Christian Economies

HAVING DISCUSSED SOME OF the dynamics of strong-arming in ideological social formation, and the special case of Christian strong-arming, this chapter will critically examine Christian movements as possible instigators of meaningful and positive change. This may seem like a strange choice for study, given the ground I've just covered, until one contemplates the other imaginable options. One option contemplated by strict Marxists is developing a rational, enlightened population capable of equitable and sustainable growth for all in society (the appropriate use of knowledge, material resources, and technology to benefit all). This is a vision that is on the surface very attractive. But we do not have good evidence that people can achieve the level of enlightened reason and concerted action necessary to make it happen. We have much more evidence that they cannot, no matter how hard they try, and that the efforts they make are often corrupted. Another option, contemplated by classical conservatives, involves a return to some sort of benevolent aristocracy/oligarchy (today, perhaps, corporate CEOs becoming more motivated by honor) and the recovery of truly human, nonmaterialistic values. But there is no good evidence that elites can be consistently benevolent enough to change things for most people. Another option, imagined by globalists, is a rational liberal world order, or even a world government. We don't have any notion of what a true world government would be like since we have never experienced it before, but past attempts at globalizing empires are not heartening precursors. At this point, I hope you can better understand why I do not think it is utopian or unrealistic, by comparison, to ask whether religious institutions could be more involved in organizing and redirecting people's values and behavior towards truly human ends. This is because churches and other houses of worship exist everywhere and represent quite a bit of actual, ongoing (albeit imperfect) human organization.

Yet the possibility for concerted Christian action seems unlikely right now. America has an estimated 380,000 Christian churches,[1] but church attendance and denominational identification are waning among the young, and at lesser but significant rates among all age brackets. Gallup reports that between 1998 and 2000, 69 percent of Americans reported being members of churches, compared with 62 percent between 2008 and 2010, and 49 percent between 2018 and 2020. For the first time in American history, less than half the US population is churched, with Catholics falling off at the highest rate.[2] The unsavory Christian behavior discussed in the previous chapter is partly to blame, not to mention all the other sources of secularization covered in chapter 4. But however much we are disenchanted, Christian churches remain among the most numerous, organized, and supported nongovernmental organizations in the United States. For that reason, it seems a shame to simply sideline them as possible agents for organizing people to help each other, their neighbors, and the larger world. Not to mention, for the sake of their own survival, churches need to change.

American churches suffer the same dynamics as American society at large. Whether populated by those on the right or left of the political spectrum, they share traits that make them currently not very effective as serious vehicles for positive societal action. This is another element that pushes people to identify as "nones." According to Stephen Bullivant, one in every four people in America is now a "none," with fully one third of all eighteen- to twenty-nine-year-olds marking "no religion" on surveys. "Nonverts" are those who used to consider themselves a part of a religion but fell away. The rate of identifications as "none" has escalated in the last twenty to thirty years, so that Bullivant can say unequivocally that "the USA is in the midst of a social, cultural,

---

1. Brauer, "How Many Congregations?"
2. Jokes, "U.S. Church Membership Falls."

THE ROLE OF CHURCH AND CHRISTIAN ECONOMIES

and religious watershed—one that today's Americans are not merely living *through*, but millions have actively *lived out* in their own stories."[3] However, being a "none" does not mean, necessarily, that one does not believe in God. In fact, Bullivant reports that 21 percent of nones told the GSS, "I believe in God and I have no doubt about it," and another 18 percent sometimes believed in God, and 27 percent did not believe in a personal God but did believe in a "higher power."[4] Many nones "genuinely miss much of what they've left behind."[5] This tendency to want to believe in God and wish things were different characterizes a lot of former churchgoers, which may suggest that secularization is not an inevitable development but a reaction to the underdevelopment of American Christianity. Those who continue to go to church tend to be older, and, for better or worse, more set in their ways, which perhaps makes coming back even less attractive to young nones.

We have already examined some of the leading causes of secularization, both recent causes and those that go back further into history. But we may still ask, why is the typical American church currently so uncompelling, so unable to keep the exodus at bay? It's not as though they haven't tried many innovations in the effort to retain membership, including the COVID and post-COVID drift into online worship. One possible cause that may be explored at more length is the neoliberal tendency of the American church touched upon earlier. This phenomenon is what makes the experience of church feel like entertainment, group therapy, or both. But there is more than the "feel" of churches at work in our inability to really attach ourselves to them and their mission. To the extent that churches think of impacting their community and beyond, they tend to do that in two ways that stem from our deep embedding in liberal values and behavior. Our liberalism, extending into our way of doing Christianity, necessarily impedes real and lasting personal and community change. Below I will examine the twin problems of liberal church politics and charitable outreach.

---

3. Bullivant, *Nonverts*, 11. See also Manning, *Losing Our Religion*.
4. Bullivant, *Nonverts*, 64.
5. Bullivant, *Nonverts*, 171.

Liberal Church Politics as Action

When it comes to addressing injustices and wrongs in society, churches often encourage or even organize left- or right-wing political activity such as voting, urging others to vote a certain way, financially supporting political organizations and lobbying groups, etc. This is an inherently liberal strategy. While it certainly is recognizable and seems practical, it has the effect of encouraging the political blaming and scapegoating we've just surveyed in the chapters on strong-arming. It also gives the government too much credit, and ordinary people too little responsibility for our moral and social order. It deflects responsibility onto an amorphous, all-powerful governing elite for what people and groups at the local level may do better. It turns people into passive petitioners, not doers. Most disturbing of all, these days this political strategy often doesn't even involve any real *action*. Instead, it involves merely talking or demonstrating. People go online and talk about their political opinions and preach to their friends about why the other side is wrong, or (if they are courageous) they occasionally go to a protest and hold up signs. This "all talk and no action" pseudo-politics takes up a great deal of energy that could be expressed in direct Christian work. Such work might include people changing their own lives in concrete ways, helping others to live better lives, cooperating with each other on real-world projects, forming more meaningful reciprocal face-to-face relationships, etc. But work is hard.

The tendency to seek change by engaging in liberal politics is of course not entirely bad, and trying to solve big problems almost always means that the government must be involved at some level. But this political strategy becomes a block to actual change when it functions, unconsciously, as a *substitute* for stronger, responsibility-taking action. It can become an excuse to not get anything productive done. Stanley Hauerwas captures the sense of entrapment and futility that can come from the liberal political strategy by noting:

> the increasing recognition that even if such churches remained socially and politically powerful, they would have nothing distinctive to say as Christians about the challenges facing this society. That such churches have nothing distinctive to contribute is not surprising, since their social and political power originally derived from the presumption that there was no or little essential difference between the church and the principles of the American experiment. That presumption may, of course,

also help explain the decline of such churches, because it is by no means clear why you need to go to church when such churches only reinforce what you already know from participation in democratic society.[6]

What do Christians look like without liberal politics as their primary mode? Here there is perhaps an ongoing real-world example that can inform us. Introduced in our last chapter because of their resistance to religious strong-arming, "exvangelicals," who are (to use one of their own terms) "deconstructing," provide us a view into what happens when people try to reject the politicization of their religion. Exvangelicals are Christians who have seen the error in combining Christianity with right- or left-wing politics and have tried in earnest to seek a more authentic faith, closer to original Christianity.

But it is more difficult to escape from liberal politics than it seems. Much exvangelical discourse gets caught up in the political tug of war by default. The goal becomes to explain how wrong right-wing politicization of Christianity is and how much more fulfilling a person's relationship to God can be once it is not obscured by bad theology. That is, much of the deconstruction movement is still identifying itself primarily by *what it is not*, which means that *its identity is still embedded in liberal politics*. This is understandable. Exvangelicals are united by a negative experience of nationalist evangelical Christianity. They left because they felt somehow uncomfortable, and that experience looms large in their minds. For instance, much of the discourse on the *Exvangelical* podcast is about the experience of having been a right-wing evangelical Christian and then deciding to leave.[7]

Deconstructing Christians who find church still worthwhile end up in a variety of other denominations and nondenominational churches formed to reconstruct Christians in a healthier, more authentic faith. But the definition of that faith, and the way it is lived, is still very much influenced by liberalism. For instance, even though many friendships form in the church context and spill over into the rest of life, it is still the case that most churches as institutions, deconstructed or not, tend to work on creating a *thin* community, based primarily on talking and understanding together but not on consistently living and working together. This observation about American churches, that

---

6. Hauerwas, *Better Hope*, 25–26.
7. See https://www.exvangelicalpodcast.com/.

overtly partisan or not, they tend to unconsciously reflect liberal values and behavior, is perhaps most starkly revealed by pointing to their tendency to centralize and grow bigger over time. American churches are, strangely enough, in a similar situation to American farms. United States Department of Agriculture (USDA) statistics tell us that most farms are still small and diversified, but also that these small farms combined produce far less food, animal feed, and other products compared to the fewer but vast industrialized farms. Similarly, the National Congregations Study (NCS) statistics tell us that there are more small churches in America than large ones, but most churchgoing Christians are members of large, even megachurches. The authors of the 2018–19 NCS survey summary put it succinctly, "In a nutshell, the largest 9% of congregations contain about half of all churchgoers."[8]

These paradoxes are resolved by realizing that farms and churches, much like businesses and government, are prone to centralization, corporatization, and monopolization in liberal capitalist economies. The impulses to keep getting more efficient through automation and centralized administration, to grow bigger by appealing to the average consumer and by weakening and eliminating competitors—cornering the market, so to speak—are all at work. The principles of anonymity and individual choice are operative in larger congregations much as in the consumer pool at large: "Megachurch growth contributes to rather than counteracts the trend towards decreasing average congregation size."[9]

So, the reason the statistics still tell us that the majority of farms and churches are small and medium-sized is summed up by Mark Twain: "There are three kinds of lies: lies, damned lies, and statistics."[10] The USDA is counting unprofitable hobby farms, demonstration farms, homesteaders, and small, largely struggling local farms as "farms," equal for purposes of their statistics to mega-farms. Similarly, the NCS is counting dying churches with fifty members or less as churches, alongside megachurches with thousands of members on multiple campuses. In both instances we are given facts, but interpreters can use those facts to paint whichever picture suits their purpose. American Christianity, politicized or not, is largely still an individualized and private affair in which people church-shop for the most comfortable experience to suit themselves, and this helps these centralizing forces. And as more of our

8. Chaves et al., *Congregations*, 10.
9. Chaves et al., *Congregations*, 11.
10. Twain attributed the quote to Disraeli (*Chapters from My Autobiography*, 471).

church experiences, as a result, come to feel like the rest of our lives, they will be boring and uninspiring, with or without overt right- or left-wing liberal politics.

The Liberal Charity Model

The second way churches engage the larger community, including churches that provide a friendly refuge to exvangelicals, is to help the poor and marginalized through liberal charity and charitable outreach (think paying for food and services, or organizing a community meal night or food pantry). But this engagement does not necessarily lead to a stronger, more involved church community. Indeed, whether in or beyond the church environment, despite increasing levels of giving and outreach in absolute terms, there has been a steady decrease in numbers of volunteers and numbers of people involved in charitable giving in America.

The University of Maryland's Do Good Institute reported in 2018 that, despite a record increase in total hours and dollars given, "fewer Americans are engaging in their community by volunteering and giving than in any time in the last two decades." This is important because the data the institute examined (from the US Bureau of Labor Statistics and the Census Bureau's Current Population Survey) was recent but pre-pandemic when one would expect a deep slide in volunteerism and charitable giving. The institute explained that fewer people volunteered more hours and gave more money, and this made up for the continual decrease in the total numbers of people involved. In other words, a small number of relatively privileged people are giving a lot because they have so much, but most people are not, perhaps because they have little extra time or money. The institute reported that "further illustrating this trend, rural and suburban areas—which traditionally exhibit much higher rates of social capital versus urban areas—experienced the most significant declines in volunteering over this period."[11]

Perhaps it is no coincidence that rural and suburban areas are also most likely to be politically "red." The same stress and anxiety that lead to political and religious radicalization may also account for the exhausted state of volunteering and donating in those areas. The fact that churches are declining in membership and giving, and that this mirrors

11. Grimm and Dietz, *Where Are America's Volunteers*, 2.

a decline in people participating in secular service work and charitable giving, is telling. Should churches look like the world when it comes to how members care for each other and their neighbors? Is it possible that when it comes to religion, liberal action such as charitable giving feels comfortable and recognizable to church members but does not hit home at the level of their souls?

It may come as a surprise that the liberal charity model is not the only way to express caritas. Loving and caring for people is good, but it can take many other forms, some of which may initially seem "selfish" because they do not seek to reach out but to draw in or incorporate. Much of liberal charity is about money—giving it, using it to buy goods (often nonlocal food that does not help the economy that could employ the local poor) and services to give to people, etc. Some of it is about time, as in volunteers giving their time to provide things to those who need them. Liberal charity works well with capitalism, because it accepts economic inequality as not only inevitable but good, and it thrives on paying money for goods and services at the cheapest price possible. Giving your time to distribute things that have been purchased is never a problem within capitalism. Neither is helping people get off the street and get low-wage jobs by helping them successfully navigate the welfare system and work.

None of this is meant to argue that we should stop giving or volunteering. If we did so in our current system, a lot of people would simply suffer even more than they do now. Liberal charity, much like government aid, transfers to those who have fewer material resources the goods they need and want, benefitting all of us economically and socially. But, as Edmund Burke might point out, liberal charity has some unintended (and sometimes intended) consequences. Perhaps the most pernicious unintended side effect is simply that the poor are not really considered part of the church community, because they are put in the position of beneficiaries and the church members in the position of benefactors. This may be a hard idea to comprehend, but there is a reason why people who need help getting enough food or other goods often feel embarrassed about, or resentful of, the charity they are given. And, conversely, there is a reason why some members of a church think, and may even openly voice, that the recipients of their charity are responsible for their situations and may be loafers or advantage-takers. It is why they typically do not think of these beneficiaries as potential members of their church. Baked into the liberal charity model is an inequality that makes true friendship and respect very difficult, especially in a culture that prizes self-reliance.

If politics weren't seen as the main means of getting things done at the societal level, and money were not the primary vehicle of aiding people at any level, what would change? I want to ask if work could get done within churches for their members, such as planting, harvesting, organizing, cooking, preserving, serving, fixing, building, childcare, eldercare, housing, etc. I suspect that if it could, the level of felt inequality among those involved would decrease, and the "poor" as a category would be hard to identify because members wouldn't immediately know and be constantly aware of who had money and who did not. Those with less money would be seen as desirable members of the church community based on their demonstrated character and willingness to help others—to give and receive work graciously. They would not be seen as people we help—they would instead be our valuable fellow community members. Hauerwas notes that Gregory of Nazianzus, in his oration "On Love for the Poor," sought to "make the poor seen, to make the poor part of the community, because unless they are seen to be integral to the community, we will fail to see Christ."[12] Gregory's model was literally to choose voluntary poverty, not simply to "do something for the poor," but to erase the distinction between himself and his fellow human beings.[13]

It may help to think in terms of Hauerwas's "politics of Jesus," as opposed to liberal politics or the politics of America. Hauerwas has argued throughout his career that Christianity is necessarily political in the sense that it is about how Christians treat each other, as well as non-Christians. It is about what Christians' stance should be towards the state, and upon which principles they collectively should agree in governing their behavior. He contends that the politics of Jesus, which translates into the polity of the church, if rightly understood, directly confronts, and often contradicts, American political priorities, and liberal politics more generally. For Hauerwas, "The Christian church is a political entity, a corporate body in the world, persisting through time. Christians must begin their thinking about politics with it. The politics of the church cannot simply be about wielding power within or beyond it. Rather, political questions for the church begin with what it means to be this body, this particular people called to follow the God of Israel and

---

12. Hauerwas and Coles, *Christianity, Democracy*, 234.
13. Hauerwas and Coles, *Christianity, Democracy*, 242.

of Jesus."[14] That is, the church is supposed to be a full community, albeit for the moment under a liberal political order.

As with Brueggemann, Hauerwas's concept is that, rather than the Christian polity being a representative of the American empire, it is a source of differential identity and prophetic truth based on submission to Jesus as the true Lord *here and now*. As such, church members are tasked with creating "an alternative political reality," resisting and opposing through how we behave towards much of what Americans hold dear.[15] Americans hold violence and domination dear; genuine Christian politics opposes them. Americans hold the freedom to choose dear, though that freedom is often applied only to those of their ideological identity. Some Americans want the freedom to choose abortion at any stage of pregnancy and the freedom to choose their gender identity, while other Americans want to stop them. But these latter Americans also want the freedom to choose to use their property exactly as they see fit, regardless of its impact on other people or the environment, and to purchase as many guns of any type as they want, while other Americans want to stop them. The politics of Jesus, on the other hand, rejects the very idea that the freedom to choose whatever we want is good. Drawing on Alasdair MacIntyre's articulation of virtue ethics, Hauerwas argues for a politics that puts Christian virtue first, not freedom of choice.

There is a reason that liberal charity is much more prevalent than a vision of genuine reciprocity. The more that a community gets away from the strategy of collecting money to provide goods and services to those "less fortunate," the more that community clashes with liberal individualism, which itself is a cultural partner of the capitalist economy. As liberal individuals, we are uncomfortable relying on others in face-to-face relationships. We feel burdened and beholden in our relationships, as though our lives were a balance sheet that should be kept even, or in our favor. It is easy for us to feel imposed upon by the suggestion we should take others' needs and wishes into account when regulating our own behavior. We want to have the option to keep relationships at arm's length, walk away from them when they become too close for comfort, are hard, awkward, tiresome, etc. Our need for privacy has been accentuated by the way we live, in which goods and services arrive seemingly out of the ether, things we've bought to consume, throw

---

14. Pinches, "Why Church Matters," 312.
15. Hauerwas and Coles, *Christianity, Democracy*, 231.

away, or do with what we wish. The faces and hands behind these goods are invisible to us. We feel no human relationship to the people who grew them, made them, and transported them. This consumer attitude is directly related to our transient and narcissistic view of human relationships generally. Our experience of freedom is based on the illusion of autonomy and self-reliance. The truth is that no one is self-reliant—we just think we are to the extent we have money.

Reliance on others rather than on our ability to summon goods and services to our doorstep requires us to have a lot of trust and patience with others, things that are in short supply because of our conditioning and societal strong-arming. However, we cannot escape the truth that the more we rely on family, friends, and neighbors, the less we need to buy goods and services. If you doubt this, look at how Hispanic immigrants and their descendants in the United States tend to live. While these values weaken through the generations after immigration to the US, in general, Hispanics rely more on family and friends in intergenerational housing and other arrangements so that they can pool resources and live better than they could if each relied only on their individual income.[16] Ironically, if enough people could really count on their family, friends, and larger community for help when they needed it, our economic system would begin to suffer. Christian communities that try this, like Catholic monasteries, Bruderhof, the Amish, and Catholic Worker farms and houses of hospitality, are considered charming oddities on the American landscape. They are often even tourist attractions appreciated for their simplicity, beauty, and/or aura of holiness. But what would happen if 20 percent of the society decided to live in similar cooperative ways, buying very little and perhaps even accumulating cash and land with the money they brought in? I suspect that even 20 percent of Americans living this way would force massive changes in our economy and deeply threaten its vital statistics. Because of this, any larger movement to reestablish and strengthen social ties involving extensive material cooperation would risk being seen as a dangerous cult, provoking the full might of the American regime. That is, I suspect such a change could not take place without some kind of conflict, political or otherwise. It is one thing to express nostalgia for a seemingly more wholesome past, or to wish with Wendell Berry that community could be restored in a return to devotion to a particular place, a pre-Cleaver simplicity with tight-knit

---

16. Becker et al., "Creating Continuity"; Landale et al., "Hispanic Families."

relationships based on an earlier, healthier occupation and use of the land. But to try to do anything like this on a large scale is another thing entirely, and probably would not be allowed.

Perhaps the possibility of conflict inherent in moving towards more community reliance or mutual aid is a good reason for churches to want to stay within the mainstream liberal practices of political lobbying and charity that relies on money, goods, and services. But again, I suspect that the toothlessness of most American churches in their adaptation to liberal politics and economics is what has bored whole generations into "nonversion." And I want to ask an even more disturbing question than why we can't move towards strong cooperation as a society: Even if we do not want to become truly revolutionary, why are most churches seemingly incapable of moving beyond the political/charity model *even a little*? For instance, many of our churches' wealthier members end up going to assisted living facilities long before they need to. This is because they do not want, and cannot get from their families, friends, and fellow church members, the socialization and physical help they need to maintain themselves comfortably in their homes. They have given their time and money to these churches their entire lives and get no care when they need it in return, and often not even moral support.

A small detour into my own family's experience may help the reader understand why this subject is important to me. Several years before my mother died, she began to slip a bit mentally and physically. She and my dad lived next door to me. She could still take care of the basic functions of life, I helped with technology and visited almost every day, and Dad did most of their cooking. But Dad and I were the only people in her life—she did not get out much, and no one else was coming in. Dad was and is still very mobile and socially active, even now in his mid-nineties. The pressure was on him to be there with Mom most of the time, and she of course preferred that. But we realized that we both needed a break, and Mom could benefit from having other people visit her. I turned to their church (this did not occur to my dad), where they had been members for years, and where my dad still volunteered to visit others in similar situations. I met with their pastor, asking for someone to visit my mother on a regular basis, like my dad did for other shut-ins. Even though they obviously had a program, nothing happened for my mother. Then the pandemic came. COVID did not help matters, and as the situation eased, we could see that Mom was slipping faster due to a lack of social stimulation. Their pastor retired and a new one was hired.

I visited the new one and asked for someone to visit my mom. This time, they came a couple of times, then stopped. Mom would ask about them, and we did not know what to say.

After that, we resigned ourselves to the situation, doing the best we could on our own, hiring hourly help from a local assisted living facility (who sent us, in many cases, teenagers whom we could have hired by walking down our own neighborhood knocking on doors). I could and did conclude from this experience, rightly or wrongly, that my parents' mainline Protestant church pastors had no way to ask anyone to do anything, and probably no real concept of what I was asking for, or why it was a request that should be taken seriously. My dad continued as a bridge builder. The folks on his list still get visited frequently because of his values, which he formed outside of his church. I suppose most folks on the list get a visit occasionally, or, perhaps more likely, a greeting card and a flower drop-off on holidays. As a result of our experience on the receiving end of church charitable outreach, Dad and I both slowly disengaged from his church. The fact is, reciprocity matters when you need it.

What would have to change to get American Christians to be more serious about creating community and helping each other so that all were truly welcome, and all benefited from the association? To answer these questions, I will first examine an iconic example of strong Christian community in the lives of Dorothy Day and Peter Maurin, cofounders of the Catholic Worker movement. I will critically examine the ideas that inspired Maurin and Day, i.e., Catholic social teaching, and how they attempted to act on these ideas. I will then look at today's Catholic Worker movement in the light of its founding and current conditions. I chose the Catholic Worker movement partly because I am associated with it through the Maurin Academy, a nonprofit that I ostensibly lead. I deem the Catholic Worker movement one of the strongest examples of Christians trying to act out a workable, and not hopelessly traditionalist or romantic, model for living and relating to our current liberal order. The Catholic Worker movement does not fulfill all its aspirations as it exists today. Often, Catholic Workers fall prey to the allure of left-liberal politics or traditionalism, and they struggle to develop stable self-governing communities. Many operate mainly at the level of liberal charity. But the fact that the movement exists at all, along with the founders' enduring vision, makes it a great inspiration for Christian solidarity.

After discussing the Catholic Worker movement as a test of meaningful and effective Christian community in action within the larger liberal society, I will move to the societal level and discuss distributism, a school of economic thought inspired by Catholic social teaching that Maurin and Day found promising. Distributism is a third-way economic theory. It is worth considering because, despite the need for more direct Christian action, it is also necessary to shape the larger economy and government in a direction that at least does not discourage such action. Distributism is useful if we want to think about a new politics beyond the left-right shouting match that Christians from both sides could get behind. For instance, it embraces the value of private property, but calls for a Christian understanding of what it means to "own." Distributism protests the tendency in modern capitalism to monopolize and drive out small and medium businesses, leading to harmful levels of inequality, but it supports the activity of businesses as a result. Distributism is intriguing to those from a variety of political orientations such as classical conservatives, libertarians, localists, anarchists, and socialists. Distributists try to adhere honestly to the teachings of Christ, and they are opposed to the way we currently live, govern ourselves, and conduct our economies. Therefore, despite distributism's limitations in our current context, it can serve as a sort of purgative, and a ground floor for thinking about our economic future.

Catholic Workers

Many people have never heard of the Catholic Worker movement, and for those who have, there are a variety of opinions about what it is and what it is supposed to be about.[17] Its identity problem is a telling characteristic of the movement. Non-Catholics reasonably think that the movement must be exclusively Catholic. It certainly has its origins in that faith, as both of its founders were Catholics who were deeply inspired by papal social teachings, mainly in the form of encyclicals. But even at its inception, and more so as the movement developed over time, it has been ecumenical, welcoming anyone who wants to be involved. It has also always been anarchistic. There are no enforced rules for becoming a Catholic Worker, and no direct support, supervision, or other connection from a church at the institutional level.

17. In two of the Maurin Academy's *Regenerative Readers*, a debate between Brian Terrell and Spencer Hess, both Catholic Workers running Catholic Worker farms, demonstrates how Catholic Workers can differ on what goals the movement should have. See Terrell, "Farmer and Agitator"; Hess, "To Face or Not."

THE ROLE OF CHURCH AND CHRISTIAN ECONOMIES

The movement got started with the initiation of a broadsheet called *The Catholic Worker* in 1933, published in response to the social and economic challenges of the Great Depression. Dorothy Day, a journalist and activist, learned radical socialist and anarcho-syndicalist ideas in her youth, because of her deep concern for the plight of the poor. She also drew inspiration from Leo Tolstoy's ideas of nonviolence and the importance of serving the least among us.[18] Witnessing widespread poverty and inequality, Day became increasingly aware of the failures of the capitalist system, and she worked for several radical socialist publications in her early years. But, to the consternation of her radical friends, Day also had a spiritual streak, and it was brought into the open at a certain point, dramatically changing her life forever. After a love affair that led to an abortion, and after the birth of her daughter Tamar in a subsequent common-law marriage, Day got Tamar baptized, left her partner, and converted to Catholicism. The main instigator for this conversion, in addition to her prior spiritual tendencies, seems to have been the desire for her daughter's stability and well-being.

Around the time she converted, Day serendipitously met Peter Maurin through a mutual editorial acquaintance. Because Maurin published so little himself,[19] it is important to articulate the spiritual and intellectual influences he brought with him in his partnership with Day. Maurin was a peasant who had left his homeland in a remote and desolate part of France, and traveled around Canada and the United States, largely working as a laborer. But there was much more to Maurin than that. Before leaving for North America, he had been a student at the St. Privat Christian Brothers school, and eventually had become a novice with the order. He went on to higher education via the brotherhood, learning the ideas of eighteenth-century religious leader Jean-Baptiste de La Salle, who wanted to bring quality education to everyone. Through these means, Maurin was imbued in the religious life and the ideals of brotherly love for all. He spent seven years teaching with the Christian Brothers. But, when he was called for military service in 1898, both his peasant background and his religious learning began to make him uncomfortable with the idea of war. And while he obeyed the law

---

18. Christoyannopoulos and Nelson, "Leo Tolstoy's Impact."

19. We have one book by Peter Maurin, his *Easy Essays*. There are some other articles in the *Catholic Worker*, but they are similar in approach, and most of them are in the *Easy Essays*.

and did his service, afterward he became even more convinced that the correct Christian stance was pacifism.

Meanwhile, Catholic education came under assault again in the Third Republic, in one of the secularizing waves that had been going on since the French Revolution. The Christian Brothers were prohibited from teaching in French schools. Having lost his job, and his association with the brothers and their educational mission, Maurin got caught up in the Sillon movement. At first an organization dedicated mainly to starting study circles and fostering local Christian community, Sillon also attempted to deal with the republican modernization of France. "In contrast to other associations, some of which favored the reinstitution of monarchy and the power of Church hierarchy, Sillon declared itself firmly in favor of the Republic, but envisioned a republic infused with Christianity."[20] Marc Ellis explains that it was around the time of joining Sillon that Maurin really absorbed the social teachings of the Catholic Church, starting with Pope Leo XIII's response to industrialization and the situation of factory workers: "*Sillon*, with which Maurin was associated for the next six years, was itself heir to a tradition of Catholic activism, a tradition awakened by the urban-industrial revolution and the forces of secularization that had attended it. A sense of urgency had been added by Leo XIII's encyclical *The Condition of the Working Classes* (Rerum Novarum, 1891), which rallied the Church to the defense of the worker and raised in a dramatic way the role of the Church in the modern world."[21]

Maurin often distributed Sillon's newspaper, working only part-time so he could dedicate most of his life to the cause, a pattern that would later be replicated by other Catholic Workers. However, Sillon's leadership started to move away from its original Catholic identity in its attempt to create a big tent in which many types of people could support the republican cause. Maurin eventually left the Sillon movement due to its increasingly secular nature.[22] Meanwhile, he continued to be called for military reserve service, and at a certain point, he decided to not answer the call, changing addresses frequently to stay ahead of authorities.[23]

Soon, he left France and emigrated to Canada, which was welcoming French immigrants with the lure of cheap land and no conscription.

20. Ellis, *Peter Maurin*, 26.
21. Ellis, *Peter Maurin*, 26.
22. For more information on the secularizing transformation of Sillon, see Myrick, "Action Libérale Populaire," 108–10.
23. Ellis, *Peter Maurin*, 28.

There, Maurin worked as a farm laborer, farmer, and a teacher. He also got involved with labor organizing. He further developed his commitment to decentralized power and agrarianism, and he deepened his "personalism," a philosophy later made famous by Emmanuel Mounier's work *A Personalist Manifesto* (1936).[24] Personalism warned against using people as means to an end and went along well with Catholic social teachings that directly contradicted the new mode of industrialized production. Peter Maurin's personalism highlighted the inherent dignity and worth of each person in their social context, and therefore the need for real relationships and strong community to live a truly good life.

In 1911, after several debacles in Canada (chief among them, the death of his farming partner in a hunting accident), Maurin migrated to the United States, usually working as a day laborer. He brought all his experience and his unique philosophical/spiritual commitment with him into this new, nomadic phase of his life. Eventually, he caught a break teaching French in Chicago, and for the first time in his life he made decent money, which caused him to fall off a bit from his religious asceticism.[25] But when he met Day, he felt reinvigorated. He began to indoctrinate her in Catholic social teachings, and he looked to her to help him get his ideas, products of his unique origins and experience, out to laboring people and the poor. The *Catholic Worker* publication was their first collaboration, and Maurin hoped that it would be a vehicle for spreading his ideas for a decentralized society built on the principles of agrarianism, distributism, and personalism. The newspaper dealt not only with Maurin's ideas, but with Day's thoughts on important economic and political issues informed by her ideological priors and her new commitment to the Catholic faith.

An example of Maurin's way of thinking, in "Easy Essay" style, appeared in the *Catholic Worker* in 1937. In it, he rejected violence in labor strikes and advised workers to engage in strikes only in the Gandhi style of the "sit-down technique." Next, he compared capitalism with a rather romantic view of the Middle Ages:

1. The capitalist system is a racketeering system.

---

24. The English edition was published two years later: Mounier, *Personalist Manifesto*. Mounier was reacting to the collectivizing tendencies in fascism and communism, and called for a "personalist communitarianism" as a way of recognizing each individual's integrity and need for social embeddedness.

25. Ellis, *Peter Maurin*, 33.

2. It is a racketeering system because it is a profiteering system.

3. It is a profiteering system because it is a profit system.

4. And nobody has found the way to keep the profit system from becoming a profiteering system.

5. Harold Laski says: "In the Middle Ages the idea of acquiring wealth was limited by a body of moral rules imposed under the sanction of religious authority."

6. But modern business men tell the clergy: "Mind your own business and don't butt into our business."

... Economic Economy

1. In the Middle Ages, they had a doctrine, the doctrine of the Common Good.

2. In the Middle Ages, they had an economy which was economical.

3. Their economy was based on the idea that God wants us to be our brothers' keepers.

4. They believed in the right to work for the worker.

5. They believed in being fair to the worker as well as the consumer.

6. They believed in doing their work the best they knew how for the service of God and men.[26]

Probably Maurin idealized the Middle Ages for rhetorical purposes and for highlighting the flaws of capitalism. But from these two segments of an easy essay, we see many of Maurin's values emerge: nonviolence, disdain for capitalist abuses of the working class, Christian love, the dignity of the person and of work, and a conservative tendency to idealize previous ways of life.[27]

Day differed from Maurin on her level of credulity regarding the Church. As Casey Cep puts it, "Day had reservations about Catholic

---

26. Maurin, "Sit-Down Technique," 1.

27. Obviously Maurin had not dwelled on the darker aspects of feudal society, such as the nobles' exercising the right of "purveyance" (aristocrats taking whatever they wanted from serfs), tax extraction methods, the (largely symbolic) *jus primae noctis* (claiming the right of first sexual encounter with newlyweds), and other abuses of peasants and their families. He also downplayed the corruptions of both church and state during the Middle Ages. See W. R. Jones, "Purveyance for War"; Wettlaufer, "*Jus Primae Noctis*"; Firnhaber-Baker, "Seigneurial Violence."

dogma, was dismayed by the faith's history of impieties and intolerance, and, above all, had no patience for its failures to live up to Christ's core teachings."[28] Day famously clashed with the New York Diocese's Cardinal Spellman over her restatement of consistent pacifism in 1942, in the midst of WWII.[29] The US Conference of Catholic Bishops continued to maintain an ambiguous stance towards the war that sought to frame it within traditional just war doctrine.[30] Day's position on the war hit the Catholic Worker movement hard, resulting in the loss of thousands of newspaper subscribers. According to Mize, the "closing of Houses of Hospitality (from 32 to 10) can at least in part be attributed to Day's unyielding commitment to pacifism during World War II. No other occasion rivals this 1942 declaration against warfare for bringing into stark relief the radical posture encountered in Day's pacifism."[31]

It is undeniable that the war did not end, and many poor were not served, by Day's absolutism on nonviolence. Her position on war arguably was most inspired by the work of Leo Tolstoy.[32] She was always saying things that were (in today's verbiage) politically incorrect. She repeatedly voiced her admiration for Fidel Castro, a position opposed to the thoroughgoing anti-communism of the American Catholic Church at the time, exemplified by the televised rhetoric of Bishop Fulton Sheen.[33] In short, Dorothy Day was a Catholic who, while personally devout in her convictions, daily Mass attendance, and most of her moral positions, nevertheless was frequently at odds with the church hierarchy over its relative conservatism, social inaction, and its position on just war.

> The same woman who attended Mass every day of her adult life, refused to hear any criticism of the Pope, and accepted Vatican teachings on all matters concerning sex, birth control, and abortion could be blistering in her remarks about priests who lived in well-appointed rectories and turned a blind eye to racial segregation in their own parishes, bishops who were allies of the rich and powerful, and Catholic writers who viewed patriotism and faith as equivalent virtues, who were

28. Cep, "Dorothy Day's Radical Faith," para. 22. Cep continues, "Still, to her mind, her politics were not contradicted but confirmed by the Catholic Church, both in the Gospels and in two of the most consequential encyclicals of the post-industrial age."
29. Mills, "Cardinal Spellman."
30. Coy, "Conscription and Catholic Conscience," 55.
31. Mize, "We Are Still Pacifists," 1.
32. Christoyannopoulos and Nelson, "Leo Tolstoy's Impact."
33. Day, "About Cuba."

more concerned with the threat of "godless Communism" than the needs of the poor.[34]

Given Day's attraction to leftism and her fraught relationship to the institutional church, it is particularly impressive that the relatively conservative Peter Maurin and Dorothy Day successfully united in the context of their concern for the working class. They were in agreement in their consistent regard for the church's social teachings, even as they continued to approach the problems of poverty and war with different styles and different toolkits. Together, they established the first Catholic Worker House of Hospitality in New York City in 1933. This part of the movement aimed to create a community where volunteers could live in solidarity with the poor and practice the spiritual and corporal works of mercy. Over time, the *Catholic Worker* newspaper became a prominent platform for advocating social change and challenging the prevailing capitalist economic order. Their shared commitment to nonviolence and their belief in the dignity of every human being led Catholic Workers to engage in various forms of activism, including protesting against war and for workers' rights, though it is safe to say that the activity of protesting was more aligned with Day's than with Maurin's prior commitments.

There has never ceased to be a split in the Catholic Worker movement about priorities and goals. The more radical-liberal activities of the movement, namely the anti-war protests and political advocacy for laudable causes such as workers' rights, racial equality, and, for some, gay rights, have disturbed some other supporters of the movement mightily. For instance, coming from the orthodox Catholic perspective in 1994, Ann O'Connor wrote in the *New Oxford Review* that "many houses and individual Catholic Workers are in varying degrees of rebellion against one or more of the Church's doctrines or disciplines. Some houses have no Catholics as Workers, and/or have Workers who are ex-Catholics or anti-Catholics. Much of the Catholic Worker has become incoherent, if not downright dishonest, in claiming the name Catholic Worker."[35]

O'Connor also complained about the feminist and gay elements in the movement, a presence that, if anything, has grown over time. But, then and now, the demand that Catholic Workers must conform to church orthodoxy runs up against the reality that the movement never was terribly obedient to the church. Remember that there is no enforcement

---

34. Loughery and Randolph, *Dorothy Day*, 178.
35. O'Connor, "Catholic Worker," 6.

mechanism that determines who is a Catholic Worker or what constitutes a Catholic Worker house of hospitality or farm.[36] Some churches have chosen to link themselves to a particular house, farm, or other project. But there is no official church policy that encourages Catholic Worker operations to depend on or affiliate with a local Catholic church or with the church at large. Ironically, Catholic critics who think the movement is not orthodox enough are demanding adherence to the doctrine of a church that has always kept the movement at arm's length. Its two devout cofounders had ideas about adhering strictly and consistently to Catholic social teaching in ways that, from the very inception of the movement, made the American church hierarchy uncomfortable. Also, as we've seen, Dorothy Day was an absolute pacifist, and Maurin identified with pacifism, though perhaps not as absolutely as Day. But the church has never agreed with strict pacifism. The bottom line: proponents of church orthodoxy will find it hard to demand control over a movement that the church has never seriously sought to aid and guide.

Today, the Catholic Worker website notes that most participants are Catholics,[37] but it is unclear how its author knows that. I cannot find any scientific survey of Catholic Workers, let alone one that determines their religious affiliations or lack thereof. It would be difficult if not impossible to do a valid survey of a movement that is so spontaneous and whose operations, and participants, come and go so frequently. Catholic Worker houses of hospitality are sometimes run by Protestant Christians and even by "nones" or atheists. In 2014, Rosalie Riegle noted the changes from the early days, which included a growing diversity in participants: "The main differences I can see are these: more families than in the early days, more diversity in religious beliefs than when most of the Workers came from Roman Catholic backgrounds, more and more successful farms than the old days when most CWs on the land simply knew little about farming, and different attitudes towards sustainability."[38] According to the official website, there are currently 187 Catholic Worker communities in the United States and other

---

36. The current Catholic Worker website suggests reading the principles statement on their website before deciding whether to call one's operation Catholic Worker, but this is an honor system, and it is not clear what authority the makers of the website claim or how much that request matters to the various people in the movement.

37. Cornell, "Brief Introduction," para. 10.

38. Riegle, "Catholic Worker Movement," para. 18.

parts of the world.[39] These communities are characterized as "committed to nonviolence, voluntary poverty, prayer, and hospitality for the homeless, exiled, hungry, and forsaken. Catholic Workers continue to protest injustice, war, racism, and violence of all forms."[40]

Today, some Catholic Worker operations follow Catholic orthodoxy in their stances on issues such as homosexuality and abortion, and some are wildly out of line with official church moral teachings. In a strange twist, right now it seems that the older Catholic Workers do more protesting of war and oppression, and the younger ones are more attracted to traditionalism and Catholic teachings. It is not unknown for these two sides to clash. The *Tradistae* podcast (no longer producing new content) is an example of a tendency within Catholic Worker, attractive to newer adherents, whose aim is to bring a Catholic sensibility and consistency to the movement, and whose "vibe" is definitely traditionalist.[41] *New Polity* is a relatively new website and journal that represents a similar, but perhaps more openly conservative stance, weighing into the typical right-liberal hot-button issues of sexual orientation, transsexual identity, and abortion, though it is also consistently anti-capitalist.[42] Dr. Larry Chapp, host of the Gaudium et Spes 22 YouTube channel and podcast, has weighed into the debate about what the Catholic Worker should be by proclaiming Day was not a socialist but "a kind of conservative Catholic, who radically sought to kick back against the notion that the call to live a life of holiness is reserved for the Church's elites in religious life."[43] But though he claims that she accepted "all of the Church's teachings,"[44] that is not exactly true. As we

---

39. But as long-term Catholic Worker and CW scholar Riegle notes, "Don't take that list too seriously as CW houses come and go. If you want to visit and don't know anyone who lives there, please call first" ("Catholic Worker Movement," para. 30).

40. Catholic Worker Movement, "About Catholic Worker Movement," para. 2.

41. For instance, its manifesto states, "Rather, we stand for the living flame of a very different traditionalism, a beautiful, living thing, ever ancient and ever new! In the words of the Holy Father, 'Here we see the authentic Tradition of the Church, which is not a static deposit or a museum piece, but the root of a constantly growing tree. This millennial Tradition bears witness to God's work in the midst of his people and 'is called to keep the flame alive rather than to guard its ashes'" (*Querida Amazonia* §66). "In every age, this living flame of Tradition has burned ever brighter by 'scrutinizing the signs of the times and . . . interpreting them in the light of the Gospel' (*Gaudium et Spes* §4)" (Barnes et al., "Manifesto of New Traditionalism").

42. See for instance Barnes, "Pope John Paul II."

43. Chapp, "Whither Catholic Worker Movement," para. 2.

44. Chapp, "Whither Catholic Worker Movement," para. 4.

have seen, she was always in tension with the institutional church, and she clearly knowingly maintained a differing position on war, which was one of the two chief problems the Catholic Worker movement meant to address. Defining Dorothy Day seems to be the arena in which the quest to define the Catholic Worker movement gets played out now. All of this means that the movement and orthodox Catholicism have always had a fraught relationship. The fact that Dorothy Day, one of the movement's two cofounders, is currently being considered for sainthood by the church makes this situation even more interesting.[45]

The current mission statement on the Catholic Worker website is quite sectarian. For instance, it says, "The aim of the Catholic Worker movement is to live in accordance with the justice and charity of Jesus Christ. Our sources are the Hebrew and Greek Scriptures as handed down in the teachings of the Roman Catholic Church, with our inspiration coming from the lives of the saints."[46] The website claims to be informed by social encyclicals from *Rerum Novarum* onward. It states that these teachings are forthrightly critical of capitalism for its exploitation of workers, the alienating effects of capitalist labor, the use of debt as a means of control, capitalism's rejection of natural limits, and its damaging effects on our environment. Capitalism pits owners and workers against each other, and heightens racism and sexism as means of control. Further, the website states that capitalism encourages society to leave those who are deemed unproductive behind, and that it has produced a "spiritual destitution" that leads to "isolation, madness, promiscuity and violence."[47] It also states that the movement opposes the enlargement and bureaucratization of both government and business and notes the growing nexus between the two. It observes that this tendency reduces our ability to influence the direction of either one, despite our supposed democratic and free-market institutions.[48] Finally, it says that Catholic Workers oppose the "arms race," seeing in our huge military structures the means not only of death in war but the

---

45. The Dorothy Day Guild was created to support the canonization of Dorothy Day, and collects all information and news related to that cause. See https://www.dorothydayguild.org.

46. Catholic Worker Movement, "Aims and Means," para. 1.

47. Catholic Worker Movement, "Aims and Means," para. 7.

48. Catholic Worker Movement, "Aims and Means," para. 6.

impoverishment of many people due to the diversion of social resources into destructive instead of life-giving activities.[49]

Putting aside the question of how orthodox the movement is, most Catholic Workers seem to agree on the core values of personalism, voluntary poverty and charity, decentralization, and the desirability of a "green revolution," Maurin's term for following ways of Irish monasticism. Wishloff explains, "Since in Maurin's mind our present age was very much like the age of the fall of the Roman Empire, he turned to the historical example of Irish Missionaries and their laying of the foundations of medieval Europe after the collapse of the ancient regime in Rome."[50] The Irish program (much like Sillon's) was to create study circles for the clarification of thought, along with houses of hospitality where the poor and the more fortunate could meet and work together, and agricultural communes where people could learn the skills of independence. Maurin also brought the philosophy of personalism into the movement. Personalism stands against "looking to the state or other institutions to provide impersonal 'charity.'"[51] He taught people to take personal responsibility for others' well-being, rather than relying on the state, and to move away from "self-centered individualism" towards acknowledging the true dignity of each human being, regardless of economic status. His advocacy for decentralization followed the church's teachings on subsidiarity: what can be done at the local level should be handled at that level rather than handed up to a higher, probably more bureaucratic, and impersonal level. For these reasons, Catholic Workers urge people to consider homesteading, operating or supporting small businesses and farms, and forming cooperatives. No doubt environmental change would result from a renewed respect for the dignity of labor and a proper relationship with the land. The Catholic Worker movement aims to rehumanize labor and social life, and to use technology appropriate to those ends rather than allowing technology to further alienate us.

From the very first Catholic Worker house started in New York City, there have been two dimensions to the houses and farms. One dimension is communal. Some of the volunteers involved in the operations stay for the rest of their lives as did Day and Maurin. Some stay for a few years, and some for far shorter stints. The general disposition of those involved is to live communally, so they usually share housing,

49. Catholic Worker Movement, "Aims and Means," para. 8.
50. Wishloff, "Hard Truths," 24.
51. Catholic Worker Movement, "Aims and Means," para. 11.

chores, and decision-making tasks. However, they do not work primarily to support one another, but to deal with the other dimension of the Catholic Worker mission, the spiritual and corporal works of mercy towards the poor. Catholic Workers usually provide for many of their own needs while they live communally. This means, while they are not typically paying rent to live at the houses or farms, they are also not relying on the work they and others do to address their other (albeit minimalist) needs. This arrangement can become stressful when Catholic Workers have families with children, a situation in which part-time work and voluntary poverty begin to clash with the interests of the family. Sometimes the situation becomes untenable, and it is time for them to leave and seek a more stable financial situation for the sake of their retirement, and their children's future.

Remember that the church does not seriously support Catholic Worker operations and never has, thereby eliminating one avenue by which Catholic Workers could give a lifetime to their mission without experiencing radical precarity. But many Catholic Workers consider voluntary poverty to be a core principle and a virtue, and they are willing to accept that they cannot stay forever. Because of this dimension of Catholic Worker beliefs and practices, and because they are primarily still acting towards the poor and not with the poor, the movement cannot clearly escape the liberal charity model. Voluntary poverty and benevolence are, by their very nature, acts of privilege, regardless of what the workers forego, because there is a tremendous difference between voluntary poverty and poverty that is inescapable. The communal element of Catholic Worker houses is largely among the givers, and they extend a comradely hand to those who largely still mainly receive.

Catholic Workers often call those they help their guests, and they make every attempt to befriend them socially and even in some cases include them at least temporarily in decision-making in their communities. They are trying to do something that is at the limits of what is possible. Most of the people served by the houses are homeless, often with mental illnesses and/or substance abuse problems, and are not good candidates for participating in decision-making. There is also another reality with which these operations are obviously dealing. There are many more poor people to help than there are those who would practice voluntary poverty by giving up at least some of their lifetime earnings and social potential to years of service. If it were possible to welcome the poor to live and work in Catholic Worker communal operations as full members, they would vastly outnumber those who were voluntarily poor.

The implication of all this is another irony: to fully accept the poor as coequal members of a house of hospitality would necessarily mean making the ideal of voluntary poverty obsolete. Instead, the emphasis would almost necessarily have to be working together, pooling resources, living better, and exiting poverty. Of course, this could happen only with those who were not so degraded by their prior circumstances that they could not muster the considerable mental and physical resolve to live in cooperation with others. Catholic Worker houses primarily serve the latter kind of person, those who are incapable of concerted cooperation, through no fault of their own. If the task was, instead, to save people before they get to that point of degradation, Maurin's communal farms would be the better inspiration. But the communal farms also have not proven to be a substantial avenue for those who hope to alleviate the poverty and insecurity of the precariat. Communal farms are up against so many obstacles it would take another book to even explain them, but chief among them is the transformation of our agricultural and food system discussed in previous chapters. This transformation makes the task of feeding oneself through one's own labor and dedicating much time to this, as opposed to making money, impractical and risky. For those of us interested in finding a model for helping the precariat achieve greater social solidarity and material security, a more promising route than either the traditional houses of hospitality or communal farms must take the concerns and the experience of the movement forward, into new forms of cooperation better suited to our current conditions.

If Catholic Workers cannot escape liberal charity in their relations to those who are poor, even less do they manage to escape the liberal political model, and the two conditions go hand in hand. The implicit charity model enacted in Catholic Worker houses depends on the existing economy and political order. Without donations of money, food, clothing, etc. coming in, houses of hospitality would not be able to continue their outreach to the poor, and those donations are predicated on an economy of excess—on people not living communally, not working part-time, and not living in a minimalist fashion. It stands to reason, then, that Catholic Worker politics would not seek to upend the political system that is intertwined with and supports that economic system on which Catholic Worker operations rely. Instead, most Catholic Worker actions fall into the category of petitioning for the redress of

THE ROLE OF CHURCH AND CHRISTIAN ECONOMIES

grievances, a wholly liberal strategy. The most radical actions Catholic Workers take towards the government come in the form of civil disobedience. Dorothy Day was famous for leading an act of civil disobedience every year on the day in New York City when everyone was supposed to practice getting into their bomb shelters. Day knew that the whole drill was futile, and thought it was about conditioning people to submit to the government's priorities through terror. So, on that day, she and others refused to go into shelters and, instead, conducted an outdoor sit-in, peacefully holding anti-war signs. Repeated every year, this demonstration grew until hundreds were joining. Eventually, NYC decided to not require the bomb shelter drills. However, nuclear weapons continued to proliferate, and the Cold War got more dangerous.

While Day's actions at least resulted in some marginal change around the (mainly perceptual) edges of the American war machine, most such protests have resulted in little more than raising awareness. The obvious exception would be the civil rights protests in the 1960s, which Day and the Catholic Worker movement supported and in which they participated. Arguably those protests were more effective in the long run (though obviously far from completely effective) because racism and racial discrimination problem in America is palpably and inescapably felt by its victims. It involves the actual, visible, and brutal treatment of Black people. Blacks and those who supported them were willing to risk their lives while engaging in civil disobedience and protests, and of course they did. Their prolonged and sometimes bloody struggle resulted in changing the minds of the American majority in favor of basic civil rights for Blacks. This was no minor achievement, even if it is still only a partial victory. Most protesters today, whether involving Catholic Workers or others, do not put their lives on the line, because they are not as immediately and directly threatened—their battle is not felt as existential.

If the Catholic Worker history is a kind of test case, then we can conclude that exiting the liberal frame is hard to do even in an organization that was founded upon anarchist lines and was and is highly critical of capitalism in the name of consistent Christianity. Even a movement that aspires to communal houses and farms, living in voluntary poverty in radical solidarity with the poor still operates within and heavily relies on the overall capitalist economy to provide its charitable outreach. Even a movement that puts a heavy emphasis on direct personal action spends a lot of time protesting for changes in government policy.

It is important to point out that these observations are not criticisms of the Catholic Worker movement so much as they are statements about what is possible. It is far from evident that moving completely away from liberal charity or politics would be a wise idea, or fruitful. As Alexandre Christoyannopoulos recently argued on a *Dustbowl Diatribes* podcast, we ought to distinguish between that which is mainly performative and futile and that which is truly efficacious. There are times when there is enough societal momentum behind a particular cause that to not head to the streets would be morally wrong. Actions such as the civil rights or Vietnam War protests in America, the mass protests that ended communism in Eastern Europe and the Soviet Union, or the Indian farmers' occupation, would be good examples of the latter.[52] Similarly, to not take advantage of the largesse of capitalism when it comes to the needs of the poor, such as food and clothing, would be irresponsible, but one could argue that there is a difference between fully relying on those methods and their results, and using them as springboards for building up actual organization and resiliency.

One influence on the early Catholic Worker movement that tends to be forgotten but may serve as a corrective to the tendency to acquiesce towards the liberal system is the proposal for a different kind of economy, one that is neither capitalist nor communist, but a third way. In the mid-twentieth century, this proposal was in the intellectual background of the criticisms Maurin and Day leveled at the US government and economy. It urged regulating the economy for human purposes instead of allowing the economy to regulate human beings for purposes of stockholder profits. This Catholic Christian economic theory, distributism, is our final stop.

Distributism

For Maurin and Day, personalism was essential to solving the problems of the poor, but it was not enough. They realized that only change at the societal level could narrow the vast gap between the rich and the poor that caused such humiliating degradation. Having rejected communism both because of its atheistic theoretical goals and because of its historic concentrations of power, they made proposals that seemed

---

52. L. Johnson and Hess, "Tolstoy Injection."

more practical, and they were attracted to the theory of distributism.[53] The theory of distributism emerged in the late nineteenth and early to mid-twentieth century in Catholic Christian circles, as people grappled with the then-obvious defects of capitalism and communism. Much of the inspiration for the theory of distributism came from the Catholic social teachings that had inspired Maurin and Day. The church long ago decided that there was nothing objectionable about private property, as long as people understood that they did not have an absolute right to use it indiscriminately and destructively.[54] As we have seen through examining D. C. Schindler's thought, the Catholic view still tends towards looking at private property as 1) an extension of the self (which is created in God's image) into the world, and therefore, 2) requiring responsible stewardship with the good of the planet and humankind foremost in mind. Though it is still theorized about in one form or another, distributism is a piece of the puzzle that was relatively downplayed early in the Catholic Worker movement, as workers tried to cope with adverse and evolving capitalist conditions. Nevertheless, it remains as part of the original Catholic Worker vision.

The distributist idea originated from a papal encyclical, Pope Leo XIII's *Rerum Novarum* (1891), and was developed further by succeeding popes such as Pius XI (*Quadragesimo Anno*, 1931), John Paul II (*Centesimus Annus*, 1991), and most recently Pope Francis (*Evangelii Gaudium*, 2013). The deep origins of the church's interest in distributism come from Aristotle, who famously disputed Plato's preference for communism in the top two classes of his *Republic*.[55] Whereas Plato had rejected the goodness of the body and posited that leaders would never think of the common good if they had private families and property, Aristotle argued that humans have souls and bodies that are inextricably intertwined. Because of humanity's worldly nature, Aristotle did not think communism of either property or people would work. It would create what Garret Hardin called the "tragedy of the commons," in which everybody used, but no one took responsibility for, shared

---

53. Zwick and Zwick, "Dorothy Day, Peter Maurin."

54. This teaching on property is associated with the Catholic idea of the "universal destination of goods," i.e., what God intended was for each person to be adequately supplied by his natural bounty. See Spieker, "Universal Destination of Goods."

55. Plato's proposal for communism can be found in *The Republic*, bk. 5. Aristotle argues against communism with practical and not moral reasons in *Politics*, bk. 2.

property.⁵⁶ Aristotle argued that people would care only about things they owned, and which they could control for the benefit of themselves and those closest to them.⁵⁷ A thriving state would ensure that people had an interest in its well-being, that they could see their interests were intertwined necessarily with the common goods of protection and peace. Aristotle's view of property fit with the church's view that there was nothing wrong, and a lot right, with people owning property if they did not abuse it or use it to impoverish others.⁵⁸

Aristotle thought that property ownership was essential to practicing many of the virtues, including generosity, magnanimity, and moderation.⁵⁹ Indeed, human beings were social animals who could not completely flourish without full citizenship in a polis or city-state. In such a community, rightly governed, people could fulfill their excellences as men and women and as citizens. But a person could not be a full citizen if he did not feel secure enough to speak freely, and that required the financial security of property.⁶⁰ Aristotle advocated for fostering a strong middle class. People could not be abjectly poor and concern themselves with the public good, because their entire lives would be preoccupied with survival. They could not be too rich and concern themselves with the public good either, because their wealth would necessarily be predicated on others being poor. In any case, the wealthy would not take kindly to admitting lesser voices into deliberation.⁶¹

Aristotle's teachings were absorbed into church doctrine through thirteenth-century Catholic theologian Thomas Aquinas's synthesis. Aquinas had never experienced capitalism, of course, and the Aquinian ethic on property worked well as a moral ideal, until the emergence of

---

56. Hardin, "Tragedy of the Commons."

57. Aristotle, *Politics*, 1261a.10–20.

58. Mary L. Hirschfeld expounds on this teaching, developed by Aquinas, applying it to today's economy. She writes, "One of the key reasons that Aquinas is a useful interlocutor for modern-day economics is that unlike much of the Christian tradition, Aquinas does not think that the institution of private property is merely a concession to our fallen nature. On the contrary, private property is fitting to our finitude—working both to assign responsibilities and to channel our proper self-interest" (*Aquinas and the Market*, 32). See also Santori, *Thomas Aquinas*.

59. Aristotle, *Politics*, 1263b.1–10.

60. Aristotle taught that for there to be a strong citizenry, a polity needed a large middle class. Leslie Rubin attempts to apply this insight to the United States' government (*America, Aristotle, and Politics*).

61. Aristotle, *Politics*, 1295b.35–1296a.5.

capitalism.⁶² Distributism was proposed only after it was clear that advancing capitalism made Aquinas's teachings on property still valuable but inadequate. It attempted to attach the older medieval ethic about the proper use of property to the new capitalist situation. Instead of calling for a welfare state, distributists proposed private property and business moderated by the government in favor of ordinary people and small- and medium-sized farms and firms. In their day (and ours), the government managed property relations and welfare in ways that encouraged the concentration of property rather than its greater distribution. Distributists pointed out that capitalism and communism both encouraged a radical secularity and deprived most people of any substantial property.

In 1926, a group of friends—Hilaire Belloc, G. K. Chesterton, Cecil Chesterton, and Arthur Penty—founded the Distributist League and collaborated to formulate core distributist proposals. Prior to forming the league in 1912, in the wake of the Industrial Revolution and not long before WWI and the Russian Revolution, Belloc had published *The Servile State*. In it, he warned that if most ordinary people did not own property, slavery would be the inevitable result. Socialism, he argued, was not the answer. Socialists proposed to collect all property into the hands of the state, which would have a similar effect as capitalism—a concentration of property and the creation of a radical dependency of the masses upon the elites. A country in which "so considerable a number of the families and individuals are constrained by positive law to labor for the advantage of other families and individuals to stamp the whole community with the mark of such labor we call the Servile State."⁶³ Belloc understood the history we have already covered: capitalism had developed out of agrarian society with the assistance of governments that forced people off their ancestral lands and threatened dire punishments if they did not work for a wage. He observed: "Our legal machinery has become little more than an engine for protecting the new owners against the necessities, the demands, or the hatred of the mass of their dispossessed citizens. The vast bulk of so-called 'free' contracts are today leonine contract arrangements which one man was free to take

---

62. Marshall Bierson and Tucker Sigourney, for instance, discuss an aspect of Aquinas's view of property that does not accord with the modern liberal understanding of property, and which justifies (or nullifies) theft in situations of dire need ("Famine, Affluence, and Aquinas").

63. Belloc, *Servile State*, 7.

or to leave, but which the other man was not free to take or to leave, because the second had, for his alternative, starvation."[64]

The "moral base" of capitalism, for Belloc, told people that they were free and equal individuals, able to make contracts or not, i.e., "free to choose." However, that moral base obscured the reality that most people did not own property and were faced with the simple choice to work or starve. To work, they naturally agreed to all conditions necessary. Belloc also pointed out the fictional equality of owners and workers in employment contracts. The law held owners responsible for any harm to workers and customers in the workplace. He saw this as a sign of paternalism towards the workers. For Belloc, they were being treated more like slaves than like truly equal contracting parties. After all, workers could not begin to pay as individuals for the damages they might do to themselves and others in the workplace.

The welfare state was another indicator of virtual enslavement, in Belloc's opinion: "Capitalism must keep alive, by non-capitalist methods, great masses of the population who would otherwise starve to death."[65] No doubt he would recognize the development of the servile state in American "workfare" policies that allow people access to many benefits only if they work a certain number of hours a week in typically precarious minimum-wage and gig jobs. These policies subsidize the corporations that use this cheap labor and do not have to provide much if any security for their low-level employees.[66] In fact, workfare is anticipated in this quote by Belloc: "Where there is compulsion applicable by positive law to men of a certain status, such compulsion in the last resort by the powers at the disposal of the State, there is the institution of Slavery."[67] Any viable basic minimum income proposal would no doubt have to include similar work requirements in order to be politically attractive to most US voters. Belloc also pointed to the problem with the liberal charity model. In his view, it helps to alleviate people's suffering, but does not fundamentally change the system in which their suffering is necessary. The only way to really change our situation, according to Belloc, is to break the cycle of dispossession, to somehow give people back enough property that they no longer are forced to work for another person simply to survive. But Belloc was not sanguine about the potential for redistribution in England

64. Belloc, *Servile State*, 36.
65. Belloc, *Servile State*, 38.
66. USDA Food and Nutrition Service, "SNAP Work Requirements."
67. Belloc, *Servile State*, 7.

or anywhere else. He thought that it was more likely that capitalism would result in some form of socialism. This was because people had already been degraded by capitalism—they were too motivated by personal security, and too accustomed to being dependent.

G. K. Chesterton gave his views on distributism in his book *The Outline of Sanity* (1912), in the same year that the *Titanic* sank in the Atlantic, killing over 1,500 people, including three quarters of the third-class travelers. He too wrote about the forced migration from country to city due to changes in land use and agriculture, emphasizing the plight of the dislocated masses in urban areas, desperate for work. Chesterton was shocked by the gross disparities between the rich in their mansions and the poor living in urban slums. *The Outline of Sanity* was written before WWI, the Bolshevik Revolution, and the Great Depression, but Chesterton warned his readers about the social dynamics that would later lead to those catastrophic events. The cheap labor of the urban poor was beginning to fuel the rise of big conglomerates, which further distorted the physical and political landscapes. He wondered even then if the situation was remediable. In his view, it was clear that most poor urbanites would be better off back on the farm, and this conclusion was partly based on the Irish land reforms occurring at the time.[68]

On the surface, Chesterton's argument sounded like he wanted society to simply return to earlier times, but this would be an unfair interpretation. He thought deeply about what work was for within the context of developing capitalism, and he pondered what made for a good human life in that context. First, he argued, work should not be menial (i.e., servile) or exploitative. Rather than being hyper-specialized, it should develop human talents and capabilities. It should not constantly work against the need for human skill through indiscriminate automation.[69] To be dignified, human work should produce real, useful things, not consumerist junk that wasted people's money and deteriorated their character. And all people should have time for leisure, time for play, in which to refresh themselves and engage in a variety of humanizing activities.

Chesterton clearly thought that rural life and diversified subsistence agriculture were more likely to yield humane values and results than urban life, with its often inhuman work. Remember our example of the Indian farmers protesting neoliberal reforms, outlined in chapter

---

68. Sparkes, "Chesterton the Economist," 41.
69. McDaniel, "Chesterton's Distributism," 525–26.

2. Surely Chesterton would have approved of the efforts of these farmers to preserve their way of life, a life that was more noble, interesting, independent, and free than that of the typical urban worker. And he would have seen the system that was in place, which those farmers want to preserve, as a form of distributism. This is because with price supports and a regulated market, prior to Narendra Modi's attempts to change to a neoliberal model, the Indian government had created the conditions for small and medium farm operators to continue to own their farms. Canada is another example of a country that is struggling with, but still resisting the pressure to, give in to free-market pressures when it comes to their agricultural products.[70]

We may ask, is Chesterton's preference for the life of subsistence farming, even if imaginable in his day, imaginable now? Before too quickly answering in the negative, we should think about the urban poor today, the homeless, the unemployed, the underemployed, and the fully employed but low-paid workers with no benefits or job security. Our cities are filled, and our economy fueled, by a huge underclass that is largely unseen by those who are not a part of it. Our underclass may not look the same now as it did in the 1910s and '20s. Now it includes baristas and Lyft drivers, administrative assistants, wait staff and cooks, clerks, seasonal construction workers and call-center staff, manicurists and hair cutters, lawn mowers and snow removal people, elder- and childcare providers. It includes everyone from the mentally ill and drug-addicted homeless, to all people "one paycheck away" from eviction, from losing their cars, from defaulting on their loans. They comprise our degraded urban poor, most of whom work to keep other urban people in their more affluent lifestyles, the rest hoping for a handout from our material largesse.

Would members of this underclass be eager for the distributist solution, if it were mainly Chesterton's solution of going back to the land? Perhaps not, if it looked like a gamble filled with debt that might not be repayable, or a life of backbreaking work. But what if, instead, the government organized and supported diversified farming with anything like the financial and market supports, regulations and institutional aid it now devotes to industrial agriculture?[71] What if it truly created a system

---

70. "Canada has tightly controlled supplies of dairy, eggs and poultry since the 1970s, restricting how much farmers can produce and limiting imports through onerous tariffs" (Reuters, "Explainer," para. 2).

71. V. Smith et al., *Agricultural Policy in Disarray* (2 volumes). Both volumes were written to influence the 2018 Farm Bill. While not everyone will agree with the AEI's

that allowed for new farmers to do their jobs in a modern, functional way, integrated with the best technology at a scale that supported truly fulfilling human labor, and with a guarantee of health care and retirement security? Then, I suspect, in the spirit of Chesterton, who thought that the desire to grow things was instinctual, the leap from being a barista or day laborer to being a farmer might look attractive.

Arthur Penty's *Distributism: A Manifesto* (1937) was commissioned by the Distributist League after Chesterton's death, so it provides a good summary of the original league's points. The manifesto makes it clear that distributists think that poverty and other problems associated with capitalism do not stem from private property per se, but from "the maldistribution of property that has come about as a consequence of laws favouring large ownership at the expense of small, and the absence of laws to prevent the misuse of money and machinery."[72] In other words, distributists believe that governments always influence economics. A "pure" market, unadulterated by politics, has never existed and is not possible. The question is, what type of economy is promoted by our politics? Likewise, the distributist position on machinery/technology is that it should be regulated and controlled so that it does not dominate the people it is supposed to serve. To allow technology to be developed without any moral oversight or control is to court disaster. For Penty, chief among the disastrous results was the loss of jobs and meaningful, humanizing work for many people, but today's distributists also point to the devastating consequences for our environment. A newly revived Distributist Party in England puts it this way:

> The National Distributist Party recognises the urgent need to address the climate crisis, both within Britain and on a global scale. We are dedicated to safeguarding our environment at all costs and fostering a harmonious relationship between our nation and the land we call home.
>
> Our green policies emphasise the importance of utilising local produce rather than relying on imports. We believe in building a nation that respects and integrates with its natural surroundings. Town planning should embrace the natural materials

---

political ideology or its goals for US agriculture, these volumes use data and facts to establish the extent to which US subsidies, farm policy, welfare policy, crop insurance, and other programs, to name a few, primarily help the wealthiest and biggest of farmers and do not encourage competition.

72. Penty, *Distributism*, 10.

available, creating communities that truly reflect the character of our people and the land they inhabit.

The NDP is resolute in its commitment to protect the environment from the scourge of plastic waste. We pledge to ban single-use plastics in Britain, contributing to a cleaner and healthier world. Our policies are designed to ensure that Britain plays its part in safeguarding not only our homeland but also the entire planet.[73]

Arthur Penty states that distributists oppose speculative investments and income from interest. Money should be used only as a "common measure of value," by fixing "prices, wages, and rents at a just level." Guilds would have to be formed to continually negotiate and enforce fixed prices, wages, and rents. In a distributist economy, it would not be impossible to make a profit, but the goal would be to disallow the leveraging of wealth to put smaller firms and property owners out of business. He reasoned that lending at interest would fade out in a system of fixed prices because "the guilds could supply credit to their members."[74] In an economy in which people fixate on making money with money through interest and dividends, the push is for constant economic growth but not an equal amount of consumption to match that growth. This would lead to events of disequilibrium in supply and demand in banking and business such as happened in the Great Depression and all the cyclical recessions we have encountered since. Penty argued that states had to find a release valve for all the labor power and wealth that expanded in capitalism beyond possible consumption. That release valve, he theorized, was war, the ultimate destroyer of excess wealth and technology, labor power and consumers. In the past, excess wealth and labor went into the building of great cathedrals, castles, and monuments. But, absurdly, in capitalism, these were far harder to justify than war. Penty called for the revival of spending on culture rather than death.[75]

Many of the difficulties and challenges explored in this book have been interwoven with the problems of the globalized economy, and

---

73. National Distributist Party, "Policy of the NDP," under "Protecting the Environment."

74. Penty, *Distributism*, 18–19.

75. One contemporary line of thought that resonates with these observations by Penty and other distributists is that of Achille Mbembe, author of *Necropolitics*. Mbembe's book set off a wave of scholarship on the phenomenon of necropolitics and its overcoming.

globalized agriculture specifically. Penty's distributist manifesto clearly sided with the idea, suggested especially in chapters 2–3, that national security and social welfare are acquired by obtaining as much self-sufficiency as possible, especially in food and raw materials, the very heart of life. He wrote, "Distributists believe that a society is only in a stable and healthy condition when its manufactures rest on a foundation of agriculture and home-produced raw material, and its commerce on a foundation of native manufactures."[76] He acknowledged that no country can be completely self-sufficient, and indeed some interdependence is an insurance policy against environmentally induced famine, but he still argued that the goal should be to grow about 80 percent of a country's food supply internally. Laissez-faire economics, he argued, is a practical impossibility. Acknowledging that economic protection has its flaws, he still argued the national fixing of wages and prices was beneficial, and that meant that imports needed to be controlled. Controlling imports was an honest form of protection, whereas "free trade" hid the many ways in which states protect corporate power. Distributists followed the principle of subsidiarity in their views of the state. A Catholic principle, *subsidiarity* teaches that what can be done at lower levels of social organization should be done at those levels.[77] It was dangerous, in Penty's view, to concentrate power into the hands of the state. But anarchism was not the answer either. He preferred the sharing of power in federal arrangements and privately governed social organizations like guilds.

The manifesto leaves us wondering how we would ever move from our much more complex and globalized economy to a more dispersed and varied system of resources and power. But Penty's views resonate, if anything, more now than when he wrote his manifesto in the 1930s, precisely because wealth and power are more concentrated in our system than ever before. We feel this, perhaps even more acutely, when our choices for how to live are constrained, and when our freedom of expression is limited, by what is socially acceptable according to our employers or social media platforms. The website of England's Distributist Party states: "The main ideologies of the NDP can be described as nationalism, social conservatism, distributism, agrarianism, and environmentalism. Through these stances, and through these stances alone, may we see Britain flourish. The

---

76. Penty, *Distributism*, 27.
77. For a brief explanation of subsidiarity, see Reno, "Subsidiarity."

mainstream political parties have abandoned us, placing their greed and profit over the people of this great nation."[78]

The sense that the old authorities are posturing but not delivering has captured our moment. We have lost faith in leaders who have clearly proven they do not know what they are doing. Under those circumstances, it is tempting to imagine we could place more responsibility into the hands of people less remote and abstract, and therefore arguably more caring and competent. However, we cannot know if an experiment like national distributism would work, or if it did work, that it would not be slowly transformed again towards centralization.

How could we change the dynamics of centralization permanently? How could we manage a more decentralized system in a time of rapid advances in information and other technologies, in a way that is fair, adequately democratic, and protective of basic universal rights? These are huge questions. We do know that sometimes people who *freely* decide to cooperate within the larger liberal, centralized system can do so successfully. Catholic Worker houses of hospitality and farms would be an example, as would older-style and modern privatized Israeli kibbutzim.[79] These experiments in living according to alternative religious and/or philosophical principles are limited, surely, by what the larger system will tolerate. That is, they can exist, and even sometimes thrive, because they are completely voluntary and because they are small, and not successful enough to pose a challenge to the existing order.

Conclusion

This chapter has been about what is truly possible within the Christian context. It may seem that I have put up roadblocks to any possible positive development by emphasizing the imperfections of people and the systems they create. The obstacles to seemingly sensible ideas for the reform of religious institutions, or Christian attempts to reinvent our

---

78. National Distributist Party, "Policy of the NDP," para. 1.

79. While I have focused on the Catholic Worker movement as an example of this type of activity, the kibbutzim of Israel also offers a robust history and current example of cooperative living in changing times. See Abramitzky, *Mystery of the Kibbutz*. There are many more such attempts at alternative communities. The Catholic Worker, however, stands out as a movement that consciously bridges into the world of those who are the most devastated by the existing order, rather than mainly focusing on retreating and protecting culture, practices, and faith within a community.

culture and economy, are numerous. But unless we understand how hard it is to really change our destructive trajectory, even among self-identifying Christians, we are going to stay on that trajectory. It is in that spirit that I have discussed two flawed but still promising elements within contemporary Christianity—the Catholic Worker Movement and the associated economic proposals of distributism. There are many more movements and ideas out there I could have highlighted, but the Catholic Worker movement seems to have more staying power than many idealistic/utopian movements in the modern capitalist era.[80] Catholic Worker operations, perhaps because of their rather anarchist nature, keep popping up like weeds, adapting to the social and economic environments at hand, dying but coming back time and again. The attractions of radical living, voluntary poverty, discovering Catholic social teaching, and even radical liberal politics, are real and compelling. Even though some of these elements would seem to get in the way of the movement's ability to contribute to our larger society's way of life, we must acknowledge that without them, it is very likely that the movement would not persist. Creating a mode of Christian living that could encompass more people over the course of their lifetimes would require what many Catholic Workers know well: persistent, often unglamorous work, realistic compromises with people's current attitudes and habits, and continual struggling with balancing material needs and desires with higher principles. I will try to describe what that may look like in my conclusion, in the spirit of contributing to a vision rather than simply analyzing problem. I hope that others will join in this imaginative conversation and open a door that has been closed for too long by capitalist realism.

---

80. Eugene McCarraher covers the amazing and painful history of American utopianism well: "The Beloved Commonwealth: Visions of Cooperative Enchantment, 1870–1920," *Enchantments of Mammon*, pt. 4.

8

Conclusions

AT THE BEGINNING OF this book, I introduced the "theory streams" I would use. I often say to people who react in fear to one or more of those streams (classical conservatism, leftism, Christianity, political psychology), "Be Not Afraid." I love how this sentiment is expressed in 2 Tim 1:7: "For God did not give us a spirit of cowardice but rather of power and love and self-control." The admonition to not fear appears in various forms in the Old and New Testament, enough to conclude that fear is an obstacle to trusting God and accomplishing good things. We know it is an obstacle to clear thinking. It tends to make people retreat, doubt their own abilities and strengths, and accept less than they are capable of or deserve. Saint Pope John Paul II admonished against fear at his papal installation ceremony on October 22, 1978. Here are his words:

> Brothers and sisters, do not be afraid to welcome Christ and accept his power. Help the Pope and all those who wish to serve Christ and with Christ's power to serve the human person and the whole of mankind. Do not be afraid. Open wide the doors for Christ. To his saving power open the boundaries of States, economic and political systems, the vast fields of culture, civilization and development. Do not be afraid. Christ knows "what is in man." He alone knows it.
>
> So often today man does not know what is within him, in the depths of his mind and heart. So often he is uncertain about the meaning of his life on this earth. He is assailed by doubt, a doubt which turns into despair. We ask you therefore, we beg

you with humility and trust, let Christ speak to man. He alone has words of life, yes, of eternal life.[1]

The pope was asking people not to be afraid to allow Christ's power to help them serve each person and all human beings. He was asking them to not be afraid to let this saving power break down borders and economic and political obstacles, trusting that Christ knows human nature better than we know it. He was asking us not to give into fear, doubt, and despair. He wanted us to do something to make the world better, not just to make ourselves as individuals better. On the hundredth anniversary of *Rerum Novarum*, the papal encyclical of Leo XIII that inspired Peter Maurin and Dorothy Day to start the Catholic Worker movement, John Paul II issued *Centesimus Annus* to commemorate and update Leo XIII's teachings for his times. Surely, he was thinking of the Catholic Worker movement, among other movements, when he referred to: "the fruitful activity of many millions of people, who, spurred on by the social Magisterium, have sought to make that teaching the inspiration for their involvement in the world. Acting either as individuals or joined together in various groups, associations and organizations, these people represent *a great movement for the defence of the human person* and the safeguarding of human dignity. Amid changing historical circumstances, this movement has contributed to the building up of a more just society or at least to the curbing of injustice."[2]

In addition to not validating the impulse to retreat into personal moral purity and quietism, John Paul II quickly demonstrated that he understood the basic Marxist analysis of capitalism. The terms he used to describe the appearance of capitalism on the world stage were also used by Marx. A "new form of property" emerged, he wrote. That form of property was "capital," whose singular aim was profit. Human labor "became a commodity" to be "bought and sold on the open market." This new type of labor, labor "for wages," threatened workers, who could not guarantee their own employment, with "death by starvation."[3] John Paul II, famously known for his anticommunism, and particularly the part he personally played in starting the revolt against communism in Soviet-occupied Poland, was not afraid to use the categories and terms previously deployed

---

1. John Paul II, "Homily of His Holiness," §5.
2. John Paul II, *Centesimus Annus*, §3; emphasis original.
3. John Paul II, *Centesimus Annus*, §1.

by Karl Marx, because he knew that it was reasonable for people confronted by the capitalist system to think in these terms.[4]

John Paul II did not agree with Marx about the solution to the problem of capital, and he obviously did not agree with the Soviet Union's methods. But he was not afraid to use these terms to capture and criticize the capitalist economic system. Previously, Leo XIII had fought back against the communist tendencies of his day with similar understanding. He understood that the complaints of the working class were valid, and he attempted to reason out an alternative to communism, a plausible way to address these problems without falling into a worldly system which did not consider human nature. In the same spirit, and one hundred years later, Pope John Paul II, who worked with Polish labor unions to set his people free from Soviet domination, proclaimed in *Centesimus Annus* the necessity of labor unions for guaranteeing workers' dignity and proper compensation.

John Paul II agreed with Leo XIII that property rights should not be absolute. Property rights should be constrained by their "original common destination as created goods." That is, God created the world for all mankind, not for some people more than others. Property rights were also constrained, the pope wrote, by "the will of Jesus Christ as expressed in the Gospel." He admonished us to see our property, though we owned it, as common to all. In other words, money and material possessions were not there for us to simply amass—they existed for our own use but also for others.[5] The general Marxist principle of "from each according to his ability, to each according to his needs" is close, at least in desired result, to the attitude Pope John Paul II called Christians to have towards their property. He argued that we should see not only our physical, but also our intellectual property in this way. He wrote:

> In this sense, it is right to speak of a struggle against an economic system, if the latter is understood as a method of upholding the absolute predominance of capital, the possession of the means of production and of the land, in contrast to the free and personal nature of human work. In the struggle against such a system, what is being proposed as an alternative is not the socialist system, which in fact turns out to be State capitalism, but rather *a society of free work, of enterprise and of participation.* Such a society is not directed against the market, but demands

---

4. Mounier agreed (*Personalist Manifesto*).
5. John Paul II, *Centesimus Annus*, §4.30.

that the market be appropriately controlled by the forces of society and by the State, so as to guarantee that the basic needs of the whole of society are satisfied.[6]

I have gone on at some length about *Centesimus Annus* because it should give right- and left-liberal Christians and Christian nationalists pause. John Paul II goes even farther in his economic understanding and analysis of capitalism than did Leo XIII. His arguments are theoretically informed and show exposure to many schools of thought, along with a strict fidelity to Catholic tradition and scriptural truth. He was bold. If there were dragons awakened in the very act of reading and understanding basic concepts of Marxist economics, the pope apparently was willing to face the dragons to make his point. If John Paul II wanted us to not be afraid to see the flaws of liberalism and capitalism, and if he wanted us to work to fundamentally improve our political economies, then we should take some inspiration and courage from that. It was in that spirit that I included all four theory streams, pouring them into what hopefully is a new river that can be drawn upon for new ideas.

Classical conservatism serves in this book as a counterweight to the deeply embedded influence of contemporary liberalism, the rising influence of the new nationalism (alt-right), as well as the religious traditionalism on offer as ideological options today, often mixed. In this book, whenever I have tried to steer the reader away from the tendency, as Eric Voegelin would put it, to "immanentize the eschaton," I have done so in the spirit of Burkean conservatism, as well as Christianity. Classical conservatives understand both that we must adapt to changing circumstances and that not everything new is actually "progress." To take a wary stance toward automation; to think about how advances in technology are inevitably woven into our social fabric in ways that could tear us apart; to call for mature, considered thinking about what is actually possible (rather than saying that we live in the "best of all possible worlds" or that we have to change our world completely to find our salvation); and to argue that human beings can take more responsibility for their own fate thereby are hallmarks of a truly conservative stance. And, taking faith back from idolatry and particularly the worship of mammon is, I would argue, a religious proposal that merits consideration by all Christians. On the other hand, faith in capitalism's autonomous market mechanisms, and the power of human beings ostensibly "free to

---

6. John Paul II, *Centesimus Annus*, §4.35; emphasis original.

choose," appears dangerously radical, naive, and strangely zealous. This faith, which proffers what Eugene McCarraher called "the enchantments of Mammon," is an instance of what Eric Voegelin would call "ersatz religion" and what Jung would call "ideological possession."

Hopefully the reader can see the streams of both faith and political psychology in these observations. I have tried to take faith seriously while not avoiding the genuinely useful observations afforded to us by political psychology as well as political theology. Human beings, it seems, are in their very nature deeply religious. It is not a question of whether they will believe in some higher power, but what that higher power will be. We have many false gods, among them technology, materialism and the market, the state, patriotism and nationalism, charismatic ministers and powerful churches, left and right political ideologies, left and right identity politics, and our own narcissism reflected in our social media posts.

When it comes to our agricultural system, the worship of bigger things and the global market has made it almost impossible to mount an argument for the smaller and more local or regional. No matter how many livelihoods have been lost or degraded, no matter how many families and communities have been decimated and dispersed, we have persisted. The state required economic globalization for the extension of national power. No matter how many people in rural *and* urban landscapes had to shift from place to place, or to deal with high levels of insecurity and social isolation, we generally believed it was all worth it, because we would continue to "grow." Ever-escalating economic growth was required for national power. No matter how misled, humiliated, and cheapened our social and spiritual lives were made by identity politics and exploitative religious and political cults, it was acceptable, because these things functioned to keep state and corporate power more secure than would sober, informed, and well-reasoned democratic citizens. A system has emerged, created piecemeal over time by those who wanted to gain and hold onto political and financial power, whose function is simply to continue to grow in wealth and power, and which allows these unpleasantries to continue because they either do it no harm or aid in its continued momentum.

Let me be perfectly clear. If you are concerned about the current state of our culture because of its contentiousness, seemingly amoral nature, the way it breaks up families, our loss of community, and the ever-swifter march of secularization, look no further for the cause than the economy that thoroughly dominates us. Our "freedom to choose" does not stop at our toothpaste brands, though it apparently increasingly does stop at being a small businessperson or small farmer. We are also free to choose to stay married or not, to be parents or not, to help our friends or not, depending on how we feel. As we have less real choice due to our mounting social stratification and precarity, our "freedom to choose" necessarily gets more and more intensely expressed in our personal moral choices and lifestyles, as well as our stylistic choices. If you don't like the way the kid down the street dyes their hair purple and wears tattoos, remember that they've been taught that the pinnacle of American freedom is in accumulation and personal expression. In effect, we are all in a constant state of flux, yet we are taught to fear the actual trans person, the one who has the courage to disregard the superficial freedoms most Americans "enjoy" every day because they feel in their interior person that they are not what their exterior says they are. Before we launch any more assaults on our trans neighbors, we need to consider the largely life-frittering ways in which the rest of us are inauthentically fluid, and change our own ways if we do not like what we see. If we do not want to stop divorcing our spouses, subsequently abandoning our children, getting cosmetic surgeries, buying excessive amounts of consumer goods in pursuit of meaning and happiness, obsessing about the latest identity fad, experimenting with ersatz and New Age religions, eating fake food of unknown origins, and keeping all our social options open, we should not say anything about the trans kid.

We tend to treat other people's gods as the ultimate threat to our own. That is why we act as though if we even hear their political or moral arguments, our entire souls will be polluted. How many people does it take to defend liberalism and capitalism? If the cloud of loud defensive voices isn't a faith response in favor of capitalism, I don't know what is. But our unwillingness to hear our neighbors really implies faithlessness, as though we are afraid our position cannot withstand any opposition, that it is empty. The best position is one that not only withstands arguments, but adapts to the parts of other arguments that are defensible and that we can live with. But this flexibility does not mean that we should adopt moral relativism. We must realize that we are inherently flawed (indeed sinful) beings for whom the best life is a struggle in which the goal is to not wholly fail, as we muddle through competing defensible ideals. If we stop trying because we reject the very concept of ideals as futile, impractical, etc., we implicitly reject our own moral nature. The most human aspect of ourselves is that part that insists on reaching upward, and which remains unsatisfied with imperfection, which knows we can be better, and does not give up. I believe we see that most human of natures in action in Catholic Worker and similar communities—people muddling through, making compromises with "reality," but still trying to determine what is right and live closer to that ideal.

Elsewhere I have argued that people often mistake talking for acting. If all we do is talk and argue about our competing values, we are wasting our time. The answer, however, is not to stop talking about what we believe, but to do so with the proper humility and with a strong prejudice for testing our talk by seeing if we can "walk the walk." *If we are not taking even small steps towards living in a way that matches up with what we say is right, then we need to stop talking until we can show our own investment in our ideals.* Walking the walk will quickly remind us of the gap between theory and practice articulated so well by Socrates in Plato's *Republic* long ago. At which practices do I think we should aim? What would life look like if we got there? In what follows I am putting forth what I consider a proposal for the sake of examination and debate, understanding that others will have arguments against it and different visions of the good life. I will focus on the individual level first, then the church, and finally the larger society.

First, for each of us, remembering that we are all too susceptible to being lured into ideological possession or cultlike followings, it would be wise for us to periodically take a bird's-eye view of our own behavior. If we have joined churches, parties, or other groups that either make us do things that run contrary to the teachings of Christ, because we want to finally find a home or have friends and feel embedded, we need to reassess our motives and choices and be willing to do as Chris Orozco did: leave them behind. For many people enmeshed in unhealthy social patterns and relationships, that can be enough for quite a while. It is an enormous step for those whose social life had largely revolved around a church, party, or both to be able to part with the sense of security they provided, at such a high price. Those of us who have not had to deal with this level of enmeshment should ask ourselves if we are also entangled in a less dramatic way in our own religious, political, and economic choices, and whether we are constrained by them from fully answering Jesus with a yes.

Once we are at least partly extricated, it is easier to see our possibilities, and we must go looking for other people. As Aristotle taught, we are social animals. But we must choose our friends wisely, and if they ask us to turn off our critical thinking capabilities, or do or say things that sow more discord than healing, we are not in the right place. Not everyone can find a church in their area that is not either divisive or corporate, or both. If so, remember that your "church" can be, and sometimes must be, the people you can find beyond the doors of the church you attend for the sacraments.

Having found some other people, think about what you can do with them, how you can cooperate with them to make everyone's lives better and easier. That may look like getting to know your neighbors and finding common ground so you can help each other. It may mean working within a church group and extending those relationships beyond the church walls. It may mean, if one has the courage to go farther, finding and joining a Catholic Worker house of hospitality or something like it to work in, and maybe even live in. It may mean starting a community like this yourself. But, for many of us, the first step must be making one-on-one connections with other well-meaning people willing to cooperate with us. To do that, we must be willing to give up some of our autonomy to deal with other people and their idiosyncrasies, and be willing to devote time and energy to doing constructive things together. This means devoting less time to other things we used to do more autonomously.

As an example, if you have a yard and can spare some ground, plant a garden with willing neighbors and share in the responsibilities and harvest. While this suggestion may seem tame, and even banal, my response is, if you can't plant a small garden with your neighbors (which is actually a very difficult social project to pull off, for many reasons I have discussed), then you certainly cannot graduate to a house of hospitality. In the garden experiment, you may very well be giving up your prior notions of private property, your choice of how and when to be in your own backyard, decisions about what food you eat, even your right to be alone. Food is intimately tied up with our lifestyles, economy, and environment. So, in another experiment, if you can afford it (and you might if you made different spending choices), purchase as much of the food you don't grow with your neighbors from local farmers. Again, this also sounds easy and even trite until you try it. It takes more time, because local purchasing is not typically a "one-stop" situation like going to the grocery store. It also takes more human contact by far, including the development of relationships and understandings between you and the growers. Bad behavior by you or the suppliers can lead to loss of reputation, and the whole arrangement means the loss of choice—the choice to buy watermelons in January, for instance. See if you can make it past a month. You may have to start over multiple times. If we cannot consistently make these types of changes because, after all, our autonomy is more important, then what else can't we do? It turns out that the utterly mundane is frighteningly difficult and, because of that, probably revolutionary.

Second, churches continue to be an important ingredient, despite their diminished capacity in recent decades. The United States is still a largely Christian country. Christianity has played a strong part in US politics throughout much of the country's history, and certainly does now. Moreover, Judeo Christianity provides the moral background of Western civilization. It is obviously important to understand the personal and social mandates of Christianity for many reasons, chief among them because the faith claims to give us the truth about ourselves and the meaning of our lives. It is obviously important to strive for better Christianity because it can either be helpful for solving our many problems, including economic precarity, cultural and political decay, and climate change, or it can cause and/or exacerbate those problems. I believe that American Christians have often politicized and distorted the religion to suit their individualism, materialism, and desire for dominance. This is certainly the case with Christian nationalists, who worship Donald Trump as a new messiah, as I hope my chapter on religious strong-arming demonstrates. But while some tend to associate "politicizing" with right-wing Evangelicals, the truth is that the term can be applied to many more denominations and orientations.

Most American mainline Protestants and Catholics, even those who consider themselves "progressive," have a view of their religion that is largely compatible with a heavy emphasis on individual autonomy, capitalist consumerism, and US foreign policy. To that extent, most American Christians are Christian nationalists. While the reader may agree that right-wing evangelical Christian nationalism is spiritually and politically problematic because the Trump phenomenon seems so destabilizing, he may have trouble seeing that his own opposing desire for stability at the cost of rejecting any serious attempt to change our economy and ways of life is also spiritually and politically problematic. For many progressive critics of Christian nationalists, government-promoted de facto censorship of the right wing in our public spaces is entirely legitimate. But if you watch news organizations that they watch, like CNN and MSNBC, you will see that they too promote capitalist realism, rampant consumerism, and an aggressive US foreign policy. In fact, the "liberals" have become more liberal on those issues than their "conservative" peers. They are, most often, ardent capitalists who believe in the efficacy of the free market, even if they hold that welfare programs are necessary. Listen to CNN's Fareed Zakaria if you have any doubts. These are not pacifists in any sense—their talk on war and international politics is usually patriotic and aggressive.[7] Timour Azhari, a Reuters news service bureau chief, puts it this way: "When you look at the reporting from Ukraine, you see a lot of journalists, whether they be from Ukraine, the U.S. or from Europe, who are extremely empathetic. They're embedded with Ukrainian troops. They're even covering Ukrainian drone strikes on Russian positions with a lot of support and a lot of empathy. Can you imagine CNN embedding with Palestinian resistance fighters in Israel, fighting against Israeli occupation? Both of those situations are essentially the same and I think that has raised questions."[8]

If most American Christians are Christian nationalists now, the solution is not to continue to hurl rocks at the other side, but to think beyond our nationalism, and our idolatrous attachment to the capitalist framework. For Christians, surely that would mean returning in humility to the source of our faith, as Brian Zahnd puts it, to the "unvarnished Jesus."[9] I am not talking about the right wing's latest penchant to warn people about the "woke Jesus," but a more serious approach that involves knowledge of early Christianity.[10] Generally, we are talking about *ressourcement* theology, a return to the words of Jesus even when they strike us as impractical, and to the early church fathers and mothers, even when their convictions seem too much for us to bear. Jesus and the early Christian sources, and anyone who has taken them seriously, seem scarily impractical. They insist on far too much holiness, including a disregard for wealth and power that, if followed well enough, would blow our world apart much as Peter Maurin thought the Church's social teachings would act like social "dynamite." Jesus also seemed to know that people could not measure up to teachings like his Sermon on the Mount, and needed forgiveness. But mercy does not absolve us from trying, and to try in a serious way and to make some long-term progress, we would need help

---

7. See Baum and Groeling, *War Stories*; Katchanovski and Morley, "Politics of U.S. Television."

8. T. Gregory, "Bias in Media Coverage," paras. 2–3. See also Olmstead, "Why Are CNN."

9. Zahnd, *Unvarnished Jesus*.

10. For the latest book arguing that Jesus was not "woke" as the "progressives" think he was, see Miles, *Woke Jesus*.

from our churches and other religious organizations. That means that our churches would have to abandon the individualizing and privatizing tendency in both Catholic and Protestant American Christianity. What we have been told is that pastors propose and inspire us, but it is not their job to tell us what to do with that inspiration. When I ask people why they think the Catholic Church does not ask parishioners to organize themselves in certain ways, and help them do so, the answer is usually that the task of the church is to teach, exhort, admonish, etc. We as individuals, having been properly admonished, are to dispose as we see fit. However, this arrangement responsiblizes us as isolated individuals in much the same way neoliberalism does generally. Somehow the burden for all social change starts with me. But is this so?

The Catholic Church's term for all the faithful who should be involved in the body of Christ in the world is the "lay apostolate." Pope Paul VI in *Apostolicam Actuositatem* clarified what the Church's relationship with the lay apostolate should be. He wrote, "Indeed, union with those whom the Holy Spirit has assigned to rule His Church (cf. Acts 20:28) is an essential element of the Christian apostolate. No less necessary is cooperation among various projects of the apostolate which must be suitably directed by the hierarchy."[11] Further, he wrote, "For in the Church there are many apostolic undertakings which are established by the free choice of the laity and regulated by their prudent judgment. The mission of the Church can be better accomplished in certain circumstances by undertakings of this kind, and therefore they are frequently praised or recommended by the hierarchy. No project, however, may claim the name 'Catholic' unless it has obtained the consent of the lawful Church authority."[12] If there was a church that would be most likely to aid, organize, and, when needed, direct the laity in their mission as Christians, it would be the Catholic Church. And yet, even as the church forges ahead with the process of canonizing Dorothy Day, there is still no official institutional connection between the church and the Catholic Worker movement that bears its name.[13] There are many reasons why this is so, and I have explored some of them in the chapter on religious

---

11. Paul VI, *Apostolicam Actuositatem*, §23.

12. Paul VI, *Apostolicam Actuositatem*, §24.

13. The directory of *International Associations of the Laity* on the Pontifical Council for the Laity website does not list the Catholic Worker movement among the recognized associations (Pontifical Council for the Laity, *International Associations*).

strong-arming. However, it must be said that the church has not really tried to make an official connection.

Supporting Catholic Worker operations at an official institutional level may involve more oversight than the workers want. The church would probably disapprove of some of the more radical liberal elements in the movement. It may very well be that this uneasy relationship must continue as it is. But what about other forms of church-supported lay organizing of the kind I argued for in chapter 7? Could Catholic and Protestant churches encourage the organization of their own people at the parish level to aid each other much more strongly? Could they create new kinds of parish communities that could bring people in, fostering in them a new sense of interdependence instead of an overreliance on money? Could they support people in their parishes who already wanted to do things like organizing community gardens and time banks, and sharing meals, work, and care? What people want, more than anything, is love, friendship, and help. Wouldn't more commitment to living and working together, which could still take place within the larger context of the capitalist system with private property, give a reality to Christianity that it often lacks when it is sequestered to services, study groups, and "volunteer opportunities"? It is disheartening to think that this proposal seems radical and even somehow dangerous, considering it is what human beings have done throughout most of human history and across cultures. We live in extraordinary times, when a sizable number of people in wealthy countries can afford to retreat to their rooms and not cooperate, and there they remain, surrounded by goods, services, and entertainment, but often miserable. That situation is truly strange, and dangerous.

If churches are dying, if more and more people are becoming "nones," it may very well be because churches are not promoting a natural, functional human community. The substitute for community, at its strongest, seems to be coffee klatches, discussion groups, and dinner meetups. It's hard for people to imagine it could mean more. But the best human communities are friendships based on common values and common activities, and the two are mutually reinforcing. Better friends are made when working side by side for a common cause, and this is where the charity model fails. There is a sense of camaraderie and purpose in cooperation, regardless of means, that you will never get writing a check or handing out a meal to someone in a line. The difference between a handout (or a hand up) and working together is immense because class differences are taken out of the equation. You can see and respect the person in front of you as true friendship material. Working together to benefit each other creates a sense of loyalty based on mutual respect and common purpose. Nothing breeds greater regard and indeed love than needing someone and being needed in return, and developing patterns of reciprocity. Giving and being given something in what we call "charity" is thin gruel by comparison.

Third, there is no substitute for government action when it comes to creating an environment in which these things can happen. There is much that the government can do, short of eliminating either private property or the market, to address the problems of the many people who are underemployed, precariously employed, working in unfulfilling jobs, and whose jobs are continuously threatened by escalating automation and artificial intelligence. However, there is no getting around the fact that anything we do that is significant enough to address the needs of our rural and urban precariat will involve increased redistribution of wealth and an openness to new win-win solutions. Not that long ago, in the Nixon administration, the top marginal tax rate was 70 percent. In 1957, the year that *Leave It to Beaver* originally aired, the top marginal rate was 91 percent. Currently, the top marginal rate is 23 percent.[14] This reflects our changed priorities as a nation as well as our willingness to continue to carry a lot of national debt to make up some of the difference. Any attempt to raise the top corporate tax rates would have to find a way to enforce that on corporations doing business in and beyond the United States. A big part of the reason we are in this mess is because corporations go to states, and other countries, where taxes are lowest and try to shelter their profits there. The result is a "race to the bottom," currently won by Barbados. Donald Trump's instincts, at least as expressed in his official rhetoric, were fairly good on the state of corporate tax dodging. It will not be easy to find the best way to stop corporations from continual tax evasion, but it is necessary to solve the problems that have led to our current political impasse and the threat of continual political instability caused by our ideological divisions.

With enough funds we could continue to take the Internet to every part of the country, allowing the many remote workers to resettle in places they or their parents and grandparents left behind, places that may look particularly attractive to families, namely small and medium-sized

---

14. Tax Policy Center, "Historical Highest Marginal Income."

towns in the rural areas of the country. With enough funds we could pursue a gradual shift away from heavy subsidization of large-scale industrial mono- and commodity-crop agriculture often aimed at export, to a more diversified agricultural base in which a good deal more land was in cultivation for our needs. This shift would not preclude the continuance of industrial agriculture in the mix, but it would move to a balanced agricultural model in which food security was a priority. With enough resources shifted towards farming at the local and regional levels, we could do it right. Small- and medium-sized farms serving their towns and regions could get enough government subsidies to support their work, and government support could also guide these farms towards producing crops and animals better able to withstand our changing climate. It seems cliché to say this, but I still find it powerful: we have sent people to the moon and can imagine someday sending them to Mars. In recent years, the US space program has been diminished by shifting priorities, but the private efforts of Elon Musk and Jeff Bezos have ramped up. Surely, by fairly taxing the likes of Musk and Bezos, and getting our priorities straight, we could do the agricultural equivalent of the moon landing and devise a way to smartly farm to employ people comfortably, and with stability, so that rural life could be revitalized. With new telecommuters and farmers populating our countryside, surely, more businesses would be drawn back into rural areas. It would be nice if the dollar store had some competition.

These changes would be good for the environment. Encouraging telecommuting for those who can do it cuts down on carbon emissions relative to people driving or riding to the office. Local and regional farming reduces the amount of shipping regular and refrigerated containers all over the country and the world. These changes would be good for people (but not for those in the shipping and hauling industry, which would need addressing). More people could experience a less polluted, more steady way of life. There would be more chances for families to stay together while not sacrificing their career goals or (in the case of farm families) having to send all but one child to work in a city. More people could eventually discover what it's like to have their extended families to really support them (i.e., not just with moral support or money, but with time and knowledge), and get to know not-so-temporary neighbors who could trade favors. Some of the urban poor would no doubt be attracted out of cities as rural employment rose, easing some of the seemingly eternal problems of the urban "surplus population." These new workers would be needed on farms and businesses if the economies in small- and medium-sized towns became stronger and more diversified. Instead of closing more and more rural religious institutions and having worship leaders travel to many locations, a revitalized rural landscape would no doubt invite the return of churches, synagogues, etc. Happier people, not in the thrall of mammon, buy fewer products for the sake of self-medication. They tend to drink less, do fewer drugs, and binge-watch less. So, there would be an impact on the most effervescent parts of our economy if this all made people feel more satisfied. But the impact on those industries would no doubt be gradual, and would involve far less job and population shifting than has been required by our ever-evolving, ever-growing consumer and entertainment economy.

Building on what is proposed above, a dose of distributism to counteract the strong neoliberal emphasis on bigger and more concentrated economic power would be required. What does this mean? First, it may very well mean a return to government action to break up and discourage monopolies. We still have the same antitrust laws on the books, but we have not used them to break up a monopoly since the 1980s, when ATT was split up into regional telephone companies, instigating a boom in telecommunications via renewed competition that is still benefiting us all today. The reason we have antitrust laws is primarily to discourage too much manipulation of our democracy by powerful financial interests. But if used correctly, antitrust actions can also encourage enough competition to spur functional innovation and increase opportunities for new businesses and new sources of employment. Breaking up and discouraging overconcentration of business power would be necessary to create more local- and regional-friendly economies where people could stay put and where strong communities could form. Eliminating monopolies and encouraging the dispersion of economic activity more evenly across the country would mean a gradual decline in, but not elimination of, the part of our economy dependent upon international trade. If our food, animal feed, and other commodity crop exports, as well as our industrial and vectoral capabilities, are a part of our overall projection of international power, then rapid change would be destabilizing to the global power balance. A shrinkage in soft power could very well mean an increase in the reliance on hard power. For that reason, any change would have to be incremental, gradual, well planned, and reversible if necessary. The very fact that this trade-off should have to be discussed should lead to an increased awareness of how much our global economic reach has been fueled by the desire for power. Ultimately, we cannot ignore our current international context, and we cannot abruptly pull away from our multifaceted empire and its military and economic entanglements without doing harm. For a shift towards national priorities to not lead to global economic instability and an increase in use and extension of hard power, we would need to change what we value as a people, from continual expanded projection of power to maintenance of power and resources. This is a hard truth that we cannot escape, and which necessitates talking about what it means to be, among other things, a Christian.

If the US and other countries could shift their priorities away from the high point of economic interdependence towards a more balanced approach in which certain national goods were fostered and protected (such as all the foods necessary for human health, and fossil and renewable fuels), no doubt we would be safer in the long run. A better lock on survival comes from knowing where these very essential things come from and being able to control them enough so that people can afford the essentials of life. A buffer between the US food economy and the international market would safeguard Americans' stomachs, and livelihoods, from market vagaries. At the same time, detaching completely from the global market in food and what it takes to grow it would be ill advised. First, a precipitous withdrawal would greatly harm food exporters in other countries. Second, if a disaster of some kind, whether caused by climate change, war, or some other reason, struck one country or region, safety would lie in the ability to access the international market, and that comes from having ongoing trade relations so that states always have an incentive to produce more than they need and to maintain good relations with each other. Therefore, the aim should really be balance, and the motive should be prudence, not an unrealizable ideal of total independence.

If the federal, state, and local levels of government created regulatory standards with which small and medium businesses could afford to comply, rather than effectively squeezing out all but the biggest firms by making the hurdles too complicated and expensive, it would be much easier for local and regional farms and businesses to get a start and stay productive. When I visited Excelsior Springs, Missouri, awhile back, locals told me that the town once had had a thriving spring water industry. People would come from all over the country to drink and soak in the waters, because of their reputed health benefits. But that all came to an end because they could not afford the level of the government-mandated testing and production of data necessary to keep up with international bottled water companies like Perrier. It was not that tourists no longer wanted to visit and drink the water. Businesses in Excelsior Springs were required to cap their springs because they could not afford the regulatory requirements. Water needs to be safe to drink, but those to whom I talked seemed to think that proving their water safe did not require a full-time staff and millions of dollars. Surely, local and state regulators could handle compliance in a way that allowed local businesses that sell products like water, cheese, kimchi, jam, chicken, etc., to survive in a competitive environment.

If the federal and state governments shifted some of their already allocated money and other resources (such as university research and support for the development of appropriate technologies at smaller scales, food aid, and welfare programs) from supporting large-scale agriculture and commodity crop production towards benefitting local and regional farming (both focused and diversified), we would be able to create a local agriculture and food delivery sector that would increase employment and stimulate the development of more local businesses. Instead of driving small businesses out of the best areas of town to make way for big-box stores (something I watched happen in Manhattan, Kansas, between 2000 and 2007),[15] municipal governments could provide similar tax abatements and incentives to innovative local and regional businesses. More people could experience business ownership and take an increased interest, as a result, in the well-being of their town or city. This would require politicians at all levels to resist the influence of corporate donors.

The fact that politicians resisting monied interests is the most unimaginable part of this scenario is precisely why localists, communitarians, and movements like the Catholic Worker fall back on their seemingly Quixotic attempts at economic and social experimentation. Their efforts are Quixotic, tending either to be very partial or to eventually fail, only because they are not supported by churches, our society, or our government. If they were supported, I believe more people would join in such efforts and would find themselves in more meaningful and satisfying relationships with other people as a result. This vision is little more, and nothing less, than a healthy community, more democratic for reducing the relative importance of money in our lives, and more Christian for providing so many more opportunities to live out the teachings of Jesus.

15. See City of Manhattan, "Downtown Redevelopment Timeline."

CONCLUSIONS

I hope that this book has made it clear how infinitely difficult it is to obtain that healthy community. It is the most difficult thing in the world to do the seemingly mundane acts that could, if done collectively, "change the world." Our institutions do not support us well in our endeavors because they have adopted the convenient "individual responsibility" position. Our liberal individual position then reinforces our distorted view of what church, other social organizations, and government are for. In our liberal social context, we have been conditioned to fear and avoid commitment and hard work whenever possible, instead of expecting to be backed up by our churches and social and political institutions. It is far easier to voice our opinions on social media, go to a protest, give a charitable donation than it is for us to consistently work over a long period of time with other people to make some material good, such as a healthier and more secure food supply, a reality. It is literally easier to riot than to maintain a community garden or, harder still, live in full cooperation with members of your own family, your church, and your neighbors and become more interdependent and therefore more economically and psychologically independent thereby. We can smile and talk all we want about the benefits of localism, farmers markets, and mutual aid, but how many of us even remotely approach consistently adopting those practices? But if we did manage to do these things, with the necessary help of our churches and our overall society, would that not be revolutionary?

Bibliography

Aaronson, Daniel, and Bhashkar Mazumder. "Intergenerational Economic Mobility in the United States, 1940 to 2000." *Journal of Human Resources* 43 (2008) 139–72.

Abbott, Norman, dir. *Leave It to Beaver*. Season 4, episode 23, "Mother's Helper." Aired Mar. 4, 1961, on ABC.

Abramitzky, Ran. *The Mystery of the Kibbutz: Egalitarian Principles in a Capitalist World*. Princeton Economic History of the Western World. Princeton, NJ: Princeton University Press, 2018.

Aleman, Richard, ed. *The Hound of Distributism: A Solution for Our Social and Economic Crisis*. Charlotte, NC: ACS, 2015.

Anderson, James E. "The Carter Administration and Regulatory Reform: Searching for the Right Way." *Congress & the Presidency* 18 (1991) 121–46.

Andersson, Ruben. *No Go World: How Fear Is Redrawing Our Maps and Infecting Our Politics*. Oakland: University of California Press, 2019.

Angel, Jacqueline L. *Inheritance in Contemporary America: The Social Dimensions of Giving across Generations*. Baltimore: Johns Hopkins University Press, 2008.

Anguelov, Chris E., and Christopher R. Tamborini. "Retiring in Debt? Differences between the 1995 and 2004 Near-Retiree Cohorts." *Social Security Bulletin* 69 (2009). https://www.ssa.gov/policy/docs/ssb/v69n2/v69n2p13.html.

Arendt, Hannah. *Eichmann in Jerusalem: A Report on the Banality of Evil*. New York: Penguin, 2006.

Aristotle. *Politics*. Translated by C. D. C. Reeve. Indianapolis: Hackett, 1998.

Armon, Adi. "Leo Strauss Reading Karl Marx during the Cold War." In *Against the Grain: Jewish Intellectuals in Hard Times*, edited by Ezra Mendelsohn et al., 32–50. New York: Berghahn, 2013.

Armstrong, Dave. *Mass Movements: Radical Catholic Reactionaries, the New Mass, and Ecumenicism*. N.p.: Lulu, 2012.

Bagby, Laurie M. Johnson. *Hobbes's "Leviathan": Reader's Guide*. Continuum Reader's Guides. London, Continuum, 2007.

———. *Thomas Hobbes: Turning Point for Honor*. Lanham, MD: Lexington, 2009.

Bagby, Laurie M. Johnson. *See also* Johnson, Laurie M.

Balfour, Danny L., et al. *Unmasking Administrative Evil*. 5th ed. New York: Routledge, 2019.

BIBLIOGRAPHY

Barcus, Holly R., and Laura Simmons. "Ethnic Restructuring in Rural America: Migration and the Changing Faces of Rural Communities in the Great Plains." *Professional Geographer* 65 (2013) 130–52.

Barnes, Marc. "Liberalism as Heresy." *New Polity*, Jan. 26, 2019. https://newpolity.com/blog/liberalism-as-heresy?rq=liberalism.

———. "Pope John Paul II against Capitalism." *New Polity*, Oct. 22, 2020. https://newpolity.com/blog/pope-john-paul-ii-against-capitalism.

Barnes, Marc, and Jacob Iman. "The Evils of Interest: Good Money." *New Polity*, Mar. 16, 2021. https://newpolity.com/podcasts-hub/the-evils-of-interest?rq=money.

Barnes, Marc, et al. "A Manifesto of the New Traditionalism." Guadiumetspes 22, Dec. 21, 2021. https://gaudiumetspes22.com/blog/a-manifesto-of-the-new-traditionalism.

Barth, Karl. *The Doctrine of Creation*. Edited by T. F. Torrance and G. W. Bromiley. Translated by A. T. Mackay et al. Vol. 3, pt. 4 of *Church Dogmatics*. Edinburgh: T&T Clark, 1961.

Bartley, Tim. "Transnational Corporations and Global Governance." *Annual Review of Sociology* 44 (2018) 145–65.

Bastani, Aaron. *Fully Automated Luxury Communism*. Repr., London: Verso, 2020.

Bauder, David, et al. "Fox, Dominion Reach 787M Settlement over Election Claims." AP, Apr. 18, 2023. https://apnews.com/article/fox-news-dominion-lawsuit-trial-trump-2020-0ac71f75acfacc52ea80b3e747fb0afe.

Baum, Matthew A., and Tim J. Groeling. *War Stories: The Causes and Consequences of Public Views of War*. Princeton, NJ: Princeton University Press, 2010.

Bauman, Zygmunt. "From Pilgrim to Tourist—or a Short History of Identity." In *Questions of Cultural Identity*, edited by Stuart Hall and Paul Du Gay, 18–36. London: SAGE, 1996.

———. *Liquid Modernity*. New York: Polity, 2000.

Beales, Derek. "Edmund Burke and the Monasteries of France." *Historical Journal* 48 (May 2005) 415–36. https://doi.org/10.1017/S0018246X05004450.

Beard, Charles A. *An Economic Interpretation of the Constitution of the United States*. London: Routledge, 1998.

Beaudreau, Bernard C., and H. Douglas Lightfoot. "The Physical Limits to Economic Growth by R&D Funded Innovation." *Energy* 84 (May 2015) 45–52. https://doi.org/10.1016/j.energy.2015.01.118.

Becker, Gay, et al. "Creating Continuity through Mutual Assistance: Intergenerational Reciprocity in Four Ethnic Groups." *Journals of Gerontology*, B ser., 58 (2003) 151–59.

Belloc, Hilaire. *The Servile State*. Coppell, TX: SRP, 2021.

Berardi, Franco "Bifo." *Heroes: Mass Murder and Suicide*. New York: Verso, 2015.

Berdyaev, Nicolas. *The Destiny of Man*. Translated by Natalie Duddington. 3rd ed. Collected Works of Nicolas Berdyaev. San Rafael, CA: Semantron, 2009.

Berlin, Isaiah. *The Crooked Timber of Humanity*. Princeton, NJ: Princeton University Press, 2013.

Berry, Wendell. *Life Is a Miracle: An Essay against Modern Superstition*. Washington, DC: Counterpoint, 2001.

———. *The Need to Be Whole: Patriotism and the History of Prejudice*. Berkeley: Counterpoint, 2022.

BIBLIOGRAPHY

———. *The Unsettling of America: Culture and Agriculture.* Berkeley: Counterpoint, 2015.

Bierson, Marshall, and Tucker Sigourney. "Famine, Affluence, and Aquinas." *Journal of Ethics & Social Philosophy* 25 (2023) 307–22.

Bilbro, Jeffrey, et al. *The Liberating Arts: Why We Need a Liberal Education.* Walden, NY: Plough, 2023.

Birch, Kean, ed. *Assetization: Turning Things into Assets in Technoscientific Capitalism.* Cambridge: MIT Press, 2020.

Birzer, Bradley J. *Russell Kirk: American Conservative.* Lexington: University Press of Kentucky, 2015.

Blake, William. "Jerusalem: ['And did those feet in ancient time']." Poetry Foundation, 1810. https://www.poetryfoundation.org/poems/54684/jerusalem-and-did-those-feet-in-ancient-time.

Blanchette, Alex. *Porkopolis: American Animality, Standardized Life, & the Factory Farm.* Durham: Duke University Press, 2020.

Block, Peter, et al. *An Other Kingdom: Departing the Consumer Culture.* Hoboken, NJ: Wiley & Sons, 2016.

Bloom, Mia, and Sophia Moskalenko. *Pastels and Pedophiles: Inside the Mind of QAnon.* Stanford, CA: Redwood, 2021.

Bluth, Rachel. "'My Body, My Choice': How Vaccine Foes Co-opted the Abortion Rallying Cry." NPR, July 4, 2022. https://www.npr.org/sections/health-shots/2022/07/04/1109367458/my-body-my-choice-vaccines.

Bock, Darrell L. "Evangelicals and the Use of the Old Testament in the New, Part 1." *BSac* 142 (1985) 209–23.

Bock, Gisela, et al., eds. *Machiavelli and Republicanism.* Ideas in Context 18. Cambridge: Cambridge University Press, 1990.

Borlaug, Norman. "Acceptance Speech." Nobel Prize, Dec. 10, 1970. https://www.nobelprize.org/prizes/peace/1970/borlaug/acceptance-speech/.

Borquez, Julio. "The Reagan Democrat Phenomenon: How Wise Was the Conventional Wisdom?" *Politics & Policy* 33 (2005) 672–705.

Brajer, Sven, and Johannes Schütz. "3 Old Concepts in Changing Societies? Continuities and Transformation of Nationalism in East Germany, 1871–2019." In *Nationalism in a Transnational Age: Irrational Fears and the Strategic Abuse of Nationalist Pride*, edited by Frank Jacob and Carsten Schapkow, 41–68. Munich: de Gruyter Oldenbourg, 2021.

Brauer, Simon G. "How Many Congregations Are There? Updating a Survey-Based Estimate." *JSSR* 56 (2017) 438–48.

Briggs, William. *A Cauldron of Anxiety: Capitalism in the Twenty-First Century.* Winchester, UK: Zero, 2021.

Brinkley, Alan. "The Problem of American Conservatism." *American Historical Review* 99 (1994) 409–29.

Brower, Jeffrey E. "Aquinas on the Problem of Universals." *Philosophy and Phenomenological Research* 92 (2016) 715–35.

Brown, Jennifer Erin. *Millennials and Retirement: Already Falling Short.* National Institute on Retirement Security, Feb. 2018. https://www.nirsonline.org/wp-content/uploads/2018/02/Millennials-Report-1.pdf.

Brown, Wendy. *States of Injury: Power and Freedom in Late Modernity.* Princeton, NJ: Princeton University Press, 2020.

BIBLIOGRAPHY

———. *Undoing the Demos: Neoliberalism's Stealth Revolution.* Near Future Series. Repr., Brooklyn: Zone, 2017.

Brueggemann, Walter. "Counterscript: Living with the Elusive God." *Christian Century* 122 (2005). https://www.christiancentury.org/article/2005-11/counterscript.

———. *Out of Babylon.* Nashville: Abingdon, 2010.

———. *The Prophetic Imagination.* 40th anniv. ed. Minneapolis: Fortress, 2018.

Bullivant, Stephen. *Nonverts: The Making of Ex-Christian America.* New York: Oxford University Press, 2022.

Bureau of Labor Statistics. "Labor Force Characteristics by Race and Ethnicity, 2020." Bureau of Labor Statistics, Nov. 2021. Report 1095. https://www.bls.gov/opub/reports/race-and-ethnicity/2020/home.htm.

Burge, Ryan. "Faith in Numbers: Fox News Is Must-Watch for White Evangelicals, a Turnoff for Atheists . . . and Hindus, Muslims Really like CNN." Conversation, May 24, 2021. https://theconversation.com/faith-in-numbers-fox-news-is-must-watch-for-white-evangelicals-a-turnoff-for-atheists-and-hindus-muslims-really-like-cnn-161067.

Burke, Edmund. *Reflections on the Revolution in France.* Edited by J. G. A. Pocock. Hackett Classics. Indianapolis: Hackett, 1987.

———. *Thoughts on the Prospect of a Regicide Peace in a Series of Letters.* London: Owen, 1796.

Burzyński, Michal, et al. "Climate Change, Inequality, and Human Migration." *Journal of the European Economic Association* 20 (2022) 1145–97.

Byrne, William F. *Edmund Burke for Our Time: Moral Imagination, Meaning, and Politics.* DeKalb: Northern Illinois University Press, 2011.

Campbell, Kelly and M. L. Parker. "Catfish: Exploring the Individual Predictors and Interpersonal Characteristics of Deceptive Online Romantic Relationships." *Contemporary Family Therapy* 44 (2022) 422–35.

Catholic Worker Movement. "About the Catholic Worker Movement." Catholic Worker Movement, n.d. https://catholicworker.org/about-the-catholic-worker-movement/.

———. "The Aims and Means of the Catholic Worker." Catholic Worker Movement, May 2019. https://catholicworker.org/aims-and-means/.

Cavanaugh, William T. "Enchantment: Charles Taylor's *Naïveté.*" *New Polity* 1 (2020) 3–23.

CDC Newsroom. "Provisional Suicide Deaths in the United States, 2022." CDC Newsroom, Aug. 10, 2023. https://www.cdc.gov/media/releases/2023/s0810-US-Suicide-Deaths-2022.html.

Center for Microeconomic Data. "Household Debt and Credit Report (Q3 2023)." Federal Reserve Bank of New York, Nov. 2023. https://www.newyorkfed.org/microeconomics/hhd.

Cep, Casey. "Dorothy Day's Radical Faith: The Life and Legacy of the Catholic Writer and Activist, Who Some Hope Will be Made a Saint." *New Yorker,* Apr. 6, 2020. https://www.newyorker.com/magazine/2020/04/13/dorothy-days-radical-faith.

Chapp, Larry. *Confession of a Catholic Worker: Our Moment of Christian Witness.* San Francisco: Ignatius, 2023.

———. "Whither the Catholic Worker Movement?" *National Catholic Register,* Apr. 5, 2023. https://www.ncregister.com/commentaries/whither-the-catholic-worker-movement.

BIBLIOGRAPHY

Chaves, Mark, et al. *Congregations in 21st Century America*. NCS. Durham: Duke University, Department of Sociology, 2021. https://sites.duke.edu/ncsweb/files/2022/02/NCSIV_Report_Web_FINAL2.pdf.

Chessman, Stuart. *Faith of Our Fathers: A Brief History of Catholic Traditionalism in the United States, from Triumph to Traditionis Custodes*. New York: Angelico, 2022.

Chesterton, G. K. *The Outline of Sanity*. Coppell, TX: Read, 2013.

Christoyannopoulos, Alexandre. *Christian Anarchism: A Political Commentary on the Gospel*. Abridged ed. London: Academic, 2011.

Christoyannopoulos, Alexandre, and Erik A. Nelson. "Leo Tolstoy's Impact on Dorothy Day and the Catholic Worker Movement." *Tolstoy Studies Journal* 33 (2020) 17–24.

City of Manhattan, Kansas. "Downtown Redevelopment Timeline." City of Manhattan, Kansas, n.d. https://cityofmhk.com/1492/Downtown-Redevelopment-Timeline.

Clegg, Geppert M., and G. Hollinshead. "Politicization and Political Contests in and around Contemporary Multinational Corporations: An Introduction." *Human Relations* 71 (2018) 745–65.

Clifford, Richard. "Changing Christian Interpretations of the Old Testament." *TS* 82 (2021) 509–30.

Cochrane, Willard W., and Walter W. Wilcox. *Economics of American Agriculture*. 3rd ed. Englewood Cliffs, NJ: Prentice-Hall, 1974.

Collen, Evelyn Jane, et al. "The Immunogenetic Impact of European Colonization in the Americas." *Frontiers in Genetics* 13 (2022) 918227.

Cooper, Kody W. *Thomas Hobbes and the Natural Law*. Notre Dame, IN: University of Notre Dame Press, 2018.

Cooper, Joseph, et al. *Agricultural Biodiversity and Biotechnology in Economic Development*. Natural Resource Management and Policy 27. New York: Springer, 2005.

Cornell, Tom. "A Brief Introduction to the Catholic Worker Movement." *Catholic Worker*, Sept. 11, 2005. https://catholicworker.org/cornell-history-html/.

Cotter, Neil. "Inside How Ireland Went from Financial Backwater to Multinational Tax Haven." *Irish Sun*, Dec. 26, 2022. https://www.thesun.ie/news/9955137/inside-ireland-financial-backwater-tax-haven/.

Coy, Patrick G. "Conscription and the Catholic Conscience during World War II." In *American Catholic Pacifism: The Influence of Dorothy Day and the Catholic Worker Movement*, edited by Anne Klejment and Nancy L. Roberts, 47–64. Westport, CT: Praeger/Greenwood, 1996.

Crane, Elaine Forman. *Witches, Wife Beaters, and Whores: Common Law and Common Folk in Early America*. Ithaca: Cornell University Press, 2011.

Crary, Jonathan. *24/7: Late Capitalism and the Ends of Sleep*. London: Verso, 2013.

C-SPAN. "Campaign 2016: Donald Trump Presidential Campaign Announcement." C-SPAN, June 16, 2015. https://www.c-span.org/video/?326473-1/donald-trump-presidential-campaign-announcement.

Cuneo, Michael W. *The Smoke of Satan: Conservative and Traditionalist Dissent in Contemporary American Catholicism*. New York: Oxford University Press, 1997.

Cutrone, Chris. "The American Revolution and the Left." *Platypus Review* 124 (Mar. 2020). https://platypus1917.org/2020/03/01/the-american-revolution-and-the-left/.

Davies, Naomi. "US MNCs Continue to Set Up Shop in China despite Rivalry." *Investment Monitor*, Mar. 5, 2021. https://www.investmentmonitor.ai/features/us-mncs-continue-to-set-up-shop-in-china-despite-rivalry/.

Day, Dorothy. "About Cuba." *Catholic Worker* (July–Aug. 1961) 1–2, 7–8. http://www.walterlippmann.com/dorothy-day.html.
DeBell, Matthew, and Shanto Iyengar. "Campaign Contributions, Independent Expenditures, and the Appearance of Corruption: Public Opinion vs. the Supreme Court's Assumptions." *Election Law Journal* 20 (2021) 286–300.
Dell'Angelo, Jampel, et al. "The Tragedy of the Grabbed Commons: Coercion and Dispossession in the Global Land Rush." *World Development* 92 (2017) 1–12.
Deneen, Patrick. *Why Liberalism Failed*. Repr., New Haven, CT: Yale University Press, 2019.
Department of Economic and Social Affairs. *World Social Report 2020: Inequality in a Rapidly Changing World*. N.p.: United Nations, 2020. https://www.un.org/development/desa/dspd/wp-content/uploads/sites/22/2020/02/World-Social-Report2020-FullReport.pdf.
DeVoto, Bernard. *The Course of Empire*. Boston: Houghton, Mifflin, 1952.
Diamond, Martin. "Ethics and Politics: The American Way." In *The Moral Foundations of the American Republic*, edited by Robert Horwitz, 39–72. 2nd ed. Charlottesville: University Press of Virginia, 1979.
Dickler, Jessica. "Boomers Have More Wealth 'Than Any Other Generation,' but Millennials May Not Inherit as Much as They Hope." CNBC, Dec. 9, 2022. https://www.cnbc.com/2022/12/09/great-wealth-transfer-why-millennials-may-inherit-less-than-expected.html.
Dimitri, Carolyn, et al. "The 20th Century Transformation of U.S. Agriculture and Farm Policy." *U.S. Dept. of Agriculture Economic Information Bulletin* (2005) 1–17.
Dome, A. J. "Manhattan City, USD 383 School Board Candidates Speak at Republican Rally." *Manhattan Mercury*, Oct. 30, 2021. https://themercury.com/news/manhattan-city-usd-383-school-board-candidates-speak-at-republican-rally/article_d9f4709b-4a56-5edb-9ee6-bf3f5b96eb4b.html.
Domencic, Sean. "Season 3, Ep. 3: Adventures in Catholic Worker-Hood (Sean Domencic of Tradistae & *New Polity*)." Maurin Academy for Regenerative Studies, June 26, 2023. https://pmaurin.org/2023/06/26/season-3-ep-3-adventures-in-catholic-worker-hood-sean-domencic-of-tradistae-new-polity/.
―――. "Trad No More." Tradistae, July 16, 2023. https://tradistae.wordpress.com/2023/07/16/a-trad-no-more/.
Donnelly, James S. *The Great Irish Potato Famine*. Thrupp, Eng.: Sutton, 2001.
Douthat, Ross. *The Decadent Society: How We Became the Victims of Our Own Success*. New York: Avid Reader/Simon & Schuster, 2020.
Douwe van der Ploeg, Jan. *The New Peasantries: Struggles for Autonomy and Sustainability in an Era of Empire and Globalization*. Earthscan Food and Agriculture. London: Earthscan, 2008.
Dreher, Rod. *The Benedict Option: A Strategy for Christians in a Post-Christian Nation*. New York: Penguin, 2018.
―――. *Crunchy Cons: How Birkenstocked Burkeans, Gun-Loving Organic Gardeners, Evangelical Free-Range Farmers, Hip Homeschooling Mamas, Right-Wing Nature Lovers, and Their Diverse Tribe of Countercultural Conservatives Plan to Save America (or at Least the Republican Party)*. New York: Crown Forum, 2006.
Dudley, Kathryn Marie. *Debt and Dispossession: Farm Loss in America's Heartland*. Chicago: University of Chicago Press, 2000.
Du Mez, Kristin Kobes. *Jesus and John Wayne: How White Evangelicals Corrupted a Faith and Fractured a Nation*. New York: Liveright, 2020.

Durward, Rosemary, and Lee Marsden, eds. *Religion, Conflict and Military Intervention*. London: Ashgate, 2000.

Dyer, Christopher. *Making a Living in the Middle Ages: The People of Britain 850–1520*. New Economic History of Britain. New Haven, CT: Yale University Press, 2003.

Edson, Rich. "Evangelical Vote at Stake for 2024 Republican Hopefuls." Fox News, Jan. 10, 2023. https://www.foxnews.com/politics/evangelical-vote-at-stake-2024-republican-hopefuls.

Eirenreich, Barbara. *Fear of Falling: The Inner Life of the Middle Class*. New York: Pantheon, 1989.

Eismeier, Theodore J., and Philip H. Pollock. *Business, Money, and the Rise of Corporate PACs in American Elections*. New York: Quorum, 1988.

Elliott, J. E. "Karl Marx on Socio-Institutional Change in Late-Stage Capitalism." *Journal of Economic Issues* 18 (1984) 383–91.

Ellis, Marc H. *Peter Maurin: Prophet in the Twentieth Century*. Catholic Worker Reprint Series. Eugene, OR: Wipf & Stock, 2003.

Ellul, Jacques. *Anarchy and Christianity*. Translated by Geoffrey W. Bromiley. Jacques Ellul Legacy Series. Eugene, OR: Wipf and Stock, 2011.

———. *The Technological Society*. Translated by John Wilkinson. New York: Knopf, 1964.

Enders, Jürgen, and Ben Jongbloed, eds. *Public-Private Dynamics in Higher Education: Expectations, Developments and Outcomes*. Science Studies. Bielefeld: Transcript, 2007.

England and Wales. Sovereign (1547–1553: Edward VI). "A proclamacion, set furth by the Kynges Maiestie with thassent of his derest vncle, Edward Duke of Somerset, gouernor of his moste royall person, and of his realmes, dominions and subiectes protector, and others of his moste honorable counsaill, concernyng certain riotes and vnlawfull assembles for the breakyng vp of enclosures." University of Michigan Library Digital Collections, 1549. Early English Books Online. https://name.umdl.umich.edu/A21512.0001.001.

Erikson, Kai T. *Everything in Its Path: Destruction of Community in the Buffalo Creek Flood*. New York: Simon and Schuster, 1976.

Fairlie, Simon. "A Short History of Enclosure in Britain." *Land* 7 (2009) 16–31.

Fecher, Benedikt, et al. "A Reputation Economy: How Individual Reward Considerations Trump Systemic Arguments for Open Access to Data." *Palgrave Communications* 3 (2017) 17051. https://doi.org/10.1057/palcomms.2017.51.

Federal Election Commission. "Citizens United v. FEC." Federal Election Commission, Feb. 2010. https://www.fec.gov/legal-resources/court-cases/citizens-united-v-fec/

Fessler, Pirmin, and Martin Schürz. "Inheritance and Equal Opportunity: It Is the Family That Matters." *Public Sector Economics* 44 (2020) 463–82.

Firnhaber-Baker, Justine J. "Seigneurial Violence in Medieval Europe." In *The Cambridge World History of Violence*, edited by Matthew S. Gordon et al., 2:248–66. Cambridge: Cambridge University Press, 2020.

Fisher, Mark. *Capitalist Realism: Is There No Alternative?* 2nd ed. Hampshire, UK: Zero, 2022.

Folmar, Chloe. "Boebert: Jesus Didn't Have Enough AR-15s to 'Keep His Government from Killing Him.'" *Hill*, June 17, 2022. https://thehill.com/homenews/house/3528049-boebert-jesus-didnt-have-enough-ar-15s-to-keep-his-government-from-killing-him/.

BIBLIOGRAPHY

Foltz, Jeremy D., et al. "Do Purchasing Patterns Differ between Large and Small Dairy Farms? Econometric Evidence from Three Wisconsin Communities." *Agricultural and Resource Economics Review* 31 (2002) 28–38.

Food and Agriculture Organization of the United Nations. *The State of Food and Agriculture 2014 in Brief.* N.p.: FAO, 2014. https://www.fao.org/3/i4036e/i4036e.pdf.

Foucault, Michel. *The Birth of Biopolitics: Lectures at the Collège de France, 1978–1979.* Edited by Michel Senellart. Translated by Graham Burchell. New York: Picador, 2004.

Fowler, Anthony, et al. "Quid Pro Quo? Corporate Returns to Campaign Contributions." *Journal of Politics* 82 (2020) 844–58.

Fox News. "Dr. Robert Jeffress." Fox News, n.d. https://www.foxnews.com/person/r/dr-robert-jeffress.

———. "Jeremiah J. Johnston." Fox News, n.d. https://www.foxnews.com/person/j/jeremiah-johnston.

———. "Jonathan Morris." Fox News, n.d. https://www.foxnews.com/person/m/jonathan-morris.

Fraad, Harriet, and Richard D. Wolff. "American Hyper-Capitalism Breeds the Lonely, Alienated Men Who Become Killers." *Salon*, Nov. 8, 2017. https://www.salon.com/2017/11/08/american-hyper-capitalism-breeds-the-lonely-alienated-men-who-become-mass-killers_partner/.

Francis, Pope. "*Evangelii Gaudium*: On the Proclamation of the Gospel in Today's World." Vatican, Nov. 24, 2013. https://www.vatican.va/content/francesco/en/apost_exhortations/documents/papa-francesco_esortazione-ap_20131124_evangelii-gaudium.html.

———. "*Laudato Si'*: On the Care of Our Common Home." Vatican, May 24, 2015. https://www.vatican.va/content/francesco/en/encyclicals/documents/papa-francesco_20150524_enciclica-laudato-si.html.

Frank, Thomas. *Listen, Liberal: Or Whatever Happened to the Party of the People?* New York: Picador, 2016.

———. *What's the Matter with Kansas? How Conservatives Won the Heart of America.* New York: Picador, 2005.

Freedman, Craig. *Chicago Fundamentalism Ideology and Methodology in Economics.* Hackensack, NJ: World Scientific, 2008.

Freud, Sigmund. *Civilization and Its Discontents.* Edited and translated by James Strachey. New York: Norton, 1961.

———. *Group Psychology and the Analysis of The Ego.* Translated by James Strachey. Project Gutenberg, 2011. eBook 35877. https://www.gutenberg.org/cache/epub/35877/pg35877-images.html.

Friedman, Hershey H. "Is Higher Education Making Students Dumb and Dumber?" *American Journal of Economics and Sociology* 80 (2021) 53–77. https://doi.org/10.1111/ajes.12372.

Friedman, Milton. *Free to Choose.* Aired Jan. 1980, on PBS. https://www.freetochoosenetwork.org/programs/free_to_choose/index_80.php.

———. "Neoliberalism and Its Prospects." Milton Friedman, 1951. From *The Collected Works of Milton Friedman*, edited by Robert Leeson and Charles G. Palm. https://miltonfriedman.hoover.org/internal/media/dispatcher/214957/full.

Fukuyama, Francis. *The End of History and the Last Man.* New York: Free, 2006.

Fullilove, Mindy Thompson. "Psychiatric Implications of Displacement: Contributions from the Psychology of Place." *American Journal of Psychiatry* 153 (1996) 1516–23.

———. *Root Shock: How Tearing Up City Neighborhoods Hurts America, and What We Can Do about It*. 2nd ed. New York: New Village, 2016.

Gaidenko, Piarna. "Medieval Nominalism and the Genesis of a New European Mentality." *Social Sciences* 46 (2015) 69–79.

Gamble, Richard M. *In Search of the City on a Hill: The Making and Unmaking of an American Myth*. London: Continuum, 2012.

Garcia-Bernardo, Janský P., and T. Tørsløv. "Multinational Corporations and Tax Havens: Evidence from Country-by-Country Reporting." *International Tax and Public Finance* 28 (2021) 1519–61.

Gardner, Bruce L. *American Agriculture in the Twentieth Century: How It Flourished and What It Cost*. Cambridge, MA: Harvard University Press, 2006.

Geddes, Katrina. "Meet Your New Overlords: How Digital Platforms Develop and Sustain Technofeudalism." *Columbia Journal of Law & the Arts* 43 (2020) 455–85.

Giddens, Anthony. *Modernity and Self-Identity: Self and Society in the Late Modern Age*. Redwood City, CA: Stanford University Press, 1991.

Gilger, Patrick, SJ. "What Rod Dreher Gets Right in *The Benedict Option* Is Just as Important as What He Gets Wrong." *America*, Mar. 16, 2017. https://www.americamagazine.org/arts-culture/2017/03/16/what-rod-dreher-gets-right-benedict-option-just-important-what-he-gets.

Global Agriculture. "Industrial Agriculture and Small-Scale Farming." Global Agriculture, n.d. https://www.globalagriculture.org/report-topics/industrial-agriculture-and-small-scale-farming.html.

Goda, Thomas. "The Global Concentration of Wealth." *Cambridge Journal of Economics* 42 (2018) 95–115.

Goldingay, John. "What Are the Characteristics of Evangelical Study of the Old Testament?" *EvQ* 73 (2001) 99–118.

Goldschmidt, Walter. *As You Sow: Three Studies in the Social Consequences of Agribusiness*. Montclair, NJ: Allanheld, Osmun, 1978.

Gordon, James M. *Evangelical Spirituality*. Eugene, OR: Wipf & Stock, 2006.

Gordon, Paddy. "Left Accelerationism, Transhumanism and the Dialectic: Three Manifestos." *New Proposals* 12 (2021) 140–54.

Goswami, Omanjana. "Farmland Consolidation, Not Chinese Ownership, Is the Real National Security Threat." Union of Concerned Scientists, Mar. 2, 2023. https://blog.ucsusa.org/omanjana-goswami/farmland-consolidation-not-chinese-ownership-is-the-real-national-security-threat.

Grace Church. "Bill Shannon." Grace Church, n.d. https://www.gracechurch.org/leader/shannon/bill.

Green, Ben. *The Smart Enough City: Putting Technology in Its Place to Reclaim Our Urban Future*. Cambridge: MIT Press, 2019.

Green, Joshua. *Devil's Bargain: Steve Bannon, Donald Trump, and the Storming of the Presidency*. New York: Penguin, 2017.

Gregg, Melissa, and Gregory J. Seigworth, eds. *The Affect Theory Reader*. Durham: Duke University Press, 2010.

Gregory, Bradley. *The Unintended Reformation: How a Religious Revolution Secularized Society*. Cambridge, MA: Harvard University Press, 2012.

Gregory, Ted. "Bias in Media Coverage of Conflict." University of Chicago Harris School of Public Policy, Jan. 13, 2023. https://harris.uchicago.edu/news-events/news/bias-media-coverage-conflict.

Grimm, Robert T., Jr., and Nathan Dietz. *Where Are America's Volunteers? A Look at America's Widespread Decline in Volunteering in Cities and States.* College Park, MD: Do Good Institute, 2018. https://dogood.umd.edu/sites/default/files/2019-07/Where%20Are%20Americas%20Volunteers_Research%20Brief%20_Nov%20.pdf.

Gross, Neil, and Solon Simmons, eds. *Professors and Their Politics.* Baltimore: Johns Hopkins University Press, 2014.

———. "The Social and Political Views of American Professors." ResearchGate, Jan. 1, 2007. https://www.researchgate.net/publication/228380360_The_Social_and_Political_Views_of_American_Professors.

Grudem, Wayne. "A Letter from Wayne Grudem." Council on Biblical Manhood and Womanhood, Sept. 28, 2020. https://cbmw.org/2020/09/28/a-letter-from-wayne-grudem/.

———. *Systematic Theology: An Introduction to Biblical Doctrine.* Grand Rapids: Zondervan, 1994.

Guastella, Justin. "We Need a Class War, Not a Culture War: A Reply to Angela Nagle and Michael Tracy." *Jacobin*, May 25, 2020. https://jacobin.com/2020/05/we-need-a-class-war-not-a-cultural-war.

Gurvis, Sandra. *Where Have All the Flower Children Gone?* Jackson: University Press of Mississippi, 2006.

Habit Stacker. "John MacArthur Net Worth and Key Habits." Habit Stacker, n.d. https://thehabitstacker.com/john-macarthur-net-worth-and-key-habits/.

Hahn, Allesia, and Jordan Tarver. "2024 Student Loan Debt Statistics: Average Student Loan Debt." *Forbes*, last updated Apr. 18, 2024. https://www.forbes.com/advisor/student-loans/average-student-loan-debt-statistics/.

Hall, Lauren. "Rights and the Heart: Emotions and Rights Claims in the Political Theory of Edmund Burke." *Review of Politics* 73 (2011) 609–31.

Haluza-Delay, Randolph. "Say No to Moralistic Therapeutic Deism." *Canadian Mennonite* 27 (2023). https://canadianmennonite.org/stories/say-no-moralistic-therapeutic-deism.

Hanschu, Jakob, and Laurie M. Johnson. "The Economic and Psychological Origins of Right-Wing Radicalism in the U.S." In *Geographies of the 2020 U.S. Presidential Election*, edited by Barney Warf and John Heppen, 25–49. Routledge Research in Place, Space and Politics. New York: Routledge, 2022.

Harder, Stephen. "Political Finance in the Liberal Republic: Representation, Equality, and Deregulation." *Annals of the American Academy of Political and Social Science* 486 (1986) 49–63.

Hardin, Garret. "The Tragedy of the Commons: The Population Problem Has No Technical Solution; It Requires a Fundamental Extension in Morality." *Science* 162 (1968) 1243–48.

Harrison, Ann E., ed. *Globalization and Poverty.* National Bureau of Economic Research Conference Report. Chicago: University of Chicago Press, 2007.

Harry, Prince, the Duke of Sussex. *Spare.* New York: Penguin, 2023.

Hart, John Fraser. *The Changing Scale of American Agriculture.* Charlottesville: University of Virginia Press, 2003.

BIBLIOGRAPHY

Harvey, David. *A Brief History of Neoliberalism*. Oxford: Oxford University Press, 2005.

Hauerwas, Stanley. *A Better Hope: Resources for a Church Confronting Capitalism, Democracy, and Postmodernity*. Grand Rapids: Brazos, 2000.

———. *Christian Existence Today: Essays on Church, World, and Living in Between*. Eugene, OR: Wipf & Stock, 2010.

———. *A Community of Character: Toward a Constructive Christian Social Ethic*. Notre Dame, IN: University of Notre Dame Press, 1981.

———. *Cross-Shattered Christ: Meditations on the Seven Last Words*. Grand Rapids: Brazos, 2004.

———. "The Good Life: If Liberalism Failed to Deliver It, What Can?" *Plough*, Oct. 13, 2021. https://www.plough.com/en/topics/life/work/the-good-life-hauerwas.

Hauerwas, Stanley, and Romand Coles. *Christianity, Democracy, and the Radical Ordinary: Conversations between a Radical Democrat and a Christian*. Theopolitical Visions. Eugene, OR: Cascade, 2008.

Havers, Grant N. "The Straussian-Thomistic Quarrel in Modernity." *European Legacy: Toward New Paradigms* 26 (2021) 535–40.

Hawn, Allison. "Escaping June Cleaver: The Domestication of Women through Advertising." MA thesis, Arizona State University, 2017.

Hayek, F. A. *The Road to Serfdom: Text and Documents; The Definitive Edition*. Edited by Bruce Caldwell. Chicago: University of Chicago Press, 2007.

Hedges, Chris. *The Death of the Liberal Class*. New York: Nation, 2010.

Hektner, Joel M. "When Moving Up Implies Moving Out: Rural Adolescent Conflict in the Transition to Adulthood." *Journal of Research in Rural Education* 11 (1995) 3–14.

Heller, Henry. "Bankers, Finance Capital and the French Revolutionary Terror (1791–94)." *Historical Materialism* 22 (2014) 172–216.

Helm, Bennett W. "Hate, Identification, and Othering." *American Philosophical Quarterly* 60 (2023) 289–310.

Hendershott, Anne B. *Moving for Work: The Sociology of Relocating in the 1990's*. Lanham, MD: University of America Press, 1995.

Hendrickson, Mary, et al. "Power, Food and Agriculture: Implications for Farmers, Consumers and Communities." In *In Defense of Farmers: The Future of Agriculture in the Shadow of Corporate Power*, edited by Sara E. Alexander and Jane W. Gibson, 13–61. Lincoln: University of Nebraska Press, 2019.

Henry Center. "Debating Trinitarian Submission: Bruce Ware & Wayne Grudem." YouTube, Aug. 1, 2013. https://www.youtube.com/watch?v=ySFrG3mOp50.

Hess, Spencer. "To Face or Not to Face Evil, or: Towards Agitating the Agitators." *Regenerative Reader* 1 (2023) 15–18.

Hewell, Rob. *Worship beyond Nationalism: Practicing the Reign of God*. Eugene, OR: Wipf & Stock, 2012.

Hirschfeld, Amy L. *Aquinas and the Market: Toward a Humane Economy*. Cambridge, MA: Harvard University Press, 2018.

Hobbes, Thomas. *Behemoth*. Edited by Paul Seaward. Clarendon Edition of the Works of Thomas Hobbes. London: Oxford University Press, 2014.

———. *Leviathan; Or, the Matter, Forme and Power of a Commonwealth, Ecclesiasticall and Civil*. Edited by Michael Oakeshott. New York: Collier, 1962.

Hochschild, Arlie Russell. *Strangers in Their Own Land: Anger and Mourning on the American Right*. New York: New, 2018.

BIBLIOGRAPHY

Hofkirchner, Wolfgang, and Hans-Jörg Kreowski, eds. *Transhumanism: The Proper Guide to a Posthuman Condition or a Dangerous Idea?* Cognitive Technologies. Cham, Switz.: Springer, 2021.

Hofmann, David C. "A Historical Case Study Analysis of the Establishment of Charismatic Leadership in a Protestant Reformation Cultic group and Its Role in the Recourse to Violence." PhD diss., Université de Montréal, 2011.

Hofstadter, Richard. *The American Political Tradition and the Men Who Made It.* Repr., New York: Vintage, 1989.

Holston, Ryan. "Burke's Historical Morality." *Humanitas* 20 (2007) 37–63.

Hoopes, Tom. "The 'Francis Option.'" *National Catholic Register*, July 8, 2015. https://www.ncregister.com/news/the-francis-option.

Hoover, Kenneth R. "The Political Thought of José Ortega y Gasset." *Midwest Journal of Political Science* 10 (1966) 232–40.

Howard, Evan B., and Daniel E Albrecht. "Pentecostal Spirituality." In *The Cambridge Companion to Pentecostalism*, edited by Cecil M. Robeck Jr. and Amos Young, 235–53. Cambridge Companions to Religion. Cambridge: Cambridge University Press, 2014.

Hudson, John C., and Christopher R. Laingen. *American Farms, American Food: A Geography of Agriculture and Food Production in the United States.* Lanham, MD: Lexington, 2016.

Ikeler, Peter. "Deskilling Emotional Labour: Evidence from Department Store Retail." *Work, Employment and Society* 30 (2016) 966–83.

IOM and UN-OHRLLS [International Organization for Migration and the United Nations Office of the High Representative for the Least Developed Countries, Landlocked Developing Countries and Small Island Developing States]. *Climate Change and Migration in Vulnerable Countries: A Snapshot of Least Developed Countries, Landlocked Developing Countries and Small Island Developing States.* Geneva: IOM, 2019. https://publications.iom.int/system/files/pdf/climate_change_and_migration_in_vulnerable_countries.pdf.

Iosif, Despina. *Early Christian Attitudes to War, Violence and Military Service.* Gorgias Studies in Classical and Late Antiquity. Piscataway, NJ: Gorgias, 2013.

Jacob, Frank, and Carsten Schapkow, eds. *Nationalism in a Transnational Age: Irrational Fears and the Strategic Abuse of Nationalist Pride.* Munich: de Gruyter Oldenbourg, 2021.

Jacobo, Julia. "This Is What Trump Told Supporters before Many Stormed Capitol Hill." ABC News, Jan. 7, 2021. https://abcnews.go.com/Politics/trump-told-supporters-stormed-capitol-hill/story?id=75110558.

James, M. R., trans. "The Infancy Gospel of Thomas: Greek Text A." Gnostic Society Library, 1924. From *The Apocryphal New Testament* (Oxford: Clarendon, 1924). http://gnosis.org/library/inftoma.htm.

Jensen, Michael. "The Link between Age and Extremism." Generations, Mar. 15, 2023. https://generations.asaging.org/link-between-age-and-extremism.

Jerolmack, Colin. *Up to Heaven, Down to Hell: Fracking, Freedom and Community in an American Town.* Focus on Climate. Princeton, NJ: Princeton University Press, 2021.

John Paul II, Pope. "*Centesimus Annus*: On the Hundredth Anniversary of *Rerum Novarum*." Vatican, May 1, 1991. https://www.vatican.va/content/john-paul-ii/en/encyclicals/documents/hf_jp-ii_enc_01051991_centesimus-annus.html.

———. "Homily of His Holiness John Paul II for the Inauguration of His Pontificate." Vatican, Oct. 22, 1978. https://www.vatican.va/content/john-paul-ii/en/homilies/1978/documents/hf_jp-ii_hom_19781022_inizio-pontificato.html.

———. "*Laborem Exercens*: On the Hundredth Anniversary of *Rerum Novarum*." Vatican, Sept. 14, 1981. https://www.vatican.va/content/john-paul-ii/en/encyclicals/documents/hf_jp-ii_enc_14091981_laborem-exercens.html.

Johnson, Kenneth M., and Daniel T. Lichter. "Rural Depopulation: Growth and Decline Processes over the Past Century." *Rural Sociology* 84 (2019) 3–27.

Johnson, Laurie M. *Honor in America? Tocqueville on American Enlightenment*. Lanham, MD: Lexington, 2017.

———. *Ideological Possession and the Rise of the New Right: The Political Thought of Carl Jung*. New York: Routledge, 2019.

———. *Locke and Rousseau: Two Enlightenment Responses to Honor*. Lanham, MD: Lexington, 2012.

Johnson, Laurie M. *See also* Bagby, Laurie M. Johnson.

Johnson, Laurie M., and Spencer Hess. *Dustbowl Diatribes*. Season 3, episode 2, "The Tolstoy Injection in the Catholic Worker Movement." Interview with Alexandre Christoyannopoulos. *Dustbowl Diatribes*, June 3, 2023. https://podcasts.apple.com/us/podcast/dustbowl-diatribes/id1613542273?i=1000615518058.

Jokes, Jeffrey M. "U.S. Church Membership Falls below Majority for First Time." Gallup, Mar. 29, 2021. https://news.gallup.com/poll/341963/church-membership-falls-below-majority-first-time.aspx.

Jones, Andrew Willard. *Before Church and State: A Study of Social Order in the Sacramental Kingdom of St. Louis IX*. Steubenville, OH: Emmaus Academic, 2017.

Jones, W. R. "Purveyance for War and the Community of the Realm in Late Medieval England." *Albion* 7 (1975) 300–316.

Jung, C. G. "After the Catastrophe." In *Civilization in Transition: Essays on Contemporary Events*, edited by Gerhard Adler et al., translated by R. F. C. Hull, 194–217. Vol. 10 of *The Collected Works of C. G. Jung*. Bollingen Series. Princeton, NJ: Princeton University Press, 1978.

———. *Aion: Researches into the Phenomenology of Self*. Edited by Gerhard Adler et al. Translated by R. F. C. Hull. Vol. 9, pt. 2 of *The Collected Works of C. G. Jung*. Bollingen Series. Princeton, NJ: Princeton University Press, 1959.

———. *The Archetypes and the Collective Unconscious*. Edited by Gerhard Adler et al. Translated by R. F. C. Hull. Vol. 9, pt. 1 of *The Collected Works of C. G. Jung*. New York: Bollingen, 1990.

———. *Civilization in Transition: Essays on Contemporary Events*. Edited by Gerhard Adler et al. Translated by R. F. C. Hull. Vol. 10 of *The Collected Works of C. G. Jung*. Bollingen Series. Princeton, NJ: Princeton University Press, 1978.

———. *Jung on Christianity*. Edited by Murray Stein. Encountering Jung. Princeton, NJ: Princeton University Press, 2012.

———. "Mind and Earth." In *Civilization in Transition: Essays on Contemporary Events*, edited by Gerhard Adler et al., translated by R. F. C. Hull, 29–49. Vol. 10 of *The Collected Works of C. G. Jung*. Bollingen Series. Princeton, NJ: Princeton University Press, 1978.

———. *Modern Man in Search of a Soul*. Translated by W. S. Dell and Cary F. Barnes. New York: Harcourt, Brace and Company, 1957.

——. "On the Psychology of the Unconscious." In *Two Essays on Analytical Psychology*, edited by Gerhard Adler et al., translated by R. F. C. Hull, 3–119. Vol. 7 of *The Collected Works of C. G. Jung*. Bollingen Series. Princeton, NJ: Princeton University Press, 1977.

——. *Psychological Types*. Edited by Gerhard Adler et al. Translated by R. F. C. Hull. Vol. 6 of *The Collected Works of C. G. Jung*. Bollingen Series. Princeton, NJ: Princeton University Press, 1990.

——. "The Undiscovered Self." In *Civilization in Transition: Essays on Contemporary Events*, edited by Gerhard Adler et al., translated by R. F. C. Hull, 245–306. Vol. 10 of *The Collected Works of C. G. Jung*. Bollingen Series. Princeton, NJ: Princeton University Press, 1978.

Kaftan, Joanna. "Religious Messages: Themes in Religious Left and Right Publications during the Obama and Trump Administrations." *Politikologija Religije* 16 (2022) 289–311.

Kang, John M. "Appeal to Heaven: On the Religious Origins of the Constitutional Right of Revolution." *William and Mary Bill of Rights Journal* 18 (2009) 281–326.

Kassel, Michael B. "Mass Culture, History and Memory and the Image of the American Family." PhD diss., Michigan State University, 2004.

Katchanovski, Ivan, and Alicen R. Morley. "The Politics of U.S. Television Coverage of Post-Communist Countries." *Problems of Post-Communism* 59 (2012) 15–30.

Kenneson, Philip D., and James L. Street. *Selling Out the Church: The Dangers of Church Marketing*. Eugene, OR: Cascade, 2003.

Keohane, Robert O., and Joseph S. Nye. *Power and Interdependence*. 3rd ed. New York: Longman, 2001.

Kessler-Harris, Alice. *Women Have Always Worked: A Historical Overview*. Old Westbury, NY: Feminist, 1981.

Keyes, Emily F., and Catherine C. Kane. "Belonging and Adapting: Mental Health and Bosnian Refugees Living in the United States." *Issues in Mental Health Nursing* 25 (2004) 809–31.

Kines, Kenneth Michael. "The Reaction to Enclosure in Tudor Policy and Thought." Master's thesis, University of Richmond, 1971. https://scholarship.richmond.edu/masters-theses/331/.

Kirk, Russell. *The Politics of Prudence*. Wilmington: ISI, 2004.

Klein, Naomi. *The Shock Doctrine: The Rise of Disaster Capitalism*. New York: Picador, 2007.

Klinenberg, Eric. *Going Solo: The Extraordinary Rise and Surprising Appeal of Living Alone*. London: Penguin, 2013.

Kloppenburg, Jack Ralph, Jr. *First the Seed: The Political Economy of Plant Biotechnology, 1492–2000*. 2nd ed. Science and Technology in Society. Madison: University of Wisconsin Press, 2004.

Kotkin, Joel. *The Coming of Neo-Feudalism: A Warning to the Global Middle Class*. New York: Encounter, 2020.

Kotsko, Adam. "Neoliberalism's Demons." *Theory & Event* 20 (2017) 493–509.

——. *Neoliberalism's Demons: On the Political Theology of Late Capital*. Stanford: Stanford University Press, 2018.

Kotz, David M. "Contradictions of Economic Growth in the Neoliberal Era: Accumulation and Crisis in the Contemporary U.S. Economy." *Review of Radical Political Economics* 40 (2008) 174–88.

Kuhn, Thomas S. *The Structure of Scientific Revolutions.* 50th anniv. ed. Chicago: University of Chicago Press, 2012.

Kutulas, Judy. "Who Rules the Roost? Sitcom Family Dynamics from the Cleavers to the Osbournes." In *The Sitcom Reader: America Viewed and Skewed*, edited by Mary M. Dalton and Laura R. Linder, 49–60. Albany: State University of New York Press, 2005.

Kwasniewski, Peter A., ed. *A Reader in Catholic Social Teaching: From Syllabus Errorum to Deus Caritas Est.* Providence: Cluny, 2017.

Landale, Nancy S., et al. "Hispanic Families in the United States: Family Structure and Process in an Era of Family Change." In *Hispanics and the Future of America*, edited by Marta Tienda and Faith Mitchell, 138–78. Washington, DC: National Academies, 2006.

Lasch, Christopher. *The Culture of Narcissism: American Life in an Age of Diminishing Returns.* New York: Norton, 1979.

———. *Haven in a Heartless World: The Family Besieged.* New York: Basic, 1977.

———. *The Revolt of the Elites and the Betrayal of Democracy.* New York: Norton, 1995.

Lears, T. J. Jackson. *No Place of Grace: Antimodernism and the Transformation of American Culture 1880–1920.* New York: Pantheon, 1981.

Le Bon, Gustave. *The Crowd: A Study of the Popular Mind.* Project Gutenberg, 1895. eBook 445. https://www.gutenberg.org/cache/epub/445/pg445-images.html.

Lee, Richard G., ed. *The American Patriot's Bible: New King James Version.* Nashville: Thomas Nelson, 2009.

Leithart, Peter J. *Between Babel and Beast: America and Empires in Biblical Perspective.* Theopolitical Visions. Eugene, OR: Cascade, 2012.

Lennox, Erin. "Double Exposure to Climate Change and Globalization in a Peruvian Highland Community." *Society & Natural Resources* 28 (2015) 781–96.

Leo XIII, Pope. "*Rerum Novarum*: On Capital and Labor." Vatican, May 15, 1891. https://www.vatican.va/content/leo-xiii/en/encyclicals/documents/hf_l-xiii_enc_15051891_rerum-novarum.html.

Lewis, Cora. "Credit Card Debt Is at Record High as Fed Raises Rates Again." AP, Mar. 22, 2023. https://apnews.com/article/federal-reserve-credit-card-debt-interest-rates-a2e1d35cb957153058d188652570c48e.

Lilla, Mark. *The Once and Future Liberal: After Identity Politics.* London: Harper Collins, 2018.

Lillico, Neil B. "Television as Popular Culture: An Attempt to Influence North American Society? An Ideological analysis of *Leave It to Beaver* (1957–1961)." Master's thesis, University of Ottawa, 1993.

Limbaugh, Rush. *The Way Things Ought to Be.* New York: Pocket, 1992.

Lind, Michael. *The New Class War: Saving Democracy from the Managerial Elite.* N.p.: Penguin Portfolio, 2020.

Lobao, Linda M. *Locality and Inequality: Farm and Industry Structure and Socioeconomic Condition.* Albany: State University of New York Press, 1990.

Locke, John. *"Two Treatises of Government" and "A Letter Concerning Toleration."* New Haven, CT: Yale University Press, 2003.

Loughery, John, and Blythe Randolph. *Dorothy Day: Dissenting Voice of the American Century.* New York: Simon & Schuster, 2020.

Lund, Dorothy S., and Leo S. Strine Jr. "Corporate Political Spending Is Bad Business: How to Minimize the Risks and Focus on What Counts." *Harvard Business Review*, Jan.–Feb. 2022. https://hbr.org/2022/01/corporate-political-spending-is-bad-business.

Luther, Martin. "95 Theses." Internet History Sourcebooks Project, 1517. https://sourcebooks.fordham.edu/source/luther95.txt.

———. *A Treatise on Good Works*. Auckland: Floating, 2009.

Lynn, Andrew. "Cultural Marxism." *Hedgehog Review* 203 (2018). https://hedgehogreview.com/issues/the-evening-of-life/articles/cultural-marxism.

Lyson, Thomas A., et al. "Scale of Agricultural Production, Civic Engagement, and Community Welfare." *Social Forces* 80 (2001) 311–27.

Ma, Li. *Babel Church: The Subversion of Christianity in the Age of Mass Media, Globalization, and #MeToo*. Eugene, OR: Cascade, 2021.

MacDonald, Daniel, and Yasemin Dildar. "Married Women's Economic Independence and Divorce in the Nineteenth- and Early-Twentieth-Century United States." *Social Science History* 42 (2018) 601–29.

MacDonald, James M., et al. *Three Decades of Consolidation in U.S. Agriculture*. Economic Research Service, Mar. 2018. EIB 189. https://www.ers.usda.gov/webdocs/publications/88057/eib-189.pdf?v=792.6.

Machiavelli, Niccoló. *Discourses on Livy*. Translated by Harvey C. Mansfield and Nathan Tarcov. Chicago: University of Chicago Press, 1996.

MacIntyre, Alasdair. *After Virtue: A Study in Moral Theory*. 3rd ed. Notre Dame, IN: University of Notre Dame Press, 2007.

Magill, Jay R. "Turn Away the World: How a Curious Fifteenth-Century Spiritual Guidebook Shaped the Contours of the Reformation and Taught Readers to Turn Inward." *Christianity & Literature* 67 (2017) 34–49.

Main, Roderick. "In a Secular Age: Weber, Taylor, Jung." *Psychoanalysis, Culture & Society* 18 (2013) 277–94.

Mak, Tim. "New York Attorney General Moves to Dissolve the NRA after Fraud Investigation." NPR, Aug. 6, 2020. https://www.npr.org/2020/08/06/899712823/new-york-attorney-general-moves-to-dissolve-the-nra-after-fraud-investigation.

Mander, Jerry. *In the Absence of the Sacred: The Failure of Technology and the Survival of the Indian Nations*. San Francisco: Sierra Club, 1992.

Manning, Christel J. *Losing Our Religion: How Unaffiliated Parents Are Raising Their Children*. Secular Studies. New York: NYU Press, 2015.

Marans, Daniel. "Why Nancy Pelosi's Comments about Capitalism Disappointed Progressives." *Huffington Post*, Feb. 1, 2017; updated Feb. 2, 2017. https://www.huffpost.com/entry/nancy-pelosi-town-hall-capitalism_n_58925a53e4b070cf8b807e28.

Martin, John E. *Feudalism to Capitalism: Peasant and Landlord in English Agrarian Development*. Studies in Historical Sociology. London: Macmillan, 1983.

Marx, Karl. *Capital: A Critique of Political Economy*. Translated by Ben Fowkes. 3 vols. Marx Library. London: Penguin, 1976.

———. "Critique of the Gotha Program." In *Selected Writings*, edited by Lawrence H. Simon, 315–32. Hackett Classics. Indianapolis: Hackett, 1994.

———. *Karl Marx's Writings on Alienation*. Edited by Marcello Musto. Marx, Engels, and Marxisms. London: Palgrave-Macmillan, 2021.

BIBLIOGRAPHY

———."Estranged Labor." Marxists Internet Archive, 1844. From *Economic and Philosophical Manuscripts of 1844*, translated by Martin Mulligan. http://spartan.ac.brocku.ca/~tmulligan/READING_Estranged_Labor.pdf.

Marx, Karl, and Friedrich Engels. *The Communist Manifesto*. Edited by Jeffrey C. Isaac. Rethinking the Western Tradition. New Haven, CT: Yale University Press, 2012.

Matthews, Gerard Paul. "Infotainment." *Encyclopedia Britannica*, Aug. 17, 2023. https://www.britannica.com/topic/infotainment.

Maurin, Peter. *Easy Essays*. Catholic Worker Reprint Series. Eugene, OR: Wipf and Stock, 2010.

———. "The Sit-Down Technique." *Catholic Worker* 4 (1937) 1, 6.

Maxwell, Grant. "A Widening of Consciousness through Integration: C. G. Jung's *Mysterium Conjunctions*." In *Integration and Difference: Constructing a Mythical Dialectic*, 165–96. Philosophy and Psychoanalysis. New York: Routledge, 2022.

Mbembe, Achille. *Necropolitics*. Theory in Forms. Durham: Duke University Press, 2019.

McCarraher, Eugene. *The Enchantments of Mammon: How Capitalism Became the Religion of Modernity*. Cambridge, MA: Belknap, 2019.

McClusky, Molly. "Public Universities Get an Education in Private Industry." *Atlantic*, Apr. 3, 2017. https://www.theatlantic.com/education/archive/2017/04/public-universities-get-an-education-in-private-industry/521379/.

McDaniel, Charles A. "Chesterton's Distributism and the Revaluation of Progress." *Christian Scholar's Review* 35 (2006) 517–35.

McGilchrist, Iain. *The Master and His Emissary: The Divided Brain and the Making of the Western World*. New Haven, CT: Yale University Press, 2018.

McGowan, Jo. "Modi Backs Down: Letter from India." *Commonweal*, Jan. 1, 2022. https://www.commonwealmagazine.org/modi-backs-down.

McGranahan, David A., and Calvin L. Beale. "Understanding Rural Population Loss." *Rural America /Rural Development Perspectives* 17 (2002) 2–11.

McKanan, Dan. *The Catholic Worker after Dorothy: Practicing the Works of Mercy in a New Generation*. Collegeville, MN: Liturgical, 2008.

McRae, Andrew. *God Speed the Plough: The Representation of Agrarian England, 1500–1660*. Past & Present. New York: Cambridge University Press, 1996.

Mercer, Alex. "John F. MacArthur Net Worth in 2022—Birthday, Age, Wife and Children." Pure Net Worth, May 25, 2022. https://purenetworth.com/john-macarthur-net-worth/.

Michels, Robert. *Political Parties: A Sociological Study of the Oligarchical Tendencies of Modern Democracy*. Translated by Eden and Cedar Paul. Kitchener, Can.: Batoche, 2001.

Milan, Babic, et al. "The Rise of Transnational State Capital: State-Led Foreign Investment in the 21st Century." *Review of International Political Economy* 27 (2020) 433–75.

Milbank, John, and Adrian Pabst. *The Politics of Virtue: Post-Liberalism and the Human Future*. Future Perfect: Images of the Time to Come in Philosophy, Politics and Cultural Studies. Lanham, MD: Rowman & Littlefield, 2016.

Miles, Lucas. *Woke Jesus: The False Messiah Destroying Christianity*. West Palm Beach, FL: Humanix, 2023.

Mills, David. "Cardinal Spellman v. Dorothy Day, at Christmas." *Catholic Herald*, Dec. 23, 2020. https://catholicherald.co.uk/ch/cardinal-spellman-v-dorothy-day/.

Minogue, Kenneth. *The Liberal Mind: A Critical Analysis of the Philosophy of Liberalism and Its Political Effects.* New York: Vintage, 1964.
Mitchell, Stacy. "The View from the Shop: Antitrust and the Decline of America's Independent Businesses." *Antitrust Bulletin* 61 (2016) 498–516. https://doi.org/10.1177/0003603X16676139.
Mitra, Esha, and Rhea Mogul. "Indian Farmers Forced Modi to Back Down on New Laws. So Why Aren't They Going Home?" CNN, Nov. 26, 2021. https://www.cnn.com/2021/11/26/india/india-farmers-protest-one-year-intl-hnk-dst/index.html.
Mize, Sandra Yocum. "'We Are Still Pacifists': Dorothy Day's Pacifism during World War II." *Records of the American Catholic Historical Society of Philadelphia* 108 (1997) 1–12.
Moltmann, Jürgen. *The Crucified God.* 40th anniv. ed. Minneapolis: Fortress, 2015.
Montanaro, Domenico. "What Does the Word 'Woke' Really Mean, and Where Does It Come From?" NPR, July 19, 2023. https://www.npr.org/2023/07/19/1188543449/what-does-the-word-woke-really-mean-and-where-does-it-come-from.
Moore, Beth. *Praying God's Word: Breaking Free from Spiritual Strongholds.* Nashville: B&H, 2009.
More, Thomas. *Utopia.* Translated by Paul Turner. London: Penguin, 1965.
Mouffe, Chantal. *The Return of the Political.* Radical Thinkers. New York: Verso, 2020.
Mounier, Emmanuel. *A Personalist Manifesto.* London: Longmans, Green, 1938.
Myrick, Richard. "Action Libérale Populaire and the Legacy of Catholic Republicans in the French Third Republic." PhD diss., Kansas State University, 2023.
Nagesh, Ashitha. "U.S. Election 2020: Why Trump Gained Support among Minorities." BBC, Nov. 22, 2020. https://www.bbc.com/news/world-us-canada-54972389.
Nagle, Angela, and Michael Tracey. "First as Tragedy, Then as Farce: The Collapse of the Sanders Campaign and the 'Fusionist' Left." *American Affairs* 4 (2020). https://americanaffairsjournal.org/2020/05/first-as-tragedy-then-as-farce/.
Nagle, Angela A. *Kill All Normies: Online Culture Wars from 4chan and Tumblr to Trump and the Alt-Right.* London: Zero, 2017.
Naipaul, V. S. "One Out of Many." In *In a Free State: A Novel*, 15–53. London: Penguin, 1973.
Nally, David. "'That Coming Storm': The Irish Poor Law, Colonial Biopolitics, and the Great Famine." *Annals of the Association of American Geographers* 98 (2008) 714–41.
Nathan, Emmanuel, and Anya Topolski, eds. *Is There a Judeo-Christian Tradition? A European Perspective.* Perspectives on Jewish Texts and Contexts 4. Berlin: de Gruyter, 2016.
National Distributist Party. "Policy of the NDP." National Distributist Party, n.d. https://www.nationaldistributistparty.com/policy.html.
NBC 26. "As 500 Wisconsin Farmers Disappear, a Fremont Family Battles to Keep Theirs Running amid Declining Sales." NBC 26, Feb. 22, 2021. https://www.nbc26.com/news/local-news/the-number-of-small-family-owned-farms-in-wisconsin-continues-to-decline.
Neel, Phil A. *Hinterland: America's New Landscape of Class and Conflict.* London: Reaktion, 2018.
Nel, Marius. "Pentacostals' Reading of the Old Testament." *Verbum et Ecclesia* 28 (2007).

Newport, Frank. "How Many Highly Religious Conservative Republicans Are There?" Gallup, Mar. 31, 2015. https://news.gallup.com/opinion/polling-matters/182210/highly-religious-conservative-republicans.aspx.

Nicholson, Shan, and Richard Lopez, dirs. *Jonestown: Terror in the Jungle*. Aired Nov. 17–18, 2018, on Sundance.

Nietzsche, Friedrich. *On the Advantage and Disadvantage of History for Life*. Translated by Peter Preuss. Hackett Classics. Indianapolis: Hackett, 1980.

———. *On the Genealogy of Morality*. Edited and translated by Maudemarie Clark and Alan J. Swensen. Indianapolis: Hackett, 1998.

Nye, Joseph S., Jr. "Soft Power." *Foreign Policy* 80 (1990) 153–71. http://www.jstor.org/stable/1148580.

Oakeshott, Michael. "On Being Conservative." In *Rationalism in Politics and Other Essays*, 407–37. Rev. ed. Indianapolis: Liberty Fund, 1991.

———. "Rationalism in Politics." In *Rationalism in Politics and Other Essays*, 5–42. Rev. ed. Indianapolis: Liberty Fund, 1991.

O'Connor, Ann. "The Catholic Worker: Is it Still Catholic?" *New Oxford Review* (Mar. 1994) 5–8.

Olmstead, Edith. "Why Are CNN, ABC, and NBC Reporters Embedding with the Israeli Military?" *New Republic*, Nov. 15, 2023. https://newrepublic.com/article/176919/cnn-abc-nbc-reporters-embedding-israeli-military-gaza.

Oreskes, Naomi, and Erik M. Conway. *Merchants of Doubt: How a Handful of Scientists Obscured the Truth on Issues from Tobacco Smoke to Global Warming*. Repr., New York: Bloomsbury, 2011.

Orozco, Chris. "The Broken Coffee Cup—I Freely Confess I Broke the Coffee Cup, but I Did Not Break the Fellowship among My Friends nor within the Church I Left; Part 3: Politics, Idolatry, Pandemic, Second Great Commandment, Theology Mantras." Writing in the Shade of Trees, Sept. 13, 2022. https://www.writingintheshadeoftrees.com/2022/09/13/everything-in-between/church-letters/the-broken-coffee-cup-i-freely-confess-i-broke-the-coffee-cup-but-i-did-not-break-the-fellowship-among-my-friends-nor-within-the-church-i-left-part-3-politics-idolatry-pandemi/.

———. "Letters, Correspondence, & Dialogue with Church & Friends on Christ, Faith, & Christian Living." Writing in the Shade of Trees, Aug. 4, 2023. https://www.writingintheshadeoftrees.com/category/everything-in-between/church-letters/.

Ortega y Gasset, José. *The Revolt of the Masses*. New York: Norton & Company, 1994.

Paarlberg, Robert, and Don Paarlberg. "Agricultural Policy in the Twentieth Century." *Agricultural History* 74 (2000) 136–61.

Parenti, Michael. *Democracy for the Few*. 5th ed. New York: St. Martin's, 1988.

Parke, Caleb. "Jonathan Morris: GOP Needs to Show Why Open Borders Is 'Morally Wrong,' or Get Branded 'Evil' by 2020 Dems." Fox News, July 23, 2019. https://www.foxnews.com/politics/jonathan-morris-gop-needs-to-show-why-open-borders-is-morally-wrong.

Parker, Kim. "The Growing Partisan Divide in Views of Higher Education." Pew Research, Aug. 19, 2019. https://www.pewresearch.org/social-trends/2019/08/19/the-growing-partisan-divide-in-views-of-higher-education-2/.

Paul VI, Pope. "*Apostolicam Actuositatem*: On the Apostolate of the Laity." Vatican, Nov. 18, 1965. https://www.vatican.va/archive/hist_councils/ii_vatican_council/documents/vat-ii_decree_19651118_apostolicam-actuositatem_en.html.

———. "*Lumen Gentium*: Dogmatic Constitution on the Church." Vatican, Nov. 21, 1964. https://www.vatican.va/archive/hist_councils/ii_vatican_council/documents/vat-ii_const_19641121_lumen-gentium_en.html.

Penty, Arthur. *Distributism: A Manifesto*. London: Real, 2019.

Peoples, Clayton D. "Contributor Influence in Congress: Social Ties and PAC Effects on U.S. House Policymaking." *Sociological Quarterly* 51 (2010) 649–77.

Perry, Barbara, et al., eds. *Right-Wing Extremism in Canada and the United States*. Palgrave Hate Studies. Cham: Springer, 2022.

Peters, Jeremy W., and Katie Robertson. "Fox Stars Privately Expressed Disbelief about Election Fraud Claims: 'Crazy Stuff.'" *New York Times*, Feb. 16, 2023; updated Apr. 24, 2023. https://www.nytimes.com/2023/02/16/business/media/fox-dominion-lawsuit.html.

Peterson, Jordan B. (@jordanbpeterson). 2023. "There is nothing Christian about #SocialJustice. Redemptive salvation is a matter of the individual soul." Twitter. Mar. 2, 2023, 2:00 a.m. https://twitter.com/jordanbpeterson/status/1631202861068570626?lang=en.

Piketty, Thomas. *Capital in the Twenty-First Century*. Translated by Arthur Goldhammer. Cambridge, MA: Belknap, 2014.

Pilsch, Andrew. *Transhumanism: Evolutionary Futurism and the Human Technologies of Utopia*. Minneapolis: University of Minnesota Press, 2017.

Pinches, Charles. "Why Church Matters: The Political Theology of Stanley Hauerwas." *Political Science Reviewer* 46 (2022) 311–27.

Pius XI, Pope. "*Quadragesimo Anno*: On Reconstruction of the Social Order." Vatican, May 15, 1931. https://www.vatican.va/content/pius-xi/en/encyclicals/documents/hf_p-xi_enc_19310515_quadragesimo-anno.html.

Plato. *The Republic*. Edited and translated by Allan Bloom. New York: Basic, 2016.

Politico Staff. "Full Text: 2017 Donald Trump Inauguration Speech Transcript." Politico, Jan. 20, 2017. https://www.politico.com/story/2017/01/full-text-donald-trump-inauguration-speech-transcript-233907.

Pollan, Michael. *The Omnivore's Dilemma*. New York: Penguin, 2006.

Pontifical Council for the Laity. *International Associations of the Faithful: Directory*. Vatican City: Vaticana, 2006. http://www.laici.va/content/laici/en/pubblicazioni/repertorio-delle-associazioni-internazionali.html.

Postone, Moishe. *Time, Labor, and Social Domination: A Reinterpretation of Marx's Critical Theory*. Cambridge: Cambridge University Press, 1993.

Porter, Clifford F. "The Interpretations of Nazi Totalitarianism by Hannah Arendt, Leo Strauss, and Eric Voegelin." PhD diss., Claremont Graduate University, 2000.

Price, Edwin, et al. *Global Food Security Is National Security: How Hunger and Malnutrition Abroad Make the U.S. Less Safe*. Washington, DC: Farm Journal Foundation, 2023. https://www.farmjournalfoundation.org/_files/ugd/cfcaf3_b59759697a054d9083e794712ea709fa.pdf.

Projectpray. "Prayer at the Heart of America 2021: Lebanon Kansas." YouTube, Mar. 28, 2022; from July 23, 2021. https://www.youtube.com/watch?v=CkSWPLnqJOY.

Rahe, Paul A. *Soft Despotism, Democracy's Drift: Montesquieu, Rousseau, Tocqueville, and the Modern Prospect*. New Haven, CT: Yale University Press, 2009.

Reed, Deborah B., and Deborah T. Claunch. "Risk for Depressive Symptoms and Suicide among U.S. Primary Farmers and Family Members: A Systematic Literature Review." *AAOHN Journal* 68 (2020) 236–48.

Reid, Melissa. "Unjust Signifying Practices: Submission and Subordination among Christian Fundamentalists." *JFSR* 29 (Fall 2013) 154–61.

Reno, R. R. "Subsidiarity." *First Things* 244 (2014) 4–6.

Retief, F. P., and L. Cilliers. "The History and Pathology of Crucifixion." *South African Medical Journal* 93 (2003) 938–41.

Reuters. "Explainer: Spilt Milk? Why Are the US and Canada Fighting over Dairy?" Reuters, Feb. 1, 2023. https://www.reuters.com/markets/commodities/spilt-milk-why-are-us-canada-fighting-over-dairy-2023-02-01/.

Rieff, Philip. *The Triumph of the Therapeutic: Uses of Faith after Freud*. Washington, DC: ISI, 2006.

Riegle, Rosalie G. "The Catholic Worker Movement in 2014: An Appreciation." *Montréal Review*, Aug. 2014. https://www.themontrealreview.com/2009/The-Catholic-Worker-Movement.php.

Rielly, Katie. "Read Hillary Clinton's 'Basket of Deplorables' Remarks about Donald Trump Supporters." *Time*, Sept. 10, 2016. https://time.com/4486502/hillary-clinton-basket-of-deplorables-transcript/.

Rinne, April. "What Exactly Is the Sharing Economy?" World Economic Forum, Dec. 13, 2017. https://www.weforum.org/agenda/2017/12/when-is-sharing-not-really-sharing/.

Ritchie, David A. *Why Do the Nations Rage? The Demonic Origins of Nationalism*. Eugene, OR: Wipf & Stock, 2021.

Robertson, Katie. "5 Times Tucker Carlson Privately Reviled Trump: 'I Hate Him.'" *New York Times*, Mar. 8, 2023; updated Apr. 25, 2023. https://www.nytimes.com/2023/03/08/business/media/tucker-carlson-trump.html.

Rogers, Richard. "Deplatforming: Following Extreme Internet Celebrities to Telegram and Alternative Social Media." *European Journal of Communication* 35 (2020) 213–29.

Romero, Paul D., and Julie M. Whittaker. *A Brief Examination of Union Membership Data*. Congressional Research Service, June 16, 2023. CRS Report R47596. https://sgp.fas.org/crs/misc/R47596.pdf.

Rosenthal, Lecia. *Mourning Modernism: Literature, Catastrophe, and the Politics of Consolation*. Bronx: Fordham University Press, 2011.

Rousseau, Jean-Jacques. *On the Social Contract*. Edited by David Wootton. Translated by Donald A. Cress. 2nd ed. Indianapolis: Hackett, 2019.

Rowe, Mike, host. *Dirty Jobs*. Aired Nov. 7, 2003–Feb. 5, 2023, on Discovery.

Roys, Julie. "John MacArthur Shamed, Excommunicated Mother for Refusing to Take Back Child Abuser." *Roys Report*, Mar. 8, 2022. https://julieroys.com/macarthur-shamed-excommunicated-mother-take-back-child-abuser/.

———. "The Prosperous Lifestyle of America's Anti-Prosperity Gospel Preacher." *Roys Report*, Feb. 3, 2021. https://julieroys.com/prosperous-lifestyle-americas-anti-prosperity-gospel-preacher/.

Rubin, Leslie G. *America, Aristotle, and the Politics of a Middle Class*. Waco: Baylor University Press, 2018.

Rutherford, Alexandra. "'Making Better Use of U.S. Women': Psychology, Sex Roles, and Womanpower in Post-WWII America." *Journal of the History of the Behavioral Sciences* 53 (2017) 228–45.

Salatin, Joel. *Folks, This Ain't Normal: A Farmer's Advice for Happier Hens, Healthier People, and a Better World*. New York: Center Street, 2012.

Sam. "John MacArthur Net Worth, Wife Patricia MacArthur and Kids." Famous Christians, June 13, 2024. https://famous-christians.com/john-macarthur/.\
Santori, Paolo. *Thomas Aquinas and the Civil Economy Tradition: The Mediterranean Spirit of Capitalism*. Routledge Studies in the History of Economics. New York: Routledge, 2021.
Sartre, Jean-Paul. *"No Exit" and Three Other Plays*. New York: Vintage, 1989.
Sautter, John A., et al. "Construction of a Fool's Paradise: Ethanol Subsidies in America." *Sustainable Development Law & Policy* 7 (2007) 26–29, 74–75.
Scheiber, Laura L., and Mark D. Mitchell, eds. *Across a Great Divide: Continuity and Change in Native North American Societies, 1400–1900*. Amerind Studies in Anthropology. Tucson: University of Arizona Press, 2010.
Schindler, David L. "Communio Ecclesiology and Liberalism." *Review of Politics* 60 (1998) 775–86.
———. *Heart of the World, Center of the Church: Communio Ecclesiology, Liberalism, and Liberation*. Grand Rapids: Eerdmans, 2021.
Schindler, D. C. *The Politics of the Real: The Church between Liberalism and Integralism*. Steubenville, OH: New Polity, 2021.
Schwarz, Jon. "The Murder of the US Middle Class Began 40 Years Ago This Week." *Intercept*, Aug. 6, 2021. https://theintercept.com/2021/08/06/middle-class-reagan-patco-strike/.
Schweiker, William. "Humanism and the Question of Fullness." In *Aspiring to Fullness in a Secular Age: Essays on Religion and Theology in the Work of Charles Taylor*, edited by Carlos D. Colorado and Justin Klassen, 127–51. Notre Dame, IN: University of Notre Dame Press, 2014.
Sedacca, Natalie. "Domestic Workers, the 'Family Worker' Exemption from Minimum Wage, and Gendered Devaluation of Women's Work." *Industrial Law Journal* 51 (2022) 771–801.
Segal, Barry. "32% of U.S. Coupled Adults Have Cheated on Their Partners Financially." Credit Cards, Jan. 24, 2022. https://www.creditcards.com/statistics/financial-infidelity-cheating-poll/.
Seidelman, James "Cid," and John Watkins. "Trump Meant the End of Neoliberalism. What Comes Next?" *Salt Lake Tribune*, May 24, 2019; updated May 25, 2019. https://www.sltrib.com/opinion/commentary/2019/05/26/commentary-trump-meant/.
Self, Robert O. *All in the Family: The Realignment of American Democracy since the 1960s*. New York: Hill and Wang, 2013.
Semuels, Alana. "'They're Trying to Wipe Us Off the Map': Small American Farmers Are Nearing Extinction." *Time*, Nov. 27, 2019. https://time.com/5736789/small-american-farmers-debt-crisis-extinction/.
Sennett, Richard. *The Craftsman*. New Haven, CT: Yale University Press, 2009.
Seybold, Peter. "The Struggle against Corporate Takeover of the University." *Socialism and Democracy* 22 (2008) 115–25.
Sgueglia, Kristina, and Steve Almasy. "Father Who Sexually and Psychologically Manipulated Victims from His Daughter's Sarah Lawrence College Dorm Doom Sentenced to 60 Years in Prison." CNN, Jan. 20, 2023. https://www.cnn.com/2023/01/20/us/sarah-lawrence-college-father-trafficking-case-sentence/index.html.

Shanahan, Murray. *The Technological Singularity*. Essential Knowledge. Cambridge: MIT Press, 2015.

Sharif, Marissa A., et al. "Having Too Little or Too Much Time Is Linked to Lower Subjective Well-Being." *Journal of Personality and Social Psychology* 121 (2021) 933–47.

Shearer, Elisha, and Amy Mitchell. "News Use across Social Media Platforms in 2020." Analysis & Policy Observatory, Jan. 12, 2021. From Pew Research Center. https://apo.org.au/node/311092.

Shellnutt, Kate. "Grace Community Church Rejected Elder's Calls to 'Do Justice' in Abuse Case." *Christianity Today*, Feb. 9, 2023. https://www.christianitytoday.com/news/2023/february/grace-community-church-elder-biblical-counseling-abuse.html.

Sirico, Robert A. "Milton Friedman and the Human Element." Acton Institute, Nov. 17, 2006. https://www.acton.org/pub/commentary/2006/11/17/milton-friedman-and-human-element.

Slezak, Rebecca. "Faithful Head to Lebanon, Kansas, Center of Mainland U.S., to Pray for America." *Kansas City Star*, July 25, 2021.

Sloterdijk, Peter. *Infinite Mobilization: Towards a Critique of Political Kinetics*. Translated by Sandra Berjan. Medford, MA: Polity, 2020.

Smith, Brian. "Edmund Burke, the Warren Hastings Trial, and the Moral Dimension of Corruption." *Polity* 40 (2008) 70–94.

Smith, Vincent H., et al., eds. *Agricultural Policy in Disarray*. Vol. 1. Blue Ridge Summit: AEI, 2018.

———. *Agricultural Policy in Disarray*. Vol. 2. Washington, DC: AEI, 2018.

Smithers, John, et al. "The Dynamics of Family Farming in North Huron County, Ontario; Part II: Farm-Community Interactions." *Canadian Geographer* 48 (2004) 209–24.

Solzhenitsyn, Alexander. "A World Split Apart." Aleksandr Solzhenitsyn Center, June 8, 1978. Commencement address, Harvard University. https://www.solzhenitsyncenter.org/a-world-split-apart.

Sourisseau, Jean-Michel, ed. *Family Farming and the Worlds to Come*. Dordrecht: Springer, 2015.

Sowell, Thomas. *Black Rednecks and White Liberals*. San Francisco: Encounter, 2005.

SpaceX. "Mars & Beyond: The Road to Making Humanity Multiplanetary." SpaceX, n.d. https://www.spacex.com/human-spaceflight/mars/.

Sparkes, Russell. "Chesterton the Economist." In *The Hound of Distributism: A Solution for Our Social and Economic Crisis*, edited by Richard Aleman, 37–50. Charlotte, NC: ACS, 2015.

Spieker, Manfred. "The Universal Destination of Goods: The Ethics of Property in the Theory of a Christian Society." *Journal of Markets and Morality* 8 (2005) 333–54.

Spock, Benjamin. *Baby and Child Care*. New York: Pocket, 1957.

Standing, Guy. *The Corruption of Capitalism: Why Rentiers Thrive and Work Does Not Pay*. London: Biteback, 2018.

———. *The Precariat: The New Dangerous Class*. London: Bloomsbury Academic, 2011.

Stanford, Peter. "Jürgen Moltmann: Man of Hope." *Tablet*, Mar. 18, 2020. https://www.thetablet.co.uk/features/2/17736/j-rgen-moltmann-man-of-hope.

Stefan, Bulgarea Candin. "John MacArthur Net Worth and Salary." Famous People, last updated Nov. 23, 2023. https://famouspeopletoday.com/john-macarthur/.

Stofferahn, C. W. "Industrialized Farming and Its Relationship to Community Well-Being: An Update of a 2000 Report by Linda Lobao." CABI Digital Library, Feb. 7, 2007. https://www.cabidigitallibrary.org/doi/full/10.5555/20073007574.

Stone, Glenn Davis, and Andrew Flachs. "The Ox Fall Down: Path-Breaking and Technology Treadmill in Indian Cotton Agriculture." *Journal of Peasant Studies* 45 (2018) 1272–96.

Strauss, Leo. *Natural Right and History*. Walgreen Foundation Lectures. Chicago: University of Chicago Press, 1968.

———. "On the Intention of Rousseau." *Social Research* 14 (1947) 455–87.

———. *The Political Philosophy of Hobbes: Its Basis and Its Genesis*. Translated by Elsa M. Sinclair. Oxford: Clarendon, 1936.

———. *The Rebirth of Classical Political Rationalism: An Introduction to the Thought of Leo Strauss*. Edited by Thomas L. Pangle. Chicago: University of Chicago Press, 1989.

———. *Thoughts on Machiavelli*. Chicago: University of Chicago Press, 1958.

———. "What Is Political Philosophy?" *Journal of Politics* 19 (1957) 343–68.

———. *What Is Political Philosophy? And Other Studies*. Glencoe, IL: Free, 1959.

Strider, Burns, 987. "Fox News Funds Research and Smear Campaign against American Pastor." *Huffington Post*, May 18, 2010; updated May 25, 2011. https://www.huffpost.com/entry/fox-news-funds-research-a_b_504433.

Swogger, Glenn, Jr. "Apocalyptic Evil and Dislocation." Unpublished manuscript in the author's possession, 2020.

Swogger, Glenn, Jr., and Henry I. Miller. "Donald Trump: Narcissist-in-Chief, Not Commander-In-Chief." *Forbes*, Mar. 30, 2016. https://www.forbes.com/sites/realspin/2016/03/30/donald-trump-narcissist-in-chief-not-commander-in-chief/?sh=2f3b39335d45.

Táíwò, Olúfẹ́mi O. "Identity Politics and Elite Capture." *Boston Review*, May 7, 2020. https://www.bostonreview.net/articles/olufemi-o-taiwo-identity-politics-and-elite-capture/.

Tax Policy Center. "Historical Highest Marginal Income Tax Rates: 1913–2023." Tax Policy Center, May 11, 2023. https://www.taxpolicycenter.org/statistics/historical-highest-marginal-income-tax-rates.

Taylor, Charles. *The Malaise of Modernity*. CBC Massey Lectures Series. Toronto: Anansi, 1998.

———. *A Secular Age*. Cambridge, MA: Belknap, 2018.

Terrell, Brian. "The Farmer and the Agitator: The Catholic Worker Needs Both." *Regenerative Reader* 1 (2023) 8, 11–13.

Thomas, Marina F., et al. "99 + Matches but a Spark Ain't One: Adverse Psychological Effects of Excessive Swiping on Dating Apps." *Telematics and Informatics* 78 (2023) 1–13.

Time Staff. "Here's Donald Trump's Presidential Announcement Speech." *Time*, June 16, 2015. https://time.com/3923128/donald-trump-announcement-speech/.

Tocqueville, Alexis de. *Democracy in America*. Edited by J. P. Mayer. Translated by George Lawrence. New York: Harper & Row, 1988.

Tokar, Norman, dir. *Leave It to Beaver*. Season 1, episode 32, "Beaver's Old Friend." Aired May 21, 1958, on CBS.

———. *Leave It to Beaver*. Season 2, episode 28, "Beaver's Hero." Aired Apr. 9, 1959, on ABC.

Trump, Donald J. "The Inaugural Address." Trump White House, Jan. 20, 2017. https://trumpwhitehouse.archives.gov/briefings-statements/the-inaugural-address/.

———. "President Donald J. Trump's State of the Union Address." Trump White House, Feb. 5, 2019. https://www.presidency.ucsb.edu/documents/address-before-joint-session-the-congress-the-state-the-union-25.

Tsing, Anna Lowenhaupt. *Mushroom at the End of the World: On the Possibility of Life in Capitalist Ruins*. Princeton, NJ: Princeton University Press, 2015.

Tumilty, Emma, and Michele Battle-Fisher, eds. *Transhumanism: Entering an Era of Bodyhacking and Radical Human Modification*. International Library of Bioethics 100. Cham, Switz.: Springer, 2022.

Twain, Mark. *Chapters from My Autobiography*. Project Gutenberg, 1906. eBook 19987. https://www.gutenberg.org/files/19987/19987-h/19987-h.htm.

Tyburski, Michael D. "Curse or Cure? Migrant Remittances and Corruption." *Journal of Politics* 76 (2014) 814–24.

Tyson Foods. "Feeding the World with America's Poultry Farmers." Tyson Foods, n.d. https://www.tysonfoods.com/who-we-are/our-partners/farmers/contract-poultry-farming.

United for Respect. "The Fight for Good Jobs." United for Respect, n.d. https://united4respect.org/campaigns/.

United States Senate Special Committee on Aging. "COVID-19 One Year Later: Addressing Health Care Needs for At-Risk Americans." United States Senate Special Committee on Aging, Mar. 18, 2021. https://www.aging.senate.gov/hearings/covid-19-one-year-later-addressing-health-care-needs-for-at-risk-americans/.

USDA Food and Nutrition Service. "SNAP Work Requirements." USDA Food and Nutrition Service, n.d. https://www.fns.usda.gov/snap/work-requirements.

Van Engen, Abram C. *City on a Hill: A History of American Exceptionalism*. New Haven, CT: Yale University Press, 2020.

Varoufakis, Yanis. "From an Economics without Capitalism to Markets without Capitalism." Yanis Varoufakis, Jan. 28, 2021. https://www.yanisvaroufakis.eu/2021/01/28/from-an-economics-without-capitalism-to-markets-without-capitalism-tubingen-university-talk/.

———. *Technofeudalism: What Killed Capitalism*. Brooklyn: Melville, 2024.

Vasilopoulos, Aristidis, et al. "Factors Underlying Denial of and Disbelief in COVID-19." *Jornal Brasileiro de Pneumologia* 48 (2022) e20220228.

Vinel, Jean-Christian. "Christopher Tomlins' *The State and the Unions* Today: What the Critical Synthesis Can Teach Us Now That the Unions Have Gone." *Labor History* 54 (2013) 177–92.

Voegelin, Eric. *The New Science of Politics: An Introduction*. Walgreen Foundation Lectures. Chicago: University of Chicago Press, 1987.

———. *Science, Politics and Gnosticism*. Wilmington, DE: ISI, 1968.

Von Mises, Ludwig. *The Anti-Capitalistic Mentality*. Edited by Bettina Bien Greaves. Indianapolis: Liberty Fund, 1956.

———. *Interventionism: An Economic Analysis*. Edited by Bettina Bien Greaves. Indianapolis: Liberty Fund, 2011.

———. *Omnipotent Government: The Rise of the Total State and Total War*. New Edited by Bettina Bien Greaves. Haven, CT: Yale University Press, 1944.

Ware, Bruce A. *Father, Son, and Holy Spirit: Roles, Relationships, and Relevance*. Wheaton, IL: Crossway, 2005.

Wark, McKenzie. *Capital Is Dead: Is This Something Worse?* New York: Verso, 2019.

Warner, John M. "The Friendless Republic: Freedom, Faction, and Friendship in Machiavelli's Discourses." *Review of Politics* 81 (2019) 1–19.

Webb, William J., and Gordon K. Oeste. *Bloody, Brutal and Barbaric? Wrestling with Troubling War Texts*. Downers Grove, IL: IVP Academic, 2019.

Weber, Max. "Science as a Vocation." In *From Max Weber: Essays in Sociology*, edited by H. Gerth and C. Wright Mills, 129–56. New York: Oxford University Press, 1948.

Weinberg, Steven. *Dreams of a Final Theory: The Scientist's Search for the Ultimate Laws of Nature*. New York: Vintage, 1994.

Weinstein, Amanda L. "Working Women in the City and Urban Wage Growth in the United States." *Journal of Regional Science* 57 (2017) 591–610.

Wettlaufer, Jörg. "The *Jus Primae Noctis* as a Male Power Display: A Review of Historic Sources with Evolutionary Interpretation." *Evolution and Human Behavior* 21 (2000) 111–23.

Williams, Walter E. *The State against Blacks*. New York: McGraw Hill, 1982.

Wilson, Jason. "Hiding in Plain Sight: How the 'Alt-Right' Is Weaponizing Irony to Spread Fascism." *Guardian*, May 23, 2017. https://www.theguardian.com/technology/2017/may/23/alt-right-online-humor-as-a-weapon-facism.

Wingfield, Mark. "John MacArthur Is Wrong about So Much More Than Keeping Women in Abusive Marriages." *Baptist News Global*, Feb. 14, 2023. https://baptistnews.com/article/john-macarthur-is-wrong-about-so-much-more-than-keeping-women-in-abusive-marriages/.

Winter, Ralph K. "Political Financing and the Constitution." *Annals of the American Academy of Political and Social Science* 486 (1986) 34–48.

Wishloff, Jim. "The Hard Truths of the Easy Essays: The Crisis of Modernity and the Social Vision of Peter Maurin." *Journal of Religion and Business Ethics* 2 (2011) 1–30.

Wolff, Edward N. "Why Piketty Is Wrong about Inheritance." *World Economic Forum*, Oct. 22, 2014. https://www.weforum.org/agenda/2014/10/piketty-inheritance-wealth-inequality/.

Wolin, Sheldon. *Democracy Incorporated: Managed Democracy and the Specter of Inverted Totalitarianism*. Rev. ed. Princeton, NJ: Princeton University Press, 2017.

Wood, Ellen Meiksins. "The Agrarian Origins of Capitalism." *Monthly Review* 50 (1998) 14–31.

———. *The Origin of Capitalism: A Longer View*. London: Verso, 2002.

Wright, Kevin. "Agricultural Consolidation Causes and the Path Forward: The 2017 Agricultural Symposium." *Ten* [Federal Reserve Bank of Kansas City], Nov. 12, 2017. https://www.kansascityfed.org/ten/2017-fall-ten-magazine/agsymposium/.

Wright, N. T. *The Original Jesus: The Life and Vision of a Revolutionary*. Grand Rapids: Eerdmans, 1996.

Wuthnow, Robert. *The Left Behind: Decline and Rage in Small-Town America*. Princeton, NJ: Princeton University Press, 2018.

Zahnd, Brian. *A Farewell to Mars: An Evangelical Pastor's Journey toward the Biblical Gospel of Peace*. Colorado Springs: Cook, 2014.

———. "God Is Like Jesus." Brian Zahnd, Aug. 11, 2011. https://brianzahnd.com/2011/08/god-is-like-jesus-2/.

———. "Good Friday: A World Indicted." Brian Zahnd, Mar. 24, 2016. https://brianzahnd.com/2016/03/good-friday/#more-5444.

———. *Postcards from Babylon: The Church in American Exile*. N.p.: Spello, 2019.

———. *The Unvarnished Jesus: A Lenten Journey*. N.p.: Spello, 2019.

———. *Water to Wine: Some of My Story*. N.p.: Spello, 2016.

Zakaria, Fareed. "Capitalism, Not Culture, Drives Economies." *Washington Post*, Aug. 1, 2012. https://www.washingtonpost.com/opinions/fareed-zakaria-capitalism-not-culture-drives-economies/2012/08/01/gJQAKtH9PX_story.html.

Žižek, Slavoj. *Sex and the Failed Absolute*. London: Bloomsbury Academic, 2019.

———. "Sex, Contracts and Manners." *Philosophical Salon*, Jan. 22, 2018. https://thephilosophicalsalon.com/sex-contracts-and-manners/.

———. "What the 'Woke' Left and the Alt-Right Share." *Project Syndicate*, Aug. 3, 2022. https://www.project-syndicate.org/commentary/woke-alt-right-fake-civil-war-between-capitalist-interests-by-slavoj-zizek-2022-08.

———. *The Year of Dreaming Dangerously*. Brooklyn: Verso, 2012.

Zuboff, Shoshana. *The Age of Surveillance Capitalism: The Fight for a Human Future at the New Frontier of Power*. New York: Public Affairs, 2019.

Zuckert, Catherine H., and Michael P. Zuckert. *The Truth about Leo Strauss: Political Philosophy & American Democracy*. Chicago: University of Chicago Press, 2006.

Zwick, Mark, and Louise Zwick. "Dorothy Day, Peter Maurin, & Distributism." In *The Hound of Distributism: A Solution for Our Social and Economic Crisis*, edited by Richard Aleman, 89–97. Charlotte, NC: ACS, 2015.

Index

abandonment from the Left, 174–89
absolute monarchy, 24, 32, 131–32
abuse, 199–205
academics, 4–5, 9, 11, 172n34
acceleration of change, 58, 95, 97, 99
action, 23, 234–37
acts of God, 126, 135
admonition to not fear, 270–71
advertising, 34, 82, 108, 128, 175, 211
AEI (American Enterprise Institute), 170n24
affect theory, 144n75
African Americans, 3n2, 5–7, 55, 117, 257
"After the Catastrophe" (Jung), 52–53
agriculture, 40, 67–68, 84–93, 105–6, 111, 115, 263–65, 274, 283, 286. *See also* farms/farmers
Airbnb, 107
alienation, 12, 29, 50n101, 52, 55, 96–99, 121, 124–29, 198
"American carnage" speech, 179–80
American Christians, 48–51, 77, 118, 174–75, 195–98, 213, 215–21, 223, 233, 235–36, 243, 278–80
American civil religion, 196–97
American Enterprise Institute (AEI), 170n24
American exceptionalism, 95, 165n13
American Patriot's Bible, 197–98
American Revolution, 22–24, 152

Angel, Jacqueline L., 110
anonymity, 236
The Anti-Capitalist Mentality (Von Mises), 162–63
anti-communism, 163, 249
anxiety, 36, 53, 98–99, 100, 108, 111, 219, 237
Apostolicam Actuositatem (Paul VI), 280
archetypal forces, 125–28, 136n47
Aristotle, 206n32, 259–61, 260n60, 276–77
Armon, Adi, 130n27
assisted living, 110
atheism, 122, 124
atomistic individualism, 143, 151
authentic religion, 52–53, 154
authoritarianism, 177
authority, 23, 45–46, 51, 79n49, 144, 147, 151–52, 155, 199, 201, 206
automation, 38–39, 42–43, 95, 96–101, 107–8, 236, 263, 273, 282
autonomy, 31–32, 65, 190, 241, 278
Azhari, Timour, 279

Baby and Child Care (Spock), 79
Bailey, Harold and Bonnie, 63–68
Balthasar, Hans Urs von, 72–73
Bannon, Steve, 173
Baptist News, 204
Barnes, Marc, 73–74
Barth, Karl, 217

INDEX

Bauman, Zygmunt, 61, 99
Bayou d'Inde, 111–12
Beaudreau, Bernard C., 35n46
Beaumont, Hugh, 77–78
Beck, Glenn, 173, 209
Belloc, Hilaire, 261–63
belonging, 192–93, 198–99
Benedict option, 68–72
The Benedict Option (Dreher), 69–70
beneficiaries, 238
Berdyaev, Nikolai, 229
Berry, Wendell, 12, 44, 49, 54, 57, 59–61, 95–96, 98–99, 100, 108, 117–18, 241–42
Biden, Joseph R., 33n38, 181–82, 210
big government, 8, 8n16, 155, 165, 170–71, 174
Black feminism, 6–7
Blake, William, 44, 146
Block, Peter, 228
blue-collar jobs, 108, 114, 178
bodies, 148–50, 148n89
Boebert, Lauren, 214–15, 214n53, 225
bomb shelter drills, 257
Borlaug, Norman, 85–88
bourgeois revolutions, 23–24
bourgeois virtues, 80, 152, 197n11
Brinkley, Alan, 162
Brooks, David, 31n33
Brown, Wendy, 168–69, 169n21, 169n23, 171
Brueggemann, Walter, 46, 49, 220–21, 228
Bullivant, Stephen, 232–33
bureaucratization, 43–46, 175–76, 253
Burke, Edmund, 22–24, 23n3, 23n6, 27–29, 27n18, 29n26, 31n32, 32, 33n41, 58–59, 124, 124n8, 238

Caesar Augustus, 222
Canada, 245–47, 264
capital campaigns, 34
capitalism
    automation, 96–101
    capitalist consumerism, 169, 278
    capitalist markets, 53–54, 121, 219
    capitalist realism, 41, 166
    capitalist socialization, 175–76

Catholic Worker movement, 253–54, 257–58
Christian faith, 165
classical conservatism, 29–31
communism, 163–64
demise of local culture, 59
distributism, 258–68
enclosure, 102–6
family dynamics and structures, 61
globalized, 118–19
Great Depression, 160–61
John Paul II, 271–73
liberal charity model, 238
Marxian critiques of, 34–44, 35n47, 53, 271–72
Maurin on, 247–48
moral base of, 262
neoliberalism, 169–70, 189–93
Strauss, 132
See also wealth
Capitalism and Freedom (Friedman), 160
Carlson, Tucker, 173, 210
Castro, Fidel, 249
Catholic Church, 103, 137–41, 144–53, 154–56, 246–55, 280–81
Catholic education, 245–46
Catholic social teaching(s), 49, 73, 243–44, 247, 251, 259
Catholic traditionalists, 68–76, 84, 192
Catholic Worker (publication), 245, 247, 250
Catholic Worker movement, 50, 71–73, 244–58
    and the church, 280–81
    distributism, 259
    houses of hospitality, 250–51, 256, 268, 277
    ideals, 276
Census Bureau's Current Population Survey, 237
Centesimus Annus (John Paul II), 271–73
centralization, 102, 132n33, 236, 268
centralized administration, 236
Cep, Casey, 248–49, 249n29
Chapp, Larry, 71–74, 252–53
charitable giving, 237–44

INDEX

cheap labor, 262–63
Chesterton, Cecil, 261
Chesterton, G. K., 40, 261–65
children, 30, 66–68, 79–84, 99, 109–11, 255
China, 36, 41, 114, 178–79, 182
Cho, Hohn, 203
Christian Brothers, 245–46
Christian community, 49–50, 202, 243–44, 246
Christian faith, 45, 51, 73, 144–45, 165, 195, 214
Christianity Today, 201–4
Christian nationalism, 214–28, 278–79
Christian right, 52, 209–11, 213, 216–19
Christian sects, 145
Christoyannopoulos, Alexandre, 258
church and state, 145, 151, 151n96, 155
church community, 198, 237–39
churches, 232–33, 276–82
    Christian political activity, 219
    church attendance, 232
    Freud on, 207
    liberal charity model, 237–44
    liberal church politics as action, 234–37
    neoliberalism, 170
Church of England, 103
church orthodoxy, 250–54
Citizens United v. FEC, 26–27, 112
city commissions, 116
city fathers, 92
civil disobedience, 257
civil rights movement, 257–58
classical (Burkean) conservatism, 22–34, 40, 231, 273–74
classical liberalism, 22, 28
Cleaver option, 79–84
climate change, 40, 42, 46, 86, 126n15, 278, 285
Clinton, Hillary, 11, 188
closed-loop or self-referential systems, 143
CNN, 90
Cochrane, Willard W., 86, 88–89
Cold War, 34, 79, 159, 163–64, 218, 257
collectivism, 159, 165
commercial values, 60

commodity crops, 64, 85, 87, 90, 102, 115, 284–86
commodity propaganda (advertising), 175
common good, 189–90
Commonweal, 89
communal living, 254–57
"Communio" movement, 72–74
communism, 34–37, 35n47, 41, 52–53, 125, 125n11, 128, 163–64, 174, 249–50, 258, 259, 261, 271–72
"communists," 74–76
complementarianism, 225
concerted action, 120, 231–32
Confession of a Catholic Worker (Chapp), 71–72
conformity, 143, 190, 198, 206, 228, 250–51
conservatism, 1–3, 162–63
conservative Christians, 69, 84, 198n13, 204, 209–13
conservative Evangelicals, 68, 215
conservatives, 4–11, 25, 92–93, 146–47, 162. *See also* classical (Burkean) conservatism; liberals
"Considerations Concerning the Common Fields and Inclosures" (Lee), 103
consumer capitalism, 169n21, 191
consumerism, 81–84, 92, 152, 219, 278–79
consumers, 28, 30, 35, 42, 90, 93, 98–99, 175, 178, 266
consumption, 40, 49, 75–76, 82, 105, 266
contracts, 261–62
cooperative community, 65, 96, 241–42
corn laws, 87
corporations, 112–15
    abuse of power, 47
    bureaucratization, 176
    corporate businesses, 8n16, 112–14, 151–52
    corporate campaign contributions, 112
    corporate donations, 26, 47, 286
    corporate funding, 9–10
    corporate power, 44, 267, 274

corporations *(continued)*
   corporate tax rates, 282
   globalized corporations, 113, 180
   and neoliberalism, 169–70
   technique, 43–44
   transnational corporations, 113–14
cosmopolitan class, 188–89
counseling, 199–204, 204n24
The Course of Empire (DeVoto), 60
COVID-19 pandemic, 50–51, 89, 233
creation, ownership of, 149–50
credit card debt, 109
crusading spirit, 48
"The Crying Sin of England, of Not Caring for the Poor" (Moore), 103
cults, 211–12, 219
cultural change(s), 7, 34, 57–62, 68, 69, 94–101, 191
cultural elites, 187, 189
cultural Marxism, 172
cultural signaling, 6
culture and politics, 218
culture of narcissism, 185–86
cynical manipulation, 210–11

Day, Dorothy, 50, 245–58, 271, 280
decision-making, 255–56
deconstructing evangelical Christians, 235–37
deep story, 100
Deism, 73
de La Salle, Jean-Baptiste, 245
democracy, 206
democratic citizenship, 79n49, 170
Democrats/Democratic Party, 2–3, 5–6, 8–9, 23n2, 25n12, 54, 75, 75n44, 92, 116, 158, 162, 184–87, 193, 196, 211
denominational identification, 232
developing world, 40
devil, 167–68
DeVoto, Bernard, 60
Diamond, Martin, 132
diffused responsibility, 125–26
direct Christian action, 72, 234, 244
disembedding, 58, 84, 140, 143, 155, 219

disenchantment, 143, 155
dislocation(s), 55, 57–59, 61–62, 68, 84, 86, 88, 117–19, 121, 125, 128, 166, 186, 190–91
displacement, 57–58, 95, 117
distributism, 244, 247, 258–68, 284–85
Distributism (Penty), 265–67
Distributist League, 261, 265
Distributist Party, England, 265–66, 267–68
disturbances, 95
diversified farming, 84, 87, 91–93, 236, 263–64, 283–84, 286
Do Good Institute, University of Maryland, 237
Domencic, Sean, 71–75
Dominion Voting Systems, 210
Dorothy Day Guild, 253n45
downwardly mobile, 92, 188
Dreher, Rod, 50n104, 69–72
Du Mez, Kristin Kobes, 215n55, 225
Dustbowl Diatribes podcast, 258

early Christianity, 148, 279
Easy Essays (Maurin), 245n19, 247–48
Eckhart, Meister, 136–37
economic class, 5–9. *See also* working classes
economy
   Catholic Worker movement, 256–58
   economic development(s), 29, 42, 54–55, 175–76
   economic globalization, 111, 274
   economic growth, 8, 34–44, 35n46, 46, 48, 127, 152, 161, 266, 274
   economic progress, 8n16
   economic systems, 50–51, 75, 106
   financially managed economy, 161
   socialized economy, 157–58
Egypt, 219–20
Eichmann, Adolf, 125–26
eldercare, 110
elites, 5–7, 99–100, 138, 140–41, 179–81, 183–89, 225, 231, 261
Ellis, Marc, 246
Ellul, Jacques, 1, 12, 43–44, 46, 150
embedded creatures. *See* social embeddedness

INDEX

eminent domain law, 92, 116
emotional trust, 65–66
emotivism, 133, 144
enchantment, 133–34
The Enchantments of Mammon (McCarraher), 166
enclosure, 101–7
Engels, Friedrich, 153
England, 32–33, 87, 101–6, 262, 265–68
English Revolution of 1642, 59n5, 152
Enlightenment, 12, 23, 26, 42, 44, 124, 138, 142, 156, 165
enmeshment, 211, 212, 217, 276
entrepreneurship, 170–71
equality of conditions, 206
essential workers, 171
Estranged Labor (Marx), 96–97
ethno-nationalism, 95, 177, 193
Europe/Europeans, 7, 40, 58–60, 122–23, 129, 135, 152, 194–95
evangelical Christianity, 68, 215, 215n55, 225, 235, 278
existentialism/ existential threat, 42, 45, 122, 129
extremism, 23, 40, 51–55, 119, 127, 128
Exvangelical podcast, 235
exvangelicals, 235, 237

Facebook, 97
factory system, 103–6
Fairlie, Simon, 101
false faith, 171
false gods, 150, 217, 274
Falwell, Jerry Jr., 211
family, 27, 40, 61, 64–67, 79–84, 175–76
farms/farmers, 59–61, 268
   classical conservatism, 33–34
   family farming, 88
   green revolution, 85–93
   liberal church politics, 236–37
   rural/urban political division, 54
   shift to diversified farming, 263–65, 283–84
   subsistence farming, 263–64
Federal Reserve, 109, 160–62
female equality, 176
Fessler, Pirmin, 109
fictional literatures of futuristic doom, 122

Fisher, Mark, 41, 166
Folmar, Chloe, 214–15
food security, 164n10, 283
food supply, 84–88, 91, 95, 267
Forbes, 109
forces of nature, 68, 126, 193, 207
forgiveness, 55, 196, 203, 222–24, 279
Foundation on Future Farming, 88
Fox News, 209–11
France, 23n3, 245–46
Francis (pope), 74, 152, 259
Francis option, 68–72
Frank, Thomas, 6n7, 184–85
freedom, 23, 51, 53–54, 150–51, 153–54, 168, 228–29, 240–41
freedom to choose, 106, 118, 158–64, 165, 167–68, 191–92, 240, 262, 274–75
free market/ free-market capitalism, 25n13, 27–28, 29, 33, 44, 92, 157–58, 160–62, 165, 172, 173, 193, 279
free marketplace, 26
Free to Choose (documentary series), 160–64, 173
free trade, 267
French Revolution, 22–24, 32, 152, 246
Freud, Sigmund, 124, 207
Friedman, Milton, 27, 106, 158–64, 165–74
Fuentes, Nick, 173–74, 173n39
Fukuyama, Francis, 121n1
fundamentalist Christianity, 199–201, 215

Galileo, 138
Gallup, 232
garage cleanups, 82–83
gender, 6, 29, 75–76, 78, 143, 149, 185, 192–93, 195, 225, 240
gig economy, 108
globalization, 107, 111, 178, 186, 231–32, 266–67, 274
   globalized capitalism, 39, 118–19
   globalized corporations, 113, 180
   globalized economy, 36–38, 47, 108, 116, 266–67

INDEX

Glorious Revolution in England, 32
God, 73, 121–22, 126–27, 135–43, 144–52, 190, 194–97, 217, 224–29
    God's freedom, 220–21
good religion, 127–28
goods and services, 240–41
good v. evil, 164, 165
government, 111–17
    Catholic Worker movement, 257–58
    and corporations, 169–70, 176
    government action, 282–85
    government bureaucracies, 49, 161, 163–64
    government regulations, 160–62
    neoliberalism, 169–71
    and Strauss, 130–32
Grace Community Church, 201–5, 212
Graeber, David, 166
"grand narrative" ideologies, 120
Gray, Eileen, 202–3, 210
Great Depression, 79–80, 158–61, 266. *See also* Catholic Worker movement
Greeks, 105, 129, 147, 151–52
green revolution, 84–93, 254
Gregory of Nazianzus, 239
gross domestic product (GDP), 111
Grudem, Wayne, 225–26, 225n79, 230n89
guilds, 266–67

Hall, Lauren, 124n8
Hannity, Sean, 173–74
Harder, Stephen, 26
Hardin, Garret, 259–60
Hauerwas, Stanley, 99–100, 217–19, 234–35, 239–40
Haven in a Heartless World (Lasch), 175–77
Hayek, Friedrich, 162
Heller, Henry, 29n26
Henry VIII, 103–4
"herd" mentality, 53–54
heresy, 216–17
The Hill, 214–15
Hispanics, 241
Hobbes, Thomas, 4, 25n9, 25n10, 131–32, 132n33, 139n58, 142

Hochschild, Arlie, 100, 100n16, 111
holiness, 72, 137–39, 141, 155, 241, 252, 279
Holy Family Catholic Worker House, 71
hope, 217–18, 219
household debt, 108–9
houses of hospitality, 250–51, 256, 268, 277
human behavior, 125, 129, 133, 142
human cost, 107–11
human emancipation. *See* freedom
human equality, 23, 131, 173
humanity, 227–28
human management, 175
human nature, 75, 97, 124n8, 134, 142, 150, 154, 166, 213n49, 219, 229, 272
human reason, 44, 124, 130n27, 212
hygienic description, 187
hyperdemocracy, 208
hyper-masculinity, 177, 214

ideals, 275–76
identity politics, 6–8, 185–86, 274
ideological crusader, 128
ideological extremism, 127
ideological possession, 48, 51, 127–28, 274, 276
ideology, 198, 213–29. *See also* liberal ideology
idolatry, 45–47, 150, 217–20
imperatives, 105–6
imports, controlling, 267
incrementalism, 33, 59, 59n6
India, 89–90
indifference, 145, 148
individual choice, 236
individualism, 141, 151, 153, 155, 159, 198, 206, 254, 278
individual responsibility, 28n22, 54, 116–17
individuation, 127
industrial agriculture, 84, 264
industrial capitalism, 106
industrialization, 106, 124–25
industrialized farming, 91–92
Industrial Revolution, 53, 58, 63

INDEX

inequality, 3, 9, 24–25, 38, 111, 111n47, 161, 219, 238–39, 244
infinite mobilization, 98
influencers, 146n82, 211, 214, 217
information asymmetry business, 107
informed citizenship, 34, 170–71
infotainment, 173
infrastructure, 158, 179, 181, 183, 196
inheritances, 40, 109–11
insurrection at the US Capitol, 33n38, 51, 177n47, 214
intensive farming, 86
interdependence, 64, 86–87, 267
international competition, 89–90, 115
international food chain, 84
international markets, 90, 285
international relations, 87n61, 112, 122
inverted totalitarianism, 154n100
Ireland, 87–88
Irish Missionaries, 254
iron law of oligarchy, 206n32
Isaiah's prophecy, 222
Islamic extremism, 119
Israel/Israelites, 219–21

Japan, 114
Jeffress, Robert, 209–11
Jesus, 49–50, 214–16, 219, 222–27, 239–40, 279–80
Jews, 125–26, 147, 223
John Paul II (pope), 259, 270–73
Johnston, Jeremiah J., 209
Jones, Alex, 173
Jones, Jim, 211–12, 228
Judeo Christianity, 129, 148, 197n11, 278
Jung, Carl, 12, 48, 52–55, 58, 119, 123, 124–29, 135n44, 136n47, 137, 137n54, 153–55, 207–8, 274

Kempis, Thomas à, 136
kibbutzim of Israel, 268, 268n79
Kirk, Russell, 25n12, 32
Kotsko, Adam, 161, 167–69, 171
Kutulas, Judy, 79–81

labor movement, 115
labor power, 266

labor unions, 6, 26, 114–15, 272
laissez-faire economics, 158, 161–62, 170n24, 267
laity, 72–73, 139, 152, 280
landlords, 105
Lasch, Christopher, 1, 12, 44, 54–55, 116, 175–77, 185–89
Laudato Si' (Francis, Pope), 152
laws and regulations, 90
lay apostolate, 280
laypeople, 136–39
leadership, 201–2. *See also* authority
Lears, T. J. Jackson, 75–76
Leave It to Beaver (television show), 77–84
Lebanon, KS, 194–96
Le Bon, Gustave, 207
Lee, Joseph, 103
leftism, 1, 9, 36–43, 189, 250, 270
Leo X (pope), 103
Leo XIII (pope), 246, 259, 271–73
LGBTQ community, 175–76
liberal charity model, 237–44, 255–58, 262, 281–82
liberal church politics as action, 234–37
liberal elite, 186
liberal God of pure potentiality, 144–45
liberal ideology, 27–28, 87, 110, 118
liberal individualism, 153, 206
liberalism, 22–23n1, 33–34, 37, 70, 73, 132, 143, 144–52, 163, 174, 191, 218, 233, 235, 273
"Liberalism as Heresy" (Barnes), 73
liberal politics, 218, 221, 234–37, 239, 242, 243
liberal progressivism, 219
liberals, 23n2, 46, 162, 172n34, 278. *See also* conservatives; right liberals/liberalism
liberal social contract, 131–32
liberal values and behavior, 233, 236
liberation, 28–31, 176
liberty, 47, 149, 160, 165
Lightfoot, H. Douglas, 35n46
Limbaugh, Rush, 5, 173
liquid modernity, 61
Listen, Liberal (Frank), 184–85
local and regional businesses, 112, 286

local culture, 57–60, 66
Locke, John, 132, 142, 195
Louisiana, 111–12
love, 55, 220, 227–28
lower classes, 130, 188
Luther, Martin, 139–40

MacArthur, John, 202–5, 210, 212, 228
Machiavelli, Niccoló, 129–34, 130n28, 142
machinery, 37–38, 86, 90, 261, 265
MacIntyre, Alasdair, 133, 144, 240
MAGA movement, 177
male leadership, 199, 214
mammon, 29, 29n25, 119, 121, 128, 171, 273–74
Mander, Jerry, 113
market competition, 162, 167
market imperatives, 38, 60, 102, 106, 118, 193, 219
marketization, 169
market logic, 192
Marx, Karl, 35n47, 96–97, 104–5, 130, 130n27, 153, 175
Marxian critiques of capitalism, 34–44, 35n47, 53, 271–72
mass behavior, 208
masses, 187–88, 206–8, 261
massification, 53, 125
mass migration, 40, 88, 96
mass-mindedness, 207
mass movements, ideological, 122, 125n11, 199
mass psychoses, 52, 55, 124–25, 127–28, 207
maternity and paternity leave, 30
Maurin, Peter, 50, 245–58, 271, 279
Maxwell, Grant, 124
McCarraher, Eugene, 124n9, 128, 163, 166, 171, 274
medieval church, 135–39, 216
medium businesses, 112, 244, 285
megachurches, 236
men, 201–2
mental health, 52
metaphysical evil, 49, 127
Michels, Robert, 206n32

Middle Ages, 50n104, 74n43, 146, 154, 247–48
middle-American cultural values, 81–84, 187–88
Milbank, John, 147
Milgram obedience study, 199
military service, 224
millennials, 108–9
minorities, 5–6, 8–9, 29, 174, 186
Mize, Sandra Yocum, 249
mob or crowd mentality, 208
modernity, 127–28, 208
Modi, Narendra, 89–90, 264
Mokarzel, Mateo, 177
Moltmann, Jürgen, 226–28
monarchies, 24–25
Moore, Beth, 212–13
Moore, John, 103
morality
    moral base of capitalism, 262
    moral freedom, 228–29
    moralistic therapeutic deism, 145–46
    morality and Strauss, 129–34
    moral relativism, 33, 144, 154
    moral responsibility, 53, 125
More, Thomas, 102–4
Morris, Jonathan, 209–11
Mounier, Emmanuel, 247, 247n24
multinationals, 114

Naipul, V. S., 61–62
National Congregations Study (NCS), 236
National Labor Relations Board (NLRB), 114
national security, 86–87, 267
nation-states, 115, 130
Native Americans, 54, 59–60, 117, 168, 168n18
natural law(s), 147–50
Nazism, 125
neighborly relations, 64–66
Nelson, Thomas, 197
neoliberalism, 54, 280
    and capitalism, 171–72, 189–93
    freedom to choose, 158–64

INDEX

Friedmanian neoliberal faith, 188–89, 190
ideological strong-arming, 167–72
Trumpian nationalist position, 177–86
New Deal, 5–6, 25, 115, 158–62
New Oxford Review, 250
New Polity, 71–74, 252
New Right/populist politics, 119
New Testament, 214–15, 217, 224–26
New York Times (newspaper), 210
Nietzsche, Friedrich, 133
nihilism, 129–34, 154
Ninety-Five Theses, 139–40
nonbinary gender identity, 193
nones, 232–33, 281
nonversion/nonverts, 232–33, 242
nonviolence, 248–50
No Place of Grace (Lears), 75
nostalgia, 69, 76, 241–42
Nye, Joseph, 113–14

Oakeshott, Michael, 24, 26, 31, 33n40
O'Connor, Ann, 250–51
Old Testament, 145–47, 217, 222–25
The Omnivore's Dilemma (Pollan), 67
online worship, 233
"On Love for the Poor" (Gregory of Nazianzus), 239
optimism, 217–19
Opus Dei Catholics, 70
Orozco, Chris, 205–6, 276
Ortega y Gasset, José, 207–8, 208n36
orthodoxy, 68–69, 73–74, 250–51
others, 127
The Outline of Sanity (Chesterton), 40, 263
overproduction, 37
ownership, 107, 148–49

pacifism, 246, 249, 251
participation mystique, 128, 207, 207n35
pastors, 208–9
pathological egoist, 128
patriotism, 179, 196–98, 220, 274
Paul VI, 280
peasants, 101–6

Pelosi, Nancy, 92, 92n77
Pence, Mike, 211
Penty, Arthur, 261, 265–67
perception of time, 99
personalism, 247, 254, 258–59
A Personalist Manifesto (Mounier), 247, 247n24
Peterson, Jordan, 196, 209
Pharisees, 223
Pius XI (pope), 259
Plato, 259, 259n55
police state, 141–42
political action committees (PACs), 26–27
political campaigns, 25–27, 112
political donations, 25–27
political ideologies, 45, 52, 125–27, 193, 196, 213–14, 274
political instability, 214, 282
political lobbying, 242
Political Parties (Michels), 206n32
political power, 52, 75, 113, 132n33, 186, 216, 223–24
political psychology, 22, 51–56, 274
political strategy, 234–35
political theology, 44–51, 217, 274
politics of Jesus, 239–40
Pollan, Michael, 67
popular culture, 187–89
populism, 11, 177
populist nationalism, 99–100
porous self, 135–36
positivism, 129
post-World War II, 127
potato famine, 87–89
poverty, 5–6, 25, 29, 87–89, 109, 161, 166, 170, 239, 254–57, 265
Prayer at the Heart of America rally, 194–96
precariat, 7–8, 116–17, 185, 189
precarity, 53, 186–87, 208, 255–56
priesthood of all believers, 139
principality, 130–31
private property, 105–6, 259–61, 260n58, 265, 281, 282
professional and managerial elites, 185–88
profit motive, 49–50, 87

INDEX

progressives, 3–7, 23n2, 39, 92–93, 116, 158, 184–89, 213, 279n10
property, 148–52
  property ownership, 107, 260
  property rights, 272–73
prophets and reformers, 128
prosperity, 78, 91, 98, 142, 163, 190, 220–21
protectionism, 179–81, 186, 189
protest, 221
Protestant Christians/Christianity, 142, 251, 278, 280–81
Protestant Reformation, 135–42, 144–45, 154–55
protests, 7, 10, 89–90, 120, 250, 257–58
psychological inflation, 127–28
psychologically healthy religion, 127
purity, 136–41, 271

QAnon, 177

racism, 3, 10, 25, 39, 74, 95, 164, 166, 252, 253, 257
radicalization, 214, 237
rationalism, 124
Ratzinger, Joseph, 72
reactionaries, 24, 27, 70, 74
Reagan, Ronald, 116, 170–71, 173–74, 184
real religion, 52, 55, 165
reciprocity, 240
red/blue division, 117–20
Reed, Ralph, 211
Reflections on the Revolution in France (Burke), 22
relativism, 133
religion and liberalism, 143
religious and lay commitments, 137–38
religious faith, 23–24, 122–23, 124–25, 128, 165, 216–17
religious left, 213
religious right, 213, 214, 217, 228–29.
  See also conservative Christians
religious traditionalism, 146n82, 177, 273
republic, 130
Republic (Plato), 259, 259n55

Republicans, 3, 6, 8–11, 25, 27, 34, 54, 92, 116, 158, 180, 182, 184–86, 193, 196, 198n13
Rerum Novarum (Leo XIII), 259, 271
resentment, 96, 99–100, 111, 143, 180, 181
responsiblization, 168–71
ressourcement, 72–74, 279
The Revolt of the Elites and the Betrayal of Democracy (Lasch), 116, 187–88
The Revolt of the Masses (Ortega y Gasset), 207–8
revolution, 60–61
Riegle, Rosalie, 251–52, 252n39
right liberals/liberalism, 25–29, 25n12, 34, 43, 158, 192, 216, 252
rights, 28–31
"right to work" laws, 116
right-wing identity movements, 119
right-wing nationalism, 146n82, 189, 273. *See also* Christian nationalism
right-wing politicization of Christianity, 209–11, 216, 235
riots, 55
Roman Catholicism, 148
Romans, 147
Romantic movement, 124
root shock, 55, 118, 125
Rousseau, Jean-Jacques, 33, 133, 133n37
Roys, Julie, 202–4
  The Roys Report, 202
rural areas, 64–65, 97, 126, 178, 237–38, 283
rural/urban division, 54–55, 117–18
Russia, 41

Salt Lake Tribune (newspaper), 177–78
scapegoating, 99, 119–20, 127, 168–69, 234
Schindler, David, 148n88
Schindler, D. C., 49, 123, 134, 144–53, 155, 195, 226, 259
Schürz, Martin, 109
science and technology, 45–47
Scientific Revolution, 58, 138, 153–54
scribes, 223

326

INDEX

Second Vatican Council, 72n34, 73
A Secular Age (Taylor), 12, 74n43, 134–35
secular faith, 51–52, 214n52
secularism, 137–38
secularity, 74n43, 122–23, 139n58, 261
secularization, 233
secular religion(s), 45, 128, 153, 164, 190, 199
secular service work, 238
secular social engineering, 142
sedevacantists, 70
self-interest, 23, 28, 123, 166–67
selfishness, 131, 166, 190, 238
self-preservation, 131–33
self-reliance, 190, 239, 241
self-sufficiency, 267
The Servile State (Belloc), 261–62
settlers, 59–60
sexuality, 149
sexual morality, 69
Shannon, Bill, 203–4, 204n24
shareholders, 90, 112, 115, 180
Sheen, Fulton, 249
Sillon movement, 246
Simon Peter, 222
singularity, 58
Sirico, Robert, 165
skepticism, 124
slavery, 24, 47, 104–5, 150, 164, 261–62
Sloterdijk, Peter, 97–98
Small, P. Douglas, 194–95
small businesses, 54, 88, 92, 112, 116, 254, 286
small government, 169–70
social change, 24–34, 58–61, 176–77, 250, 278–84
social chaos, 141, 155
social disembedding, 143
social embeddedness, 57–58, 136, 140
social engineering, 155
social fabric, 31, 58–59
socialism, 177, 261, 263
socialization of production and reproduction, 175
social justice warrior, 36–37
social media, 118
social problems, 37, 141, 166

Social Security Administration, 108–9
social stability, 23, 59, 101, 129, 192, 205
social teachings, Catholic, 73, 148, 151, 244, 246–47, 250, 259, 279–80
social welfare and programs, 7, 159, 176, 267
soft power, 113–14, 284–85
Sojourners Magazine, 209–10
Solomon (King), 221
Solzhenitsyn, Aleksandr, 34–35, 153–54, 218
Soviet communism, 153–54, 159, 163
Soviet Union, 36, 43, 272
Sowell, Thomas, 5–6, 5n4
speech codes, 116
Spellman (Cardinal), 249
Spencer, Richard, 173–74
Spock, Benjamin, 79
Standing, Guy, 7, 116
Stanford prison experiment, 199
statistics, 236
Strangers in Their Own Land (Hochschild), 111–12
Strauss, Leo, 122n4, 123, 129–34, 142, 144, 154–55, 218
strong-arming, ideological, 157–93
strong-arming, religious, 195–96, 198–211, 235, 280–81
strong-arming, social, 219, 241
strong-arming, spiritual, 213, 216, 228
strongholds, 211–13, 216, 219
student loan debt, 109
subordination of Christ, 225
subsidiarity, 267
subsistence farming, 85–89, 111, 263–64
subtraction story, 138
suffering, 227
suicides, 50, 63, 90–91
surplus population, 283
surveillance capitalism, 97
survival, 131–32
Swogger, Glenn, 57–58
systemic problems, 95

Taylor, Charles, 12, 28, 54–55, 57–59, 123, 127, 134–43, 146, 153, 154–55

INDEX

technical rationality, 35n47, 43
technique, 43–44, 150
technofeudalism, 171n27
technological advancement, 42–46, 58, 85–86, 95, 97–99, 121–23. *See also* automation
The Technological Society (Ellul), 43
technological treadmill, 86, 88–89
teleology, 129
Thatcher, Margaret, 170–71
theodicy, 168
therapeutic culture, 75–76
Third Republic, French, 246
Thomas Aquinas, 145n78, 151, 260–61, 260n58
Tocqueville, Alexis de, 143, 206
Tolstoy, Leo, 249
totalitarian communism, 52, 125
totalitarianism, 154, 174
tower of Babel, 217
trad-Catholics, 70
Tradistae, 71, 74, 252
traditionalism, 70, 74–76, 143, 252, 252n41
traditional religious faith, 128–29
Traditiones Custodes, 74
transcendent God, 51–53, 126, 190
transhumanists, 62–63
Tridentine (Latin) Mass, 70, 72n34, 74–76
Trump, Donald, 11, 39n59, 51, 52, 94, 177–86, 189, 193, 209–11, 213–14, 278, 282
truth, 130, 133–34
Turning Point USA, 10n22, 11, 172n31
TV shows, 76–84
Twain, Mark, 236
Tyson Foods, 107, 107n32

United States Department of Agriculture (USDA), 236
universal destination of goods, 259n54
universities, 170–72
unrest, 94–95
The Unsettling of America (Berry), 57–59, 96, 100
UN's Food and Agricultural Organization, 88

upward mobility, 78, 81–82, 111
urban areas, 55, 95, 118, 207–8, 237, 263
urbanization, 52–53, 90, 118, 125
urban poor, 6, 263–64, 283
US Bureau of Labor Statistics, 237
US Conference of Catholic Bishops, 249
US conservatives. *See* right liberals/liberalism
US foreign policy, 113, 278–79
US space program, 283
usury, 73
utopia, 130
Utopia (More), 102

vectoralists, 107
Voegelin, Eric, 54–55, 125n11, 137n53, 141–43, 141n65, 141n66, 142n70, 171, 273–74
voluntary poverty, 239, 254–57
volunteerism, 237–38
von Mises, Ludwig, 162–63
voter fraud, 183, 210
vulnerability, 32, 37, 40, 91, 97, 117, 118–19, 190

Wagner Act, 114
Wallace, Jim, 209–10
Ward and June Cleaver, 77–84
Ware, Bruce, 225–26
wealth, 40, 42, 85–86, 109–11, 109n42, 248, 260, 266–67, 274, 279, 282
Weber, Max, 138
Weinstein, Amanda, 30
welfare spending, 160–61
welfare state, 25, 40, 53–54, 172n43, 262–63
Wesley, John, 140
white-collar jobs, 3, 108
William of Ockham, 144–45
Wishloff, Jim, 254
wokeness, 185–86, 210
Wolin, Sheldon, 154n100
Wolsey (cardinal), 103
women, 29–31, 60–61, 84, 175–77, 225
Wood, Ellen, 101–6
work, Marx on, 35n47
work and automation, 107–8

328

workers' rights, 73, 250
workfare policies, 262
working classes, 3, 6, 8–9, 38–39, 158, 185–87, 248, 250, 272
world government, 231–32
World War I, 52, 122, 125
World War II, 52, 79, 122, 125–27, 249

Yahweh, 220
Yiannopoulos, Milo, 215n56

Zahnd, Brian, 46n85, 49, 119–20, 196–97, 222, 279
Zakaria, Fareed, 172, 172n33, 279
Žižek, Slavoj, 37n51, 48n91, 186
Zuckert, Catherine and Michael, 134

www.ingramcontent.com/pod-product-compliance
Lightning Source LLC
Chambersburg PA
CBHW032050220426
43664CB00008B/944